P9-ASK-694

# COMPARATIVE STUDIES IN SOCIOLOGY

*Volume 1* • 1978

# COMPARATIVE STUDIES IN SOCIOLOGY

*An Annual Compilation of Research*

*Editor:* RICHARD F. TOMASSON
*Department of Sociology*
*The University of New Mexico*

---

VOLUME 1 • 1978

JAI PRESS INC.
*Greenwich, Connecticut*

*321 Greenwich Avenue*
*Greenwich, Connecticut 06830*


*ISBN NUMBER: 0-89232-025-7*

*Manufactured in the United States of America*

# CONTENTS

## TWO-CASE STUDIES

# INTRODUCTION

The mode of comparison is central not only to the practice of sociology, but to the whole of science and everyday human reasoning. This is not, however, what we generally mean when we talk of comparative sociology. Less ambiguous terms for what we *do* mean are cross-societal (e.g., Marsh, 1967; Payne, 1973) or cross-national, a term particularly favored by political sociologists and political scientists (e.g., Allardt and Littunen, 1964; Merritt and Rokkan, 1966). A broader yet more precise term is cross-system sociology which, without controversy, might be defined as the comparison of values, structures, processes, and behaviors across social systems "to distinguish between those regularities . . . that are system-specific and those that are universal" (Grimshaw, 1973, p. 5). Comparative sociology (I will continue to use the established term) is also a means whereby we can trace cultural borrowings between social systems together with the study of their comparative development. It is no coincidence that the sociology of development, or more narrowly *modern-*

**Comparative Studies in Sociology—Vol. 1, 1978, pages 1–15**

**ISBN 0-89232-025-7**

*ization,* has expanded in tandem with comparative sociology since the late 1950s.

Comparative sociology is not, though it is frequently so regarded, a "field" of sociology. Rather it is a methodological orientation which is, or at least should be, warp and woof of the approaches of all the substantive areas of sociology. Looking about our disparate discipline we find marked differences in the use of the comparative perspective. It is well-developed in demography and political sociology, less so, for example, in the family and criminology.

There are also degrees of "comparativeness" in this sociology we call comparative. In the strictest sense it systematically compares two or more, and sometimes all, cases of a particular type. Here the various studies of sociologists such as Bendix, Eisenstadt, Goode, Inkeles, Lipset, Marsh, Barrington Moore, and Rokkan come to mind. Yet much of what we commonly put under the rubric of comparative sociology is merely study of some "other" society. This is true of the articles in *Comparative Studies in Society and History,* the ten or twelve other social science journals specializing in comparative studies,[1] and of the papers presented in the Comparative Sessions at the meetings of the American Sociological Association. (See Table 1). The more comparative of the single case study type involves seeing the particular case in a comparative context or explicitly showing it to support or to be an exception to some theory or other. Less comparative are those which deal with the "foreign" case without an explicit comparative orientation or without relation to some general proposition. We might call these studies "materials for comparative study." Most of the work we commonly attribute to comparative sociology is really not of the strictly comparative sort. Single case studies of "other" societies predominate.

The method of cross-system comparison as it is understood in sociology is in no way unique to our field. It is just as fundamental to all of the other social sciences and is indeed more substantively developed in some of them, certainly in political science which has at least six journals explicitly devoted to comparative study (see Footnote 1) and in anthropology (see Bibliography in Marsh, 1967, pp. 375–496). The study of literature, too, has become more comparative over past decades (Wellek, 1968; Nichols and Vowles, 1968), so has history (Hofstadter, 1968; Lipset, 1968), though in both these disciplines, as in sociology, there is much less strictly comparative study than one might expect.[2]

The word comparative in the sense in which it is used in the social sciences and humanities goes back to Middle English (Wellek, 1968, p. 3). The earliest use of the term found by Wellek is in a 1598 work by Francis Meres entitled "A Comparative Discourse of Our English Poets with the Greek, Latin, and Italian Poets." But the method of comparison goes back to antiquity, at least to Aristotle's *Politics* (Books IV–VI) in which he made a genuine comparative analysis of the stability, downfall, and *coups d'etat* of actually existing states. But the Greeks, unlike the Romans, were essentially inhibited in their comparative perspective by their ethnocentric attitudes of superiority over non-Greeks or barbarians. A rich comparativist orientation came out of the Renaissance. It was later fundamental to the precursors of modern social science from the sixteenth century on, from Machiavelli and Jean Bodin through Montesquieu, Vico, Adam Smith, and countless others in the eighteenth century.

Virtually all of the nineteenth and early twentieth century "pioneers" (Rokkan's word, 1964) of modern sociology, at least all of those in the macrosociological tradition, were comparativist. Toqueville was intimately acquainted with Britain and America in addition to his native France, a stance fundamental to his two major works—*Democracy in America* and *The Old Regime and the French Revolution*. Marx and Engels were highly knowledgeable about the major western European countries and had many corrrespondents throughout the world. Weber and Durkheim were centrally comparative and historical in their methodologies, even if neither travelled much. The cross-national orientation of the pioneers of modern sociology, however, came to be replaced by a "wave of hardheaded empiricism." Sociologists in particular

> . . . had to establish their methodological status and to win recognition in the academies of each nation and in this very struggle had to abandon the initial comparative perspective: the result was a long succession of local and national studies, often at a high level of methodological sophistication but with only incidental bearing on the central problems of a comparative sociology. (Rokkan, 1964, p. 6)

There has been a dialectical transformation from the comparative orientation of the early American sociologists (Sumner, Small, Ward, etc.) to a stage of "national empiricism," and then a partial return to a comparative orientation but at a higher level of methodological rigor. Westie (cited in Armer and Grimshaw, 1973, p. xi) studied the work of all the presidents of the American Sociological Society/Association from the beginning (1905) through 1972 and found "that (by contrast with the early period) of the 20 ASA presidents from 1931 through 1950 [up to the time of their election to office], *not one is known primarily or substantively for comparative work.*" (p. xi, my italics.) This has certainly not been the case with the presidents since the late 1950s (e.g., Davis, Sorokin, Turner, Bendix, Goode).

How relatively recent is the involvement of North American sociologists with comparative sociology can be seen in Table 1 which provides data on the frequency of comparative papers presented at the 1956, 1966, and 1976 ASA Annual Meetings. At the 1956 Meetings only one percent of the papers presented, just two of a total of 198, were "strictly comparative" in orientation, at least as judged by their titles. These were Paul Oren's "Social Structure and the Socialization of Adolescents: A Contrast between Paris and Urban U.S.A." and E. Franklin Frazier's "Race Relations in World Perspective." An additional four percent of the papers (8 of 198) dealt with non-North American societies or cultures. Two examples of this genre are Richard Conrad's "A Newspaper Study of Church-State Relationships in Communist East Germany" and Arnold S. Feldman and Melvin M. Tumin's "Theory and Measurement of Occupational Mobility in Puerto Rico." For another one percent of the papers (2 of 198) it is not clear from the title whether they contain comparative data or are just statements of "things to consider," new "perspectives," or what have you. I call these "possibly comparative." Here we have Lowry Nelson's "Rural Life in the Mass Industrial Society" and Philip M. Hauser's, "Cultural Obstacles to Economic Development in the Less-Developed Areas."

The percentages in Table 1 for the 1956 papers (as well as for the 1966 and 1976 papers) are minimal figures because there are probably some papers, though I don't think they are many, which are in some sense comparative but do not indicate this in their titles. In any case, we can conclude from these data that there was amazingly little comparative sociology being done in North America as recently as the mid-1950s. Some corroborative support for this view is the study by Marsh (1962) in which he found that out of 1,479 doctoral dissertations presented to the 23 most productive sociology departments between 1950 and 1960, 12 percent (175) dealt in some way with societies (including Canada) other than the United States. Most of these "comparative" dissertations came from

*Table 1.* Comparative Papers Presented at the 1956, 1966, and 1976 Meetings of The American Sociological Association.

(Percentages)

| | 1956 | 1966 | 1976 |
|---|---|---|---|
| Strictly comparative papers | 1 (2) | 7 (22) | 4 (24) |
| Papers dealing with non-North American countries or cultures | 4 (8) | 5 (18) | 8 (56) |
| Possibly comparative papers | 1 (2) | 2 (5) | 3 (17) |
| | 6 | 14 | 15 |
| | (N = 198) | (N = 332) | (N = 674) |

*Source:* Calculated from the 1956, 1966, and 1976 Annual Programs of the American Sociological Association Meetings.

a handful of universities. Two institutions alone, Harvard and Columbia, were responsible for 35 percent of them. My guess, though one cannot tell from Marsh's data, is that the large majority of these dissertations were concentrated in the last years of the decade.

By the mid-1960s there was appreciably more strictly comparative sociology being done and more engagement with non-North American topics than a decade earlier. Two-thirds more papers were presented in 1966 than in 1956, 332 compared with 198, with 7 percent (22) of them being strictly comparative and another 5 percent (18) dealing with non-North American topics; an additional two percent of the papers were "possibly comparative." These three categories total 14 percent of the 1966 papers.

Between 1966 and 1976, the number of papers formally presented (always excluding roundtable discussions, didactic seminars, and the like) more than doubled, from 332 to 674. However, there was a relative decline, if not an absolute decline, in the number of strictly comparative papers presented, from 7 to 4 percent; the absolute number, however, increased slightly from 22 to 24. The percentage of papers dealing with non-North American topics, on the other hand, increased both proportionately and absolutely, from 5 to 8 percent or from 18 to 56 papers, a really big jump. The number of "possibly comparative" papers reached three percent (17 of 674). The 1976 total for the three categories was about the same as a decade earlier, 15 percent. A great proportion of the increase in the total number of papers between 1966 and 1976 is accounted for by the areas of ethnicity, sex roles, women, and aging; 7 of the 24 strictly comparative papers in 1976 dealt with these topics.

Other ways of measuring the attenuation of national empiricism from North American sociology would be to make content analyses of the sociology journals, book reviews, and textbooks, particularly the mass of introductory ones. My general observation of the latter is that they are becoming somewhat less ethnocentric. My hunch, without making any formal analysis, is that the leading sociology journals contain fewer comparative studies than is reflected in the ASA programs because of the "methodological" and "theoretical" concern of these journals and the observation that so many of their articles are based on survey data, albeit occasionally of a comparative sort. Books and monographs in the discipline, on the other hand, probably show more comparative sociology. The practice of comparative sociology generally requires knowledge in depth of an aspect of another society or access to survey data, both commonly combined with fieldwork or at least foreign travel. The practice of comparative sociology, then, is expensive both in terms of time and money and is often undertaken with a view toward publication of a book or monograph.

One more point about the extensiveness of comparative sociology: there is relatively more of it being done in North America than elsewhere in the world. I reviewed the contents of the articles in recent volumes of the *British Journal of Sociology, Kölner Zeitschrift für Soziologie und Sozialpsychologie* (Germany), *Revue française de Sociologie* (France), *Acta Sociologica* (Scandinavia), and *Sociologia Neerlandica* and became convinced that Western European sociology has not moved as far out of the stage of national empiricism as even the modest moves of North American sociology. One must not be deceived by the relative catholicity of the articles in some of these journals; many of the contributions are by foreigners.

Scandinavian sociology, about which I am somewhat knowledgeable, did not, with the exceptions of the Norwegians Johan Galtung and Stein Rokkan, begin to move out of the stage of national empiricism until the late 1960s. Edmund Dahlström in Gothenburg was instrumental in beginning the comparative study of the social structures of Denmark, Finland, Norway, and Sweden and Erik Allardt at Helsinki began a large-scale survey research study of the realization of welfare values in the same four countries. (A paper based on data from this latter study is contained in this volume.) About Britain, Payne (1973, p. 13) has written that "relatively few sociologists particularly in this country actually use the cross-societal comparative method in their research." Indeed hardly any do.

* * *

Besides the fact that there is not being much of it done, there are some criticisms of the current state of comparative sociology that I think should be made. These can be delineated as follows: (1) the overemphasis on method at the expense of substantive work, (2) the trained incapacity of many (most?) sociologists to do comparative sociology in depth, (3) the non-utilization of the vast resources of existing and pertinent demographic, economic, and social data, on the one hand, and of the genuinely comparative sociology done *outside* of academic sociology, on the other, and (4) the politicized and moralistic orientation that informs, or doesn't inform, some comparative sociology. Let me ignore in this brief Introduction all the positive things that might be said.

(1) Sociology is the methodological social science *par excellence,* a pervasive characteristic of the discipline that is both dominant virtue and dominant vice. There is nothing original in this criticism. Many sociologists have criticized the overdevelopment and misuse of sophisticated methodology in the field (e.g., Coser, 1975; Duncan, 1975). In few areas of the discipline, however, is an emphasis on sophisticated methodology less appropriate than in comparative sociology; in few areas has the concern with methodology so far outrun the mountains of existing

materials (sociological studies in many countries, histories, journalistic accounts, statistics, etc.) that have not even been subject to the most primitive comparative analysis. Yet of the four general volumes devoted to comparative sociology published in the last decade and with which I am familiar, three are specifically devoted to methodology (Vallier, 1971; Armer and Grimshaw, 1973; Smelser, 1975); the fourth is more substantively oriented (Marsh, 1967). Vallier's volume contains an annotated bibliography (pp. 423–467) in which about half of the items are listed under the rubric "Theoretical, Methodological, and Technical Works," and the remaining half under "Comparative Studies," many of which are heavily methodological. Marsh's much longer bibliography (1967, pp. 375–496), does not show as great a methodological emphasis as Vallier's because the contents are so heavily anthropological. Some of the exercises in the "methods and strategies" of comparative sociology remind me of the nasty old German saying: "Weiss man nichts, so schreibt man über Methode" (cited by Trewartha, 1953, p. 71).

(2) Besides the emphasis, or rather overemphasis, on methodology in contemporary sociology, other factors contribute to a trained incapacity of sociologists to do comparative sociology in depth. Most important, I propose, is the enormous distance between sociology and history. Not only do we and they show little knowledge of each other's work and methods (Hofstadter, 1968), the two disciplines are ecologically and structurally separate on most campuses with history being with the humanities and sociology with the social sciences and psychology. Few sociologists receive training in history or historical methods. There is more exchange the other way. It may be banal to say, but the two disciplines need each other and each other's methods and styles. "Sociology," Lichtheim (1967, p. xviii) once wrote, "is history with the hard work left out, while history is sociology with the brains left out."

Few non-émigré sociologists ever have the intellectual security or the comparative perspective provided by an intimate knowledge of another society, historical or contemporary, or even another period in the life of their own society. A ritualistic obeisance to the comparative and historical sociology of Max Weber is no substitute. History, which should be the discipline closest to those in the macrosociological tradition, is even more distant from the world of contemporary sociology than is economics. Political science has within itself a greater, though much attenuated, historical tradition. The involvement of so many sociologists with social psychological concerns, the enormous emphasis on narrow non-historical methodologies and techniques, and the "presentism" of most of our concerns are pervasive characteristics of our field which inhibit comparative study. Like members of any subculture, most sociologists follow the ways of their group.

Historians and political scientists often study the same topics as comparative sociologists but they are more substantively oriented, to a greater extent than we they deal upclose with concrete historical functioning social structures. And when they turn to comparative analysis they have a depth and detailed knowledge not commonly found in the work of contemporary comparative sociologists. We sociologists are mostly oriented toward testing some theory or other in a methodologically sophisticated way or in creating some abstract typologies. Much of the time the result is a pretty thin soup.[3]

(3) There is great value in sociology placed on obtaining "new" data and rather little concern on learning of the enormous riches of already existing data. Most sociologists, comparative and otherwise, make little use of the census, vital statistics, and the monthly surveys of the Current Population Survey, and much less of the similar, and in some instances better resources of other developed societies (e.g., Sweden, England). An example: the possibilities for the comparative study of family and household structure from census and vital statistics data has barely been touched by family sociologists. (Chaplin's article in this volume does this.) Also, where are the comparative studies of crime statistics? (One is the article by Archer and his associates also in this volume.)

Another source of unused riches available to comparative sociologists are studies done outside of the sociological tradition. Let me note two examples, not quite taken at random, that have come my way. One is Ernst Robert Curtius's *The Civilization of France* (1962; originally published in 1930), a brilliant work comparing French and German institutions and values and their development by one of the greatest literary comparativists of this century. Another is Salvador de Madariaga's (1927) *Englishmen, Frenchmen, Spaniards,* a superb treatise by a noted Spanish historian on that treacherous topic of national character.

On the one hand, we comparative sociologists should know more about and make greater use of statistical data existing in our fields of study; on the other hand, we need to seek out the comparative sociology in our specialties *outside* of academic sociology.

(4) Sociologists, after social psychologists (many of whom are in fact sociologists), are the most moralistic of the social scientists (see Ladd and Lipset, 1976, pp. 93–124). We are also more given to political radicalism and activism than those in other disciplines.

Actually disturbing, however, are the politicized comparative studies now making their appearance in sociology which attempt to compare "capitalist" and "socialist" societies along various dimensions. They discover greater egalitarianism in the socialist societies, findings often at variance with the observations of those who know much about Eastern European societies (e.g., Smith, 1976; Kaiser, 1976), or anyone who is a careful reader of the reportage from Eastern Europe in the *New York Times*. Here we have the meeting of narrow methodology, moralism, and Marxism. Two examples: Stack (1976, cited in Appendix) utilizes the Gini Coefficient of Equality to compare the income distributions of 44 nations. He finds that the "socialist" nations manifest "considerably more" income equality than do the "capitalist" nations! This generalization, while true of some countries, is a biased simplification of a complex reality (see, e.g., Wiles, 1974). (Day, in this volume, finds through qualitative and quantitative analysis that old-age pensions are *more* egalitarian in the Western European capitalist than in the Eastern European socialist countries.) In an analogous study Nuss (1976, cited in Appendix) compares the demographic position of women in industrialized capitalist and socialist countries. She finds substantially greater equality of the sexes in the socialist compared with the capitalist societies. (Compare her findings with those of Smith [1976, pp. 124–146] on "emancipated" Russian women.)

* * *

The articles in this first volume of *Comparative Studies in Sociology* are a particularly good selection of contemporary comparative sociology of the strictly comparative sort. All represent fresh, unpublished, and original research. It was, by the way, no easy task obtaining the thirteen papers of the generally high quality that make up this collection. I wrote scores of letter to comparative sociologists and to comparativists who are not formally sociologists. I scoured the 1975 and 1976 programs of the American Sociological Association Meetings. Some of the papers submitted were no more than "materials for comparative sociology" and were not considered. Hopefully, as *Comparative Studies in Sociology* becomes more widely known, the problem of finding such papers will become easier. As I have already noted there is not much to be found. But even if such works were more plentiful, this would not be reason to limit contributions to scholars who are formally sociologists. Scholars in related disciplines also do good comparative sociology. Of the 21 authors of the thirteen articles in this volume, seven have an affiliation outside of sociology: three in political science, two in geography, and one each in history and education.

The diverse studies in this collection are placed under three loose rubrics: Modernization, Social Indicators and the Quality of Life, and a residual category of Two-Case Studies. The first paper in the Modernization section is the most globalistic of all the papers in the volume. Cutright and Kelly utilize demographic data from all countries in the world with populations in excess of one million. Their paper is devoted to understanding the components that enter into the differential growth rates of these 117 nations; the factors are mainly those which influence the crude birth rate. Inkeles develops a strictly comparable cross-national Scale of Individual Modernization (IM) based on data from six developing nations collected in the Harvard Project on Social and Cultural Aspects of Development. He supports the conclusion that individuals living in a more modern society become more modern "merely by sharing a *generally* modern ambience." (p. 66). This is a continuation of work presented in Inkeles and Smith's (1974) *Becoming Modern.* Archer and his colleagues deal cross-nationally with the issue of city size and homicide rates. They present a complex set of conclusions to what is sometimes mistakenly regarded as a simple and direct relationship. Chaplin deals descriptively with the role of domestic service in a number of different countries at varying levels of industrialization, an immensely interesting and important topic on which there has been little research. Eckstein and Evans present a "controlled comparison" in depth of Brazil's "elite revolution" and Mexico's "social revolution." Glick, both an historian and a geographer, deals with the relations between ethnic systems in three periods of Spanish history: the Islamic (eighth through thirteenth centuries), the Christian feudal (eleventh through fifteenth centuries), and the Christian imperial (sixteenth and seventeenth centuries).

Three papers follow which deal with an area of much current concern: social indicators and the quality of life. Inglehart, a political scientist, finds that subjective satisfaction is no greater among "Post-Materialists" than among "Materialists" in his study utilizing survey research data from nine Western European countries. From data collected in his study of the realization of welfare values in the Nordic countries, Allardt finds a lack of correspondence between the objective circumstances of people and their subjective satisfaction-dissatisfaction. His findings and interpretations neatly support those presented in the previous study by Inglehart. Day evaluates the adequacy of government pension schemes in 19 industrialized nations while demonstrating a method of making cross-national comparisons using disparate materials.

The third and final category of papers consists of four two-case comparisons. First is Bell and Robinson's study of the evaluation of equality in England and the United States, a topic about which there is surprisingly little empirical data, but many assertions. Their findings are in the expected direction, but the differences are consistently small. They develop a new instrument, the Index of Evaluated Equality, which is a contribution to the empirical study of equality. Fein finds numerous contextual and structural similarities in the Turkish genocide of the Armenians in 1915 and the German killing of the Jews and gypsies. Field and Higley, a political scientist and a sociologist, continue an earlier collaboration and compare two cases of modern societies, France and Italy, where a national unification of elites has not been achieved. The final paper is another joint product, this one between a sociologist knowledgeable about Puerto Rico and a geographer specializing in the Soviet Union. Levine and Clem here demonstrate a number of remarkable parallels in what they call the "imperial development" of Puerto Rico and Soviet Georgia.

I hope that Volume I of *Comparative Studies in Sociology* meets with the approval of sociologists and other social scientists with comparative interests. In addition, I hope it will be both an avenue for the continued presentation of comparative sociology and a catalyst for encouraging more of it.

In conclusion let me thank those—several of them historians—who helped me read, evaluate, and edit the papers for this volume.

Richard F, Tomasson
The University of New Mexico
November 1977

## APPENDIX

Strictly Comparative Papers Presented at the 1956, 1966, and 1976 Annual Meetings of the American Sociological Association

### *1956*

1. Race Relations in World Perspective. (E. Franklin Frazier)
2. Social Structure and the Socialization of Adolescents: A Contrast between Paris and Urban U.S.A. (Paul Oren)

### *1966*

1. Equivalence and Variance in Cross-Cultural Research: A Quest for Data Relating to the Impact of Translation on Comparability. (R. Bruce W. Anderson)
2. Social Change and the Position of French and Flemish in Belgium. (Jacques Brazeau)
3. Development of Sociology of Law in Japan, with Comparison to U.S. and Europe. (Masaji Chiba)
4. Social Security Systems and the Status of Non-Working People. (Phillips Cutright)
5. Cross-Cultural Studies in Child Rearing: A Research Report. (Edward C. Devereaux, Jr.)
6. Social Differentiation and Role Allocation in African Social Systems. (St. Clair Drake)

7. UNESCO and the International Development of Sociology. (Charles E. Glick)

8. Cross-Cultural Distributions of Cancer. (Saxon Graham)

9. Intellectuals and the Larger Society: United States and Soviet Union. (Jan Hajda)

10. The Soviet Family Allowance Program: Comparison with Family Programs in the United States and Other Nations. (David M. Heer and Judith G. Brydan)

11. Youthful 'Survivals' and Destructive 'Innovators': the Problems of Delinquency in the USSR and USA. (Paul Hollander)

12. A Comparative Measure of Attitudinal Modernity. (Alex Inkeles and David Horton Smith)

13. U.S. and U.S.S.R. Representation in Non-Governmental Organizations. (Louis Kriesberg)

14. Fertility and Mobility in Cross-Cultural Perspective. (George C. Myers)

15. The Ecology of Future International Relations. (Bruce M. Russett)

16. Polarity in the Approach to Comparative Research in Ethnic Relations. (R. A. Schermerhorn)

17. Family Help Patterns and Social Class in Three Countries. (Ethel Shanas)

18. The Methodology of Comparative Analysis of Economic Activity. (Neil J. Smelser)

19. The Two Great Rural Sociocultural Systems in Latin America: Problems of Stability and Change. (T. Lynn Smith)

20. Family Interaction in a Laboratory Setting in Three Societies. (Murray A. Straus)

21. Social and Political Structures of the Soviet Union and United States. (D. A. Tomasic)

22. International Criminal Statistics: A Proposal. (Marvin Wolfgang)

## *1976*

1. International Comparisons of National Divorce Rates. (Theodore R. Anderson and Kay M. Troost)

2. Unemployment and Homicide: A Comparative Approach. (Dane Archer and Rosemary Gartner)

3. The State and Capitalist Development in Brazil and Peru. (Tom Bamat)

4. Proximity and Commuting Immigration: An Hypothesis Explored Via the Bi-Polar Ethnic Communities of French Canadian and Mexican Americans. (Elliott Robert Barkan)

5. On the Causes and Solution to the Problem of World Hunger and Starvation: Comparative Evidence from China and Other Developing Countries. (Shirley Cereseto)

6. Monopoly Capitalism and Women's Labor Force Participation: The Case of the U.S., Argentina, and Guatemala. (Norma Chinchilla)

7. Sex-Role Images in Children's Picture Books: China, France, and the United States. (Esther N. L. Chow)

8. A Formula for Genocide: A Grounded Theory Comparing the Turkish Genocide (1915) and Nazi Germany's Holocaust (1939–45). (Helen Fein)

9. Theater as a Medium for Critical Expression in the Soviet Union, Poland, and the United States. (Jeffrey Goldfarb)

10. National Development and the Development of the Self: A Cross-National Perspective. (Alex Inkeles)

11. Economic Attitudes of the English and French Aristocracies Before 1800. (Jerry A. Jacobs)

12. Weber, Durkheim, and the Comparative Method. (Robert E. Kapsis)

13. A Durkheimian Analysis of International Crime Rates. (Marvin D. Krohn)

14. Imperial Development: The Cases of Puerto Rico (U.S.A.) and Georgia (U.S.S.R.). (Barry B. Levine)

15. The Political Economy of Conservatism: A Comparison of the Effects of the Korean, Algerian, and Vietnamese Wars. (Clarence Y. H. Lo)

16. The Position of Women in Industrialized Socialist and Capitalist Countries: A Comparative Study. (Shirley A. Nuss)

17. Dreams and Sex Roles in Two Cultures. (Deborah I. Offenbacher)

18. Attitudes Toward Social Inequality in England and the United States. (Robert V. Robinson and Wendell Bell)

19. Population Measures and Social Control: Singapore, China, and Pluralist Systems. (Janet W. Salaff)

20. Comparative Role of the Bourgeoisie in the Development of Poor and Rich Countries. (Saskia Sassen-Koob)

21. Income Inequality and Political Violence: A Cross-National Analysis. (Lee Sigelman and Miles Simpson)

22. Income Stratification and the Type of Economic System: A Cross-National Study of Fourty-Four Countries. (Steven Stack)

23. From Prussia to Yenan: A Comparison of the Modern Western and the Maoist Views on Interorganizational Relations. (Barriman Taraki and David L. Westby)

24. The Mortality of Swedish and U.S. White Males: A Comparison of Experience, 1969–71. (Richard F. Tomasson)

## FOOTNOTES

1. These are *Studies in Comparative Religion, Studies in Comparative Communism, Studies in Comparative International Development, Studies in Comparative Local Government, Comparative Education Review, Comparative Education, Comparative Political Studies, Comparative Politics, International Journal of Comparative Sociology, Journal of Comparative Family Studies, and Journal of Commonwealth and Comparative Politics.*

2. See, for example, *Comparative Drama, Comparative Literature Studies,* and *Comparative Literature;* also *Comparative Studies in Society and History.*

3. Similar observations have been made by Landsberger (1976, p. 789).

## REFERENCES

Allardt, Erik and Littunen, Yrjö (eds.) (1964) *Cleavages, Ideologies and Party Systems.* Helsinki: The Academic Bookstore.

Aristotle (1943) *Politics*. Trans. by Benjamin Jowett. New York: Modern Library.

Armer, Michael and Grimshaw, Allen D. (1973) *Comparative Social Research: Methodological Problems and Strategies*. New York: Wiley.

Andreski, Stanislav (1964) *The Uses of Comparative Sociology*. Berkeley: University of California Press.

Coser, Lewis A. (1975) "Presidential Address: Two Methods in Research of a Substance." *American Sociological Review* 40:691–700.

Curtius, Ernst Robert (1962) *The Civilization of France*. New York: Vintage Books.

Duncan, Otis Dudley (1975) *Introduction to Structural Equation Models*. New York: Academic Press.

Grimshaw, Allen D. (1973) "Comparative Sociology: In What Ways Different from Other Sociologies?" Pages 3–48 in Michael Armer and Allen D. Grimshaw, (eds.), *Comparative Social Research: Methodological Problems and Strategies*. New York: Wiley.

Hofstadter, Richard (1968) "History and Sociology in the United States." Pages 1–19 in Seymour M. Lipset and Richard Hofstadter, (eds.), *Sociology and History: Methods*. New York: Basic Books.

Inkeles, Alex, and Smith, David (1974) *Becoming Modern: Individual Change in Six Developing Countries*. Cambridge, MA, Harvard University Press.

Kaiser, Robert G. (1976) *Russia: The People and the Power*. New York: Atheneum.

Ladd, Everett Carll, Jr. and Lipset, Seymour M. (1976) *The Divided Academy: Professors and Politics*. New York: Norton.

Landsberger, Henry A. (1976) "Review of John Wilson Lewis (ed.), *Peasant Rebellion and Communist Revolution*." *Contemporary Sociology* 5:788–790.

Lichtheim, George (1967) *The Concept of Ideology and Other Essays*. New York: Vintage Books.

Lipset, Seymour M. (1968) "History and Sociology: Some Sociological Considerations." Pages 20–58 in Seymour M. Lipset and Richard Hofstadter, (eds.), *Sociology and History: Methods*. New York: Basic Books.

Madariaga, Salvador de (1927) *Englishmen, Frenchmen, Spaniards*. London: Oxford University Press.

Marsh, Robert M. (1962) "Training for Comparative Research in Sociology." *American Sociological Review* 27:147–149.

——— (1967) *Comparative Sociology: A Codification of Cross-Societal Analysis*. New York: Harcourt, Brace and World.

Merritt, Richard L. and Rokkan, Stein (eds.) (1966) *Comparing Nations*. New Haven: Yale University Press.

Nichols, Stephen G., Jr. and Vowles, Richard B. (1968) *Comparatists at Work*. Waltham, MA.: Blaisdell.

Payne, Geoff (1973) "Comparative Sociology: Some Problems of Theory and Method." *British Journal of Sociology* 24:13–29.

Rokkan, Stein (1964) "International Cooperation in Political Sociology: Current Efforts and Future Possibilities." Pages 5–18 in Erik Allardt and Yrjö Littunen, (eds.), *Cleavages, Ideologies and Party Systems*. Helsinki: The Academic Bookstore.

Smelser, Neil J. (1975) *Comparative Methods in the Social Sciences*. Englewood Cliffs, NJ: Prentice-Hall.

Smith, Hedrick (1976) *The Russians*. New York: Quadrangle.

Trewartha, Glenn T. (1953) "A Case for Population Geography." *Annals of the Association of the American Geographers* 43:71–97.

Vallier, Ivan (ed.) (1971) *Comparative Methods in Sociology*. Berkeley: University of California.

Wellek, René (1968) "The Name and Nature of Comparative Literature." Pages 3–27 in Stephen G. Nichols, Jr. and Richard B. Vowles (eds.), *Comparatists at Work.* Waltham, MA: Blaisdell.

Wiles, Peter (1974) *Distribution of Income: East and West.* Amsterdam: North Holland Publishing Co.

# MODERNIZATION AND OTHER DETERMINANTS OF NATIONAL BIRTH, DEATH, AND GROWTH RATES: 1958–1972

Phillips Cutright and William R. Kelly*

---

Understanding the causes of differences among nations in annual rates of population growth requires analyses of the components of these rates. Birth and death rates determine the growth rate in most populations. The effect of international migration on national population growth can be ignored in nearly all countries (Teitlebaum, 1975). Historical trends in world growth rates are discussed first, followed by a review of the current world situation. Next is an outline of the main features of the "demographic transition"—an ideal type model that describes past trends in birth, death, and growth rates in now-developed countries. The major emphasis of this study, however, is to develop and test models of birth,

**Comparative Studies in Sociology—Vol. 1, 1978, pages 17–46**

**ISBN 0-89232-025-7**

death, and growth rates among the world's nations in recent years.

For most populations the annual growth rate was low until the 20th century. Estimates of world growth rates and population size since 8,000 B.C. are shown in Table 1. The average annual growth rate for each time period in the first column can be converted into a statistic which gives the number of years before a population with such a rate will double in size. The lower the growth rate, the more years it takes to double. The third column gives the number of millions of people in the world at the end of each period; this number times the annual growth rate (column 1) estimates the number of millions of people being added to world population each year at the end of each period.

The first period with an annual growth rate greater than one per 1000 is 1751–1800. By 1800, world population was about one billion and was increasing by approximately four million each year. The 1901–1950 period shows a growth rate more than double that of 1751–1800; about 2.5 billion people were alive in 1950. The 1950–1974 period shows a doubling of the growth rate over that of the preceding period, with nearly 3.9 billion people alive in 1974 and a doubling time of only 40 years.

Estimates of 1975 world population and growth rates vary primarily because universally acceptable Chinese data are not available. Sources other than those used here may, therefore, yield somewhat different numbers because estimates of Chinese data vary. Data for 1975 in the bottom three rows show that the world is not homogeneous; by dividing the world into the developed ("rich") and the underdeveloped ("poor") categories commonly used, sharp demographic differences are shown. Growth rates are three times greater in poor as compared to rich countries; doubling times average 28 and 91 years respectively. Rapid population growth (a rate of 15 per 1000 or higher) is restricted to underdeveloped nations. No developed nation had a rate of 15 or more in 1975. With nearly 29 percent of world population, the developed countries contribute only 11 percent ot its annual increase. The difference in growth rates between rich and poor nations and the likely stability of this difference for some time to come is cited (e.g., Keyfitz, 1976; Heilbroner, 1974) as a cause of current and future inequalities in wealth among nations.

Although the long-run trend in growth rates since the adoption of agriculture (Neolithic Period) is up, this trend may be reversed in the near future (Freedman and Berelson, 1974; Coale, 1974; Keyfitz, 1976). A reversal is expected in the near term (say, by the year 2000) because rapid population growth cannot continue indefinitely. For example, if a growth rate of 19 persists to the year 2000, world population will then equal 6.4 billion. At least 90 percent of the 2.5 billion increase from 1975 levels will occur in countries least able to cope with rapid growth. The 1975–2000 increase equals total world population in 1950. Increases in energy pro-

*Table 1.* World Population Growth: 8,000 B.C.–1975 A.D.

| Years | Annual Growth Rate per 1000 | Years to Double Population | Population (millions) at End of Period | Millions Added per Year |
|---|---|---|---|---|
| | (1) | (2) | (3) | (4) |
| 8,000 B.C.–1 A.D. | 0.4 | 1,925 | 300 | 0.1 |
| 2 A.D.–1750 | 0.6 | 1,237 | 800 | 0.4 |
| 1751–1800 | 4.4 | 157 | 1,000 | 4.4 |
| 1801–1850 | 5.2 | 133 | 1,300 | 6.8 |
| 1851–1900 | 5.4 | 123 | 1,700 | 9.2 |
| 1901–1950 | 7.9 | 87 | 2,500 | 19.7 |
| 1950–1974 | 17.1 | 40 | 3,860 | 66.7 |
| 1975 World | 20.0 | 35 | 3,930 | 78.6 |
| Rich nations | 7.6 | 91 | 1,130 | 8.6 |
| Poor nations | 25.0 | 28 | 2,800 | 70.0 |

*Sources:* Freedman and Berelson, 1974; Coale, 1974; Keyfitz, 1976.

duction, agricultural and industrial technology, water and food, needed to avoid increased mortality in many poor nations, may not be forthcoming. Unless birth rates decline, death rates will increase in some populations and their growth rates will then decline.

Developed nations are now very close to replacement levels of fertility (Westoff, 1974) which will produce a near zero rate of growth by perhaps 1990; therefore, most change in rates of population growth after 1975 will occur in nations now classified as underdeveloped. These nations are not homogeneous. They differ widely in the extent to which they are approaching that stage in the transition which is favorable to declining fertility and to a reduction of the rate of population growth from declining fertility rather than increasing mortality.

Somewhat arbitrary "stages" of the demographic transition are shown in Figure 1. This diagram includes a scale of birth and death rates, although these rates differ among populations before and during the transition to long-run declines in either rate. Also, the number of years each population spends in Stage II or III varies (Kirk, 1971; Matras, 1973). In Stage I crude birth rates often vary (Wrigley, 1969; Lee, 1973) according to food supply and other factors, but the variation is generally small compared to changes in the death rate. Populations with birth rates of 35–45 and death rates of 30–35 may, in famine or plague years, have crude death rates of 150, or even 300 per 1000 (Keyfitz, 1976). Although an excess of births over deaths would occur in most years, periodic disasters would reduce the population and the result is a very low rate of growth.

*Figure 1.* Four stages in the demographic transition from high to low vital rates.

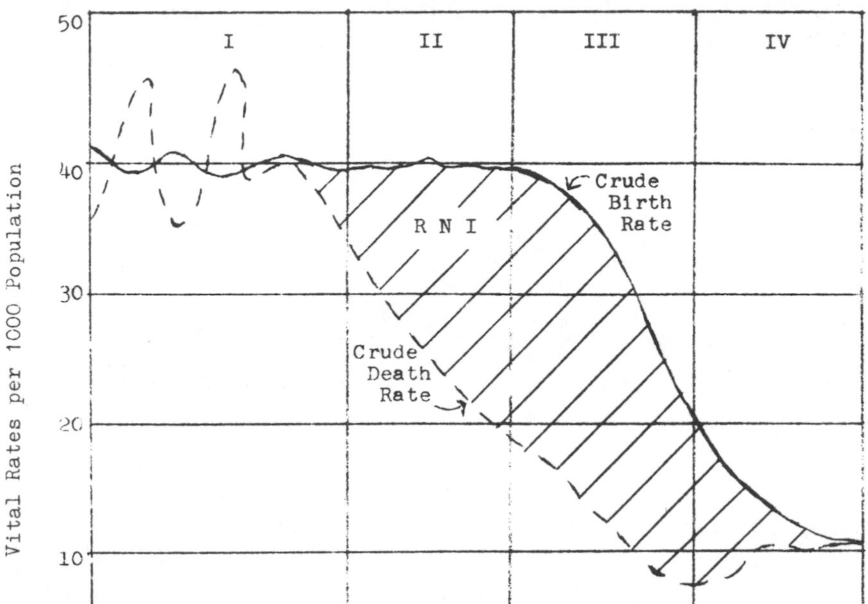


Stage II is characterized by a decline in the crude death rate, continuing high levels of fertility, and a resulting rapid rise in the rate of natural increase, depicted by the hatched area between the two vital rates. Stage III is characterized by further declines in mortality, and substantial declines in fertility. The final stage completes the transition. In Stage IV birth rates finish their downward trend. Crude death rates gradually increase as low fertility and high life-expectancy gradually produce an older population. The population has both low fertility and mortality, resulting in a low or zero rate of population growth.

This model of the transition is largely based on the European experience. The form of the transition in underdeveloped nations differs in several important respects. First, in Europe the decline in mortality during Stage II and III was largely the result of gradual improvement in material conditions. Stability and then reduction of crude death rates from about 30 to 15 required a century of slow economic progress. The slow pace of mortality decline gave European populations several generations to adjust fertility with regard to the new mortality levels.

In contrast, nations that were underdeveloped at the end of World War II experienced large and very rapid declines in mortality. Improvements in life expectancy, which required a century in Europe, occurred in just 15–20 years in many poor countries (Stolnitz, 1964; Goldscheider, 1971). The result of this rapid drop in mortality is a startling rise in the annual rate of world population growth after 1950 (Table 1).

No nation with 1 million or more people in 1972 was in Stage I. Crude death rates in the 30 range are confined to a few African nations and these rates are below traditional levels (U.S. Bureau of the Census, 1974). Most African countries are in the early-to-middle Stage II period. In contrast, most Latin American, Middle Eastern and Asian countries are in late Stage II and early Stage III—they have relatively low mortality and may or may not have begun the fertility decline, Nations such as Chile, China, Costa Rica, Cuba, Singapore, Sri Lanka, and Taiwan have birth rates in the 23–35 range and appear to be moving from Stage III toward Stage IV. The developed nations are the last cluster of countries, and all are in the early-to-late Stage IV condition, with East and West Germany having small negative rates of natural increase in the mid-1970s. Differences among these countries' rates of growth are partially due to age structure (Westoff, 1974).

Because fertility rather than mortality is the primary component determining the rate of natural increase (RNI), a model is first developed which explains national differences in fertility. We then examine death and growth rates.

## FERTILITY ANALYSIS

The modernization theory of fertility is largely based on efforts to understand the causes of the decline of fertility in Europe (Coale, 1969; 1973; Van de Walle and Knodel, 1969). Both early (Davis, 1955; Freedman, 1963) and recent (Goldscheider, 1971; Coale, 1973; Cutright, Hout, and Johnson, 1976) expositions of the theory emphasize structural modernization. The principal components of the structural modernization concept are education, urbanization, levels of economic well-being, and mortality.

Theorists argue that because increasing structural modernization reduces mortality, it compels a population to reduce fertility; declines in child mortality lower the number of births needed to achieve a given number of surviving children. Modernization breaks down traditional kinship domination of reproductive goals and nuclear-family decision-making; it also changes traditional sex roles and generates alternatives to early marriage and large family size for women. Finally, modernization motivates adults' aspirations, for themselves and their children, to participate in the new achievement-oriented socioeconomic institutions. Achieving these new goals is facilitated by small family size. If increasing modernization does not affect kinship domination, sex roles, or aspirations, it will not lower fertility (Goldscheider, 1971, Chapter 6). Theorists believe that continuing structural modernization will destroy barriers that maintain high fertility.

Historical studies of the transition from high to lower fertility in Europe have expanded modernization theory to include factors that accelerate or retard fertility declines in given populations. The revised theory is necessary because fertility declines do not occur at a common level of modernization; a search for factors that affect the *timing* of fertility changes is necessary. The revised theory (Goldscheider, 1971; Coale, 1973; Cutright, Hout, and Johnson, 1976) has incorporated geographic, cultural, and demographic factors, in addition to structural modernization.

Previous work is reviewed first, followed by strategies which attempt to reduce methodological and conceptual problems. Then a model of the modernization theory is tested. An alternative conceptualization of the fertility transition is then examined.

*Problems with Early Fertility Studies*

Previous multivariate empirical studies of world-wide 1950 and 1960 fertility rates (e.g., Adelman and Morris, 1966; Heer, 1966; Friedlander and Silver, 1967; Janowitz, 1971; Kasarda, 1971; Ekanem, 1972; Hohm, 1975) suffer one, and usually several of the following deficiencies: (1) tests of hypotheses are applied only to a small and poorly defined sample of the world's populations; (2) a limited theoretical perspective leads to inadequate statistical control which introduces a strong potential for spurious conclusions (see Kelly, Cutright, and Hittle, 1976); (3) efforts to establish the relative importance of one aspect of modernization over others do not adequately consider the nature of the modernization process or estimation problems related to high multicollinearity among indicators (see Oechsli and Kirk, 1975); (4) cross-sectional studies use independent variables measured in the same year as the dependent variable, thus, assuming no time lag for causal impact (see Beaver, 1975); (5) data from only one point in time are used, and change over time is ignored (see Cutright, Hout, and Johnson, 1976; and Janowitz, 1973a, for discussion); (6) measures of cultural and regional factors that may affect institutions that regulate fertility are omitted; and (7) researchers ignore basic assumptions of the estimation method by not testing the specification of the functional form, for example, non-linearity in linear models.

Fertility rates for the early 1970s and the necessary independent variables for 117 of the 120 world countries with one million or more inhabitants in 1965 are now available. The new data invite analysis of change over time in fertility rates as a check on the causal effects inferred from cross-sectional analyses. As Blalock (1964, p. 131) comments, ". . . we will have additional faith in the conclusions if two studies, one of which involves change data and the other comparative data, both give similar results."

*Variables in Fertility Analysis*

*Crude birth rates* (births per 1000 population) for 1955–1959 (Office of Population Research, 1966, Table 1; Rothman, 1970, p. 24; United Nations, 1965) and circa 1972 (U.S. Bureau of the Census, 1974; Nortman, 1975, Tables 3 and 4; Orleans, 1976, Table 3) are the basic dependent variables. Estimated rates are used for those nations with faulty birth and population records. The two measures are labeled 1958 and 1972 CBR, respectively. Mean 1958 CBR was 38.9 (S.D. = 11.9); 1972 CBR was 35.9 (S.D. = 13.3).

A 1972 general fertility rate (births per 1000 women aged 15–49) was computed and found to be correlated 0.99 with 1972 CBR. Bogue and Palmore (1964) report a comparably high correlation using fifty nations for the 1955–1960 period. Such high correlations make analyses of both crude and general rates redundant. Despite the likelihood that lack of age and sex standardized fertility rates may result in errors among a few populations with unusual age-sex structures, only the crude rates in 1958 and 1972 are used. General fertility rates are not available for 1958.

*Structural modernization.* All empirical and theoretical work indicates a negative relationship between indicators of modernization and fertility (e.g., Friedlander and Silver, 1967; Coale, 1973). The main indicators of modernization relevant to fertility are urbanization, education, and living standards. Indicators of these theoretical components are used to construct two modernization indices—one for analyses of 1958 and a second for analyses of 1972 birth rates.

The literate percentage of the population 15 years and older (Russett et al., 1964, Table 64; UNESCO, 1968, Table 32; Taylor and Hudson, 1972, Table 4.5; Banks, 1971, Segment 7) and newspaper circulation per capita (Banks, 1971, Segment 9; Taylor and Hudson, 1972, Table 4.8) measure the education component. The proportion of the population living in urban areas (Davis, 1968, Table C) measures urbanization.

Living standards refer to health and economic conditions. Physicians per capita (Banks, 1971, Segment 9; Taylor and Hudson, 1972, Table 4.12) is a proxy for life expectancy and development of health resources.

Economic standards are measured by the natural logarithm of telephones per capita (see Barbera, 1973 for discussion; data from Banks, 1971, Segment 5; Taylor and Hudson, 1972, Table 4.7; United Nations, 1957) and the natural logarithm of gross national product per capita, labeled GNP/C (Taylor and Hudson, 1972, Table 5.4; Russett et al., 1964, Table 44). The negative correlation of fertility with telephones and GNP/C increases when the variables are logged, indicating that their relationship to fertility is nonlinear before the transformation. This is expected because fertility cannot reasonably be expected to become zero or negative as the number of telephones or the GNP/C becomes very large. Logging did not substantially improve the correlation of other modernization indicators with fertility.

Because theory dictates a lag between the timing of modernization change and a fertility decline, each of the six indicators was lagged about ten years before the measurement of fertility. For example, we used the 1950 and 1960 percentage urban in indices of modernization for analyses, respectively, of 1958 and 1972 fertility.

Following Cutright, Hout, and Johnson (1976), each modernization scale was constructed by standardizing each indicator to a mean of zero and variance one, summing the standardized items and dividing by the sum of their standard deviations. The higher the score, the higher the modernization level. The two indices are labeled modernization 1950 and modernization 1960. The mean intercorrelation of the six indicators was 0.815 for modernization 1950 and 0.831 for modernization 1960. These scales are internally consistent: Cronbach's alpha (Cronbach, 1951) is 0.964 for the 1950 index; it is 0.967 for 1960.

*Agricultural land per capita.* Population density is usually measured by the ratio of population per land area and, thus, is subject to estimation error when other variables in the same analysis use population in their denominators (Schuessler, 1974). We take the natural logarithm of the ratio of agricultural land per capita as our measure. Agricultural land is defined as ". . . arable land and land under permanent crops plus those reported as permanent meadows and pasture" (Taylor and Hudson, 1972, p. 287). It has a surprisingly small (−0.20) correlation with urbanization. This variable may be a reversed proxy for the "cost of living space" (Friedlander and Silver, 1967, p. 53) or "population pressure" (Adelman and Morris, 1966). The expected relationship to fertility is positive, i.e., the greater the agricultural land area per inhabitant, the higher the fertility. Because fertility rates have upper limits, the relationship of fertility to land per capita should be curvilinear. By using the logged rather than the untransformed ratio, higher correlations were found. The variable is expected to be positively related to fertility in each time period. Thus, the effect is to inhibit declines in fertility over time.

The 1950 and 1965 measures are computed using 1950 and 1965 population data (Davis, 1969, Table A; Taylor and Hudson, 1972, Table 5.1) and a 1965 measure of agricultural land (Taylor and Hudson, 1972, Table 5.3). A 1950 measure of agricultural land is not available. This is not a serious loss because in most nations the amount of agricultural land is fairly constant over short periods.

*Population size.* The natural logarithm of 1950 and 1965 population was used to control spurious effects that might occur if this variable was omitted. Spurious effects could occur if population size was related both to fertility and other independent variables (Blalock, 1968). Previous studies have not introduced size as a variable affecting vital rates. Size may affect fertility if governments of large populations are more aware of population problems and possibly are better able to introduce policies to lower fertility. Or couples may have lower desired family size in large rather than smaller populations for reasons yet to be understood. The effect of size on fertility, if it exists, is expected to be negative.

*Islamic culture.* As a proxy for Islamic culture in 1958 and 1972, the percentage of the population of Islamic religion around 1965 was used (Taylor and Hudson, 1972, Table 4.17). Data for 1950 are not available but the 1965 statistics should be an acceptable estimate for 1950 if the assumption of high stability over time is correct. Islamic culture is expected to increase fertility because Moslem family and economic institutions tend to be pronatalist (Kirk, 1966; Yousef, 1972). Supporting this view is the sharp subordination of women to men, emphasis on traditional goals of the kinship group over those of the couple, and the lack of female participation in the labor force.

*Low-literacy Latin America.* A common history of Iberian conquest and Roman Catholicism suggests (Cutright, Hout, and Johnson, 1976; Stycos, 1971) that these Latin countries may have higher fertility than would be expected on the basis of their level of modernization. However, several Latin countries are heavily populated by European immigrants and tend to have relatively high levels of modernization and low fertility. Tests for interaction showed a significant effect among Latin nations with less than 70 percent literate in 1950. The first five nations with high literacy (Argentina, Chile, Costa Rica, Cuba, and Uruguay) all have large "white" populations and small "mixed," Indian, or black populations (Johnson and Cutright, 1973, Table 1)—a consequence, in part, of past levels of European emigration. The 13 Latin nations with low literacy, formerly ruled by Spain or Portugal, were coded 1; all other countries are 0.

*Southern Europe.* If fertility control practices diffused (Coale, 1969, Figure 2) from Northern to Southern Europe, then proximity to Northern European nations with early fertility transitions should reduce Southern Europe's fertility below what would be expected solely from the effects of modernization. Although the rest of Europe was modernizing in the 19th and early 20th centuries, Southern Europe lagged behind. Nonetheless, by 1910 or 1920 (Matras, 1973) most of Southern Europe had moved to a later age at marriage and lower fertility. We test whether or not this measure of geographic location continues to have an effect on fertility, net of modernization and other factors after World War II. Portugal, Spain, Italy, Yugoslavia, Albania and Greece are coded 1; all other nations are coded 0.

*Legal abortion.* By the late 1950s eight nations (Bulgaria, Czechoslovakia, Hungary, Japan, Poland, Rumania, the USSR, and Yugoslavia) had laws allowing legal abortion on request for other than medical indications. In analyses of 1958 CBR, these nations are coded 1; all others are 0 (Tietze, 1969). By 1972 legal abortion rates per 1000 women aged 15–44 were available in most nations with liberal abortion laws and the medical personnel needed to implement such legislation. Thirty nations with missing data (all at low levels of development) are coded zero (Tietze and Murstein, 1975, Table 1). Their legal aboriton rates must be very low because they lack legislation and the medical resources needed to achieve high legal abortion rates. Nations with known 1971–1972 legal abortion rates under 10 per 1000 are also coded 0. The eight countries with rates of 10.0 to 29.9 are scored 1; the eight scored 2 have rates of 30 or higher. Expecting a negative relationship between legal abortion and fertility is not tautological. Legalization of abortion may only replace formerly uncounted legal abortions with counted legal abortions (Tietze, 1972). Therefore, differences among populations in legal abortion rates may not directly cause differences in their fertility rates.

*Transition potential.* We are also interested in identifying countries likely to experience declining birth rates *before* such declines occur. A measure labeled transition potential was developed. We reasoned that nations with much higher fertility rates than would be expected on the basis of their level of modernization and other characteristics in 1958 should, by 1972, be more likely to experience a drop in fertility than nations without unusually high rates. Therefore, the errors of prediction

from the equation used to estimate 1958 birth rates were used to identify those countries with "much higher rates than would be expected" from their characteristics. (See Table A.2 for 1958 errors and the equation used to generate 1958 CBR predicted values.) The eighteen nations with a positive error greater than one standard deviation (4.6) of the 1958 CBR errors of prediction are coded 1; all others are coded 0. High transition potential countries are not exclusively underdeveloped. For example, Canada, New Zealand, and the United States are among the 18 high transition potential countries in 1958. These developed nations experienced birth rates in 1958 that were temporarily inflated by short term shifts in age at marriage and the timing of fertility (Campbell, 1975; Ryder, 1974). The 1972 errors of prediction (Table A.2) may identify nations likely to exhibit fertility declines over the next decade.

*Cross-Sectional Differences in Fertility: 1958 and 1972* Equation (1) exhibits the form of the model we employ to estimate the effect of the several independent variables on cross-sectional differences in fertility for both 1958 and 1972.

$$Y_{1958} = a + \Sigma b_i Z_i + e_{1958} \tag{1}$$

where: $Y_{1958}$ is the CBR for 1958 (or 1972); the $Z_i$ are indicators (with appropriate lags) of modernization, agricultural land (logged), population size (logged), the interaction term for literacy/Latin American, Southern Europe, percent Islamic, and legal abortion; $e_{1958}$ is the disturbance. Examination of Table 2 (which shows the year of measurement and both types of coefficients from ordinary least squares regression) shows that the most important influence on cross-national differences in fertility is the level of structural modernization. In the 1972 analysis, explained variance using only the modernization index is 0.826, compared to an $R^2$ of 0.098 when all the remaining variables are included. The 0.082 increase in $R^2$ suggests a substantial influence of the remaining factors net of modernization, but also reaffirms the dominant role of modernization. All variables have statistically significant relationships with fertility. We report significance levels with the knowledge that they should not be interpreted in the conventional sense (i.e., generalization to a population), because our case base constitutes a population rather than a sample. We prefer to rely on substantive significance (see Frideres and Taylor, 1972) and employ statistical significance as indicators of the variability of the estimates of the population parameters.

The effect of land per capita is positive, while population size has a relatively small negative effect. The metric coefficient in column 1 show that net of other factors, Latin nations with low literacy have a CBR 6.

*Table 2.* Regression Analyses of 1972 and 1958 Crude Birth Rates—Cross-Sectional Model: 117 Countries.

| Independent Variables | 1972 CBR Year | 1972 CBR Metric (b) Coeff. | 1972 CBR Stand. (beta) Coeff. | 1958 CBR Year | 1958 CBR Metric (b) Coeff. | 1958 CBR Stand. (beta) Coeff. |
|---|---|---|---|---|---|---|
| Modernization | 1960 | −9.80[a] | −0.74 | 1950 | −8.90[a] | −0.75 |
| Log Land per Capita | 1965 | 1.85[a] | 0.09 | 1950 | 0.40 | 0.02 |
| Log Population | 1965 | −1.68[a] | −0.16 | 1950 | −1.06 | −0.05 |
| Low Literacy Latin America | 1960 | 6.85[a] | 0.16 | 1950 | 6.52[a] | 0.17 |
| Southern Europe | 1960 | −6.41[a] | −0.12 | 1950 | −7.40[a] | −0.16 |
| Percent Islamic | 1965 | 0.05[a] | 0.13 | 1965 | 0.03[b] | 0.08 |
| Legal Abortion | 1971 | −2.60[a] | −0.11 | 1957 | −0.08[a] | −0.17 |
| Constant | — | 39.82[a] | — | — | 42.16[a] | — |
| $R^2$ | | 0.91 | | | 0.86 | |

[a]p = 0.05 and metric coefficient is greater than twice its standard error.
[b]p = 0.10 and of "borderline" significance.

points higher than that of non-Latin countries with similar characteristics. The metric coefficient for Southern Europe is −6.4, indicating that southern European populations had an average CBR 6.4 points lower than comparable nations outside that region. The metric coefficients for Islamic culture show that a nation whose population was 100 percent Islamic would be expected to have a crude birth rate 5 points higher than a comparable non-Islamic nation.

Finally, 1971 legal abortion had a negative effect on 1972 CBR. Nations with moderate levels of legal abortion, such as the United States, were coded 1; their CBR averaged 2.6 points lower than the CBR of nations with even lower legal abortion rates. Countries with the high abortion code of 2 averaged a CBR of 5.2 points less than comparable nations with low legal abortion rates.

Analyses of 1958 CBR show that modernization is again the dominant influence. However, the effects of land per capita and population size are relatively trivial and Islamic religion has only a marginal effect on CBR although it remains positive. "Latin America," "Southern Europe" and "legal abortion" have effects similar to those observed on 1972 fertility. The 1958 results reinforce most findings from the 1972 analysis. Both analyses find that the main variable affecting fertility is level of modernization. Cultural and geographic factors also have a substantial indepen-

dent impact on fertility. A lack of *complete* stability of all the relationships is expected because minor fluctuations result from the impact of processes that differentially affect the system over time.

*Longitudinal Analysis of Fertility: 1958 to 1972*

Although several analysts (Blalock, 1964; Lieberson and Hansen, 1974) have emphasized the necessity of comparing longitudinal results with those from cross-sectional analyses, most studies of national fertility differentials ignore change over time or examine trends in only a few countries. This section reports the procedure employed and the results obtained from the analysis of change over two points in time for our population of nations.

A major methodological problem involved in the analysis of change is the dependence of change on initial standing. That is, change is usually negatively correlated with the time one value, resulting in the so-called "regression effect." Bohrnstedt (1969) has determined that the most satisfactory method of measuring change, and eliminating the correlation of change and initial standing, is the residualization of the dependent variable at time two in terms of time one. Once the effect of time one fertility (CBR 1958) is removed, the variance in time two CBR reflects changes over the period of measurement. The net effect of the other independent variables in the equation reflects their relation to change. Equation (2) shows the form of the lagged dependent variable model employed to estimate the effect of the exogenous variables on fertility change over the time span 1958–72.

$$Y_{1972} = a + b_{1958}\, Y_{1958} + \Sigma\, b_i Z_i + e_{1972} \qquad (2)$$

where: $Y_{1972}$ is CBR for 1972; $Y_{1958}$ is the lagged CBR; $Z_i$ represents time one measures of the independent variables employed in the cross-sectional analysis above (the specification of this model requires that the independent variables be time-one lagged, [Heise, 1970]); and $e_{1972}$ is the disturbance term.

The lagged dependent variable model exhibits several other characteristics which render it a reasonable method for measuring change. First, Heise (1970) shows that this model is relatively insensitive to measurement and sampling error. Second, due to the upwardly biased estimates of the autoregression term (correlation of the time one and time two errors), the lagged dependent variable model will downwardly bias the estimates of the other independent variables and, thus, should provide a conservative test of hypotheses (see Chase-Dunn, 1975). Finally, coefficients from this model reflect the impact that independent variables have on absolute change rather than the percentage change. Percentage change treats all nations which had, for example, a 10 percent decrease in fertility as equivalent, regardless of the magnitude of the change. The absolute change measure is preferred because processes which result in a change in CBR of 5 from a level of 50 (a 10 percent change) are probably quite different (Stolnitz, 1964) from those which cause a change of 2 from a level of 20 (also a 10 percent change).

Mean 1958 to 1972 CBR change was −3.0 (S.D. = 4.4). Although 1958 to 1972 is a brief period, it is one of substantial fertility change and may be used to test the impact of variables which were found to influence fertility in the cross-sectional analyses.

Ordinary least squares regression is used to estimate the effect of the independent variables on change in fertility (see Table 3). As expected, time one CBR is the best predictor of 1972 fertility (beta = 0.64). However, the impact of the time one control does not overwhelm the variables of substantive interest.

Of the remaining variables, structural modernization is the second most important (beta = 0.23). Modernization, high transition potential, population size, and legal abortion all promote declines in fertility over time. Countries with high agricultural land per capita ratios and Islamic religion are less likely to experience fertility declines. Neither regional variable affects 1958–1972 fertility change. Because the direction of effects of variables in the cross-sectional and fertility-change analyses are the same,

*Table 3.* Lagged Dependent Variable Model of Fertility Change—Coefficients from Regression of 1972 CBR on Independent Variables: 117 Countries.

| Independent Variables | Regression Coefficients: Metric (b) Coefficient | Standardized (beta) Coeff. |
|---|---|---|
| 1958 CBR | 0.71[a] | 0.64 |
| 1950 Modernization | −3.07[a] | −0.23 |
| 1950 Log Land per Capita | 2.22[a] | 0.10 |
| 1958 High Transition Potential | −3.18[a] | −0.09 |
| Percent Islamic | 0.02[a] | 0.06 |
| 1950 Log Population | −1.02[b] | −0.05 |
| 1957 Legal Abortion | −2.68[b] | −0.05 |
| Low Literacy Latin America | 1.08 | 0.03 |
| Southern Europe | −1.66 | −0.03 |
| Constant | 11.79[a] | |
| $R^2$ | 0.94 | |

[a]p = 0.05 and metric coefficient is greater than twice its standard error.
[b]p = 0.10 and of "borderline" significance.

the conclusion is that most variables that explain fertility differentials at particular points in time also influence changes in fertility over time.

This analysis was supplemented with one directly measuring 1958 to 1972 change in CBR. The set of variables in Table 3 explained 49 percent of the variance in change scores. All variables significant at the 0.05 or higher level in Table 3 were significant at the 0.05 level, while the two borderline variables were also borderline in the change score analyses. Neither regional variable was significant in the change score analyses. All variables of substantive interest take the same sign in both analyses: the four variables with the largest beta coefficients in the change score analysis are 1958 CBR, 1950 modernization, high 1958 transition potential and log land per capita, in that order. This is virtually the same order yielded by the lagged dependent variable analysis. Both methods of measuring change produce comparable results.[1]

### *Summary*

Structural modernization is the most important variable in analyses of 1958 and 1972 crude birth rates. "Latin America," Southern Europe," "Islamic religion" and "legal abortion" have substantial independent effects on fertility in both years, while land per capita and population size are significant only in 1972. The analysis of fertility change provides the basis for concluding that the factors which explain cross-national variation in the level of fertility were also important influences on change over time. These findings provide added confirmation of the model.

This analysis of the world's nations adds to earlier support for modernization theory based on a longitudinal analysis of 20th century fertility differentials among Latin American countries (Cutright, Hout, and Johnson, 1976). Claims of empirical disproving of modernization theory by researchers (e.g., Janowitz, 1973b) seem premature, and may originate from methodological and conceptual problems identified earlier.

### *An Alternative Model of Fertility*

An economic model of historical change in national fertility rates provides an alternative conceptual scheme to that employed here; it takes similar empirical indicators, but interprets them in a different light. Rather than interpreting relationships between measures of structural modernization or other factors in terms of their effects on traditional kinship domination over nuclear family fertility decisions, sex roles, mortality, and level of living aspirations, the economic view speaks of preferences, prices and resources.

Spengler's (1966) economic theory of historical declines in fertility rates has been tested and carefully reviewed by Heer (1966; 1975, Chapter 5). The *preference system,* or the value a couple sets on an additional birth in relation to their desire for alternative goods, is one of three pillars of the theory. The second is the *price system,* or the costs of achieving alternative goods. The last is *resources,* or the time, energy, and money a couple has to acquire for what they want from life.

The theory holds that in modernizing nations, decreases in child mortality, the declining contribution of children to family income, mass education, child labor laws, the effective demand children make on family income to develop their skills and, thus, compete in an increasingly achievement-oriented economy, a decline in social rewards for large family size, all act to change the preference system and reduce fertility. With increasing modernization the *price system* also becomes less favorable to large families because of the impact of urbanization on housing and other costs of large families, including rising direct and indirect costs of child care as the value of female labor increases (see Heer, 1975, pp. 74–79 for additional discussion).

The negative effects of modernization on fertility, related to the preference and price system, tend to be offset by the increase in real per capita income, leisure time, better parental health, and longevity. Couples are less likely to be shattered by death and have more time, energy, and money to rear children in rich than in poor countries.

This appealing theory is difficult to test. The only explicit effort is by Heer (1966), using fertility around 1953 from 41 populations. Summarizing his empirical work Heer (1975, p. 64) states: ". . .when the relation of income to fertility is considered in a simultaneous statistical analysis holding constant the effects of four other variables, per capita income is found to have a positive rather than a negative relation with the national fertility level." However, the source for this claim (Heer, 1966, Table 3) indicates that net national product per capita (aged 15–64 years) was *not* significantly related to fertility in either an additive or a multiplicative model.

To test the economic view that increasing "resources" will increase fertility net of other factors, cross-sectional data is used following Heer's example, but these data have more adequate statistical controls, a larger case base, two cross-sectional and one change analysis. The measures of resources are untransformed gross national product per capita and the natural logarithmic form.

Table 4 shows the results. To simplify data presentation, only the coefficients for GNP/C from each regression are displayed. Each cross-sectional analysis uses the independent variables listed in Table 2, but the 1950 or 1960 modernization index omits GNP/C. The GNP/C measure is included as a separate predictor. The results of a lagged dependent variable analysis of 1972 CBR test the hypothesis that GNP/C affects change in fertility over time.

*Table 4.* Standardized (Beta) Coefficients of Two Measures of GNP/CAPITA on 1972 and 1958 Crude Birth Rates: 117 Countries.

| | 1972 CBR | | 1958 CBR |
|---|---|---|---|
| Statistics | Cross-Section | Includes 1958 CBR | Cross-Section |
| | | GNP/C | |
| Beta coefficient | −0.09 | −0.02 | −0.02 |
| Significance (p) | 0.16 | 0.76 | 0.74 |
| | | Log GNP/C | |
| Beta coefficient | −0.08 | −0.10 | 0.06 |
| Significance (p) | 0.40 | 0.15 | 0.56 |

*Note:* GNP/C coefficients are from equations including a modernization index that excludes GNP/C, low literacy Latin America, Southern Europe, log land, log population, Islamic religion, and legal abortion. CBR for 1958 and time one measures of independent variables are used in the lagged dependent variable analyses of 1972 CBR.

In the upper panel of Table 4, the GNP/C measure is not transformed, following Heer's example. Neither the 1972 nor the 1958 GNP/C beta coefficients have a significant independent effect on fertility, and GNP/C is not significant in the lagged dependent variable equation.

The lower panel shows the results using the natural logarithm of GNP/C. The regression coefficients for log GNP/C are not significant in either cross-sectional equation. The sign of the negative coefficient in the lagged analysis is opposite to the effect expected from the theory.

We conclude that these tests for an independent positive effect of national income on fertility fail to support the hypothesis. However, the economic rationale for preference and price effects on fertility is consistent with the finding that structural modernization decreases fertility.

Because the empirical measures used in the economic model are virtually identical to indicators of structural modernization, and these variables are so highly intercorrelated, a test or set of tests is unlikely to indicate whether the economic or modernization theory is "correct." Given the results of the above tests of the independent effect of the resource concept, the conclusion might well be that the economic theory elaborates our understanding of the consequences of structural modernization that cause fertility declines. Thus, if increasing levels of modernization break down traditional kinship domination and sex roles and increase aspirations, the preference and price system will change. These changes then facilitate the social-psychological processes seen by Coale as necessary preconditions for marital fertility declines. Coale (1973, p. 65) says marital rates will decline when (1) parents balance advantages against disadvantages before having another child; (2) they conclude that smaller family size is beneficial; and (3) they can use methods to effectively control their fertility. Changes in the preference and price system probably work most strongly on the first two preconditions. But changes in the preference and price system are caused by prior societal changes induced by structural modernization.

## MORTALITY ANALYSES

*Crude Death Rates and Life Expectancy in 1972*

Because mortality is rapidly changed by improvements in sanitation, public health programs, and nutrition, and these causes are all products of structural modernization, the index of modernization should be the key determinant of mortality. A study of mortality differentials among nations is needed to better understand differences in population growth rates. A model using two measures of mortality (U.S. Bureau of the Census, 1974) is now estimated.

The first mortality measure is the 1972 crude death rate (CDR), the number of deaths in 1972 per 1000 population. Mean 1972 CDR is 14.5 (S.D. = 6.2). The second mortality measure is life expectancy at birth in 1972 (mean is 56.9, S.D. = 11.9). Life expectancy is age standardized. Removing the effects of age differences on mortality among nations is important. Because populations in developed countries have lower fertility and mortality, the percentage under age 15 is much smaller and percentage over age 60 is much larger than in developing countries. The older populations of developed nations, therefore, have inflated crude death rates, while the younger populations of underdeveloped countries have deflated rates. Cross-national comparisons of factors affecting mortality should use an age-standardized mortality rate such as life expectancy.

Structural modernization is expected to be the most important predictor of mortality and regional effects, net of modernization, is also expected to be significant because the effective diffusion of mortality control knowledge and programs should vary among less developed populations. These differences are expected because some less developed nations are closer culturally and geographically to centers of modern health care and should benefit from this proximity. Other less developed nations (for example, those recently under colonial rule) should have unusually high mortality. If land per capita is related to mortality, the relationship should be positive because health care is more difficult to provide for a sparsely-settled than a densely-settled territory.

African countries have higher mortality than underdeveloped nations of other regions. African nations (excluding those on the Mediterranean and South Africa) are scored as 1 and all other countries are scored as 0.

Nations on the Mediterranean are less isolated from European influence, while South Africa clearly is unlike countries to the north.

Table 5 shows variables with significant relations to mortality. Explained variance in the crude death rate is 0.75, a figure far below 0.91 when life expectancy is used. Because life expectancy is the superior analytical measure, the results for it are reported in some detail while only passing comments are made about the CDR statistics.

The standardized coefficients (betas) in Table 5 reveal the overwhelming importance of modernization on life expectancy. The beta for modernization is 0.77, while the second largest beta is the −0.20 effect for Africa; a coefficient of −.11 is the effect of the log-land measure. The Southern European region has a significant and positive effect on life expectancy, while Latin America is also positive, but is not significant. Population size, Islamic culture, and legal abortion have no relationship to life expectancy and are omitted from this model. Taking modernization alone as the sole predictor of variation in life expectancy, 85 percent of the differences in national longevity can be explained. The additional variables add 6 percent.

Geographic and cultural proximity to other more developed European nations is assumed to explain the favorable effect of Southern European location on mortality. Perhaps the inability of most newly independent African governments to quickly develop death-control programs after independence (and the lack of attention to such programs by their former rulers) explains the unfavorable relationship of African location with life expectancy. The negative effect of high land per capita ratios on life expectancy may be related to the difficulty of providing care to sparsely settled populations.

*Table 5.* Regression Analyses of 1972 Life Expectancy and 1972 Crude Death Rates: 117 Countries.

| | Measure of Mortality | | | |
|---|---|---|---|---|
| | Life Expectancy | | Crude Death Rate | |
| Independent Variables | Metric (b) Coeff. | Stand. (beta) Coeff. | Metric (b) Coeff. | Stand. (beta) Coeff. |
| Modernization 1960 | 9.14[a] | 0.77 | −3.12[a] | −0.50 |
| Log Land per Capita 1965 | −2.06[a] | −0.11 | 1.24[a] | 0.12 |
| Low Literacy Latin America | 1.17 | 0.03 | −2.71[a] | −0.14 |
| Southern Europe | 4.32[a] | 0.09 | −2.47[a] | −0.10 |
| Africa | −5.35[a] | −0.20 | 5.28[a] | 0.37 |
| Constant | 59.92 | | 12.40 | |
| $R^2$ | 0.91 | | 0.75 | |

[a]p = 0.05 and metric coefficient is greater than twice its standard error.

Analysis of CDR finds lower explained variance in CDR than life expectancy. The zero-order correlation of modernization is much lower using crude death rates (−0.76 v. 0.92) rather than the age-adjusted measure—a difference expected because of the positive relationship of modernization to older age structures. This large difference in correlations explains much of the lower explained variance when CDR rather than life expectancy is the dependent variable. Latin America is significant only in the CDR analysis and this effect is probably related to the very young age structure of low-literacy Latin nations relative to modernization.

## ANALYSIS OF THE RATE OF NATURAL INCREASE

Do factors that affect fertility and mortality also have significant impacts on the rate of natural increase (RNI)? For example, the negative effect of modernization on fertility could conceivably be canceled by an equally large negative effect on crude death rates, with a resulting zero net effect on the rate of natural increase. The cross-sectional model is now applied to 1972 RNI, the only year for which both crude birth and death rates are available.

The 1972 crude death rate subtracted from 1972 CBR yields the rate of natural increase (RNI) per 1000 population. The data have a mean 1972 CBR of 35.9, mean CDR of 14.5 and a resulting RNI mean of 21.4 (S.D.= 9.9). The 1972 death and birth rates are correlated 0.706 and their respective correlations with the RNI are 0.317 and 0.895. The impact of the birth rate on the rate of natural increase is *far* more important than is the effect of the death rate.

The effect of factors related to fertility and mortality on the RNI is now measured. Regression equations using a common set of independent variables, first taking the CBR and then the CDR as the dependent variable show how each independent variable achieves its impact on the RNI. The results are displayed in Table 6.

Comparison of columns 1 and 2 in the first row finds the negative effect of modernization on CBR stronger than its negative effect on the CDR. Subtracting the CDR coefficient from the CBR coefficient equals the metric coefficient for modernization on the rate of natural increase. The conclusion is that the negative impact of modernization on mortality does not increase the RNI because an ever larger negative effect of modernization on fertility exists.

A different pattern of effects is shown for land per capita. The positive relationship of land on fertility is offset by its positive effect on the death rate, yielding an insignificant effect on natural increase. Population size has no significant effect on the CDR, and its significant negative effect on

*Table 6.* Regression Analyses of the 1972 Rate of Natural Increase: 117 Countries.

| Independent Variables | Dependent Variables, 1972 | | | |
|---|---|---|---|---|
| | Crude Birth Rate (Metric) | Crude Death Rate (Metric) | Rate of Natural Increase (Metric) | (beta) |
| Modernization 1960 | −9.62[a] | −2.74[a] | −6.88[a] | −0.70 |
| 1965 Log Land per Capita | 1.71[a] | 0.97[b] | 0.74 | 0.05 |
| 1965 Log Population | −1.63[a] | 0.37 | −2.00[a] | −0.12 |
| Low Literacy | 7.13[a] | −1.78[b] | 8.91[a] | 0.28 |
| Latin America | | | | |
| Southern Europe | −6.30[a] | −2.18[b] | −4.12[a] | −0.11 |
| Africa | 0.62 | 6.10[a] | −5.48[a] | −0.24 |
| Percent Islamic | 0.05[a] | 0.02[b] | 0.03[b] | 0.10 |
| Legal Abortion 1971 | −2.63[a] | 0.16 | −2.79[a] | −0.16 |
| Constant | 39.50 | 10.36 | 29.14 | |
| $R^2$ | 0.91 | 0.76 | 0.76 | |

[a]p = 0.05 and metric coefficient is greater than twice its standard error.
[b]p − 0.10 and of "borderline" significance.

the CBR translates directly into a negative effect on the rate of natural increase.

The large positive coefficient of "Latin America" on the CBR is accompanied by a large negative coefficient on mortality; the absolute sum of the two (8.9) equals the net direct effect of the "Latin" variable on the RNI. The negative impact of Southern European location on the CBR is partially negated by its negative effect on the CDR. African location depressed the rate of national increase because this variable is related to high death rates.

Neither Islamic religious composition nor legal abortion affect mortality and their effects on the RNI are primarily a reflection of their differing impacts on fertility. Most variables with significant impact on 1972 birth rates also had a significant effect on the 1972 rate of natural increase.

The beta coefficients from the RNI analysis show "modernization" as the most important predictor followed at some distance by "Latin America" and "Africa." "Legal abortion" is the fourth ranked predictor.

## CONCLUSION

We have developed and tested a model that provides good theoretical and empirical fit with national fertility differentials. The model depends on a modernization theory of the European fertility transition and is sociological in origin. It explains the relationship of structural modernization to fertility by positing an impact of modernization on the nuclear family, sex roles, mortality, and individual aspirations. The theory recognizes that the timing of fertility transitions is not automatically triggered by achieving some threshold level of modernization. Timing differences exist because cultural, geographic, and demographic factors peculiar to given populations will inhibit or accelerate the impact of modernization on fertility rates. Our basic model of fertility differentials included an index of modernization and measures of cultural, demographic, and geographic variables.

Because the crude birth rate is the primary cause of national differences in the rate of population growth, most variables that affect the birth rate affect population growth in the same way. Variables that affect death rates also increase or decrease the growth rate. Modernization was the overwhelming variable explaining mortality, and was especially important in analysis of life expectancy. Other variables had only a small role in raising explained variance of national differentials in life expectancy.

Despite the dominant role of modernization on decreasing mortality, this variable had even larger effects on fertility; consequently, modernization emerged as the most important variable depressing the rate of natural increase. Low literacy Latin America, Southern European, and African location had net effects on the rate of natural increase, with the African effect solely due to higher mortality, the Latin American effect due largely to higher than expected fertility, and the Southern European effect primarily from lower than expected fertility. Islamic culture increases growth rates because it increases fertility net of other factors.

Nations with laws and medical resources able to deliver legal abortion on request have lower fertility and lower growth rates than expected. Nations with abortion on request are in the more developed category. The abortion effect on growth rates means that nations with relatively high levels of modernization will have lower fertility than expected net of other characteristics if they also have laws and practices allowing abortion on request. Whether nations at lower levels of development would experience such large effects on birth and growth rates by changing their abortion laws and providing medical resources is unknown.

Regional effects on fertility and growth rates are believed to result from diffusion of birth control practices interacting with time and cultural factors. Our findings suggest that Teitlebaum (1975) may be correct in suggesting that the availability of mass media as a new and effective means of diffusion, and deliberate efforts by governments to encourage practices that reduce fertility, may accelrate fertility declines in underdeveloped countries, even in the absence of rapid improvements in modernization. China, for example, may fit Goldscheider's (1971) example of a population where substitutes for structural modernization are developed by government and rapidly reduce mortality, kinship domination, traditional sex roles, and increase aspirations. Deliberate and direct efforts to change the socio-demographic factors that mediate effects of modernization change on fertility characterize Chinese population activities over the past 15 years. The Chinese approach emphasizes delayed marriage, moves the locus of reproductive goal setting from the kinship group and family to the state, presses equal rights for women, effectively preaches and implements a noticeable increase in living standards for the masses, and provides the full range of birth control services. This rapid and successful organization of the largest population on earth, and provision of relatively cheap substitutes for structural modernization, suggests that socio-political organizations, directed at controlling vital rates, may be more important than structural change in modernization (as measured here) for future fertility and growth rate declines in much of the underdeveloped world. If this shift occurs, it would *not* disprove modernization theory. The theory states that increasing modernization will depress fertility only if it affects primary groups and individuals in certain ways. But changes in kinship domination and the other intermediate factors can be achieved by effective government. If substitutes for modernization are not implemented fairly soon, the future of much of the underdeveloped world is probably as bleak as Heilbroner (1974) and others have suggested. The Appendix to this chapter follows (page 40).

*Table A.1* Correlation of Variables in Analyses of 1958 and 1972 Crude Birth Rates: 117 Countries.

| | | 1[a] | 2[a] | 3[a] | 4 | 5 | 6 | 7[a] | 8 | 9[a] |
|---|---|---|---|---|---|---|---|---|---|---|
| Modernization[a] | 1[a] | 0.981 | −0.190 | 0.216 | 0.207 | −0.003 | −0.436 | 0.472 | 0.223 | −0.906 |
| Log Land/Capita[a] | 2[a] | −0.223 | 0.994 | −0.257 | 0.028 | 0.088 | 0.217 | −0.210 | −0.087 | 0.307 |
| Log Population | 3[a] | 0.248 | −0.284 | 0.994 | 0.066 | −0.083 | −0.068 | 0.265 | −0.020 | −0.314 |
| Southern Europe | 4 | 0.179 | 0.002 | 0.090 | 1.000 | −0.096 | −0.109 | 0.009 | 0.072 | −0.309 |
| Low Literacy Latin America | 5 | −0.005 | 0.116 | −0.109 | −0.096 | 1.000 | −0.229 | −0.142 | −0.151 | 0.178 |
| Percent Islamic | 6 | −0.438 | 0.234 | −0.084 | −0.109 | −0.229 | 1.000 | −0.231 | −0.106 | 0.474 |
| Legal Abortion[a] | 7[a] | 0.221 | −0.134 | 0.270 | 0.061 | −0.096 | −0.142 | 0.715 | −0.130 | −0.553 |
| 1958 High Transition Potential | 8 | 0.255 | −0.054 | −0.052 | 0.072 | −0.151 | −0.106 | −0.116 | 1.000 | −0.137 |
| CBR[a] | 9[a] | 0.868 | 0.264 | −0.331 | −0.332 | 0.196 | 0.419 | −0.392 | 0.030 | 0.943 |

[a]Measures of modernization, area per capita, population, legal abortion and CBR are for different years—see text. The main diagonal shows correlations of these variables at two points in time.

*Note:* Correlations for anlysis of 1958 CBR are below the diagonal and those for 1972 CBR are above the diagonal.

Table A.2. Crude Birth Rates and Errors of Prediction from Equations for 1972 and 1958 CBR'S: 117 Countries.[a]

| | 1972 | | 1958 | |
|---|---|---|---|---|
| Country | CBR | Error[a] | CBR | Error[a] |
| 1. Afghanistan | 51 | 0.1 | 51 | −0.2 |
| 2. Albania | 35 | 2.9 | 42 | 6.4 |
| 3. Algeria | 50 | 5.3 | 48 | 4.1 |
| 4. Angola | 50 | 3.6 | 50 | 1.9 |
| 5. Argentina | 21 | 2.9 | 24 | 4.8 |
| 6. Australia | 19 | −0.8 | 23 | 2.5 |
| 7. Austria | 14 | −6.5 | 17 | −7.8 |
| 8. Belgium | 14 | −4.1 | 17 | −5.3 |
| 9. Bolivia | 44 | −4.0 | 43 | −6.7 |
| 10. Brazil | 37 | −3.3 | 43 | −0.9 |
| 11. Bulgaria | 15 | −6.0 | 19 | −5.5 |
| 12. Burma | 40 | −1.9 | 46 | 0.5 |
| 13. Burundi | 48 | 0.2 | 50 | 1.0 |
| 14. Cambodia | 44 | 0.9 | 47 | 0.6 |
| 15. Cameroon | 39 | −8.4 | 40 | −7.6 |
| 16. Canada | 16 | −4.2 | 28 | 6.0 |
| 17. Central Africa Republic | 46 | −1.2 | 48 | 0.4 |
| 18. Chad | 48 | −4.6 | 46 | −4.0 |
| 19. Chile | 25 | −4.0 | 37 | 4.9 |
| 20. China | 31 | −6.2 | 40 | −5.7 |
| 21. Colombia | 43 | 3.4 | 45 | 1.3 |
| 22. Costa Rica | 32 | −2.4 | 47 | 11.9 |
| 23. Cuba | 26 | 1.7 | 32 | 0.5 |
| 24. Czechoslovakia | 17 | 2.5 | 19 | −0.1 |
| 25. Dahomey | 50 | 2.8 | 50 | 3.1 |
| 26. Denmark | 15 | −0.1 | 16 | −4.9 |
| 27. Dominican Republic | 46 | 10.7 | 46 | 5.5 |
| 28. Ecuador | 44 | 0.2 | 47 | 0.6 |
| 29. Egypt | 37 | −2.9 | 49 | 5.5 |
| 30. El Salvador | 42 | −1.7 | 48 | 1.5 |
| 31. Ethiopia | 51 | 1.4 | 51 | 1.5 |
| 32. Finland | 13 | −5.8 | 20 | −7.4 |
| 33. France | 17 | −3.0 | 18 | −7.6 |
| 34. Germany (East) | 12 | −0.3 | 16 | −11.4 |
| 35. Germany (West) | 11 | −4.5 | 17 | −7.2 |
| 36. Ghana | 47 | 6.5 | 50 | 6.2 |
| 37. Greece | 16 | −3.7 | 19 | −5.3 |
| 38. Guatemala | 42 | −2.8 | 49 | 0.0 |
| 39. Guinea | 47 | −2.7 | 47 | −3.0 |
| 40. Haiti | 44 | −0.6 | 45 | −1.0 |
| 41. Honduras | 49 | 0.8 | 50 | 1.2 |
| 42. Hong Kong | 19 | −2.4 | 36 | 4.9 |
| 43. Hungary | 15 | −3.0 | 18 | −3.8 |
| 44. India | 37 | −2.5 | 42 | −3.9 |
| 45. Indonesia | 45 | 1.2 | 43 | −5.1 |

*(Table A.2. continued)*

| Country | 1972 | | 1958 | |
|---|---|---|---|---|
| | CBR | Error[a] | CBR | |
| 46. Iran | 47 | 4.6 | 48 | 1.6 |
| 47. Iraq | 48 | 3.5 | 48 | 2.9 |
| 48. Ireland | 23 | −2.8 | 21 | −7.4 |
| 49. Israel | 28 | 8.9 | 28 | 7.5 |
| 50. Italy | 16 | 0.5 | 18 | −3.5 |
| 51. Ivory Coast | 46 | 2.3 | 46 | −1.3 |
| 52. Jamaica | 34 | 1.4 | 39 | 3.6 |
| 53. Japan | 19 | 8.1 | 18 | −0.8 |
| 54. Jordan | 46 | 3.7 | 45 | 0.3 |
| 55. Kenya | 49 | 5.8 | 50 | 4.5 |
| 56. Korea (South) | 29 | 0.1 | 45 | 3.9 |
| 57. Laos | 42 | −4.4 | 42 | −5.7 |
| 58. Lebanon | 40 | 7.7 | 40 | 2.9 |
| 59. Liberia | 50 | 2.1 | 50 | 2.1 |
| 60. Libya | 46 | 0.0 | 46 | −1.4 |
| 61. Malagasy Republic | 46 | 1.2 | 49 | 3.2 |
| 62. Malawi | 49 | 2.1 | 48 | −1.2 |
| 63. Malaysia | 38 | −0.6 | 44 | 1.1 |
| 64. Mali | 50 | −1.4 | 50 | 0.6 |
| 65. Mauritania | 44 | −11.0 | 45 | −5.4 |
| 66. Mexico | 43 | 5.1 | 46 | 3.0 |
| 67. Mongolia | 40 | 4.2 | 40 | −2.0 |
| 68. Morocco | 49 | 5.0 | 46 | 1.5 |
| 69. Mozambique | 44 | −3.9 | 45 | −3.6 |
| 70. Nepal | 45 | −0.1 | 45 | −3.5 |
| 71. Netherlands | 16 | −2.7 | 21 | −3.1 |
| 72. New Zealand | 20 | 0.7 | 26 | 4.9 |
| 73. Nicaragua | 47 | 3.0 | 46 | −0.5 |
| 74. Niger | 52 | −0.8 | 52 | 2.0 |
| 75. Nigeria | 49 | 3.8 | 50 | 2.1 |
| 76. Norway | 17 | 0.3 | 18 | −4.4 |
| 77. Pakistan | 45 | −0.6 | 48 | −1.5 |
| 78. Panama | 36 | −3.9 | 41 | −0.7 |
| 79. Papua/New Guinea | 44 | −1.3 | 44 | −5.0 |
| 80. Paraguay | 45 | 1.2 | 44 | −2.3 |
| 81. Peru | 41 | −0.5 | 46 | 0.4 |
| 82. Philippines | 43 | 7.4 | 50 | 10.9 |
| 83. Poland | 17 | −4.7 | 27 | 3.7 |
| 84. Portugal | 20 | −4.6 | 24 | −4.3 |
| 85. Rhodesia | 48 | 7.5 | 48 | 2.9 |
| 86. Rumania | 19 | −5.1 | 23 | −0.8 |
| 87. Rwanda | 50 | 2.2 | 50 | 1.7 |
| 88. Saudi Arabia | 50 | 0.5 | 50 | 0.7 |
| 89. Senegal | 45 | −1.5 | 43 | −3.6 |
| 90. Sierra Leone | 45 | −1.8 | 45 | −1.8 |
| 91. Singapore | 23 | −2.0 | 43 | 14.5 |

*(Table A.2. continued)*

| Country | 1972 CBR | 1972 Error[a] | 1958 CBR | 1958 Error[a] |
|---|---|---|---|---|
| 92. Somalia Republic | 45 | −8.2 | 45 | −5.3 |
| 93. Sri Lanka | 30 | −7.6 | 37 | −3.7 |
| 94. South Africa (Republic) | 40 | 6.3 | 41 | 5.6 |
| 95. Spain | 19 | 0.5 | 21 | −2.8 |
| 96. Sudan | 49 | 1.3 | 50 | 1.1 |
| 97. Sweden | 14 | 0.5 | 15 | −6.5 |
| 98. Switzerland | 14 | −0.7 | 18 | −3.1 |
| 99. Syria | 48 | 5.6 | 49 | 5.9 |
| 100. Taiwan | 24 | −7.3 | 43 | 5.5 |
| 101. Tanzania | 47 | −0.5 | 46 | −2.8 |
| 102. Thailand | 37 | −2.0 | 46 | 1.7 |
| 103. Togo | 51 | 4.3 | 51 | 2.6 |
| 104. Tunisia | 40 | −4.4 | 43 | −0.6 |
| 105. Turkey | 39 | −2.5 | 42 | −2.2 |
| 106. Uganda | 45 | 0.9 | 42 | −5.6 |
| 107. U.S.S.R. | 18 | 3.4 | 25 | 4.1 |
| 108. United Kingdom | 15 | 3.2 | 16 | −2.1 |
| 109. U.S.A. | 16 | 3.4 | 25 | 6.4 |
| 110. Upper Volta | 49 | 0.3 | 50 | 0.7 |
| 111. Uruguay | 22 | 3.5 | 22 | 1.7 |
| 112. Venezuela | 40 | 3.5 | 44 | 2.9 |
| 113. Yemen | 50 | 0.9 | 50 | −1.7 |
| 114. Yeman (South) | 50 | 0.0 | 50 | −0.5 |
| 115. Yugoslavia | 18 | −2.1 | 25 | 3.0 |
| 116. Zaire | 44 | −1.7 | 44 | −2.8 |
| 117. Zambia | 50 | 6.8 | 51 | 7.7 |

[a]Observed minus CBR values predicted from equations in Table 2 that omit variables below borderline significance. The standard deviation of the errors in 1958 was 4.6; in 1972, 4.1.

# FOOTNOTES

* Phillips Cutright is a Professor and William R. Kelly a graduate student in the Department of Sociology, Indiana University, Bloomington. They are currently working on time-series analyses of trends in U.S. fertility since World War I. Cutright and F. S. Jaffe's 1977 book, *Family Planning Programs and the Reduction of Fertility: The United States Experience,* evaluates the impact of family-planning programs on U.S. fertility rates.

The generous support of Indiana University, Bloomington, is gratefully acknowledged. We also thank Michael Hout for comments on an earlier draft.

1. It can be shown algebraically that the lagged dependent variable model is directly derivable from the gain score model. That is, the unstandardized coefficient for the time one control in the lagged dependent variable model differs by a factor of 1.0 from the time one control in the gain score model.

## REFERENCES


Adelman, Irma and Morris C. (1966), "A Quantitative Study of Social and Political Determinants of Fertility." *Economic Development and Cultural Change* 14:129–157.

Banks, Arthur S. (1971) *Cross Polity Time Series Data*. Cambridge: Massachusetts Institute of Technology Press.

Barbera, Henry (1973) *Rich Nations and Poor in Peace and War*. Lexington, MA: Lexington Books.

Beaver, Steven E. (1975) *Demographic Transition Theory Reinterpreted*. Lexington, MA: Lexington Books.

Blalock, Hubert M., Jr. (1964) *Causal Inferences in Nonexperimental Research*. Chapel Hill: University of North Carolina Press.

——— (1968) "Theory Construction and Causal Inferences." Pages 155–198 in Hubert M. Blalock, Jr. and A. B. Blalock, (eds.), *Methodology in Social Research*. New York: McGraw-Hill.

Bogue, Donald and Palmore, J. A. (1964) "Some Empirical and Analytic Relations Among Demographic Fertility Measures, With Regression Models for Fertility Estimation." *Demography* 1:316–338.

Bohrnstedt, George W. (1969) "Observations on the Measurement of Change." Pages 113–136 in E. F. Borgatta (ed.), *Sociological Methodology 1969*. San Francisco: Jossey-Bass.

Campbell, Arthur (1975) "Beyond the Demographic Transition." *Demography* 11:549–561.

Chase-Dunn, C. (1975) "The Effects of International Dependence on Development and Inequality: A Cross-National Study." *American Sociological Review* 40:720–738.

Coale, Ansley, J. (1969) "The Decline in Fertility in Europe from the French Revolution to World War II." Pages 3–24 in S. J. Behrman, L. Corsa, Jr., and R. Freedman (eds.), *Fertility and Family Planning*. Ann Arbor: University of Michigan.

——— (1973) "The Demographic Transition Reconsidered." Volume 1, pages 53–72 in *Proceedings of the International Population Conference*. Liège, Belgium.

——— (1974) "The History of the Human Population." *Scientific American* 231:41–51.

Cronbach, Lee J. (1951) "Coefficient Alpha and the Internal Structure of Tests." *Psychometrika* 16:297–334.

Cutright, Phillips, Hout, M., and Johnson, D. R. (1976) "Structural Determinants of Fertility in Latin America: 1800–1970." *American Sociological Review* 41:511–527.

Davis, Kingsley (1955) "Institutional Patterns Favoring High Fertility in Underdeveloped Areas." *Eugenics Quarterly* 3:33–39.

——— (1969) *World Urbanization 1950–1970*. Volume 1: *Basic Data for Cities, Countries and Regions*. Berkeley: University of California Press.

Ekanem, Ita I. (1972) "A Further Note on the Relation Between Economic Development and Fertility." *Demography* 9:383–398.

Freedman, Ronald (1963) "Norms for Family Size in Underdeveloped Areas." *Proceedings of the Royal Society* 1959B:220–245.

——— and Berelson, B. (1974) "The Human Population." *Scientific American* 231:31–39.

Frideres, J. and Taylor, K. M. (1972) "Issues Versus Controversies: Substantive and Statistical Significance." *American Sociological Review* 37:464–471.

Friedlander, Stanley and Silver, M. (1967) "A Quantitative Study of the Determinants of Fertility Behavior." *Demography* 4:30–70.

Goldscheider, Calvin (1971) *Population, Modernization, and Social Structure*. Boston: Little, Brown.

Heer, David (1966) "Economic Development and Fertility." *Demography* 3:423–444.

——— (1975) *Society and Population*. Englewood Cliffs, NJ: Prentice-Hall.

Heilbroner, Robert L. (1974) *An Inquiry into the Human Prospect*. New York: Norton.

Heise, David R. (1970) "Causal Influence from Panel Data." Pages 3–27 in E. F. Borgatta and G. W. Bohrnstedt (eds.), *Sociological Methodology 1970*. San Francisco: Jossey-Bass.

Hohm, Charles F. (1975) "Social Security and Fertility: An International Perspective." *Demography* 12:629–644.

Janowitz, Barbara S. (1971) "An Empirical Study of the Effects of Socioeconomic Development on Fertility Rates." *Demography* 8:319–330.

——— (1973a) "Cross-Section Studies as Predictors of Trends in Birth Rates: A Note on Ekanem's Results." *Demography* 10:479–481.

——— (1973b) "An Econometric Analysis of Trends in Fertility Rates." *Journal of Development Studies* 9:413–425.

Johnson, David R. and Cutright, P. (1973) "Problems in the Analysis of Latin American Illegitimacy." Pages 377–408 in Michael Armer and A. D. Grimshaw (eds.), *Comparative Social Research: Methodological Problems and Strategies*. New York: Wiley.

Kasarda, John D. (1971) "Economic Structure and Fertility: A Comparative Analysis." *Demography* 8:307–330.

Kelly, William R., Cutright, P., and Hittle, D. (1976) "Comment on Charles F. Hohm's 'Social Security and Fertility: An International Perspective.'" *Demography* 13:581–586.

Keyfitz, Nathan (1976) "World Resources and the World Middle Class." *Scientific American* 235:28–35.

Kirk, Dudley (1966) "Factors Affecting Moslem Natality." Pages 561–680 in Bernard Berelson et al. (eds.), *Family Planning and Population Programs*. Chicago: University of Chicago Press.

——— (1971) "A New Demographic Transition?" Pages 123–147 in National Academy of Sciences, Study Committee of the Office of the Foreign Secretary, *Rapid Population Growth*. Baltimore: Johns Hopkins Press.

Lee, Ronald (1973) "Population in Preindustrial England: An Economic Analysis." *Quarterly Journal of Economics* 87:581–607.

Lieberson, Stanley and Hansen, L. (1974) "National Development, Mother-Tongue Diversity and the Comparative Study of Nations." *American Sociological Review* 39:523–547.

Matras, Judah (1973) *Populations and Socities*. Englewood Cliffs, NJ: Prentice-Hall.

Nortman, Dorothy (1975) *Population and Family Planning Programs: A Factbook*. Reports on Population/Family Planning. New York: Population Council.

Oechsli, Frank W. and Kirk, D. (1975) "Modernization and the Demographic Transition in Latin America and the Carribean." *Economic Development and Cultural Change* 23:391–419.

Office of Population Research (1966) "Table 1: Birth Rates." *Population Index* 32:473–487.

Orleans, Leo A. (1976) "China's Population Figures: Can the Contradictions be Resolved?" *Studies in Family Planning* 7:52–58.

Rothman, Ana Maria (1970) *Evolutión de la Fecundidad en Argentina y Uruguay*. Buenos Aires: Instituto Torcuato Di Tella Centro de Investigaciónes Sociales.

Russett, Bruce M. et al. (1964) *World Handbook of Political and Social Indicators*. New Haven: Yale University Press.

Ryder, Norman B. (1974) "The Family in Developed Countries." *Scientific American* 231:123–132.

Schuessler, Karl (1974) "Analysis of Ratio Variables: Opportunities and Pitfalls." *American Journal of Sociology* 80:379–398.

Spengler, Joseph J. (1966) "Values and Fertility Analysis." *Demography* 3:109–130.

Stolnitz, George (1964) "The Demographic Transition: From High to Low Birth Rates and Death Rates." Pages 30–46 in R. Freedman (ed.), *Population: The Vital Revolution.* Garden City, N.Y.: Doubleday.

Stycos, J. Mayone (1971) *Ideology, Faith, and Family Planning in Latin America: Studies in Public and Private Opinion on Fertility Control.* New York: McGraw-Hill.

Taylor, Charles L. and Hudson, M. C. (1972) *World Handbook of Political and Social Indicators.* 2d ed. New Haven: Yale University Press.

Teitlebaum, Michael S. (1975) "Relevance of Demographic Transition Theory for Developing Countries." *Science* 188:420–425.

Tietze, Christopher (1969) "Induced Abortion as a Method of Fertility Control." Pages 311–337 in S. J. Behrman, L. Corsa, Jr., and R. Freedman (eds.), *Fertility and Family Planning.* Ann Arbor: University of Michigan.

——— (1972) "The Potential Impact of Legal Abortion on Population Growth in the United States." Pages 581–585 in Commission on Population Growth and the American Future, Volume 1: *Demographic and Social Aspects of Population Growth.* Edited by Charles F. Westoff and R. Parke, Jr. Washington, DC: Government Printing Office.

Tietze, Christopher and Murstein, M. C. (1975) *Induced Abortion: 1975 Factbook.* New York: Population Council.

UNESCO (1968) *Compendium of Social Statistics: 1967.* New York: United Nations.

United Nations (1957) *Statistical Yearbook.* New York, United Nations.

——— (1965) *Population Bulletin of the United Nations.* 1963, no. 7.

U.S. Bureau of the Census (1974) *World Population: 1973.* Washington, DC: Government Printing Office.

Van de Walle, Etienne and Knodel, J. (1969) "Demographic Transition and Fertility Decline: The European Case." Pages 47–55 in *Conference of the International Union for the Scientific Study of Population* Sydney, Australia, 1967, *Proceedings.*

Westoff, Charles F. (1974) "The Populations of the Developed Countries." *Scientific American* 231:108–120.

Wrigley, E. A. (1969) *Population and History.* New York: McGraw-Hill.

Yousef, Nadia H. (1972) "Differential Labor Force Participation of Women in Latin America and Middle Eastern Countries: The Influence of Family Characteristics." *Social Forces* 51:135–153.

# NATIONAL DIFFERENCES IN INDIVIDUAL MODERNITY

Alex Inkeles*

## INTRODUCTION

In *Becoming Modern* we reported that in a set of six developing countries we were able to "explain" a median of 47 percent of the variance in individual modernity (OM) scores by weighing the contribution of a series of eight variables, of which education, occupational experience, and mass media were most notable.[1] Since our basic design committed us to looking at the phenomenon one country at a time, we were of necessity precluded from utilizing national membership as one of the explanatory variables.[2] Yet the question of how far national (or indeed ethnic) groups vary in their

**Comparative Studies in Sociology—Vol. 1, 1978, pages 47–72**

**ISBN 0-89232-025-7**

relative modernity is one of the oldest and most basic of those raised in the standard works on economic development (see, e.g., McClelland, 1961; Lerner, 1958; Hagen, 1962). In this paper we use the data of the former Harvard Project on Social and Cultural Aspects of Development to answer that question insofar as it applies to a comparison of men from Argentina, Chile, India, Israel, Nigeria, and East Pakistan (now Bangladesh).

In the research reported here we took as our task to establish whether and how far individuals who were rather strictly comparable in occupation, education, and other respects might nevertheless be more or less psychologically modern merely by virtue of being Argentinian, Chilean, and so on. We also meant to see whether taking account of national origin would permit us to explain more of the variance in individual modernity than we could earlier, and to compare the relative contribution of such national membership with that of membership in other groups, educational and occupational.

Our approach to this phase of our research was frankly exploratory rather than being oriented to the testing of an explicit hypothesis. Thus, we considered it quite possible that once we took account of the educational and occupational differences in our samples, the different national groups would be equal in modernity. On the other hand, if national character, religion, or some other cultural factor really was an important force in shaping individual modernity, then the national groups might vary considerably in their psychological modernity even after being matched on education. But there was no obvious principle which could guide us in deciding in what order the countries would stand and whether they would be widely spread out or bunched up in special ways. Another possibility was that some simple principle such as the level of economic development measured by GNP per capita would account for any underlying order which might emerge. But it was not clear how such a principle, if it operated, might interact with distinctive cultural factors.

Therefore, to prepare the ground for more effective systematic hypothesis testing, we set ourselves two more limited tasks. First, we took on the responsibility of working out the difficult methodological challenge of measuring the quality of individual modernity in such a way that a given score assigned to a person in one country would have exactly the same meaning when assigned to someone in another country. Second, using this new measure, we meant to discover the relative modernity of our six national samples after we had rendered them equivalent in average education, occupation, and so on. This done, we intended to study any pattern in the national rankings which might emerge, in order to draw out its implications for a theory as to the qualities of nations which make them more or less likely to produce psychologically modern citizens.

To live comfortably with our findings, however, and to understand the limitations of how far one can generalize our results, it is first necessary to know the basic facts about our larger study, and, in particular, the characteristics of the samples with which we worked. The description given here must, of course, be very brief, but full details are available in *Becoming Modern* (Inkeles and Smith, 1974).

## THE SAMPLE AND RESEARCH DESIGN

The main objective of the Project on Sociocultural Aspects of Development was to test a theory concerning the social forces producing "psychosocial modernity." Individual modernity is here conceived of as a complex set of interrelated attitudes, values, and behaviors fitting a theoretically derived model of the modern man, at least as he may appear among the "common men" in developing countries. In all six countries studied, we found that basically the same set of personal qualities which we had identified theoretically as defining the psychologically modern man cohered as a syndrome. The central elements of this syndrome were:

> (1) openness to new experience, both with people and with new ways of doing things such as attempting to control births; (2) the assertion of increasing independence from the authority of traditional figures like parents and priests and a shift of allegiance to leaders of government, public affairs, trade unions, cooperatives, and the like; (3) belief in the efficacy of science and medicine, and a general abandonment of passivity and fatalism in the face of life's difficulties; and (4) ambition for oneself and one's children to achieve high occupational and educational goals. Men who manifest these characteristics (5) like people to be on time and show an interest in carefully planning their affairs in advance. It is also part of this syndrome to (6) show strong interest and take an active part in civic and community affairs and local politics; and (7) to strive energetically to keep up with the news, and within this effort to prefer news of national and international import over items dealing with sports, religion, or purely local affairs (Inkeles, 1969, p. 210).

These and other related qualities were measured by a long series of questions, and the results summarized in an Overall Modernity (OM) score for each individual running from a low of zero to a high of 100.[3]

Having established the empirical existence of the syndrome of individual modernity, the Project sought to determine its antecedents, concomitants, and consequences. We were particularly interested to find out whether, and how, work in factories or similar enterprises changed attitudes, values, and habits in ways relevant to the individual's adjustment in and contribution to a modern or modernizing society. At the same time we tested the role of other "modernizing" experiences such as education, contact with urban living, and exposure to the mass media. In the research to be reported in this paper we extend the analysis in an effort to ascertain how far the nation as a setting determines individual modernity.

Our interview included almost 300 entries. Some 160 of these elicited attitudes, values, and opinions, or reported the behavior of others and oneself. We touched on almost every major aspect of daily life. Our questions were largely fixed choice, but we avoided the agree-disagree type answer, and instead presented basic human situations and dilemmas which could be responded to in the language of everyday speech. The questionnaire included various tests of verbal ability, literacy, political information, intelligence, and psychic adjustment. In some cases it took four hours of interviewing to complete—a demanding experience for both interviewer and interviewee.[4]

This questionnaire we then administered to some 5,500 young men in the six developing countries cited above. The samples were highly purposive, with the men to be interviewed selected to represent points on a presumed continuum of exposure to modernizing influences. The main groups were the cultivator of the land still rooted in his traditional rural community; the migrant from the countryside just arrived in the city but not yet integrated into urban industrial life; the urban but nonindustrial worker still pursuing a more or less traditional occupation, such as barber or carpenter, but now doing so in the urban environment even though outside the context of a modern large-scale organization; and the experienced industrial worker engaged in production using inanimate power and machinery within the context of a more or less modern productive enterprise.

Industrial workers were to be the largest sample in each country, some 600 to 700, whereas the other subgroups were to be 100 each. The targets were not, however, always reached. Within and across these sample groups we exercised numerous controls in the selection of subjects and in the analysis of our data. The selection of cases, therefore, was on the basis of the respondents' meeting certain common characteristics as to sex (all male), age (18–32), education (usually 0–12 years), religion, ethnicity, rural or urban origin, residence, and, of course, the occupational characteristics already mentioned.

Respondents were chosen within "sites," the most important being the factory. Up to 100 factories were included in each country. In practice virtually everyone meeting the sample criteria was selected from each factory, except the very largest. In those, up to 20 men were selected at random from among the pool of eligible subjects. Factories were selected on the basis of differentiation by size (5 categories), product (7 categories), and relative "modernity" (2 categories). Villages were chosen on the basis of being either the same as those from which the migrant industrial workers had come originally, or as being equivalent in region, culture, crop, and the like. Urban nonindustrials (UNI's) had to work outside large-scale production organizations in the same cities as the workers, and otherwise meet the general sampling criteria.

Because of constraints arising from the limits on our budget and personnel, these target groups could not be sought wherever they might be. Instead we operated within some territorial constraints. Thus, in selecting our worker sample, we were limited to the three main industrial cities within each geographical field of operations. In Argentina, Chile, East Pakistan, and Israel that field was the entire nation. In Nigeria, however, we were limited to the Southwest provinces, and in India to the province of Bihar. In addition, local circumstances sometimes dictated some specialization in the ethnic and religious composition of the samples. Thus, in Bihar half the sample was drawn from the group legally classified as the "scheduled tribes."[5] In Nigeria the sample was exclusively Yoruba speaking. And in Israel, Jews of European origin were excluded in favor of the so-called Oriental Jews who had more recently entered the country, mainly from North Africa, the Middle East, and Asia Minor.[6] Consequently, when we refer to Nigerians, Israelis, or Indians, the terms should always be understood to apply only to these particular subsets of nationals of those countries.

Although this sample design was well suited to some purposes, it was obviously not so appropriate for others. Normally, to compare nations, one would prefer that each country sample be strictly representative of its parent national population. Unfortunately, the main objective of the larger project, as noted, made a highly purposive sample more appropriate. Nevertheless, we believe the samples we did collect are not only relevant to our purpose, but even have some special virtue.

We pursued our national comparison in order to assess the extent to which any given society produces a more or less distinctive human product whose personality and orientation to the world express some essence of his culture or some distinctive features of the characteristic institutions of his nation. However, other factors than national tradition were known to shape the very qualities we were studying. It was important, therefore, not to confuse the issue by attributing to the "national setting" what should more accurately be attributed to some force like individual education. Consequently, to discern what was the distinctive role of nationality in shaping the modernity of Argentinians and Pakistanis, we were under obligation to consider only men who had had about the same amount of schooling and who pursued comparable occupations. Otherwise, we ran the risk of attributing to nationality what really should be attributed to formal education or to work experience. From this perspective, therefore,

the fact that our samples had the same general "structure" in all countries, being more or less alike in average education, age, sex, and occupation, was an advantage. We did not, however, rest in that position. Rather we undertook, through matching and regression analysis, to bring under statistical control any remaining differences in the relative advantage or disadvantage any of our national samples might suffer in education, occupation, and the like. We hoped thus to isolate as far as possible the "pure" influence, if any, of the national setting as a factor shaping individual modernity.

## CONSTRUCTING A STRICTLY COMPARABLE CROSS-NATIONAL SCALE OF INDIVIDUAL MODERNITY (IM)

Although the measures of individual modernity, called OM, used in the main part of our study were all constructed by the same method and were highly comparable in content, they were nevertheless not identical from country to country. Indeed, the OM scale had been calibrated separately within each country.

In constructing the OM, as against the IM scale used in this article, each item was dichotomized as close as possible to the midpoint of the distribution of answers *within* each country taken separately. Thus on a question concerning the ideal family size the "modern" answer could have been two or less in one country and four or less in another. The summary modernity or "OM" score for each individual, therefore, told us how far above or below the average he was *as compared to his own countrymen only*. An OM score of 80 was a "high," or "modern" score in all countries, but there was no clear-cut way of saying what the man who got 80 in India would have got if he had been scored using the coding criteria utilized in Argentina or Israel. That procedure was appropriate, indeed desirable and even necessary, to attain the goals set by our initial research design. In that design, we treated the research in each country as a separate replication of the basic study. Since we were mainly testing for the existence of an OM type syndrome in all six nations, and correlating that with a comparable set of independent variables, we wanted a scale which best discriminated *within* each national sample. By using variable cutting points and eliminating some items which were obviously not understood in a particular country we maximized certain objectives. Each country's scale had maximum reliability; we obtained scales with a normal distribution in each country, and ones in which all items were being given equal weight in the total scale. But calibrating the OM scale separately for each national group had the disadvantage of precluding systematic comparison of the OM score of an individual from any one country with that of someone from another country. To make possible such comparisons we had to construct a new scale which was exactly the same for all the countries, not only in content, but in the standard used to classify answers as modern or traditional. That scale, which we labeled IM, for International Modernity measure, must now be at least briefly described before we proceed with our analysis.

To suit our purpose we needed a scale which met the following requirements:

(a) It covered basically the same ground as did the OM scale, treating modernity as a complex multidimensional attitude, value, and behavior syndrome in which more or less equal weight was given dimensions such as: a sense of efficacy, openness to new experience, active participation as a citizen, and acceptance of birth control.

(b) It used only those questions which had been worded in more or less exactly the same way from one country to another, thus reducing the variability of the stimulus presented by the questions.[7] This similarity of question wording extended to the requirement that, for a given question, the number and form of the alternatives offered in a "closed alternative" type question were also identical from country to country.

(c) It scored the alternative answers to questions as "modern" or "traditional" on a strictly comparable basis from country to country. For example, in scoring the question about the ideal number of children, we would consider those who mentioned three or less to have given the modern answer in all countries.

(d) It weighed responses identically from country to country, and preferably by the method used in scoring OM, so that each individual's score would fall in the range from 0, indicating all his answers were "traditional," to 100, indicating all his answers were "modern."

(e) It yielded a scale having comparable reliability in all the countries, in no country falling below the level of 0.60.

Insofar as we could construct a scale meeting these requirements, we felt it would be reasonable to advance to the next stage of searching for and attempting to explain similarities and differences in the modernity of individuals representing different national groups. We recognized, of course, that there were a host of theoretical and methodological issues raised by any effort to score men from different cultures and societies on a single unified measure of a quality as complex as individual modernity. The discussion of these issues could easily take up all the space allotted us in this article, indeed could easily fill a modest sized volume.

*Constructing the Scale*

Our first step in constructing the IM scale was to compile a list of all questions used in the six national versions of our OM questionnaire which had consistently demonstrated that they were part of the modernity syndrome and, in addition, had been asked in a more or less identical way in all six countries.[8] How many questions met this qualification depended, of course, on how strictly we applied the test of what was an "identical" wording. Although the six country field directors were committed to fairly strict adherence to the general form of the questionnaire, they were free to make adaptations to suit local conditions. This sometimes led to changes in wording and variations in the number or the form of the alternative answers from among which people were asked to make their choices. Using the strictest criterion, we could count on 55 items, asked in exactly the same way in all countries. By recoding some answers to make the items more comparable, we could increase to 93 the number of questions appropriate for international scale construction.[9] Finally, if we relaxed our standard to include questions which were merely "more or less" comparable everywhere, we could bring the pool of items up to 125.[10]

In deciding which of these sets of items to use in which combinations we faced the usual kinds of trade-off. A longer scale might yield higher reliability, but at the possible cost of reduced comparability. A shorter and more selective scale promised maximum comparability, but was more prone to distortion if even a few questions were widely misunderstood in some countries. We could find no obvious rule dictating which set of advantages and disadvantages to prefer. We therefore compromised on the middle ground. Our candidate, used throughout the analysis in this paper, was our scale IM2A.

We selected IM2A because it had a very large number of items, 93 to be exact, yet excluded those which our staff thought to be of somewhat questionable comparability.[11] These qualities earned it a higher reliability than most other IM scales we constructed, its range across six countries going from K-R 0.59 to 0.80 with the median at 0.63.[12] In addition, IM2A, being rather long, could include questions representing all the subthemes which we had included in our theoretical conception of individual modernity and had found empirically to be part of the syndrome.[13] Moreover, the length of the scale made it less likely to be overresponsive to the influence of a single question or a subset of questions which, in a short scale, could have a disproportionate effect on the standing of one or another country.[14] IM2A had an observed range of 70 points from a low score of 6 to a high of 76 across the total set of men, and the scale had a standard deviation of 9.1 for the total sample of some 5,500 men.[15]

Given that the content of the scale for all countries was virtually identical, and the scoring scheme likewise; that the individual items used had all shown themselves part of the modernity syndrome when modernity scales had earlier been constructed separately within each country; and that the reliability and the standard deviation of the scale were basically alike within each country—we felt confident in accepting IM2A as an international measure of individual modernity suitable for the sort of analysis we anticipated making.

## BASIC QUESTIONS AND BASELINE DATA

Accepting IM2A as a reasonable measure of individual modernity permitting meaningful cross-national comparisons put us in a position to answer the following questions:

1. Holding other things constant, are there significant differences in individual modernity manifested by sets of men from the six different countries in our study? In other words, how much of a bonus on his modernity score does a man somehow secure by virtue of his membership in a national group or his residence in a given country?
2. Insofar as such differences are manifested, what weight should we assign to "national" origin, as against other factors such as education and mass media exposure, as explanations of differences in individual modernity?
3. How far can we attribute the contextual effect of nationality to visible and "objective" factors such as greater national wealth and more widespread diffusion of the mass media, and how far to some ineluctable residue of advantage built into the "culture" which any person shares as a member of a given national community?

There are, of course, other interesting questions which might be put to these data. For example, it is intriguing to consider how far the men from each country earn their standing as modern men on the basis of a different profile of psychological characteristics, some countries producing people more modern in their independence from family control, others in their openness to new experience. We are obliged, however, to leave that issue for another presentation.

### *Baseline Differences*

To establish our baseline we calculated the mean IM score for each national sample. The differences were notable. The Israelis and the Argentinians were as much as 13 points, almost 1½ standard deviations, ahead of the men from East Pakistan, with Nigerians, Chileans, and Indians, respectively, occupying the middle ranks. The details are given in Table 1, on the lines 1 and 3 for "Unadjusted Country means."

The full significance of these differences in mean scores can probably be better appreciated by considering the proportion of each national sam-

*Table 1.* Six Country Mean Scores in Individual Modernity (IM2A): Unadjusted and Adjusted.

| | Argentina (A) | Chile (C) | India (I) | Israel (S) | Nigeria (N) | East Pakistan (P) |
|---|---|---|---|---|---|---|
| 1. Unadjusted Country Means F = 298*** | 52.3 | 47.9 | 46.9 | 53.5 | 49.2 | 40.7 |
| 2. Adjusted Means (Controlling for 6 Covariates)[a] F = 75.5*** | 50.1 | 47.3 | 48.5 | 50.7 | 47.2 | 44.5 |

3. Unadjusted Means: 40 P — 45 I C N — 50 A S — 55

4. Adjusted Means[a]: 40 — P 45 — NC I — 50 AS — 55

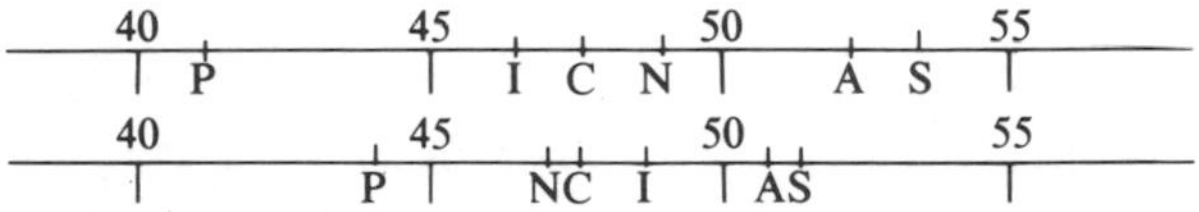

***Significant at the 0.001 level.

[a]See footnote 25 and Johnston (1972) for a description of the covariates, and the procedures used to calculate the adjusted means and significance levels.

ple qualifying as modern. To that end we arbitrarily classified as modern anyone whose IM score placed him in the upper third of the distribution for the total sample of almost 6,000 men. Using that criterion we found 57 percent of the Israelis and 51 percent of the Argentinians to be modern, while a mere 5 percent of the men from Bangladesh could so qualify. The other three countries were bunched on the middle ground, the percent modern in those samples being, respectively: Nigeria 34, India 33, and Chile 28.

We felt, however, that it might be quite misleading to draw any conclusions from these mean scores because of differences we knew to exist in the composition of our several national samples. Our samples were broadly similar in occupational composition, as per our design, but despite our efforts they were sometimes unequal on other critical dimensions. For example, the median years of schooling in the East Pakistan group was only about two years, in the Chilean about six, and in the Nigerian it reached eight. Since the number of years of schooling a man had received had shown itself in all the countries to be the most powerful fact in explaining individual modernity, all comparisons of the national samples not controlling for this factor invited confusion as to whether any observed differences in modernity should be attributed to the education of the respondents rather than to their national environment and cultural heritage. There were less extreme but comparable disparities in the national patterns of mass media exposure, again an important variable in explaining individual modernity.[16]

## PERSISTENCE OF NATIONAL DIFFERENCES

To answer the question, as to whether individual modernity differs by country when other things are held constant, we utilized two relatively independent methods for adjusting the IM scores to take account of educational, occupational, and other sampling disparities.

### *The "Match" Adjustment*

First, we used the technique of matching. By this method we simultaneously controlled for up to five background variables, thus enabling us to compare men who were alike in a number of key characteristics—such as education, degree of mass media exposure, occupation, rural origin, and father's education—yet who were differentiated on the variable of interest, in this case nationality.[17]

The match results, presented in Table 2, indicate some variation in the outcome, depending on which subgroup—such as worker or cultivator—is used as the basis for the match.[18] This is itself an interesting issue to which we will return systematically in a later publication.[19] Nevertheless, Table 2 also gives evidence of a clear-cut pattern, about which we may observe the following:

1. *Nationality does make a statistically significant difference in predicting a man's level of individual modernity, even when the men compared are matched to be more or less exactly alike on up to five other basic characteristics.*

This is indicated by the F ratios, most of which were significant at the 0.001 level. Typically the spread between the highest and lowest scoring national groups was 5 or 6 points on the IM scale. This meant that an individual from the high performing country, compared to someone from a low scoring country, would have given modern answers to five or six more questions out of every hundred even though the two individuals were otherwise identical in education, mass media exposure, and other characteristics.[20]

These contrasts may perhaps be more readily grasped if we express the differences in terms of the percent of each national group which qualified as "modern men." This designation, as noted above, was assigned to anyone whose score put him in the upper third of the overall distribution on the IM scale. A typical contrast was that shown in Match A-1 representing all occupational subgroups, in which the proportion who scored as modern rose from a low of 8 in East Pakistan to a high of 30 percent in India. Similarly, in Match F-2, restricted to the better educated industrial workers, the proportion qualifying as modern rose from a low of 58 to a high of 78 percent, as one moved from Nigeria to Argentina.[21]

*Table 2.* Mean Scores on IM2A for Various Matched Groups, by Country.[a]

| Matched Group | Match Number | Argentina | Chile | India | Israel | Nigeria | East Pakistan | F[d] | No. of Pairs in Match |
|---|---|---|---|---|---|---|---|---|---|
| Cultivators | C1 | 45.5 | 40.1 | 44.0 | — | 44.9 | 40.6 | 6.82*** | 53 |
| | C2 | — | — | 46.4 | 53.7 | — | — | 14.8** | 31 |
| Urban | U1 | — | — | — | 52.8 | 48.4 | — | 7.31** | 40 |
| Nonindustrials | U2 | 51.2 | 52.5 | — | 50.3 | 45.5 | — | 3.30* | 17 |
| | U3 | — | — | 41.6 | — | — | 38.8 | 1.42 | 15 |
| Factory | F1 | 55.3 | 52.4 | — | 55.6 | 52.0 | — | 6.73*** | 105 |
| Workers[b] | F2 | 57.1 | — | 54.2 | 57.5 | 53.7 | — | 4.36** | 50 |
| All | A1 | 46.8 | 42.6 | 45.7 | — | 46.0 | 41.8 | 6.96*** | 80 |
| Occupations[c] | A2 | 52.4 | 48.7 | — | — | 49.3 | — | 20.3*** | 293 |
| | A3 | 54.4 | 51.9 | — | 54.1 | 50.6 | — | 8.5*** | 145 |

[a]Empty cells indicate that that country was not included in a particular match. See footnote 18 for details.

[b]Only workers with three or more years of industrial experience could enter Match F1; in F2 the additional restriction was placed that they be relatively better educated.

[c]All occupations includes cultivators, new workers, urban non-industrial workers, and experienced workers in A1 and A2. In Match A3, however, cultivators were excluded.

[d]Significance is indicated as follows: * = 0.05, ** = 0.01, *** = 0.001.

2. *Within the pattern of overall differentiation there appears to be a definite structure in the placement of the several countries. Indeed, we found a more or less invariant rank order regardless of the occupational or educational subgroups being compared.*

The East Pakistan group was consistently the least modern. The Chilean, Nigerian, and Indian samples generally represented an intermediate position. These three, usually not statistically distinguishable from each other, were, nevertheless, generally significantly different from the people of Bangladesh.[22] Argentina fell substantially further along on the continuum, generally at a statistically significant level.[23] The Israelis were still a bit further on, but generally were not significantly different, statistically, from the Argentinians.[24]

*Regression Based Adjustments*

Since every method achieves its advantages at the cost of developing peculiar weaknesses and distorting propensities, we used a second quite independent method to check the results obtained by matching. The B weights, i.e., the unstandardized regression coefficients, from a regression analysis based on the total of some 5,500 cases were utilized to calculate an adjusted mean score for each national group. By this process we adjusted for differences in the observed characteristics of national subsamples on five important variables such as education.[25] The result, in effect, answers the following question: if a group from each of the six countries in turn was either "compensated" or "penalized" for being above or below average in education, mass media exposure and the like, what would its resultant IM score then look like? Clearly, if nationality made no difference, the resultant adjusted scores would all come out statistically indistinguishable from one another. The actual outcome was quite different.

It is immediately apparent from Table 1 that adjusting the country means to take account of differences in the composition of the sample in the several countries had substantial consequences. As compared to the array of unadjusted means on line 1, the adjusted set, on line 2, reveals the gap separating the high from the low scoring groups to be substantially reduced. Moreover, the rank order of Chile, Nigeria, and India changed. At the same time, however, these shifts brought the data more into line with the basic patterns observed when we had used the matching process to adjust for differences in sample characteristics. As a result of the adjustments based on the regression, the gap separating the high and low scoring groups, being 5.6 IM points, fell into the same range as the gap shown in the typical match. The adjusted country means still yielded a highly significant F ratio, indicating nationality does make a real difference (see Johnston, 1972, p. 196). The rank order previously observed in the matches was preserved, with Argentinians and Israelis indistinguishable from each other in the front rank, Nigerians, Chileans, and Indians, bunched in the middle, and the East Pakistanis trailing behind by a substantial margin.

## THE RELATIVE IMPACT OF NATIONALITY IN COMPETITION WITH OTHER VARIABLES

We have established that taking nationality into consideration makes a significant difference. But how much of a difference? In particular, what portion of the variance does it account for? Is it as important as education, or twice as important as occupation, in accounting for a man's modernity? To answer these questions, we again utilized two methods.

First, we performed a regression analysis in which nationality was entered as a variable along with six other standard explanatory variables our research has shown to be important predictors of modernity.[26] The results are presented in Table 3.

As was the case in our within-country studies (Inkeles and Smith, 1974) education had by far the most substantial Beta weight, at 0.34. The variable measuring nationality yielded a more modest Beta of 0.22. Nevertheless, it was actually larger than the 0.18 Beta for mass media, generally the second most powerful variable in our within-country analysis, and was considerably larger than the Beta for the variable measuring occupational experience in the modern sector of the economy. All in all, this outcome identified the "nation factor" as a major element in accounting for psychological modernity even in the context of powerful competing variables.[27]

*Table 3.* Regression on IM2A of Six Background Variables and Nationality.[a]

| | Beta | B | (Standard Error) |
|---|---|---|---|
| Country (Nationality) | 0.22 | 0.49 | (0.03) |
| Years of Education | 0.34 | 0.95 | (0.04) |
| Years of Factory Experience | 0.13 | 0.28 | (0.02) |
| Age | 0.03 | 0.06 | (0.03) |
| Mass Media | 0.18 | 0.94 | (0.06) |
| Urban/Rural Origin | 0.06 | 1.30 | (0.22) |
| Consumer Goods Possessed | 0.04 | 0.30 | (0.08) |
| K | | 62.2 | |

$R^2 = 0.43$

[a]See footnotes 25 and 26.

These results, while indicating that national membership was a consequential contributor to the modernity rating of individuals, left open the question of the extent to which nationality made a *unique* contribution. In order to get at that issue we looked at the stepwise increment to $R^2$ due to "country" when it was pitted against the composite influence of all the individual background variables. With six background variables already taken into account, putting "country" into the regression still added four percent to the variance explained. This distinctive contribution of country was very much less than that of the background variables. The unique variance explained by the background variables as a set was 22 percent, as indicated in Table 4.

Actually, we were gratified by this outcome because our project, from its very inception, rested on the assumption that an individual's position in social structure, rather than his distinctive culture, would be the *prime* determinant of his psychological modernity. Nevertheless, the finding that the set of individual background factors, such as education and occupation, was much *more* important than the variable national-cultural milieux, should not be allowed to obscure the fact that the latter are nevertheless quite significant influences in their own right. To get additional perspective on this issue, and in addition to gain the advantage of being able to judge the extent of interaction effects in our data, we utilized a second method, namely an analysis of covariance. By using the analysis

*Table 4.* Partition of Explained Variance ($R^2$) in IM2A into Unique and Joint Components, Due to Country and to Background Variables.

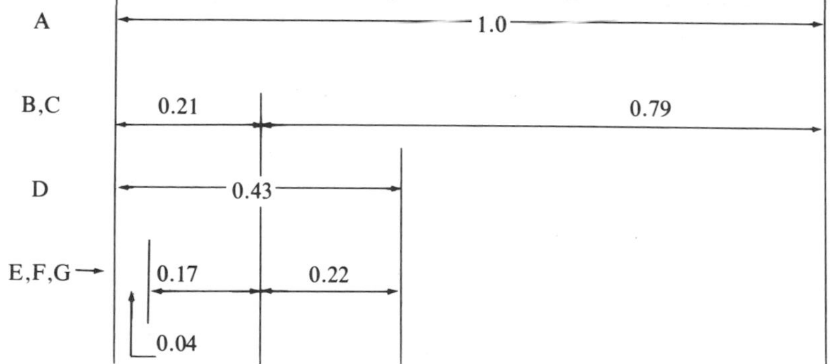


A: Total variance (standardized).
B: Between country variance.
C: Within country variance.
D: Variance explained by country and 6 background variables.
E: Variance unique to country.
F: Joint variance (country and 6 background variables).
G: Variance unique to background.

of covariance we were able to gain perspective on the meaning of moving up a step on the educational ladder, as compared to moving from one country to the next. We could do this by looking at the mean of the sample, on IM2A, in each education-country category. Table 5 presents the results.

We again see substantial evidence for the importance of nationality as a determinant of individual modernity, even when the scores of the groups compared have been adjusted to equalize the effect of differences in education, mass media, and the like. Thus, even in the narrow range of those with six to eight years of education, and with five additional covariates controlled, the East Pakistanis lagged 9 points behind the Israelis and almost 8 points behind the Argentinians, equivalent to almost a full standard deviation. The greatest gap from the lowest to the highest *education group* within any country was about 10 points. But with men matched on education, the greatest gap between the most modern and the least modern *country* was of comparable magnitude. Although the main effect of education, overall, was much the larger, the main effect of country was quite substantial, with an F of 0.89 significant well above 0.001.

It seems clear that merely by virtue of their nationality the men from certain countries received a substantial bonus toward their IM scores *above and beyond whatever they might have earned by virtue of their individual profile of education, factory experience, and the like.* A man from Argentina who had not gone to school at all apparently scored as modern as an East Pakistani who had completed more than eight years of schooling, and a Chilean with about seven years of schooling did only as well as an Israeli who had only been to school for three years. How can one account for such a powerful effect arising from the mere difference in a man's national citizenship?

*Table 5.* Adjusted Means[a], with Interactions[b], for IM2A by Education and Country.

| Years of Education | Argentina | Chile | India | Israel | Nigeria | East Pakistan |
|---|---|---|---|---|---|---|
| 0 | — | — | 43.2 | — | — | 40.5 |
| 1–5 | 48.4 | 45.0 | 46.2 | 48.4 | 46.9 | 41.4 |
| 6–8 | 51.1 | 48.6 | 48.7 | 52.4 | 48.5 | 43.4 |
| 9–15 | 54.0 | 50.5 | 53.8 | 54.9 | 51.7 | — |

[a]The covariates controlled in this regression were Factory Experience, Mass Media, Age, Urban/Rural Origin, Consumer Goods Possessed.

[b]The main effect of education yields an F of 401, significant at the 0.001 level. The main effect of country yields an F of 89, also significant at the 0.001 level. The interaction of education and country yields an F of only 2.3, significant at the 0.01 level.

## EXPLAINING THE ADVANTAGE OF SOME COUNTRIES IN CONFERRING INDIVIDUAL MODERNITY

After extensive working and reworking of our data we found no way to escape the fact that the men from some countries consistently scored higher in individual modernity than those from other countries, even when the individuals compared were apparently alike in certain characteristics which had previously been shown to be the most powerful determinants of such scores. Since we could neither wish away, nor wash away, these facts, we would like to be able to explain them. At the present juncture, however, we cannot offer a definitive conclusion. We can only point to a series of plausible alternatives, one or all of which may be the true explanation, and indicate our best estimate as to the probable contribution of each.

1. The first alternative runs as follows:

"All that these results show is that, after all, the modernity syndrome is really a specification of the Western man, hence the more Western a country the more its citizens get a bonus on the scale."

This raises a complicated issue much broader than its manifestation in this particular set of data. We hold that the modernity syndrome is not culture specific, and feel that our published work has demonstrated its relevance in a variety of societies (Inkeles and Smith, 1974, *passim;* Inkeles, 1976). To say that, however, is not to say that explanation Number 1 is wrong. On the contrary, we always assumed that individual modernity, as we defined and measured it, would be more *prevalent* in Western countries while not being *exclusively* present there. We feel that being from a "Western" culture is neither a necessary nor a sufficient condition for being psychologically modern. Quite apart from any theoretical objections, the assumption that IM scores are adequately explained by some purported Western bias in the scale must face several important bits of contradictory evidence.

First, we note that our Chilean group, coming from a country as much "Western" as any other in our sample, nevertheless did not generally fall in with the presumably more Western Israelis and Argentinians, but rather stood closer to the very "un-Western" Nigerians and Indians. Second, we call attention to the sharp separation of the Indian from the East Pakistani groups, even though they were both certainly very much "non-Western."[28] And third, we need to reckon with the fact that the Israeli group was only nominally Western, being so only in the sense that Judaism is linked to Christianity, and thus to Western culture. Otherwise, those in our Israeli sample were almost exclusively "Oriental" Jews, who had not many years before emigrated to Israel from countries such as

Iran, Iraq, Syria, Turkey, Lebanon, and Egypt. Their values and living patterns quite often reflected strong Arab influence. The European Jews in Israel consider these people to be "Orientals," and often express the view that they are rather alien to, and do not readily assimilate to, "European" culture. The fact that such Israelis scored high on the modernity scale cannot, therefore, be convincingly explained on the premise of their being so much more "Western."

2. The second alternative argues that:

"The trouble lies in assuming that the independent variables other than nationality really were controlled. For example, a man who had six years of school in East Pakistan may not have had an experience truly equivalent to six years of schooling in Argentina, even though the project scored them as equal in education."

This argument seems quite plausible. A "year" in school in Argentina could well mean attendance during 180 days, whereas the school in Bangladesh may have operated only during 90 days. The one school might have been staffed by well-trained teachers, equipped with books and paper and maintained at a comfortable temperature, while the other may well have lacked all these amenities. Under the circumstances, granting equal weight in both countries to the response "I completed six years of schooling," might certainly be misleading.

Although, as indicated, we find this argument appealing, it seems contradicted by one of our main findings. Our Indian and East Pakistanian samples included a substantial number of people who had never been to school. Yet, as may be seen from the first line in Table 5, the illiterate group from India was considerably more modern than the strictly comparable set of men from East Pakistan. Differences in the quality of schooling can have had nothing to do with that outcome, since none of the men compared had been to school. There seems no escaping the conclusion, therefore, that something about a country or region other than the effectiveness of its schools can contribute to making its citizens more or less modern.

In addition, if school quality were a key factor, we should have found a powerful effect for the interaction of education and country in our analysis of covariance. Actually, the observed effect, noted in Table 5, while statistically significant, was very modest compared to the separate main effects for education and country.

Admittedly, such statistical inferences leave something to be desired as a method for settling the issue. We acknowledge that a definitive resolution would require more direct measures of the actual quality of schools, newspapers and other institutions in different countries. In the meantime we note that some studies in the West have failed to show that sheer length of the school year, or even the quality of the school, make very much difference in cognitive development [Husén, 1972; Coleman, 1966]. It may be that those factors are not so important in the attitude-value realm either.

3. The third alternative explanation holds that:

"The observed differences are real, and reflect differences in culture and national character, which are distinct from and independent of level of national economic development."

Anthropologists, sociologists, and psychologists interested in group personality and in culture have often noted that certain groups have a distinctive ethos, a culturally defined systematic personality bent, or national character (Inkeles and Levinson, 1969; LeVine, 1973). Indeed, from the time of Weber on such tendencies have been of particular interest because of their presumed implications for economic growth and national development. In the past, efforts to compare the national character of different groups have been impeded by lack of a cross-culturally standardized measure of important personality dimensions. We see the IM scale as overcoming this difficulty in good part, and feel that IM scores may be interpreted as showing the relative standing of our respective national samples on this particular measure of group character.

While we acknowledge that our data present some surprises and some anomalies, we do not, on the face of it, see the results as patently contradicting common assumptions about where the six societies should have fallen on a scale measuring qualities such as those encompassed in the modernity syndrome. Even the departures from popular expectation may be explained on culturological grounds. For example, the Indian sample's advantage over the East Pakistani sample might be attributed to the differential effect of the Hindu and Islamic religions, or to the fact that half the Indian sample was "tribal." And Argentina's lead over Chile might be attributed to the greater diffusion of American Indian influence in the Chilean working class population.[29]

Certainly, in principle, we have no inclination to contradict the line of reasoning which seeks in distinctive cultural properties or in national character, an explanation for the differences in modernity we observed. We can, however, readily anticipate the argument that our samples are not sufficiently representative of the respective parent populations to justify any such conclusion. Representing the full range of Indian and Nigerian groups might certainly alter the rankings those countries attained in our samples. But each of our samples certainly constituted a distinctive national group or subgroup, each different from the other even if not representative of any entire nation. Moreover, our statistical controls corrected for the possibility that any lack of representativeness was expressed mainly in unique advantages in education or occupation. Yet, even after such controls were applied, the several national samples were significantly differentiated on our measure of modernity. It might well be, then, that each man's national or ethnic heritage had conferred on him a bonus, or a handicap, as the case might be, when he came to complete the interview leading to the assignment of his IM score.

4. The fourth alternative is to assume that:

"The differences are real, and they exemplify the impact on individual modernity of the general character of the social milieu in which each individual lived. Those who lived in more modern societies, with more opportunity for contact with modern institutions and objects, and more interaction with decidedly modern men, should have become more modern as a result. In other words we have observed true 'contextual' effects."

Of the explanations offered, this is the one we find most convincing.

Of the forces which make a man modern, we measured mainly the qualities one normally thinks of as individual properties, such as a man's education, occupation, or age. If, however, becoming modern is a process of socialization, and therefore depends, in part, on following role models, then individuals living in a more modern setting should become more modern merely by sharing a *generally* modern ambience. And one important factor in making a modern ambience may be the *average* level of modernity of the individuals who live in the environment. This line of reasoning seems most germane to our findings because the research reported in this paper utilized as its main indicator of a country's development the average modernity score of the men from that country. But basically the same sort of reasoning would apply if we used other more "objective" indicators of a nation's level of development such as its GNP, the extent of its newspaper and radio networks, or the average schooling of its population. Thus, a man surrounded by individuals with above average education might well acquire modern ideas by mere contact with his presumably more modern peers even if he himself had had little schooling. And whether or not he himself reads the newspaper, a man surrounded by people who do so every day will hear more about world news events just as part of the general conversation around him. Similarly, whether they work in a modern organization or not, individuals who live in an environment in which such organizations are widespread should more likely be aware of, and possibly incorporate in their own value scheme, the principles of the rational legal order. And so on.

The most commonly used indicator of these types of objectively measured enrichment of national environments is GNP per capita. We therefore re-ran our regressions with each country represented in the variable for "nation" by its GNP per capita in the mid 60s, the era when our field work was done. The same six additional variables entered the regression as had been used earlier. This way of recording each nation's standing gave "country" somewhat less importance. Nevertheless, the Beta weight for the "nation" factor, at 0.16, was still highly significant statistically; it held third place, close behind mass media exposure, at 0.18; and it was well ahead of our own favorite, namely years of factory experience, which had a Beta weight of 0.10.[30]

In effect then, each individual living in such an "enriched" environment thereby enjoys a bonus on the modernity scale over and above the points he earns from his own profile of schooling, mass media, and the like. If, in turn, the psychological modernity of a nation's citizens has the power to increase the efficiency of the economy, then the richer countries will enjoy a double advantage. In the first instance, the countries which are wealthier, or have otherwise developed a modern social system, will provide more of their citizens with more education, more newspapers, and more factory jobs. But *in addition,* the wealthier countries can evidently count on a "spill-over" or "trickle-down" effect. As a result, even their more disadvantaged citizens will be more modern than are comparably educated people from poorer or less developed countries. We may have uncovered here yet another reason why the gap between the have and the have not nations seems to grow ever wider.

## FOOTNOTES

*Alex Inkeles is the Margaret Jacks Professor of Education and Professor of Sociology at Stanford University. An authority on the sociocultural aspects of economic development in the developing nations, and on the Soviet social system, he is also an expert in the field of personality and social structure. Inkeles directed the Project on the Sociocultural Aspects of Development which led to *Becoming Modern,* written with D. H. Smith (1974). Currently he is investigating the effect of national development on personal development.

Paper presented in the session on "Comparative Study of Society," at the 69th Annual Meeting of the American Sociological Association meeting, Montreal, Canada, August 1974. Larry Meyer and Amnon Igra rendered creative research assistance in the preparation of this paper, which also benefited from a critical reading by the latter. The Spencer Foundation and the Institute for Advanced Study at Princeton kindly provided support for a major part of the analysis presented here.

1. This was in a regression on OM500. The range in variance explained was from 32 percent in Israel to 62 percent in India (Inkeles and Smith, 1974, Chapter 20).

2. This was true only in the sense that we could not meaningfully compare the OM score of a man in one country with that of a man in any other country. However, we could, and did, show that the structure of relations between the "explanatory" and the dependent variables was basically the same across all six countries (Inkeles and Smith, 1974, *passim*).

3. The empirical nature of the OM syndrome is fully described in Inkeles and Smith (1974, Chapter 7). A principal components factor analysis (of OM519) yielded firm evidence of the existence of a coherent factor of individual modernity in all six countries. Further evidence of the coherence of the syndrome of attitudes and values included in the OM scale is provided by the high reliability of the scale. Thus, OM500, the main scale used in the analysis for *Becoming Modern* (Inkeles and Smith, 1974, Chapter 7), had a median K.R. of 0.82.

4. A detailed discussion of each of the themes we tested and the rationale for including it will be found in Chapter 2, and a complete set of the questions asked is given in Appendix A of *Becoming Modern.*

5. The "scheduled *tribes*" constitute both a social and legal category in India, alongside the better known "untouchables," now classified as "scheduled *castes.*" People in the scheduled tribe category are further divided socially into those who have become Hindu and those who are Christian. The cross cutting of caste and religion in our sample design for India therefore yielded four groups of more or less equal size: high caste Hindu, low caste Hindu, Hinduized tribals, and Christian tribals.

6. By country of origin, the main sources were: Morocco 209, Iraq 154, Yemen/Aden 104, Tunisia 49, Iran 43, others 180.

7. The goal of attaining truly *equivalent* measures across cultures and countries, rather than striving for literal translation, is generally stressed by comparative researchers (Przeworski and Teune, 1970; Manaster and Havighurst, 1972; Brislin, et al. 1973).

8. To establish its relevance a question had to have an item to scale correlation (adjusted for autocorrelation) significant at least at the 0.05 level in all six countries. The scale used was OM3, our longest. For details about that scale, see Inkeles and Smith (1974, Chapters 6 and 7).

9. An example of a question rendered comparable by minor recoding is EF-14, which asked for an evaluation of scientific research into such things as what makes a child come out as a boy or a girl. In four of the countries only two alternative answers were presented: "good" or "bad." In the two remaining countries, the respondent was asked to select his preference from among four alternatives on a continuum from good to bad. We collapsed the four alternatives into two, thus making it possible to score the question following exactly the same procedure in all six countries.

10. Question CH-3 is an example of a question which could not be rendered strictly comparable by any simple recoding, but which nevertheless could be treated as if it were "more or less alike" in all countries. The question was designed to test the readiness of people to accept technical innovations in agriculture. What obliged us to classify this question as only "more or less comparable" across countries was the fact that the field directors had varied the description of the situation in which the innovation came up for discussion. In one country, for example, the father was talking to a boy of only 12, but in another country the son was described as being 18 years of age. Although we could, in all the countries, code the answers as being simply "for" or "against" the innovation, we could not be sure how far the context in which the innovation had been presented in the question might have influenced people in different countries to be more pro or con.

11. The only departure from exact duplication in constructing IM2A was in the recoding of alternatives so that the number in each country was the same as described in footnote 9. Questions considered only "more or less" comparable, as described in footnote 10 were excluded. The code letter and number of the 93 questions, listed immediately hereafter, may be used to ascertain their wording by reference to Appendix A of *Becoming Modern:* AC-4; AC-6; AG-2; AS-3; AS-6; AS-8; AS-11; CA-2; CA-3, CA-6; CA-7; CA-8; CA-11; CH-1,2; CH-10,11; CH-12, 13; CH-14; CI-2; CI-7; CI-13; CI-14; CO-7; CO-8; DI-6; DI-7; DI-8; DI-11; EF-1; EF-2; EF-3; EF-4; EF-8; EF-9; EF-11,12; EF-13; EF-14; EF-15; EF-16; FS-1; FS-3; GO-1; GO-2; GO-3; GO-4; GO-5; GO-6; GO-7; IN-7; KO-2; KO-3; KO-4; KO-5; KO-6; MM-6; MM-7; MM-10,11; NE-1; NE-2; NE-3; NE-7; PL-1, PL-2; PL-3; PL-4; PL-5; PL-9; RE-2, RE-3; RE-4; RE-8; RE-9; RE-11; RE-12; SC-2; SC-8; ST-9; TI-3; TI-4; TI-5; TI-7; TS-14; WC-13,14; WR-1; WR-3; WR-4; WR-6; WR-7; WR-8; WR-9; WR-11; WR-12; WR-13; WR-14. Entries with two numbers such as CH-1,2 or MM-10,11 indicate that the answers to two questions were in our coding, combined as if they had been in response to a single question.

12. The reliability of the IM scale was lower than that of the OM scales in all six countries. Clearly we paid some price for insisting that the IM scale everywhere use exactly the same questions and codings. However, the OM scales had been cleaned by eliminating the items in any country which showed relatively low item to scale correlations. Since those were replaced by other items with similar content but of greater reliability, the OM scales remained basically alike across all countries while yet being maximally reliable. Since the IM scale permitted no substitutions and was scored by an inflexible international rule, it showed lower reliabilities.

13. As reported in *Becoming Modern* (Inkeles and Smith, 1974, p. 101) OM3, from which IM2A was derived, included questions representing 24 of the themes we considered relevant to an overall conception of individual modernity. The questions which qualified for inclusion in IM2A represented 22 of those themes. The two topics which did not qualify were: "understanding production," and "work commitment." As Chapter 7 of *Becoming Modern* makes clear, no one element of the modernity syndrome was indispensable for defining the syndrome empirically. But even if there had been either theoretically or empirically indispensable themes, these two would certainly have not been among them.

14. Such effects were observed in the process of our examination of the several variants on the IM scale which we initially constructed. Thus, when we used any one of four longer versions of the IM scale, the Nigerians obtained a mean score (unadjusted) which put them ahead of the Indians and Chileans. However, on the two short forms of the scale which had only 12 and 17 items, respectively, Nigeria was behind Chile and India. Inspection of the short scales, item by item, revealed that our Yoruba respondents were especially sensitive to questions which pitted luck against other forces. Evidently, without intending it, we had used a disproportionate number of such questions in the very short scales. By very consistently giving less modern answers to those questions, the Nigerians drove down their overall score, and emerged as a seemingly less modern group than they were when tested on the longer scales. Their few extreme answers had, in a short scale, outweighed the otherwise general propensity of the Nigerians to give answers at least as modern as those usually given by Chileans and Indians.

15. By country the standard deviation of IM2A was, respectively: Argentina 7.3, Chile 7.6, India 10.1, Israel 8.3, Nigeria 7.0, East Pakistan 6.8. We consider these to be very similar. Even the Indian case seemed not an anomaly, but rather stemmed from the fact that the Indian sample had a more U-shaped distribution, containing an extra large number of cases with no schooling and an extra large number with some high school education. This evidence on the standard deviation, along with that on the reliabilities, supported our confidence in the cross-national IM scale as appropriate for use in all six countries.

16. Across our six countries, the median Pearsonian correlation of individual modernity (OM500) with education-literacy was 0.52, with mass media exposure 0.45, and with occupation 0.41. These three measures accounted for about 80 percent of the variance in OM scores which could be "explained" by our full battery of measures. For detailed evidence concerning the role of these measures as predictors and presumed causes of individual modernity see Inkeles and Smith (1974).

17. The matching technique is more fully described in Inkeles and Smith (1974, Chapter 8; see also Althauser and Rubin, 1970). The standard of matching quality was quite rigorous. On each quality controlled the matched groups had to have means scores so close that any difference would fail to test as statistically significant at the 0.05 level. On education, for example, this generally meant that the average education of the groups matched could not differ by more than two or three months.

18. The matches presented in Table 2 were drawn from a much larger pool. We actually constructed a total of 56 international matches, focused on different combinations of occupation and education, such as "high educated cultivators," or "rural origin urban non-

industrial workers." Some of these combinations were applicable in only two countries. Others yielded matched groups with extremely few cases, and it was our general rule not to use matches with an N of less than 10. The matches in Table 2 were not selected in advance from the larger pool to make any particular point, but to save space and simplify the presentation. The criteria for inclusion in Table 2 were that the match have a large N, include as many countries as possible given the occupational and educational range covered by the match, and be minimally redundant. That the matches thus selected led to conclusions consistent with those drawn using the larger set will be evident from data given in footnotes, 22, 23, and 24 below.

19. One interpretation of convergence theory might lead one to expect that industrial workers from different countries should be more alike than sets of peasants from those same countries would be. An alternative interpretation would deny that prediction. This would be done on the grounds that peasant villages in different countries actually have a great deal in common. Following from the assumption that like organizational milieux produce like personal dispositions one should, therefore, predict that a cross-national comparison of peasants will produce no greater diversity than cross-national comparisons of workers, *at least on a general psycho-social measure such as the modernity scale*. The extensive set of cross-national matches we have developed for each occupational group permits some initial testing of these competing theories.

20. The scoring system for the IM scale, as for the OM scales on which it was modeled, was designed to permit this simple interpretation of score differences. Regardless of the number of questions asked, all OM and IM scores are expressed on a scale from 0 to 100. This results from the fact that all answers are scored 1.00 for traditional responses, 2.00 for modern responses, with the total then averaged by the number of questions the individual answered. On a scale with 100 items, a five point difference means precisely five more questions answered in the modern or traditional direction. For shorter or longer scales, containing less than or more than 100 items, a process of extrapolation is obviously involved in making the sort of statement made in the text.

21. It will be noted that the order in which the countries stand when they are ranked according to the percent modern does not accord perfectly with their relative standing when mean scores are used as the basis for ranking, as in Table 2. Thus, Argentina had the highest mean scores on Match A-1, but India and not Argentina had the highest proportion qualifying as "modern." Such anomalous findings can arise because the same mean can result from a different assortment of high and low scores. Consequently, the same group mean can yield different proportions labeled modern, depending on the *distribution* of the scores which yielded the mean. For example, with the same overall average you could have a large number of individuals bunched just above *or* just below the cutoff point defining the "modern" man. Other scores could smooth out, or equalize, the average, but would not equalize the percent considered modern in the two cases. Because of the smaller numbers used in the matches, we found the "percent modern" figures to be more volatile than the means, and hence in Table 2 preferred to use the mean scores.

22. As noted above, for lack of space Table 2 does not present all the available match comparisons we could make. Using our largest set of matches, we had available a total of 65 comparisons of any pair from the set: Chile, Nigeria, India. Of that total, 83 percent were not significant, even at the 0.05 level. By contrast, in 41 matches pitting East Pakistan against *either* Chile, Nigeria, or India, 34 percent favored the other country over Bangladesh at 0.05 or better. Indeed, in not a single match were the East Pakistanis ahead of any one of these three competitors, even at a statistically non-significant level.

23. In the thirteen available matches comparing the East Pakistanis and the Argentinians, the latter were ahead in 100 percent of the cases, and 54 percent of those matches gave the Argentinians a statistically significant advantage at 0.001 or better. Comparisons of the

Argentinians with either Chileans, Indians, or Nigerians were made in a total of 100 matches, of which 46 percent favored Argentina, significant at 0.05 or better. By contrast, in not even a single contest were the Argentinians significantly *behind* the Chileans, the Nigerians, or the Indians.

24. In seventeen matches permitting comparison of the Argentinians and the Israelis, each alternated being ahead pretty much 50/50. Of the total, none of the comparisons was statistically significant at even the 0.05 level.

25. The regression equation for which IM2A was the dependent variable contained the following independent variables: years of education, years of factory experience, mass media (a scale measuring radio listening and newspaper reading), age, consumer goods possessed, and urban versus rural origin. In addition, the equation contained five dummy variables for "country." These are variables which take on the value 1 or 0, depending upon whether a man *is* in a certain country or not, respectively. For the logic of this procedure see Searle (1971, Chapters 4 and 8). The B weights (unstandardized regression coefficients) of the dummy variables, and of the above listed covariates, enabled us to calculate adjusted means for each country. The B's and Betas for the covariates are given in Table 3. Note that all these variables were coded so as to be strictly comparable cross-nationally, except for consumer goods possessed. That variable actually is based on possession of different items in different countries, and each individual was coded as falling above or below the mean in his own country. In a later analysis we plan to replace this variable with income, for which we have data strictly comparable across countries, although for factory workers only.

26. This "nationality" variable was based on the mean modernity score of each country on IM2A. The resulting B and Beta weights for the six additional explanatory variables, given in Table 3, were the same as when we entered nationality in the form of five dummy variables as described in the previous footnote. Incidentally, the same six variables were used as covariates in calculating the adjusted means in Table 1.

27. It is worth noting that the Beta weights from the regression on the original OM scale, *done separately within each country,* were, in the median case, quite close to those obtained using the total sample for a regression on the IM scale. Giving the six country median Beta for OM first, followed by that for the total 5,500 case IM regression, the results were: education 0.37/0.34; mass media exposure 0.18/0.18; occupation 0.16/0.13. The basic eight variables used in the regression on OM yielded a median $R^2$ of 0.47, whereas, as may be seen in Table 3, a set of six variables, including country, yielded an $R^2$ of 0.43 for the combined multi-country sample. Any regression of this type may be much affected by problems of multi-colinearity. The available space does not permit dealing in detail with such problems here. They are, however, dealt with extensively in the analysis presented in Inkeles and Smith (1974).

28. Both the Indian and the East Pakistan samples were Bengali in culture, and their respective countries stand moderately close on a scale of national economic development. Yet Indian and East Pakistani samples manifested significant differences in individual modernity. In eighteen match comparisons which controlled for most important variables, the Indian sample was ahead of the East Pakistani 94 percent of the time, and in 50 percent of those matches the difference was statistically significant.

29. The ethnic and religious composition of each of our six national samples is described in some detail in Inkeles (1977). That paper also deals with ethnic and religious membership as an influence on individual modernity, but the analysis is limited to comparisons *within* each country separately.

30. The assumption of an effect due to culture or national character, the position taken in our third alternative explanation, is to some extent supported by the fact that in making this substitution of GNP for the country dummy variables we reduced the Beta weight for country from 0.21 to 0.16 and the unique variance explained by "country" from the former

four percent to between one and two percent. That portion of between country variance not explained by GNP might well be due to cultural differences. GNP per capita clearly is not sufficient to capture or summarize all the qualities of a country which influence the psychological modernity of its citizens.

## REFERENCES

Althauser, Robert, and Rubin, Donald (1970) "The Computerized Construction of a Matched Sample." *American Journal of Sociology* 76:325–346.

Brislin, R. W. et al. (1973) *Cross-Cultural Research Methods*. New York: Wiley-Interscience.

Coleman, James (1966) *Equality of Educational Opportunity*. Washington, DC: U.S. Office of Education.

Hagen, Everett E. (1962) *On the Theory of Social Change*. Homewood, IL: Dorsey Press.

Husén, Torsten (1972) "Does Time in School Make a Difference?" *Saturday Review* 55:32–35.

Inkeles, Alex (1969) "Making Men Modern." *American Journal of Sociology* 75:208–225.

——— (1976) "Understanding and Misunderstanding Individual Modernity." Pages 103–130 in Lewis A. Coser and Otto Larsen (eds.), *The Uses of Controversy in Sociology*. New York: Free Press.

——— (1977) "Individual Modernity in Different Ethnic and Religious Groups: Data from a Six Nation Study," *Issues in Cross-National Research* 285:539–564. *Annals of the New York Academy of Science*.

——— and Levinson, D. (1969) "National Character." Pages 418–506 in G. Lindzey and E. Aronson (eds.), *The Handbook of Social Psychology* 2d ed. Volume 4. Chicago: Aldine.

——— and Smith, D. (1974) *Becoming Modern: Individual Change in Six Developing Countries*. Cambridge, MA: Harvard University Press.

Johnston, J. (1972) 2nd Ed. *Econometric Methods*. New York: McGraw-Hill.

Lerner, Daniel (1958) *The Passing of Traditional Society*. Glencoe, IL: Free Press.

LeVine, R. A. (1973) *Culture, Behavior, and Personality*. Chicago: Aldine.

McClelland, David C. (1961) *The Achieving Society*. New York: Van Nostrand.

Manaster, G. J. and Havighurst, R. J. (1972) *Cross-National Research: Social Psychological Methods and Problems*. Boston: Houghton Mifflin.

Przeworski, A. and Teune, H. (1970) *The Logic of Comparative Social Inquiry*. New York: Wiley-Interscience.

Searle, S. R. (1971) *Linear Models*. New York: Wiley.

# CITIES AND HOMICIDE: A NEW LOOK AT AN OLD PARADOX

Dane Archer, Rosemary Gartner, Robin Akert, and Tim Lockwood*

Cities have long been regarded as centers of crime and violence. This unfavorable reputation is at least as old as the Bible. For example, in Ezekiel (7.23), one of the explanations God is said to have given for his wrath is that "the land is full of bloody crimes and the city is full of violence."

Over several centuries, many other writers have contrasted the immorality of cities with the innocence and purity of rural life. In many of these accounts, the city is described as seducing its new arrivals into a life of crime. For example, Adam Smith wrote that a man of "low moral charac-

**Comparative Studies in Sociology—Vol. 1, 1978, pages 73–95**

**ISBN 0-89232-025-7**

ter'' could be constrained to behave properly in a village environment, "but as soon as he comes into a great city he is sunk in obscurity and darkness . . . and he is very likely to . . . abandon himself to every sort of low profligacy and vice'' (quoted in Mannheim, 1965, p. 545).

This image of the city has been extremely influential in the history of sociology and, with some refinement, constitutes today the dominant theory about crime in cities. In sociology, this perspective is particularly identified with Durkheim and Wirth. In *The Division of Labor in Society,* Durkheim suggests that the "common conscience'' is diluted as a city grows in size:

> . . . local opinion weighs less heavily upon each of us, and as the general opinion of society cannot replace its predecessor, not being able to watch closely the conduct of its citizens, the collective surveillance is irretrievably loosened, the common conscience loses its authority and individual variability grows. (1933, p. 300)

Wirth (1940) accepted this view of cities and discussed the mechanisms by which cities dissolved traditional forms of social control. According to Wirth, the effects of cities included an increase in residential mobility, isolation, and anonymity as well as a breakdown of kinship ties and other informal sources of social control.

In addition to this Durkheim-Wirth view of the city as a place where traditional social controls are minimized and anonymity is maximized, no fewer than six additional theoretical explanations have appeared in the literature on urban crime. These six hypotheses can be stated in abbreviated form as follows: (1) cities foster the development of criminal subcultures; (2) cities produce class, cultural, and racial conflict as a function of greater population heterogeneity; (3) cities increase criminal opportunities because of population size and the large numbers of commercial establishments; (4) cities have relatively impersonal police-civilian relations which lead to rigid law enforcement and arrest practices; (5) the age and sex composition of cities have been altered by the arrival of immigrants (from rural areas, other nations, etc.) who are predominantly young males; and even (6) the possibility that the population density of cities might by itself increase the likelihood of pathological behavior.

The relationship between cities and violent crime is, unfortunately, an area of sociology where theory seems to have outdistanced empirical evidence. Despite the existence of at least seven quite plausible theoretical explanations for why cities might have a higher rate of violent crime, the nature and origins of urban crime remain far from well understood.

Much of this confusion is a function of the way in which different sociologists have tried to answer the deceptively simple question: "Do cities have high rates of violent crime and, if so, why?'' Like many other areas in sociology, this topic has been clouded by a confusion between cross-sectional and longitudinal ways of answering the question.[1]

The difference between the cross-sectional and longitudinal approaches to this question can be illustrated easily. There are two ways in which cities and homicide could be related. There would be a cross-sectional relationship between the two if, at any one time, *city size* and homicide rates were related—e.g., if in a given year large cities had higher homicide rates than small cities. The cross-sectional effect of city size has been called "urbanism" (Lodhi and Tilly, 1973).

By contrast, there would be a longitudinal relationship between cities and homicide if, over time, *city growth* and homicide rates were related—e.g., if, in a given century, a city's homicide rate rose as its population grew. The longitudinal effect of city growth is often called "urbanization."[2]

With extremely few exceptions, sociological theories about urban crime rest upon only cross-sectional studies of city size—e.g., static comparisons of the homicide rates of different size cities in a single year. For example, Wolfgang (1968) reviewed U.S. crime statistics for cities of different size in 1965 and concluded that "the larger the city category, the higher the crime rate for all 'serious' crimes combined" (p. 246). Using more recent data, Clinard (1974) has also found a monotonic relationship between city size and homicide rates—i.e., small cities have lower homicide rates than large cities. This relationship between city size and homicide appears to hold consistently in the U.S. (Ogburn, 1935; Boggs, 1966; President's Commission on Law Enforcement and the Administration of Justice, 1967; Glaser, 1970; McLennan, 1970; Sutherland and Cressey, 1970; and Harries, 1974), and is also found in other societies (Szabo, 1960; Mannheim, 1965; and Tarniquet, 1968).

The finding of a positive cross-sectional association between city size and homicide rates has become one of the most widely accepted maxims in sociology. Unfortunately, this finding has encouraged some sociologists and others to infer that (1) rural areas have lower homicide rates than all cities, and that (2) individual cities will experience an increase in homicide rates as they grow in size.[3] Neither of these two conclusions is logically warranted solely on the basis of the cross-sectional evidence discussed above and, in fact, there is little empirical support for either conclusion. Each will be discussed in turn.

Since rural areas are obviously less urban than even small cities, there has been a natural tendency to assume that their homicide rates are lower than the rates of small cities. This assumption has probably been strengthened by the Durkheim-Wirth hypothesis, discussed above, which tends to portray rural areas as more innocent, tranquil, and law-abiding than cities.[4]

Evidence on this question is, however, mixed. For example, Wolfgang (1968) reported slightly higher homicide rates for rural areas in the U.S. in 1965 than for small cities—but he indicated that this pattern had been somewhat unstable over time. Several researchers have reported finding that rural homicide rates can be higher than urban rates, both in the U.S. (Frankel, 1939; Vold, 1941; and Sutherland and Cressey, 1970, p. 178) and abroad (Dhanagare, 1969; Clinard and Abbott, 1973; Scherer, Abeles, and Fischer, 1975). In summary, even though it is theoretically reasonable to expect rural homicide rates to be lower than the rates of all cities, there is no robust evidence for this proposition.

The second inference, that cities experience increased homicide rates as they grow, also cannot be justified on the basis of cross-sectional studies. This question is clearly a longitudinal question about the effects of city growth, and it can be answered only by studying how homicide rates change as cities grow over time.

Some longitudinal studies have been made, and the results of these investigations constitute the other half of the paradox of cities and homicide. These few longitudinal studies are paradoxical because they have not found the expected—i.e., they have not found that individual cities experience homicide rate increases as they grow in population.

Three of these longitudinal studies have examined individual cities over a period of roughly one century. For example, Powell (1966) studied Buffalo between 1854 and 1956; Ferdinand (1967) studied Boston from 1849 to 1951; and Lane (1969) studied both Boston and Massachusetts from the mid-nineteenth to the mid-twentieth century. These three studies of American city growth found a consistent decline in murder and other serious crimes over the century studied.

There have also been a few longitudinal studies of crime and homicide rates for entire nations. For example, Christiansen (1960) studied Denmark for the period 1940–1955; Venter (1962) studied South Africa between 1913 and 1960; Tobias (1967) used qualitative sources to study English crime over the eighteenth and nineteenth centuries; and Lodhi and Tilly (1973) completed the most comprehensive study of this kind using the case of nineteenth century France. In general, these studies of nations provide no evidence that city growth and homicide rates are related—e.g., Lodhi and Tilly (1973) found that crimes against the person in nineteenth century France fluctuated mildly but had no discernible trend.

This, then, is the paradox of cities and homicide rates: Why do large cities currently have higher homicide rates than small cities, if there is no evidence of increasing homicide rates as a city grows? The cross-sectional evidence on city size and homicide seems at first to suggest that cities must grow to some absolute size (e.g., 100,000 persons) before having a high homicide rate. But this apparently reasonable proposition is contradicted by the longitudinal evidence which shows that cities don't in fact show homicide rate increases as they grow. In short, if larger cities currently have higher homicide rates than small cities, how did they get these high rates—if not by growing in population size?

This paper attempts a new interpretation of this paradoxical relationship between cities and homicide rates. Both cross-sectional and longitudinal evidence will be examined in an effort to explain the apparent contradictions produced by these two approaches. In addition, although American data will be examined briefly, the analysis will depend primarily upon homicide data from other societies. This comparative approach, which is intended to maximize the generalizable nature of the analysis, is only now made possible by the recent creation of a 110-Nation Comparative Crime Data File.

## METHOD

The cross-sectional effects of city size can be examined using both American and cross-national homicide data. The American data used in this analysis were obtained from the FBI's annual *Uniform Crime Report*. This report provides aggregate homicide rates for the entire nation, rates for individual cities, and rates for cities in several categories of population size (e.g., 10,000 to 25,000, 25,000 to 50,000, etc.). For this analysis, the rates of different categories of city size were averaged over a five-year period to smooth the effects of idiosyncratic annual fluctuations. These rates were examined to determine whether, as reported by previous researchers, (1) large American cities have consistently higher homicide rates than small cities; (2) whether the cross-sectional relationship between city size and homicide rates appears to be linear or follows some other form, and finally (3) whether rural U.S. homicide rates are higher than the rates of large cities, lower than the rates of small cities, or somewhere between these two extremes.

With the recent creation of the 110-Nation Comparative Crime Data File (CCDF), it is also possible to examine some cross-sectional effects of city size in other societies. The development of this comparative file has been reported in some detail elsewhere (e.g., Archer and Gartner, 1976), and only a brief description of the file will be given here. The CCDF contains time series data for approximately 110 nations on their annual incidence of five types of offenses: homicide, assault, robbery, theft, and rape.

The time series in the CCDF begin in the year 1900, although many of the nations in the file did not begin maintaining crime data until much later. For example, developing nations generally have data in the CCDF only for relatively recent periods. In addition, the records for some nations contain interruptions due to national emergencies and bureaucratic lapses. These factors mean that for any given year or period, the CCDF has effective data for fewer than 110 nations.

The principal sources for the creation of this massive comparative file have been: (1) correspondence with national and metropolitan governmental sources in essentially all societies in the world; (2) examination of documents and annual reports of those nations which have published data on their annual incidence of various offenses; and (3) correspondence with other record-keeping agencies.

As part of the collection of the 110-Nation CCDF, we have reviewed the literature on possible sources of unreliability and invalidity in official crime data. The implications of these concerns for comparative research with the CCDF have been discussed elsewhere, and efforts have been made to identify research designs which minimize these problems (Archer and Gartner, 1976). For example, the most conservative design using the CCDF is one which (1) examines homicide rather than other offenses, (2) examines only longitudinal trends within each of several societies rather than absolute levels across several societies, and (3) controls for the variable validity of different offense indicators (e.g., offenses known versus arrests).

With these methodological precautions, the CCDF makes it possible to investigate the effects upon offense rates of a great number of possible antecedent variables. In addition, the CCDF can maximize the comparative rigor of research on the origins of homicide by maximizing a researcher's chances of identifying both internationally general relationships and also relationships which hold only for certain types of societies. An example of the kind of analysis made possible by the CCDF is an investigation of the effects of wars upon homicide rates in postwar societies (Archer and Gartner, 1976).

In addition to aggregate data for entire nations, the CCDF includes offense data for 44 "primary" cities—cities which are either the largest or one of the largest cities in a society. This feature of the comparative file makes it possible to compare homicide rates in each primary city with the national homicide rate of the corresponding society.

If these two rates differ, it will be a conservative test of a relationship between city size and homicide rates for two reasons: (1) the national homicide rate obviously includes the primary city rate and this fact will diminish the observed difference between the two rates, and (2) the national homicide rate reflects both rural areas and other urban areas, in addition to the primary city itself. The effects of these two facts is conservative. Differences will only be observed if the primary city homicide rate differs from the aggregate homicide rate of all national sectors combined—rural areas, small cities, other large cities, and the primary city itself. This comparison will provide a cross-national answer to the cross-sectional question of whether large cities have homicide rates which are higher than their national averages.

The longitudinal question of whether city growth is related to changes in homicide rates can be restated in two component questions: (1) Have the homicide rates of primary cities borne a *consistent* relationship to national homicide rates over time?, and (2) Have the homicide rates of the primary cities themselves increased over time as these cities have grown in population size? A separate analysis is necessary to answer each of these two questions.

Because of the large volume of CCDF data needed to answer the first of these two longitudinal questions, a simple data reduction strategy was adopted. For any given year, the median primary city homicide rate was compared with the median national homicide rate. This is a controlled comparison strategy since each national rate acts as a "control" for each primary city rate—i.e., a primary city is only included in the median for a given year if its corresponding national rate is also available for that year. This controlled comparison prevents any bias due to the partial entry (e.g., only for cities) of homicide data from a society with unusually high or low homicide rates. This analysis will answer the question of whether primary city homicide rates have differed in a consistent manner from national homicide rates over time.

The second longitudinal question, of whether the rates of primary cities have increased with their population growth, has to be answered using a slightly different approach. The key question here is whether the primary cities show a positive correlation over time between changes in their population size and changes in their homicide rate. This correlation can be calculated separately for each primary city. Since most cities show consistent population increases over time, this correlation will be very similar to the slope of the homicide rate for each city.

In summary, the relationship between cities and homicide will be examined using two cross-sectional analyses and two longitudinal analyses. These four steps will examine: (1) U.S. cross-sectional data on city size and homicide rates; (2) comparative cross-sectional data contrasting the homicide rates for primary cities and the rates for entire nations; (3) comparative longitudinal data on the relationship between primary city homicide rates and national rates over time, and (4) comparative longitudinal data on the slope of primary city homicide rates over time.

## RESULTS AND DISCUSSION

*Cross-sectional Evidence*

Cross-sectional data in the U.S. has the advantage that homicide rates are available for each of several city-size categories. In addition to general comparisons of urban and rural homicide rates, therefore, it is also possible to speculate about the precise shape of the relationship between levels of city size and homicide rates. This cross-sectional relationship is shown for U.S. cities for the period 1971–1975 in Table 1.

For cities alone (i.e. excluding suburban and rural areas), Table 1 shows a strong and perfectly monotonic relationship between U.S. city size and homicide rates. Each category of city size has a higher homicide rate than all smaller city-size categories and a lower rate than all larger city-size categories. This analysis replicates earlier findings about homicide rate variations among U.S. cities of different sizes.

The suburban and rural areas in Table 1, however, have homicide rates which are unexpectedly high. Even though these areas of the U.S. are less urban than all other categories of city size, they exceed the rates of some of these categories. For example, the rural U.S. homicide rate is higher than the rates for the three smallest city-size categories—i.e., rural homicide rates in the U.S. are as high as the homicide rates of cities with a population between 50,000 and 100,000. At least for this one country, therefore, rural homicide rates are higher than the rates of small cities but not as high as the rates of large cities.

The relationship between U.S. city size and homicide rates becomes even more interesting when graphed. The mean homicide rates from

*Table 1.* City Size and Homicide Rates in the U.S.: 1971–1975.[a]

| City Size | Homicide Rate (per 100,000) |
|---|---|
| Over 1,000,000 | 23.2 |
| 500,000 to 1,000,000 | 20.2 |
| 250,000 to 500,000 | 16.8 |
| 100,000 to 250,000 | 11.5 |
| 50,000 to 100,000 | 6.5 |
| 25,000 to 50,000 | 5.4 |
| 10,000 to 25,000 | 4.3 |
| Under 10,000 | 3.6 |
| Suburban Areas[b] | 4.9 |
| Rural Areas | 6.4 |

[a]Adapted from the FBI's *Uniform Crime Reports*, 1971–1975. To smooth the effects of annual fluctuations, the rates shows are the means of the murder and non-negligent manslaughter rates for the five years 1971–1975.

[b]Includes suburban, city, and county police agencies within metropolitan areas. Excludes core cities. Suburban cities are also included in other city groups.

Table 1 are graphed in Figure 1, using a logarithmic scale for city size because of the non-arithmetic nature of the population category intervals.

Except for the rates of suburban and rural areas, Figure 1 indicates that the categories of city size and homicide rates are logarithmically related—i.e., when graphed on semi-logarithmic paper, the points approach a straight line. This shows that the most dramatic increases in homicide rates (rate increases per population increases) occur at the lower end of the city size categories. Starting with the smallest cities, therefore, one observes the greatest homicide increases with relatively small increases in city size categories.[5] For more populous cities, it takes much larger "increments" in city size categories to produce homicide rate increases of the same size. In summary, the most striking aspect of Figure 1 is the regularity of the logarithmic relationship between city size and homicide rates.

When suburban and rural homicide rates are included in Figure 1, the relationship between U.S. city size and homicide rates is something like a

*Figure 1.* City Size and Homicide Rates in the U.S.: 1971–1975[a]

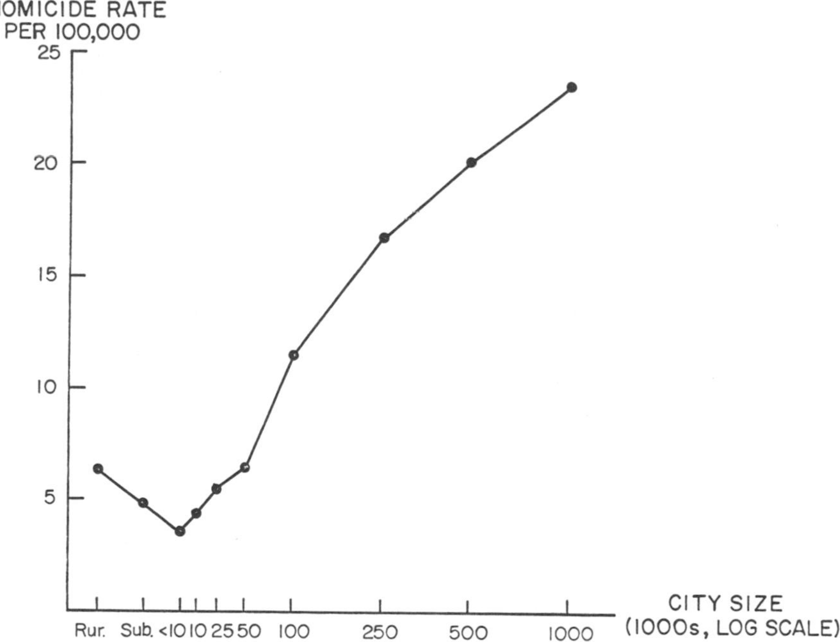


[a]*Source:* Adapted from the FBI's *Uniform Crime Reports,* 1971–1975. Rates shown are the means of the five-year period 1971–1975.

logarithmic J-curve.[6] This curve reaches a minimum for cities with fewer than 10,000 persons and increases for both rural areas and for larger cities. At least in the U.S., therefore, city size and homicide rates are related by the logarithmic J-curve shown in Figure 1.

It would be fascinating, of course, to see if city size and homicide rates in other societies are also related by the logarithmic J-curve in Figure 1. However, although the CCDF does include time series homicide rates for 44 cities, it does not in general include more than one city in each society. It is not possible, therefore, to use the CCDF to test for the presence of this logarithmic J-curve within each of several societies. Researchers with homicide rates for individual cities in a given society could, of course, test for the presence of this distinctive curve.

As discussed earlier, however, it is possible to complete a somewhat different cross-sectional test for the effects of city size in other societies. The homicide rates of the primary cities in the CCDF can be contrasted with the aggregate rates of the corresponding societies to see whether large cities have higher homicide rates than their national averages. A comparison of this kind is shown for 24 "pairs" of primary cities and nations in Table 2. In order to smooth the effects of erratic annual fluctuations, the rates shown in Table 2 are the averages of (in general) the five-year period 1966–1970—the most recent period in the CCDF.[7]

In general, the cross-sectional analysis in Table 2 indicates that the homicide rates of primary cities exceed the rates of nations as a whole. This was true for 75 percent (18 out of 24) of the pairs of cities and nations in Table 2. As discussed earlier, it should be noted that the differences in Table 2 understate the actual differences between large city rates and non-urban rates—because the national rate actually includes the primary city rate and the rates of other cities as well as the rates of non-urban areas.

With some exceptions, the comparative evidence in Table 2 is in agreement with cross-sectional evidence for the U.S.—in both cases, large cities have homicide rates which are higher than their national averages. While these cross-sectional comparisons do not by themselves explain the origins of the higher homicide rates of large cities, it is still encouraging to see that comparative data is consistent with American data on this question.

It is also interesting that although all the cities in Table 2 are large cities, there is obviously great variation among the cities in their homicide rates, just as there is great variation among the nations in their rates.[8] This variation indicates that absolute city size does not correspond in any direct way to the absolute magnitude of a city's homicide rate—i.e., cities of 500,000 people do not necessarily have a homicide rate of, say, 17 per 100,000 people.

This suggests the intriguing possibility that large cities have homicide rates which are unusually *high only in terms of the overall homicide rates of their societies*. A primary city, therefore, can have a homicide rate which is remarkably low (when compared to other large cities worldwide) but which is still a high rate for this specific society. This pattern can be convincingly illustrated using two of the cases in Table 2. Both Paris and New York City had over 7,000,000 inhabitants for the period 1966–1970. But as Table 2 indicates, these two cities have dramatically different homicide rates. In both cases, however, the homicide rate of the primary city is higher than the rate of the entire society.

If this observation is generally correct, the relationship between city size and homicide rates is relative rather than absolute—i.e., there is no formula relating specific homicide rates to specific city sizes. Sociologists are unlikely, therefore, to identify a theoretical model which can predict an international city's homicide rate purely from its population. On the basis of the evidence in Table 2, it seems more promising to pursue theories which try to explain why large cities have homicide rates which are only high relative to the entire nation's homicide rate, whatever that rate is. In summary, we cannot know in advance what a large international city's homicide rate will be, but we can be fairly certain that it will be higher than the average rate of the nation.

Finally, it is interesting to note that five of the six exceptions in Table 2 are developing nations. This could mean that the factors which produce relatively higher rates in most primary cities do not operate in developing societies. It is not difficult to illustrate some hypothetical explanations for this difference. In terms of the Durkheim-Wirth hypothesis discussed earlier, it might be that primary cities involve a weakening of kinship and community ties in developed societies but not in developing societies. Perhaps developing societies have lower rates of mobility, or perhaps people moving to cities in developing societies move with intact families rather than alone. Developed societies might also have greater controls over rural homicides—e.g., decentralized law enforcement which reduces blood feuds, marauding gangs, etc. Whatever the reason, all but one of the exceptional cases in Table 2 are developing societies.

### *Longitudinal Evidence*

Longitudinal evidence on cities and homicide can be examined to answer two related questions. The first of these questions is whether the pattern shown in Table 2 has been consistent over time—i.e., have primary cities always had relatively high homicide rates?

This question was addressed using the method of controlled comparison described earlier. For each year, a median homicide rate was calculated for primary cities, and a second median rate was determined for the

*Table 2.* Primary City Homicide Rates and National Homicide Rates: A Cross-Sectional Comparison.[a]

City Homicide Rate Lower than National Rate ($n = 6$)

| | Homicide Rate[b] |
|---|---|
| 1. Guyana (1966–1970) | 6.18 |
| Georgetown | 5.21 |
| 2. Japan (1966–1970) | 2.23 |
| Tokyo | 1.78 |
| 3. Kenya (1964–1968) | 5.67 |
| Nairobi | 5.27 |
| 4. Panama (1966–1970) | 11.07 |
| Panama City | 4.96 |
| 5. Sri Lanka (1966–1970) | 6.09 |
| Colombo City | 5.59 |
| 6. Turkey (1966–1970) | 9.65 |
| Istanbul | 4.84 |
| Median Country Rate: | 6.14 |
| Median City Rate: | 5.09 |

City Homicide Rate Higher than National Rate ($n = 8$)

| | Homicide Rate |
|---|---|
| 1. Australia (1966–1970) | 1.28 |
| Sydney | 1.57 |
| 2. Austria (1966–1970) | 0.73 |
| Vienna | 0.89 |
| 3. Belgium (1965–1969) | 0.29 |
| Brussels | 0.45 |
| 4. Finland (1966–1970) | 0.35 |
| Helsinki | 0.65 |
| 5. France (1966–1970) | 0.45 |
| Paris | 0.61 |
| 6. India (1966–1970) | 2.72 |
| Bombay | 2.85 |
| 7. Ireland (1966–1970) | 0.34 |
| Dublin | 0.35 |
| 8. Mexico (1962, 1966, 1967, 1972) | 13.24 |
| Mexico City | 13.34 |
| 9. Netherlands (1966–1970) | 0.50 |
| Amsterdam | 1.23 |
| 10. New Zealand (1966–1970) | 0.16 |
| Wellington | 2.32 |
| 11. Northern Ireland (1964–1968)[c] | 0.20 |
| Belfast | 0.35 |
| 12. Philippines (1966–1970) | 7.98 |
| Manila | 23.86 |
| 13. Rhodesia (1966–1970) | 5.33 |
| Salisbury | 7.20 |
| 14. Scotland (1966–1970) | 0.78 |
| Glasgow | 1.56 |
| 15. Spain (1964–1968) | 0.49 |
| Madrid | 0.56 |
| 16. Sudan (1961–1964, 1968) | 5.67 |
| Khartoum | 30.25 |
| 17. Trinidad & Tobago (1966–1970) | 14.00 |
| Port-of-Spain | 15.31 |
| 18. United States (1966–1970) | 6.62 |
| New York City | 11.54 |
| Median Country Rate: | 0.76 |
| Median City Rate: | 1.57 |

*Table 2*. Footnotes:

[a]Because of national idiosyncrasies in definition and reporting, the reader is cautioned against making direct cross-national comparisons of homicide rate levels. As explained in the text, this is not a problem for urban-national comparisons within the same society.
[b]Source for all data is the 110-Nation Comparative Crime Data File. Homicide rates are given in offenses per 100,000 population. In order to smooth the effect of annual fluctuations, the rates are the means of the years shown. The difference in rates between nations and cities is conservative for two reasons: (1) the national rate includes the urban rate, and (2) the national rate also includes other urban areas (i.e., the national rates aggregate both urban and rural areas).
[c]The period 1966–1970 also shows Belfast as having a higher homicide rate. This period was not used in this analysis, however, because Northern Ireland's most recent political violence began in 1969.

nations as a whole. In the computations for each year, therefore, the national homicide rate serves as a paired control for the primary city rate. The longitudinal relationship between the homicide rates of primary cities and the rates of entire nations is shown in Figure 2. Because of missing or incomparable homicide indicators, particularly in the early part of this century, only the period 1926–1970 is reflected in Figure 2. The number of pairs (one pair consists of one city and one nation) in the analysis is indicated at five-year intervals.

The most striking pattern in Figure 2 is that primary cities consistently have had homicide rates higher than their national averages. The gap between the solid and broken lines in Figure 2 is a conservative index of the effect of city size on homicide rates. It is conservative, again, because the dotted line actually includes the rate of the solid line, and it also includes the rates of other large and small cities as well.

The median homicide rates in Figure 2 show that the main finding of Table 2 (that primary cities have homicide rates higher than their national averages for 1966–1970) could be replicated for any period between 1926 and 1970. If anything, Figure 2 shows that the effect of city size was even more pronounced earlier in this century than during the period 1966–1970.[9]

The consistent difference reflected in Figure 2 is our most important longitudinal finding. Although we do not have homicide data reaching back into the eighteenth and nineteenth centuries, the consistently higher rates of the primary cities in Figure 2 encourage us to make the following extrapolation: In general, large cities have always had homicide rates higher than their national averages, and this was true even when primary cities were much smaller than they are today. If this interpretation is correct, it suggests that the homicide rates of large cities are higher than national rates not because of the absolute population size of these cities, but because of their *relative* size. Even when primary cities were much smaller than they are today (e.g., in 1926), they were still relatively more urban (densely populated, etc.) than their societies as a whole. We are

*Figure 2.* Primary City Homicide Rates and National Homicide Rates: A Longitudinal Comparison.[a]

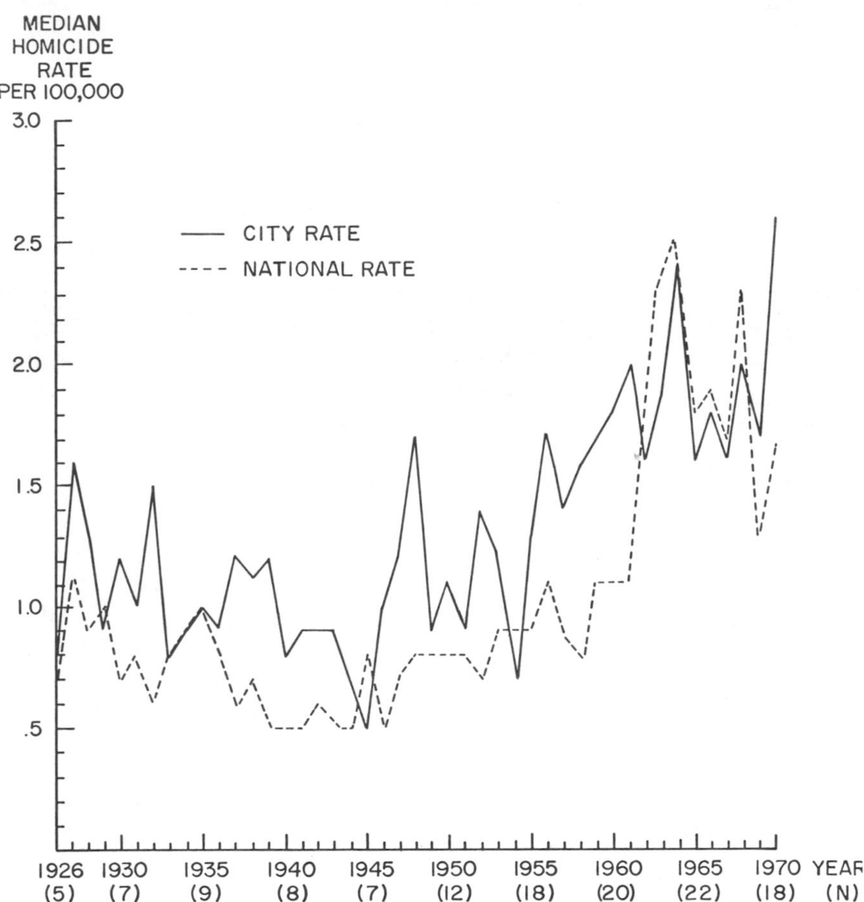


[a] *Source:* The 110-Nation Comparative Crime Data File. The solid line shows the median homicide rate of primary cities for each year; the broken line shows the median rate of the corresponding nations. The number of pairs (each pair is one city and one nation) in the analysis is indicated at five-year intervals.

suggesting, therefore, that it is the relative size of "large" cities at any moment in time—rather than their absolute population in thousands—which is responsible for their consistently high homicide rates.

In summary, the effects of city size first identified in Table 2 have clearly been consistent over time—i.e., at least for the time period covered in Figure 2, the homicide rates of primary cities have always been higher than national homicide rates.

A final cautionary note should be mentioned concerning Figure 2. Because different intervals in Figure 2 reflect different cities (depending on the availability and comparability of city data), the slope of the solid line in Figure 2 is not meaningful. Since different cities are included in this median line in various years, the line cannot provide an indication of how primary city rates have changed in absolute terms over time.

The question of whether primary cities have experienced any absolute increases in homicide rates over time is a second longitudinal question, and one which cannot be answered from Figure 2. The three longitudinal case studies of single American cities cited earlier (Powell, 1966; Ferdinand, 1967; Lane, 1969) found no homicide increases for these three cities, and a similar conclusion was reached in the study of nineteenth century France by Lodhi and Tilly (1973).

In order to provide a rough answer to this question for each primary city in the CCDF, a simple zero-order correlation was calculated between: (1) the city's population, and (2) the city's homicide rate. Since almost all the cities increased continuously in population during this period,[10] this correlation provides a crude index of the homicide trend during the period. A positive correlation indicates homicide rate increases during this period; a zero correlation indicates essentially no change; and a negative correlation indicates homicide rate decreases.

This analysis produced 34 correlations, each one roughly analogous to the single-city studies of Buffalo and Boston discussed earlier. Since fewer than 100 years were available for these 34 cities, however, our analysis is not as deep as these previous case studies. This analysis is much broader, however, in that it examines 34 cities in 28 countries.[11] The results of this analysis are shown in Table 3.

As Table 3 clearly indicates, there is no general relationship between city growth and changes in absolute homicide rates. The correlations range from a low of ×0.66 to a high of 0.98, and the 34 cases are evenly divided into 17 positive *r*'s and 17 negative *r*'s. This broad scatter is responsible for the essentially zero median correlation of ×0.01.

The inconsistency of these 34 longitudinal analyses suggests that there is no invariant tendency for the homicide rates of large cities to increase as these cities grow in size. Table 3 shows that homicide rates are just as likely to decrease with city growth as they are to increase.

Even though the time periods reflected in Table 3 are all shorter than the century-long studies of individual American cities cited earlier, several cities have data for more than 50 years. This variance in time periods can be used for a kind of data quality control procedure. If one limits the comparison to the four cities with 50 or more years of data, for example, the median correlation is still only ×0.46. Even for cities with a half-

*Table 3.* Homicide Rates and Population Size for Primary Cities: A Longitudinal Analysis.[a]

| City | Correlation Between City Population and City Homicide Rate[b] | Number of Years in the Analysis | Significance |
|---|---|---|---|
| New York[c] | 0.98 | 8 | 0.001 |
| Istanbul | 0.88 | 19 | 0.001 |
| Manila | 0.79 | 23 | 0.001 |
| Quezon City[d] | 0.64 | 8 | 0.090 |
| Calcutta | 0.51 | 16 | 0.044 |
| New York[c] | 0.47 | 12 | 0.121 |
| Panama City | 0.45 | 11 | 0.167 |
| Salisbury[d] | 0.41 | 22 | 0.058 |
| Port-of-Spain | 0.38 | 25 | 0.061 |
| Johannesburg | 0.33 | 10 | 0.360 |
| Georgetown | 0.27 | 18 | 0.273 |
| Sydney | 0.27 | 40 | 0.090 |
| Quezon City | 0.26 | 11 | 0.437 |
| Wellington | 0.16 | 17 | 0.542 |
| Colombo | 0.15 | 74 | 0.198 |
| Khartoum | 0.13 | 13 | 0.683 |
| Amsterdam | 0.02 | 43 | 0.911 |
| Port-of-Spain[d] | −0.04 | 25 | 0.851 |
| Mexico City | −0.13 | 12 | 0.697 |
| Dublin | −0.15 | 47 | 0.315 |
| Brussels | −0.17 | 27 | 0.409 |
| Oslo | −0.18 | 14 | 0.541 |
| Salisbury | −0.21 | 22 | 0.361 |
| Munich | −0.26 | 28 | 0.181 |
| Vienna | −0.32 | 21 | 0.155 |
| Montevideo | −0.36 | 31 | 0.045 |
| Glasgow | −0.38 | 72 | 0.001 |
| Paris | −0.45 | 39 | 0.004 |
| Nairobi | −0.50 | 21 | 0.022 |
| Belfast | −0.54 | 52 | 0.001 |
| Madrid | −0.57 | 16 | 0.021 |
| Tokyo | −0.57 | 73 | 0.001 |
| Helsinki | −0.58 | 43 | 0.001 |
| Bombay | −0.66 | 16 | 0.005 |
| Median *r*: | −0.01 | | |

[a]Source: the 110-Nation Comparative Crime Data File. This analysis tests for the presence of any linear relationship between changes in population size and changes in homicide rates for these primary cities.
[b]Since most of these cities have grown consistently over time, the correlations are easily interpreted. A positive correlation means that the city's homicide rate has increased over time; a zero *r* indicates no consistent change in homicide rate; and a negative *r* means that the city's homicide rate has decreased over time.
[c]New York City appears twice because a change in recording procedures created two series: one before 1966 and one after.
[d]Indicates that a rate for "murder" was used for this city; other rates are homicide rates.

century or more of data, therefore, there is still no strong evidence that homicide rates increase with city growth.

It is possible, of course, that the near-zero median in Table 3 conceals some lawful differences among different types of societies. For example, a casual reading of Table 3 indicates that primary cities in developing societies seem to be overrepresented among the positive correlations—i.e., primary cities in developing nations may be more likely than other cities to experience increasing homicide rates as they grow. This purely speculative observation does not, of course, alter the general lack of a consistent pattern in Table 3.

In passing, it is also interesting to speculate about the different conclusions which would have resulted from independent studies of different single cities in Table 3. For example, a researcher examining twentieth century data for Tokyo would have concluded that homicide rates declined with city growth; a different researcher studying data for Amsterdam would have found no relationship between the variables and would have concluded that previous researchers (e.g., Ferdinand, 1967) were correct; but a third researcher doing a case study of Manila would have found homicide rate increases with city growth and would have concluded that previous researchers were wrong. The unique strength of the CCDF for sociological research on homicide rates is that it can maximize a researcher's view of the range of possible outcomes across several societies and also indicate whether any general pattern occurs. In this case, the CCDF data in Table 3 demonstrates that city growth can have an extremely wide range of implications for homicide rates and that, in general, there is no evidence that cities and homicide rates grow together.

Seven of the primary cities in Table 3 have essentially uninterrupted homicide data for the entire period 1926–1970. These seven cities are Amsterdam, Belfast, Colombo City, Dublin, Glasgow, Helsinki, and Tokyo. The homicide rates of these seven cities can be represented, therefore, by a median rate for each year. This median rate (unlike the solid line in Figure 2) is not affected by the inclusion or exclusion from year to year of cities with unusually high or low homicide rates. When graphed, therefore, the median rate of these seven cities has an interpretable slope. The median rate for these seven cities between 1926 and 1970 is shown in Figure 3.

Just as Table 3 provided evidence that urban homicide rates do not in general increase with city growth, Figure 3 indicates that these seven primary cities do not show any consistent increase in homicide rates over time. The slope of the graph in Figure 3 is essentially zero (×0.006)—i.e., there is no evidence of progressively higher homicide rates over time. Since time and city growth are almost perfectly correlated (i.e., almost all

*Figure 3.* Trends in Primary City Homicide Rates, 1926–1970.[a]

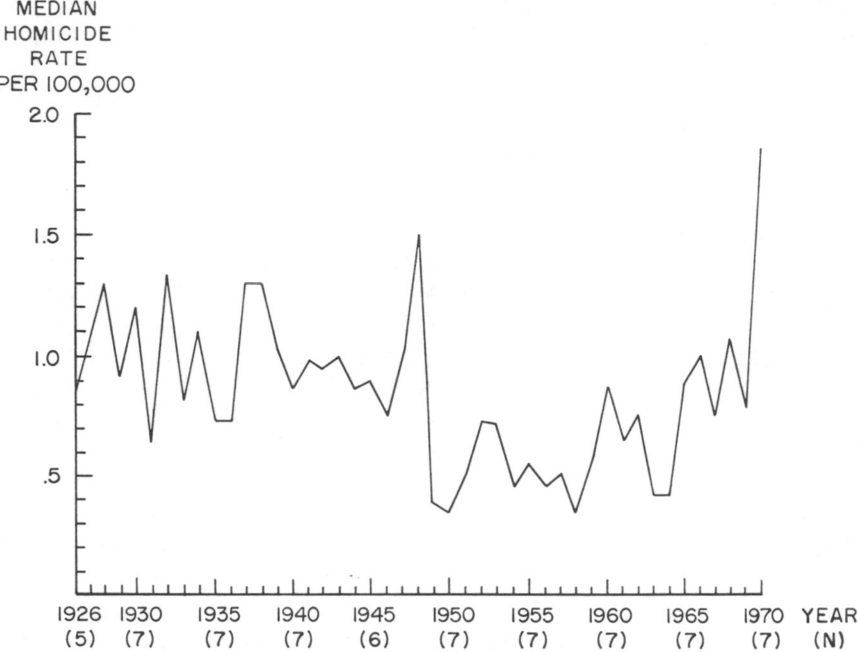


[a]*Source:* The 110-Nation Comparative Crime Data File. The cities in this trend line are Amsterdam, Belfast, Colombo City, Dublin, Glasgow, Helsinki, and Tokyo. These seven cities have essentially uninterrupted homicide data for this entire period.

cities in the file have grown consistently or even monotonically over time), these two analyses are in agreement: there is no evidence that city growth has any consistent implications for a city's homicide rate.

## SUMMARY AND CONCLUSIONS

The sociological literature on urban homicide rates contains a paradox. Cross-sectional research on city size and homicide rates has found higher homicide rates in large cities than in small cities. The few longitudinal studies of city growth in individual cities, however, have not found increases in homicide rates as these cities grow. The paradox is this: If larger cities currently have high homicide rates, how did they acquire these high rates if not by growing in size?

This question was investigated using data from a newly created Comparative Crime Data File (CCDF). This file has time series rates of homicide and other offenses beginning in 1900 for 110 nations and 44 primary cities. Data from the CCDF, along with data on U.S. homicide rates, were used to investigate both (1) the cross-sectional relationship between city size and homicide rates, and (2) the longitudinal relationship between city growth and homicide rates.

These analyses produced the following conclusions:

1. Cross-sectional evidence for the U.S. indicates that city size and homicide rates are strongly related. The form of this relationship is a highly consistent logarithmic J-curve—the highest homicide rates are found in the largest cities and the lowest rates are found in cities with fewer than 10,000 people. Rates for each city size are higher than the rates of smaller cities and lower than the rates of larger cities. Homicide rates in suburban and rural areas, however, are higher than the rates of small cities—e.g., rural homicide rates in the U.S. are roughly equal to the rates of cities with populations between 50,000 and 100,000. For the U.S. in general, this analysis strongly supports the conclusion that city size and homicides are related—large U.S. cities have high rates of homicide.

2. Comparative cross-sectional evidence from the CCDF also indicates a relationship between city size and homicide rates. For the period 1966–1970, primary cities in 24 societies generally have homicide rates higher than their national averages. This analysis actually understates the relative magnitude of the primary city homicide rates since the national rate includes data from the primary city and from other large and small cities as well.

3. This cross-sectional analysis also reveals wide variation among primary cities in terms of their absolute homicide rates. Variation in homicide rates even occurs among primary cities with the same population size. This suggests that two international primary cities of equal size can have radically different homicide rates, but that both these rates will be higher than their national average. The link between city size and homicide rates is, therefore, country-specific or relative, and not absolute.

4. Comparative homicide data were also examined longitudinally. The homicide rates of primary cities were compared to the rates of entire nations. In this analysis, a median city homicide rate and a median national rate were calculated for each year between 1926 and 1970. This comparison reveals that the homicide rates of primary cities have consistently exceeded national rates over time. The observed difference in this analysis again understates the actual difference in rates because the national rate includes the primary city and other large cities. This difference in rates is particularly impressive since the primary cities were much smaller in absolute terms at the beginning of this period. This suggests that urban homicide rates exceed national rates not because of the abso-

lute population size of these cities, but because of their *relative* size. Even when they were much smaller than their present size, these primary cities were highly "urban" compared to their societies.

5. Comparative longitudinal data were also used to test for a relationship over time between city growth and homicide rate changes in each of 34 international primary cities. Exactly half of these cities show homicide rate increases with city growth, and half the cities show rate decreases with city growth. The median correlation between city population growth and homicide rates over time, therefore, is essentially zero. This analysis provides no evidence for the general proposition that city size and homicide rates increase together.

6. Finally, longitudinal data were used to examine the homicide rate trends of seven primary cities with uninterrupted homicide data from 1926–1970. The slope of the median homicide rates of these seven cities over time is essentially zero. This is further evidence that the absolute homicide rates of primary cities have not shown any consistent increases over time, despite the population increases of these cities.

Considered together, these findings appear to provide a new interpretation of the paradox of cities and homicide rates. The core of this paradox is the apparent contradiction between the results of cross-sectional studies and the results of longitudinal studies. Previous cross-sectional studies of city size have found high homicide rates in large cities; while previous longitudinal studies of city growth have not found homicide rate increases as a city grows. This paradox has left unanswered the question of how large cities acquired their high homicide rates.

In part, our analyses provide broad comparative support for some earlier research on the two aspects of the paradox. Our cross-sectional analyses are consistent with earlier work in finding high homicide rates in large cities, not only in the U.S. but also in many other societies. However, we found that the rates of large cities were only high relative to the rates of their societies and not necessarily high in any absolute or international sense. Our longitudinal analyses of 34 international primary cities also support earlier work in finding no evidence that city growth and homicide rates increase together.

We believe that a solution to this paradox lies in our longitudinal comparison of the homicide rates of primary cities with the rates of entire nations. This analysis showed that city rates have consistently exceeded national rates, even when the cities were much smaller in absolute terms. This is the key to our interpretation of the paradox: The determinant of a city's homicide rate is not the absolute size of the city, but its size *relative* to its contemporary society. Even when these primate cities were small, by current standards, they were extremely "urban" compared to their societies at that time.

This, then, is our interpretation of the paradox. We believe this interpretation explains why homicide rates do not necessarily increase as a city grows. Large cities have always had high homicide rates relative to their societies because these cities have always been more urban than their national environments.

This interpretation suggests that sociologists have been misled—undoubtedly by cross-sectional evidence—into the unwarranted assumption that absolute city sizes during a city's growth would correspond in some way to absolute homicide rates. In light of previous cross-sectional research, it does seem intuitively reasonable to assume that a city would have to grow to a certain size before it could have a certain homicide rate.

Our analysis, however, suggests that this assumption is invalid, despite its apparent reasonableness. Based on our evidence, we believe that a city's relative population size determines its relative homicide rate. Any city more urban than its national environment will have a homicide rate higher than its national average. The relative nature of this relationship, we believe, is the answer to the paradoxical question of why large cities have high homicide rates which do not grow higher as the cities grow larger.

## FOOTNOTES

*Dane Archer is Associate Professor of Sociology at the University of California, Santa Cruz. Rosemary Gartner is a graduate student in Sociology at the University of Wisconsin. Robin Akert and Tim Lockwood graduated from Santa Cruz in 1976. Archer and Gartner recently published an article on the effects of war on homicide rates (*American Sociological Review*, December 1976). Archer and Gartner are now working on a 110-nation study of the antecedents of homicide. Archer and Akert are collaborating on a study of different factors in the social psychology of communication and interpretation.

This project was made possible by NIMH Research Grant MH27427 from the Center for Studies of Crime and Delinquency. The conclusions are, of course, those of the authors. Helpful comments on this project were received from several people, including particularly Marshall Clinard and Claude Fischer.

1. For a recent discussion and examples of the differences between these two research designs, see Lieberson and Hansen (1974). Even when addressing the same question, these two methods are capable of producing different or even opposite answers. In studies where both designs are possible, the longitudinal design is more powerful and more capable of identifying causal relationships.

2. In this paper the terms "city size" and "city growth" will be used in place of "urbanism" and "urbanization" in the interests of terminological simplicity. In this paper, "city size" refers to cross-sectional designs, and "city growth" refers to longitudinal designs.

3. For example, Clinard (1942; 1964) found a cross-sectional relationship between criminal offenders and urban background and, from this finding alone, predicted a longitudinal increase in crime rates as urbanization occurred.

4. It should be mentioned that rural areas do appear to have a lower rate of most non-

homicide crimes, with the possible exception of rape (Wolfgang, 1968; Clinard and Abbott, 1973; Scherer, Abeles, and Fischer, 1975).

5. It should be emphasized, of course, that these are not genuine homicide "increases" (in the longitudinal sense) since this particular comparison is only cross-sectional.

6. Since suburban and rural areas are not associated with precise population sizes, they could not be included in any appropriate location on the logarithmic scale in Figure 1. Instead, they are shown at an arbitrary distance from the smallest city category.

7. Even though the CCDF contains crime data for 44 primary cities, several of these cities could not be included in Table 2 for one of two reasons: (1) one (or both) of the city and nation time series were not available in the CCDF for the period 1966–1970; or (2) even if both series were available for this period, the nation reported a different homicide indicator than was available for the primary city—e.g., homicide offenses known for the entire nation, but homicide convictions for the primary city. For example, in both Germany and South Africa, the primary city rates exceeded the national rates—but these cases were excluded from Table 2 because the city indictors differed in type from the national indicators in the CCDF.

8. Although it is tempting to try to make direct homicide rate comparisons across the primary cities or across the nations shown in Table 2, such comparisons are hazardous without a careful inspection of the CCDF. Although the same indicator (e.g., offenses known) was used *within* each pair in Table 2, not all pairs used the same indicator. In addition, national idiosyncracies in homicide classification and definition make cross-national comparisons of absolute homicide rate levels far from uncomplicated.

9. A plausible interpretation for the narrowing of this gap after 1960 is suggested by the exceptional cases in Table 2. After roughly 1960, developing nations are increasingly represented in the CCDF, and Table 2 suggests that developing nations may not have the same relationship between city size and homicide as is found in developed nations.

10. Two of the very few cities to decline in population or show discontinuous growth are Belfast and Glasgow.

11. Some of the 44 primary cities in the CCDF have data points which are too few in number or too scattered to permit calculation of this correlation.

## REFERENCES


Archer, D. and Gartner, R. (1976) "Violent Acts and Violent Times: A Comparative Approach to Postwar Homicide Rates." *American Sociological Review* 41:937–963.

Boggs, S. (1966) "Urban Crime Patterns." *American Sociological Review* 30:899–908.

Christiansen, K. C. (1960) "Industrialization and Urbanization in Relation to Crime and Delinquency." *International Review of Criminal Policy* 16:3–8.

Clinard, M. B. (1942) "The Process of Urbanization and Criminal Behavior." *American Journal of Sociology* 68:202–213.

——— (1964) "The Relationship of Urbanization and Urbanism to Criminal Behavior." Pages 541–558 in E. Burgess and D. Bogue (eds.), *Contributions to Urban Sociology*. Chicago: University of Chicago.

——— (1974) *Sociology of Deviant Behavior*. New York: Holt, Rinehart and Winston.

——— and Abbott, D. (1973) *Crime in Developing Countries: A Comparative Perspective*. New York: Wiley.

Dhanagare, D. N. (1969) "Urbanism and Crime." *Economic and Political Weekly*, July: 1239–1242.

Durkheim, E. (1933) *The Division of Labor in Society*. Translated by G. Simpson. New York: Free Press.

Ferdinand, T. (1967) "The Criminal Patterns of Boston since 1849." *American Journal of Sociology* 73:84–99.

Frankel, E. (1939) "One Thousand Murders." *Journal of Criminal Law and Criminology* 29:672–688.

Glaser, D. (1970) *Crime in the City*. New York: Harper and Row.

Harries, K. (1974) *The Geography of Crime and Justice*. New York: McGraw-Hill.

Lane, R. (1969) "Urbanization and Criminal Violence in the 19th Century: Massachusetts as a Test Case." Pages 468–484 in H. D. Graham and T. R. Gurr (eds.), *The History of Violence in America*. Washington, DC: Government Printing Office.

Lieberson, S. and Hansen, L. K. (1974) "National Development, Mother Tongue Diversity, and the Comparative Study of Nations." *American Sociological Review* 39:523–541.

Lodhi, A. Q. and Tilly, C. (1973) "Urbanization, Crime and Collective Violence in 19th Century France." *American Journal of Sociology* 79:296–318.

McLennan, B. (1970) *Crime in Urban Society*. New York: Dunellen.

Mannheim, H. (1965) *Comparative Criminology*. London: Routledge and Kegan Paul.

Ogburn, W. F. (1935) "Factors in Variation in Crime among Cities." *Journal of the American Statistical Society* 30:12–13.

Powell, E. (1966) "Crime as a Function of Anomie." *Journal of Criminal Law, Criminology and Police Science* 57:161–171.

President's Commission on Law Enforcement and the Administration of Justice (1967) *Crime and its Impact: An Assessment*. Washington, DC: Government Printing Office.

Scherer, K. R., Abeles, R. P. and Fischer, C. S. (1975) *Human Aggression and Conflict*. Englewood Cliffs, NJ: Prentice-Hall.

Sutherland, E. and Cressey, D. (1970) *Criminology*. Philadelphia: Lippincott.

Szabo, D. (1960) *Crimes et villes*. Louvain: Université Catholique.

Tarniquet, H. (1968) "Crime in the Rapidly Industrializing Urban Environment." *Revue internationale de criminologie et de police technique* 22:49–58.

Tobias, J. J. (1967) *Crime and Industrial Society in the 19th Century*. London: Batsford.

Venter, H. J. (1962) "Urbanization and Industrialization as Criminogenic Factors in the Republic of South Africa." *International Review of Criminology* 20:59–71.

Vold, G. B. (1941) "Crime in City and Country Areas." *Annals of the American Academy of Political and Social Sciences* 217:38–45.

Wirth, L. (1940) "Urbanism as a Way of Life." *American Journal of Sociology* 47:743–755.

Wolfgang, M. (1968) "Urban Crime." Pages 245–281 in J. Q. Wilson (ed.), *The Metropolitan Enigma*. Cambridge, MA: Harvard University Press.

# DOMESTIC SERVICE AND INDUSTRIALIZATION

David Chaplin*

## INTRODUCTION

Domestic service has only recently received scholarly attention. In the 1960s a concern with an occupational approach to poverty led to an examination of this category which still employed ten times as many workers (over two million) as did coal mining (Chaplin, 1964; 1969). Prior to this, it received only sporadic attention from historians (Salmon, 1897; Eaton, 1899; Haynes, 1923; Hecht, 1956; Davidoff, 1974; McBride, 1974; 1976). Those most continuously concerned have been economists (e.g., Stigler, 1946; Boserup, 1970; C. A. Anderson and Bowman, 1953) and the Women's Bureau of the U.S. Department of Labor. Few sociologists

**Comparative Studies in Sociology—Vol. 1, 1978, pages 97–127**

**ISBN 0-89232-025-7**

have taken domestic service seriously, notwithstanding our traditional concern with the poor and minority groups (Addams, 1896; Bossard, 1954; Aubert, 1955–1956; Broom and Smith, 1963; Mehta, 1960; Nett, 1966; Useem, 1966; Whisson and Weil, 1971; Coser, 1973). There is a more substantial literature on seventeenth and eighteenth century indentured service, which was predominantly male, but until the advent of the women's movement and increased field research outside their home countries, sociologists have neglected this crucial transitional occupation. It should "go without saying" that a full understanding of minority and women's employment, industrialization and urbanization, middle and upper class child rearing practices, and other issues, cannot be obtained without the comparative and historical study of domestic service. Here we shall summarize a variety of theoretical perspectives and present research findings for a number of countries.

With respect to the process of industrialization in both western historical experience and "Third World" development, domestic service was the primary source of urban employment for women. In Lima, Peru 60 percent of all employed recently-arrived migrant females in 1965 were domestic servants (Peru, . . . 1966, p. 58). In a comparative historical study, McBride (1974) reported that the percentage of servants in France, of all economically active workers, fell from 14.6 to 4.6 percent between 1866 and 1911, while the comparable English figures were 14.3 and 13.9 percent for 1861 and 1911. The peak of domestic service employment in London reached 20 percent in 1861, while Parisian domestic workers had increased to 24 percent by 1921, although, as in England, the national level had declined sharply by this time (McBride, 1976, pp. 35–36). Overall, 16 to 20 percent of the workers in currently developing countries are in this type of work at any one time (Galenson, 1959, p. 265). Therefore, given the high level of turnover in domestic service, a much higher percentage of women have ever been employed as servants, thus making it the major setting for female urban labor force participation during the transitional stages of industrialization. It occupies this unique status in part by default for this is the period when the lowest proportion of women engage in paid employment according to most census definitions. At an earlier stage a high percentage of all women work, largely as unpaid family workers in agriculture and artisan handicraft (United Nations, 1962, pp. 6–10). At a later stage, as in the United States in recent years, the proportion of women working again rises as married women increasingly seek employment.

Domestic service is interesting not only as the most usual occupation of women at this stage in industrialization, but also because it serves as a useful entry point for analyzing the rationalization of the domestic economy as the production of goods and services is gradually removed from familial control. In this respect this study complements that of Smelser (1959) who investigated textile factory work as it affected the family life of British manual workers.

Historically, all economic activity was at one point familial. Subsequently trade or distribution became extra-familial followed by the production of most goods and many services. Most individuals consume as part of family households although many, as in the military or religious orders, function as single units of consumption through non-familial distributive institutions. Most domestic servants were primarily concerned with the production of goods until the industrial revolution. They eventually became specialized in those personal services which resist packaging or mechanization. At this stage they became a source of what Reynolds (1951, p. 11) has called "disguised unemployment," or the core of Veblen's "conspicuous consumption" pattern.

Those who live-in continue to resist the general contractualization of labor-management relationships by virtue of payment partly in kind (room and board plus gifts and tips) as well as having to face an employing family increasingly specialized in affect and status maintenance.[1] M. Anderson (1971, p. 89) calls attention to the blurred line between kinship, apprenticeship, and domestic service in mid-nineteenth century England in discussing the "lending of children" which involved both welfare and exploitive aspects.

Another way of approaching this problem would be to clarify *what* is being purchased. A worker can hire out his physical strength, appearance, character, personality, and skills. Each type of occupation calls for a different mix of these traits or services. Most occupations tend to require more of one than of the others, thus simplifying the problem of self-esteem and objective evaluation of the worker and his work.

Domestic service, though essentially manual labor, can be as demanding of personality involvement as is selling, and of character as clerking in a bank. In addition, "These different (domestic service) occupations for the most part call for different types of workers. A butler or chambermaid-waitress who is tall and comely may have access to a larger number, and to better places, than one who is short . . ." (Haynes, 1923, p. 428).

At this point the labor and welfare legislation bearing on this occupation should be examined. In the United States, domestic service did not come under social security until 1950 (Myers, 1975, p. 84), and even today many are still not covered as a result of the part-time structure of this type of employment. In some countries laws and regulations have attempted to control this employer-employee relationship. In France and England domestics were not accorded full citizenship until the late nineteenth or early twentieth centuries on the grounds that anyone in this dependent child-like employment was not a responsible adult, hence any extension of suffrage to them would merely reinforce the political power of the established elites.[2] Germany under Bismarck introduced elaborate welfare protection for domestic servants. The Scandinavian countries (Drake, 1969) instituted a licensing system to control them and in Norway, according to Aubert (1955–1956), there was an abortive turn-of-the-century effort to re-establish some traditional level of discipline. Norwegian law in this respect, until recently, seems to have had a predominantly repressive character. Until the twentieth century servants were treated as familial dependents, not freely contracted employees (p. 416). Until 1864 the unmarried children of farmers not busy with agriculture were obliged to seek this sort of employment and runaways were punished. Obedience to the master's will was a categorical requirement with only two exceptions, the military draft and acts clearly illegal. Physical punishment was not forbidden until 1891. Aubert also observes that the belated recent efforts to contractualize this occupation in Norway took place when labor law in general was in the process of reintroducing some non-contractual status elements (p. 419). However, only 3 percent of a sample of servants surveyed in Oslo enjoyed the legal requirement for a contract.

In Peru there are a variety of laws which intentionally, or in fact, affect the lives of servants. Also, as in continental Europe, this class of workers received the attention of special labor and welfare laws long before (1901/1937) the rest of Peru's manual workers. At one extreme, adoption was abused as a way of securing the "purchase" of an Indian child as a prospective servant. On the other hand, in contemporary Lima there is a special government employment agency for servants and several schools set up to provide adult education in literacy and home economics skills. There is a considerable divergence of opinion as to their function between those sponsoring these schools and those directing them. The former hope to produce better servants while the latter hope to provide an escape from their being servants.

Although no country has seen successful unions of domestics develop, the existence of labor protest is not in doubt. One question about its form is whether the retreat from a traditional noblesse oblige relationship was initiated from the "managerial" or labor side. In the case of British factory workers, the earliest protest initiated by workers was against the failure of management to fulfill traditional paternalistic obligations—only later did a more modern bread and butter labor protest arise (Bendix, 1956, p. 46). The popular employer's view of servants would argue that it was the servants who took the initiative in trying to emancipate themselves. At the aggregate level the only way the study of such protest could be operationalized would be through the analysis of labor turnover rates, assuming one could differentiate "quits" from "fireds" (Chaplin, 1968a, pp. 75–78).

During the colonial period in Massachusetts, Towner (1962) found considerable evidence of servant protest. There, the law, labor shortages, and abundant land prevented the institutionalization of stable master-servant relationships. As a result, the English domestics—largely indentured or "bound in" as criminals, paupers, or orphans—made ample use of legal proceedings, and in fact won 55 percent of the 200 cases whose records are still available (for the period 1629–1750) (p. 208).

A smaller number of the growing proportion of non-English servants or slaves (Irish, Scottish, and black) in the eighteenth century have recourse to law. By 1750, 75 percent of the cases of servant protest were runaways as compared with only 26 percent in 1660 (p. 214). In the later period the non-English whites were more likely to run away (86 percent), while black slaves were more likely to be viewed by the law as "unruly."

Towner interprets the increase in servant protest to the growing social distance between the English employing family and the increasingly non-English servants or slaves (p. 215). On the contrary, it seems more likely that the greater the social distance the easier the legitimation of such subordination would have been. Religion may well have been the major factor. As in Latin America, the Puritan family attended the same church as did their servants. However, the Puritan Ethic, unlike Latin Catholicism, never fully accepted servitude except on a contractual basis between presumably voluntarily consenting parties (p. 217).

Domestic service can also be viewed as the major acculturating or socializing agency for rural and foreign migrants during the early stages of industrialization. This period was probably the era when a larger percentage of the labor force was employed in domestic sevice than ever before or ever again. In this respect, it was comparable to the situation in currently developing countries. In "processing" migrants, its function is often viewed as generally negative in that it presumably constitutes a traditionalizing dead-end job. Broom and Smith (1963) challenge this view with respect to England by viewing domestic service as the principal "bridging occupation" facilitating first sideways and then vertical mobility. They focus on horizontal situs mobility as a prerequisite for successful vertical mobility for most migrants in an urban industrial setting. It serves to resocialize the incumbents and, among those who live-in, loosens primary ties to family and lower class friends. Most crucial were the opportunities for a significant minority to be launched in upper-lower class or lower-middle class service or commercial trades with or without the help of former employers. Most of the schools for domestic servants, common in the United States half a century ago and in predominantly Catholic developing areas today, functioned the same way, even when their intention was generally to train domestic workers for this type of work.

In Spain and Peru, various Catholic orders have training schools specifically for domestics, or use domestic service as the preferred first placement for lower-class female orphans. In 1970 there was an organizational struggle in Spain between the women's branch of the Falange and of Opus Dei for control over the training schools for domestics. The superior financial and organizational advantages of Opus Dei led to its predominance.

Another perspective on domestic service is that offered by Goode (1967). He argues that the primary basis for the efficiency of the urban industrial system is not so much its attraction for genius, but rather its more effective utilization of the "inept." Bureaucracy and technology serve the double function of more fully utilizing whatever talents the inept possess while protecting society from their potentially parasitical or destructive behavior. Goode, however, begs the question of the social origin of aptitude. Barring genetic control over innate ability, Young's suggestion (1961, p. 20) in *The Rise of the Meritocracy* that the feeble-minded serve as the domestics for the geniuses comes to mind. In fact, it has been common for institutions for the feeble-minded to hire out their more capable charges to presumably sympathetic employers at nominal wages. It would appear, however, that those intelligent enough to be of any practical help as domestic servants and yet not sensitive to their menial status or loss of conventional social opportunities, constitute a narrow segment of the intelligence spectrum, if, indeed, tests could measure such things. Such a suggestion, however serious or humane in intent, would not really solve either the "servant problem" or the problem of economic incompetence.

The role domestic service plays in socializing middle and upper-class children constitutes an additional perspective for a full analysis of this strategic occupation. The socializing function can involve a variety of roles: mother-surrogate, intermediary, playmate, diffusers of "exotic" culture ("superstitions"), seducers or at least verbal diffusers of sexual information, symbols of racially, ethnically or socially inferior groups, and faithful family retainers (Bossard, 1954). Servants, especially if resident, tend to lower the emotional intensity of otherwise isolated nuclear families by introducing a third adult in a somewhat more formal role. If the servant has the primary task of caring for children up to adolescence, the ideal typical middle-class American character structure would be less likely to develop, especially if the child was shielded from the universalistic morality of games (formal rules and technical competence) with serious peer competitors. This situation is still the norm in middle and upper-class Latin American families, producing adults, especially males, with well fed egos but poorly prepared for an objectively competitive university education. Thus, while Latin American students have many justified complaints against the present state of their universities, one factor in the protest may be a discordant "character structure."

An analysis of domestic service could also benefit from the numerous insights developed by Goffman (1956; 1959). Next to mental patients, the resident unmarried multi-purpose servant in a middle-class household probably suffered the lowest level of privacy. Whether this represented a loss depends on the amount of privacy the worker enjoyed in his or her own family. In many societies this may have been equally low, so that conflicts would arise more on the basis of the type of control being exerted rather than on the degree of privacy. Nevertheless, this occupation does offer a setting in which the limits of human needs for privacy can be exposed. Aubert (1955–1956, p. 420) noted that it was not until after World War II that Norwegian law required that servants not be obliged to sleep in the children's room.

The reactions to this invasion of personal privacy would often include a reciprocal defensive intrusion into the life of the employing family. A common defense of children's nurses faced with the need to maintain discipline yet forbidden to use effective force or meaningful rewards has been to teach children a set of "superstitious" beliefs through which the servant could threaten them. Goffman's analysis presents us with a long list of defense measures such as excessive deference, avoidance rituals, and behind-their-back burlesques (1956, pp. 478, 481, 494). One of the central issues in this respect is the "zombie" servant ideal cultivated in nineteenth century England. [The "dumb waiter" had been invented in an *earlier* period because of a feeling that the presence of servants made intimate conversations, especially about the servants, impossible (1959, p. 213).] Somehow that upper-class sensitivity was overcome in the nineteenth century as the social distance between it and its servants widened. Servants could be tolerated in intimate settings as they became sufficiently socially distant. However, in contemporary society they decreasingly exhibit "professional" commitment to confidentiality, hence celebrities occasionally pay a high price in objectionable exposés by former servants.

A standard question, then, which might be asked in any society is what topics may be discussed within the hearing of servants. To what extent have they been made into non-people? How oblivious were their masters to their unavoidable eavesdropping, and what did the servants think and do with such information? Can anyone maintain sanity if he enjoys no ecological niche where he may let his guard down? Historical analyses of these questions are difficult because of the rarity and unrepresentativeness of servant diaries. However, contemporary studies may offer some clues. In the case of language barriers the problem can be "solved" structurally at the expense of a considerable level of defective communication on relevant matters (Useem, 1966, p. 4; Goffman, 1959, p. 177). There are interesting variations in this area: 1) the master speaks the servants' language, hence can invade their lives unilaterally; 2) the servant speaks the master's language; 3) they both speak a third lingua franca. Each would have different consequences for the relationship and each would be open to alteration depending on which party chose to restructure their power by extending their linguistic fluency.

Goffman's dramaturgical analogy also suggests the following issues with respect to servant-master relationships:

1. Does the servant have his own backstage area which the master will not violate? The Kitchen in British India was so off limits to the mistress that it was physically separated from the main house (Useem, 1966, p. 15). Do the servants' backstages have to be physically delimited or is it a symbolic or mainly a temporal matter? How often are they left alone with the "run of the house"? How differently are they treated when in *the master's* on-stage area, when guests are present, and in *his* off-stage area, which is still on-stage for them?

2. What sorts of family matters are discussed with servants and which, by a conspiracy of silence, are avoided? Do the same people use their servants to obtain the same type of gossip on other families?

3. What are the settings which permit servants to turn the tables on masters? In Barrie's *The Admirable Chrichton,* a shipwreck elevated the butler to the master's role, but on returning to England he gracefully retired to "his place." More usual occasions for such a reversal would be: a single servant caring for an aged or infirm master or mistress (a group of servants possibly would keep some check on each other), sexual liaisons, and perhaps the Mary Poppins situation in which a strong-minded governess takes over from a weak-willed mistress by becoming uniquely indispensable.

4. What are the relations among servants in multi-servant households? For employers they tend to be a constant challenge and headache. If a related group is hired, their commonality may weaken the mistress' hand. If, on the other hand, each is hired separately, endless squabbling may ensue. Such households are and evidently always were rare, however common in popular literature. The basic historical trend in this respect was a continuous reduction in the number of servants per household (among those living in) during the transitional stages of industrialization. In this sense a derationalization of the domestic economy occurs as fewer servants are asked to undertake a wider range of jobs. This derationaliza-

tion is compounded by the increasing strangeness of the master-servant relationship to both parties as waves of unskilled rural or foreign migrants meet a rising middle class. In the case of Western experience the increasing diffuseness of the servant's duties was gradually countered by the development of external or mechanical substitutions together with a decline in the size of employing households. In currently developing societies, appliances and packaged services are already available for the wealthy but their tendency to replace servants is slowed by the abundant supply of surplus unskilled labor in the larger cities as well as by inflation and the decline of the foreign exchange value of local currency.

A final topic highly suited to comparative analysis is that of the fertility of domestic servants. The pressures against marriage and childbearing are well documented for England and Norway. Many masters preferred single servants and the law and custom supported obstacles to servants marrying (Glass, 1966, p. xxxv). Thus it seems possible that during Western industrialization, employment in this occupation would have significantly accelerated the decline in urban lower class fertility—by postponing or preventing marriage and discouraging childbearing among the resident servants. The greater tendency for servants to live out in Latin America today may mean that this fertility-depressing effect will not operate, thus helping to account for the higher natural increase in the cities of these countries.

## THE UNITED STATES

The general pattern of private household employment in the United States has been one of decline during the twentieth century. Note from Table 1 that the percentage of women in private household employment declined from 28.6 percent in 1900 to 3.4 percent in 1970. Note also that a reversal of the general trend occurred during the Great Depression. In 1960 this decline was again arrested by a sharp increase in "professional" babysitting which parallels the rising percentage of working mothers.

The apparent sharp drop in female household employment between 1960 and 1970 is somewhat misleading. One aspect of declining occupations is that of "casualization," which makes them appear to be disappearing even faster than is the case. As a larger percentage of workers, whose primary employment was still domestic service, worked more often part-time and seasonally, they were thus less likely to be enumerated as private household workers by the census. Also, as the number of live-in servants declined (who could *only* be classified as domestics) the increasing number of non-resident day servants were freer to report themselves unemployed or in other occupations. In addition, welfare and so-

*Table 1.* Evolution of Private Household Employment in the United States, 1900–1970.

(Percentages)

| | 1900 | 1910 | 1920 | 1930 | 1940 | 1950 | 1960 | 1970 |
|---|---|---|---|---|---|---|---|---|
| Percent of Labor Force | 5.4 | 4.9 | 3.3 | 4.1 | 4.6 | 2.5 | 2.7 | 1.3 |
| Number (1000's) | (1,579) | (1,851) | (1,411) | (1,998) | (2,412) | (1,411) | (1,725) | (1,164) |
| Percentage Female in Private Household Employment | 96.6 | 96.3 | 96.3 | 95.5 | 94.4 | 94.8 | 96.4 | 97.0 |
| Percentage in Private Household Employment of all Employed Females | 28.6 | 23.9 | 15.7 | 17.7 | 18.1 | 8.5 | 7.9 | 3.4 |
| Percentage Living In[a] | | | | | | 15.3 | 9.3 | |
| | Percentage Living In: | | | | Male | 17.1 | 13.5 | |
| | | | | | Female | 15.1 | 9.1 | |

*Source:* U.S. Bureau of the Census, 1960; 1972.
*Note:* [a]Not available for 1970 or before 1940.

cial security regulations have made it even more desirable for many workers to hide this source of income. A sizable proportion of the sharp increase in illegal immigrants from Latin America and the West Indies hide out as unreported domestic servants.

Between 1960 and 1970 the percentage of employed women in private household employment declined much more rapidly for white than for minority women, 56 percent among the former compared with 35 percent among the latter (Table 2). As domestic service has declined in the United States, it has become increasingly stereotyped as a minority occupation.

From Table 3 note that workers of Spanish origin are closer to whites than blacks in their patterns of participation in private household

*Table 2.* Employed Female Private Household Workers, by Ethnicity, 1960 and 1970.

(in thousands)

| | 1960 | | 1970 | | |
|---|---|---|---|---|---|
| | Number | Percentage of All Employed | Number | Percentage of All Employed | Percentage Decline 1960–1970 |
| White | (1,182) | 6.1 | (522) | 2.1 | 56 |
| Minority | (990) | 35.1 | (642) | | 35 |
| (Black = 17.9) | | | | | |
| (Spanish Origin = 4.6) | | | | | |

*Source:* U.S. Department of Labor, Women's Bureau, 1974.

*Table 3.* Unemployment Rates by Ethnicity, United States, 1973. (Percentages)

| | Spanish Origin | White | Black |
|---|---|---|---|
| | Average Annual Unemployment Rate | | |
| Private Household Workers | 3.2 | 2.9 | 6.8 |
| All Workers | 6.6 | 3.7 | 7.8 |
| | Employed in Private Household Employment | | |
| | 1.8 | 1.1 | 6.3 |
| | No. Employed as Private Household Workers (in thousands) | | |
| | (59) | (828) | (505) |

*Source:* U.S. Department of Labor, 1974.

employment and in the resulting rates of unemployment in this occupation. Mexican workers, as can be seen in Table 4, have unemployment rates higher than blacks. (Table 3 includes both sexes, but the data on private household workers is overwhelmingly made up of women.) There is, however, some historical evidence that suggests that Latin women have relied less often than others, such as the Irish or Scandinavians, on domestic service as an "agency of acculturation" to American society, especially as live-in servants.

In terms of secondary jobs among women, in May 1973, private household workers had an above-average rate of multiple job holding (Michelotti, 1974, p. 67). The data do not permit one to determine what the distribution of secondary occupation was for those for whom private household employment was their primary job, but the aggregated figures suggest that more women came into this occupation as "moonlighters" than moved in the opposite direction. It seems reasonable to assume that private household service is a moonlighting occupation for many more

*Table 4.* Employment of Spanish Origin Women, United States, 1973.

| | Total Spanish Origin | Mexican Origin | Puerto Rican Origin | Other Spanish Origin |
|---|---|---|---|---|
| Employed | 39.7 | 38.7 | 31.8 | 45.5 |
| Unemployed | 7.7 | 8.7 | 6.3 | 6.7 |
| In Private Household Employment | 4.8 | 6.4 | 0.7 | 3.7 |

*Source:* U.S. Bureau of the Census, 1974.

women than will admit to it to official interviewers either to avoid revealing their income or for reasons of stigmatization.

Domestic service has long played a bridging or acculturation function for immigrants, especially those from ethnic groups similar to the local majority. Today it seems less likely to do so owing to (1) its increasingly minority composition, and (2) the specialized training needed to enter related paraprofessional occupations (such as practical nursing). However, the 1965 immigration law still had the undesired and unanticipated effect of attracting large numbers of domestic workers, especially from the West Indies. This source of domestic servants is included under "North America" in the official statistics. From Table 5 note that the percentage of all immigrants who were private household workers increased from 7.0 percent in 1960–1965 to 10.9 percent in 1966–1968, but declined to 7.8 percent in 1969–1972. A recent report comments on this decline:

> The Labor Department was issuing certifications for applicants with job offers as live-in maids due to a shortage of such workers in the United States. Various forms of questionable and even illegal placement service practices, the high turnover rate once the immigrants entered the United States and the policy issue of using scarce visas for domestic servants for the wealthy, all led to pressure to make certifications for live-in household workers more difficult, including requiring demonstrated previous experience and conformity to wage and hour standards in the United States. These steps had their effect in 1970 and after, when the percentages in this category returned to approximately the levels of the McCarran-Walter period (1961–1965) (Keely, 1974).

As the number and proportion of workers in domestic service declines, the structure of employment changes. An occupation which once normally meant living in, now rarely requires or allows servants to be resident (St. C. Drake and Cayton, 1962, p. 244). The replacement of physical distance, as far as black homes are concerned, for the narrowing

*Table 5.* Private Household Workers as a Percentage of All Immigrants to the United States, by Origin.

| | *1961–1965* | *1966–1968* | *1969–1972* |
|---|---|---|---|
| Total | 7.0 | 10.9 | 7.8 |
| Europe | 4.6 | 6.3 | 5.6 |
| Asia | 1.8 | 3.1 | 2.9 |
| Africa | 1.6 | 2.2 | 1.3 |
| Oceania | 2.9 | 4.2 | 3.7 |
| North America (includes Mexico) | 10.2 | 17.0 | 13.9 |
| South America | 9.1 | 17.4 | 8.9 |

*Source:* Keely, 1974, Table 3.

caste distinction, added to the general absence of servants' quarters in modern urban homes, has meant that most employers prefer help by the day.

The next stage in the dissolution of the full-time resident servant tradition is that servants come only part-time, sometimes for only a few hours a week, and increasingly for more specialized duties.

The implications of this shift for the paternalistic master-servant relationship are profound. First of all, new categories of employers, many with no experience in handling servants or employees of any type, are now able to afford some domestic service. This is especially the case since the effective employer is normally the woman of the house, who at any class level is unlikely to have had outside administrative experience. Secondly, part-time domestics need to have numerous employers, thus seeing too little of any one to establish the personal ties on which the old relationship was based. In this respect the work relationship was become more "business-like." However, Noble (1967) found that those working full-time for one employer were much more likely to receive the benefits required by law.

The primary reason for a focus on the black domestic has been the fatal lure this relationship offers to the unemancipated. It presumably selects those blacks least prepared or able to go out on their own and rewards them at a modest level for their subservience. In 1970, as has presumably always been the case, private household workers had the lowest median educational level of any occupational category, 8.6 years of completed schooling, compared with a national average of 11.7 years (U.S. Bureau of the Census, 1972, p. 131).

In her survey of domestic servants in Harlem, Noble (1967, p. 42) found that 22 percent of all households had one or more occupants who worked "out" as servants. Their median age was 46, and they had been working in this occupation for an average of 10 years. Many of these women lived in boarding houses catering largely to servants. In 1960, 53 percent of all female servants in the U.S. were black and over a third of all employed black women worked in this field (U.S. Department of Labor, Women's Bureau, 1974).

As for white domestic servants, the current trend is also for fewer and fewer to live-in. Serious career domestics increasingly work for agencies who hire them out by the hour as part of catering services. Others have gone into hotels and luxury all-service apartment buildings which provide domestic services for tenants.

A phenomenon peculiar to the United States is the widespread taking of full-time summer jobs by college students. Many work in summer camps and resorts. The demand for their services arises not only from the large scale and short-term expansion in this employment, but in many cases also because their nonprofessional touch is preferred. Many middle class resort guests would be uncomfortable faced with a waiter skilled in intimidating them into leaving large tips. Warner (1940, p. 256) observed in New Haven, "There is a Southern Negro eagerness to please and ingratiate which some people find confusing or resent as untruthfulness."

Some of these college students enjoy the peculiar experience of serving their social inferiors. In this case they are playing a part somewhat comparable to the trained black domestics hired by New Haven's nouveau riche industrial elite. Here the blacks were expected to teach their employers upper class manners. In the college students' case such a diffusion of manners is probably quite unconscious on their part.

Several patterns of interest to the sociologist appear in Stigler's (1946) study of the economics of domestic service. Within the United States the ratio of servants to families varied directly with income, as expected. However, internationally, the wealthiest countries are not those with the highest servant ratios. The crucial factor was the degree of social inequality, at least among the Western European countries for which fairly good data exist (pp. 4, 6). Social inequality turns out to be the primary basis for a high servant-employer ratio.

It also appears that while the absolute number of workers classified as domestics has decreased up to the present (except for the Great Depression), the ratio of servants to the population peaked in the United States about 1910. The gradual increase in the proportion of blacks in this occupation, since immigration was largely cut off by World War I, was checked during the Depression. It seems that the "last hired, first fired" pattern of black employment applies even in this field.

Stigler also noted that the money income for women was higher in domestic service than in factory work in 1900, while by 1940 a reversal had taken place (p. 12). This suggests that in spite of the popular outcry about the shortage of servants, the demand was not serious enough to have resulted in an effective increase in the wage level. The imperfections of this market are such that employers and their agents persist in resorting to every alternative *but* that of effectively higher wages in order to attract more workers (Haines, 1960).

In short, we are obliged to agree with Levenstein (1962, p. 38) when he asserts that:

> The moralists who lament the refusal of people to take menial jobs forget that we have cut off the traditional American sources of supply of such labor. . . . The virtual disappearance of domestics in this country, which makes conversation under the beauty parlor dryers, is somehow believed to be evidence of a change in the American character. It is evidence principally of a change in our immigration laws. . . . Certain

> types of labor could be obtained only through immigration. The servant class was never native American; even in Colonial days domestics came as indentured servants who ultimately moved up to higher-status jobs once their service was over.

The most effective forces operating against domestic service have been: 1) the closing of supplies of foreigners, many of whom were obliged to enter American culture through Victorian cellars, 2) the equalization of income which had reputedly taken place in the United States, and 3) income maintenance programs for the poor or unemployed.

Some implications of changes in the organization of domestic service are the following:

1. The kitchen again is the center of the American middle-class family which constitutes a return to nineteenth century rural custom.
2. The status of housework has been raised due to the vast improvement in home appliances and packaged services as well as the resulting performance of middle-class wives of such work, however unwillingly.
3. On the other hand, in areas of the United States and in countries such as England, where the improvement of domestic facilities lagged behind the disappearance of domestic servants, middle-class wives, indeed, become the "slaves" of their families. So concerned was even the post-war Labour government with the plight of servantless housewives that special permits were issued for the importation of foreign girls in spite of a general policy of restricting immigration (Lewis and Maude, 1950, p. 311).
4. Another consequence of the disappearance of the servant has been the increasing participation of American husbands (and children?) in housework as well as a lessening of the formality of middle-class family life. These changes have several aspects. In the first place, with no servants present, adults need not feel obliged to strike as dignified a posture before their children and guests. Also, parties have to be less formal if the hosts are to have the time to mingle with their guests. There may well have been a time when, due to a lag in standards of hospitality behind the loss of servants, pretentious or proud families simply ceased entertaining (Lynes, 1963, p. 51).
5. A more diffuse consequence (at least in England) is noted by Chapman:

> Up to the outbreak of the First World War a high proportion of all working class women living outside the great areas of women's industrial employment, spent several years before marriage living in the homes of the middle and upper classes as domestic

> servants. . . . The decline of domestic service has (thus) greatly reduced the direct influence of the middle class on the working class, who now furnish in what they believe, rather than in what they know, to be the style of the higher classes (1955, pp. 19–20).

## SPAIN

The legal status of domestics in Spain prior to 1959 was almost as anomalous as in the United States. In fact, more attention was paid to their status in the colonial *Laws of the Indies* than in recent centuries. These regulations, like so much of Spanish social legislation, were designed primarily to preserve social and cultural institutions rather than to protect individuals. Employers were responsible for religious education and the preservation of family life of their domestics. Orphans could not be removed from their villages for domestic service "against their will." "Negroes" were not allowed Indian servants nor should an Indian mother leave her village to raise a Spaniard's child if it meant leaving her own behind (Vazquez, 1960, pp. 62–63). Needless to say, these proscriptions were rarely if ever heeded except possibly for the one involving blacks.

Until they were finally given a special social security program in 1959, domestics continued to be treated in the paternalistic spirit of the laws of the Indies (which in any event did not apply to Spain). While they were given certain rights as creditors on the death of their employers, as pseudokin they were prohibited from testifying (along with relatives to the fourth degree) on matters involving wills (p. 68).

In 1614, three homes were established in Madrid to house migrant women in order to lock them into domestic employment. As in rural Norway in the nineteenth century, they were not allowed to remain "abroad" more than a week without either taking employment or registering with this agency, nor could they refuse to accept employment with a "master" on the grounds of his having "stairs to climb" or "children to look after." They also could not agree to terms of employment of less than six months. In spite of the repressive nature of these regulations in current terms, Vazquez views them as a great step forward for their period, in that they implied, for the first time, a limited range of contractual independence for these workers (p. 64).

Contrary to what would be expected from Spain's level of economic development, the percentage of households with live-in servants is extremely low. Three independent surveys carried out in the 1960s found only two to three percent of Spanish households still employed live-in servants (Spain, 1966, p. 1164; 1968a, p. 125; 1968b, pp. 165–168). The FOESSA (Fomento de Estudios Sociales y de Sociología Aplicada) survey found an additional five percent who hired servants by the day or even hour, while the I.N.E. (Instituto Nacional de Estadística) survey found that among the upper and upper middle classes a considerable proportion had several live-in servants. However, since these three categories amounted to only three percent of the nation's households, their weight was insufficient to affect significantly the national totals on plural-servant households, as is revealed in Table 6. This table also shows how closely the employment of servants is related to high occupational status.

At this point in the study, only conjectures can be offered as to the basis for these low figures.

1. In spite of their independent convergence on this level of domestic service, both surveys could be mistaken. The present author's study (1969) of domestic service in the United States suggests that underenumeration is common with respect to this occupation. Both the workers and the wealthiest families (who are most likely to hire *any* servants, especially live-ins, as well as more than one servant) are especially difficult groups to reach through the usual survey-interview techniques. A reason for "hiding" domestics has arisen from the fact that by 1969 Spanish household income had risen so far above Portugal's that illegal or semi-illegal Portuguese workers were replacing the Spanish domestic workers who in turn were becoming increasingly common in Paris and London. In any case, it seems fairly certain that even the correct figure would remain significantly below that of most Latin American countries. Therefore, the following additional hypotheses are offered.

2. Spain does not have a "population problem" in the popularly understood sense of an annual growth rate of over two percent, such as that suffered by most Latin American countries. Its fertility began to fall, even in rural areas, as early as the eighteenth century. Neither Leasure (1963)

*Table 6.* Upper and Upper Middle Class Spanish Households by Occupation of Head and Number of Servants, Mid-1960s.

| Occupation | Number of Servants (Percentages) | | | | |
|---|---|---|---|---|---|
| | 1 | 2 | More than 2 | None | Total |
| Liberal Professions | 37 | 4 | — | 59 | 100 |
| Upper Level Executives | 35 | 8 | 2 | 55 | 100 |
| Directors of Firms | 29 | 3 | 2 | 66 | 100 |
| TOTAL POPULATION | 3 | — | — | 97 | 100 |

*Source:* Spain, 1968a, p. 125.

nor Bacci (1968) offer any conclusive explanation for this decline, but both demonstrate that, unlike the case of Ireland, a late age-at-marriage and a low percentage married were not the most important factors. Marital fertility fell significantly, indicating voluntary control over fertility in both rural and urban areas long before the advent of modern contraceptive techniques. Fertility research in Latin America indicates that where families are weak, fertility tends to rise. The Spanish case suggests that, faced with objectively or subjectively difficult or unfavorable conditions, especially the unavailability of land, a strong family tradition can result in controlled fertility, religious strictures notwithstanding.

Spain has had a population problem, however, in the relative sense of insufficient employment. Hence, a large proportion of its work force has responded to the opportunity to work outside of the country in recent years. The timing of this exodus would seem to match that of the onset of a "severe servant shortage." Between 1948 and 1967, about 700,000 Spaniards emigrated to the Western hemisphere. Emigration to the rest of Europe rose from an annual level of 24,000 in 1959 to a peak of nearly 200,000 in 1964. Of the latter number, 83,818 were permanent emigrants, the balance returning to Spain (Spain, 1968c, pp. 106–107). Spanish government statistics on the occupations of the emigrants lump domestic servants with other types of services. However, a more detailed survey by Guy Hermet (1970) indicates that Spaniards are a major source for this occupation in France. This specialization has apparently increased due to what Hermet calls the "meridionalización" of Spanish emigrants over the past decade, i.e., the relatively greater proportion coming from the poorer areas of Spain and who are "less adaptable to this (industrial) work which awaits them in France (p. 347)" (hence the resort to domestic service).

3. The Spanish economic development policy is based partly on the maintenance of a comparative advantage in cheap labor in exported manufactured products. This has taken the form of the extensive employment of women in branches of industry which are predominantly male in Latin America. In addition, tourism, as one of Spain's major "exports," employs many women of the background and skills who would otherwise be working as domestic workers in private households. The number of foreign tourists in Spain rose from 2.8 million in 1959 to 16.2 million in 1969 (Spain, 1970, p. 347), a figure more than half the size of Spain's population of 30 million.

4. Unlike the United States, which has a larger percentage of domestics than its level of development would indicate, Spain has no segregated racial or ethnic minority (with the possible exception of the Gypsies) who would constitute a pool of reserve labor for this menial occupation.

5. On the demand side, the only significant depressing factor would be

the sharp increase in the cost of housing, reflected in the reduction in living space designed for resident servants. The typical upper middle and upper-class Spanish urban residence still has a socially segregated servant's bedroom and bathroom, but the trend is away from the luxury of having so much apartment space designed to be "unusable" for a member of the family should a live-in servant become too expensive. As in the United States, the modernization of domestic service means an increasing "casualization" in its structure. As such, many disappear from official statistics as domestics, showing up instead as other types of manual service workers or as housewives. Other sources of demand are presumably on the increase: a larger urban middle class and a larger proportion of employed mothers.

Overall, the incidence of live-in domestic servants in Spain is much lower than would be "normal" for its level of economic development. This factor exerts an accelerated pressure for the "rationalization" of urban family life, taking the form of lower fertility, a relatively high expenditure for packaged services and a larger proportion living in small apartments than is the case in equally underdeveloped countries with an abundant supply of servants. The rapidity with which the current generations of middle class and middle-aged urban housewives have had to adjust to this "crisis" in the economic support for their preferred style of life deserves more than literary analysis, especially since the predominant ideology of the Franco regime heavily favored a style of femininity which presumably could not cope with the demands of a servantless household (Falcón, 1969, p. 421).

Spain does not deviate, however, from a pattern found in contemporary and nineteenth century societies at all levels of industrialization. The highest proportions of servants in the labor force and of households with servants are found in the largest cities. The FOESSA survey found a direct relationship between a wide set of indicators of industrialization and the percentage of households with servants, living in and living out. The percentage of households (Table 7) with servants (resident and nonresident) increases from 8 percent in the "preindustrial" regions to 16 percent in the "postindustrial" regions (largely Madrid).

Madrid, as expected, had the highest percentage of households with servants (21 percent). Within the country, domestic service is an indicator of relative degrees of development at any one point in time. But cross-nationally and historically, the relationship is quite different since it peaks at the transitional point during industrialization. Spain's "premature" population growth rate decline, and the other factors mentioned above, have apparently brought about an early decline in this development indicator (although a reliable time series is not available). The low level of domestic service in Spain in the late 1960s does, however, accurately

*Table 7.* Level of Provincial Development and Domestic Service, Spain, Mid-1960s.

| Provincial Development | Households With Domestic Service (Percentages) |
|---|---|
| Pre-industrial | 8 |
| Sub-industrial | 9 |
| Semi-industrial | 9 |
| Industrial | 15 |
| Post-industrial | 16 |

*Source:* Spain, 1966, p. 1064.

reflect Spain's remarkable decade of economic development. Spain is no longer a candidate for "Third World" status but has at least an economic claim to European membership.

## SOUTH AFRICA

The major differences among societies with respect to servants is whether they come from the same ethnic group as their employers, whether there is a buyers' or a sellers' market, and the extent to which employer-employee relationships are effectively regulated, whether exploitively or protectively. South Africa offers sharp differentials in all three respects. Servants in 1970 were almost exclusively female and increasingly African rather than coloured. The government's apartheid policy permits the hiring of Africans only if no "coloured" worker is available and then only through an elaborate permit and control system (Whisson and Weil, 1971, p. 44). The general apartheid inconsistency of striving to make the labor of Africans fully available for the white-run economy without having them co-reside with whites is, of course, impossible in the case of live-in servants. Therefore, the implacable need of white families for the status and convenience of round-the-clock service from highly isolated women creates a special control problem. Coloured women are preferred by government policy as a buffer against the Africans, but 1) white families find Africans more tractable and deferential, and 2) coloured women are also more desirous of, and needed in, factory employment.

Many of the elements of African domestic service are similar to the situation in the United States, especially in the Old South. In the paternalistic tradition, those black workers who needed a white protector and could accept the style of submissiveness expected, found a viable existence. For their employers, these servants also provided a crucial behavioral validation of apartheid:

> The humble domestic servant, dropping a cup at the end of a 10-hour day, whispering "master" and "madam" when summoned, perpetually insolvent, occasionally drunk, meets all these needs. She is the dependent whose homage is balm and honey, the instrument which frees her employer for the good life and the justification for apartheid. (Whisson and Weil, 1971, p. 40).

Crucial to this demeaning dependence is the amount and type of payment in kind rather than cash. Not being expected to be able to responsibly plan for their lives, "good" servants could be rewarded by free medical care, old clothes, tips, and legal help when they broke the law. As in India, extraordinarily crowded living conditions in the servants' home areas made the prospect of a room of her own a considerable advantage. Their total income (wages plus room and board) in 1970 in the Capetown area was better than those of unskilled factory workers in absolute terms, but not in terms of hours of work (p. 5).

Only four percent of the households with live-in servants had more than one in a sample survey of three Capetown suburbs, two of which were wealthy (p. 28). Recruitment was predominantly through informal personal contacts rather than newspapers or government employment offices. This meant that many of the Africans were illegally employed, a greater risk to the worker than the employer, since the latter faced only a small fine.

The primary social significance of domestic service in South Africa is that it constitutes virtually the only personal contact most white women and children have with Africans. Those with education and skills are limited to "their own" areas by fiat, so whites have provided themselves with the highly distorted view of African society which impoverished detribalized African women cannot help but present.

## INDIA

Aristocratic, military, and nouveau riche Victorian standards of domestic service from England and India's caste system probably resulted in the world's most complex variety of this institution. As Sofer and Ross (1951) noted for East Africa:

> On the whole, non-economic factors probably play a greater part in inducing the European immigrant to prolong his stay or to return to the country than in motivating his first arrival. . . . the existence of lowpaid domestic service and the psychological gratification arising from membership in the top status group in a multi-racial society become realities difficult to relinquish (pp. 319–321).

India's greater population pressure and indigenous tradition of elegance offered unparalleled opportunities for whites to live far better abroad than in their home countries.

As in all other countries, domestic service reached its peak in the largest cities. In Sen's (1960) survey of Calcutta, as reported in Goldthorpe (1975, pp. 123–126), only 2.8 percent of the labor force was employed in factory manufacturing, while 8.8 percent were residential servants which along with owners of retail shops (9 percent) constituted the two largest and fastest growing occupations. In Table 8 we again see a direct relationship between status and the employment of resident servants. Six percent of the poorest employers hired such servants while 70 percent of the wealthiest did.

In Bombay and Calcutta resident servants are predominantly male. Goldthorpe (1975, pp. 123–126, following Sen) reports that 80 percent of the resident servants in Bombay were males in the 1950s. However, for the 20 percent who were women, domestic service still constituted "by far" the single largest female occupation. Three-fourths were migrants. "The average monthly income of servant-employing households was about 530 Rupees, of which . . . they were paying out about 50 Rupees on servants' food and wages (p. 124)." Of the nonagricultural labor force in 1951, 7.0 percent were servants in Bombay compared with 10.8 percent in Calcutta and 4.4 percent for the entire country (cited in Mehta, 1960, p. 41).

Based on a sample of 500, Mehta (1960) provides unusually useful detail on residence patterns of servants in Bombay. Note from Table 9 that there are sharp differences by sex and ethnicity which determine whether servants live with their employers. No Gujerati and almost no Marathi women servants live with their employers; on the other hand, 83.0 percent of Christian women do.

*Table 8.* Servants in Calcutta by Monthly Income of Employers, Late 1950s.

(Percentages).

| Monthly Income (Rupees) | Households With Resident Servants |
|---|---|
| 201–350 | 6.0 |
| 351–750 | 21.5 |
| 751–1200 | 36.0 |
| Over 1200 | 70.0 (50.0 have 2 or more) |
| | 100.0 |
| | N = 500 |

*Source:* Goldthorpe, 1975, pp. 123–126, from Sen, 1960.

*Table 9.* Servant Residence in Bombay, Late 1950s. (Percentages)

| Residence | Servants' Ethnicity | | | | | | | |
|---|---|---|---|---|---|---|---|---|
| | Christian | | Gujeratis | | Marathis | | Total | |
| | M | F | M | F | M | F | M | F |
| With Employer | 86.3 | 83.0 | 86.3 | 0 | 90.0 | 5.0 | 87.5 | 24.5 |
| Own Home | 8.7 | 5.6 | 12.5 | 100.0 | 10.0 | 95.0 | 10.4 | 72.4 |
| Communal Club | 5.0 | 11.4 | 1.2 | 0 | 0 | 0 | 2.1 | 3.1 |
| | 100.0 | 100.0 | 100.0 | 100.0 | 100.0 | 100.0 | 100.0 | 100.0 |
| Number | (80) | (70) | (80) | (75) | (80) | (115) | (240) | (260) |

*Source:* Mehta, 1960, pp. 116–117.

In spite of the buyers' market facing employers of servants, these groups are differentially available for residence with employers. The communal clubs, like so much else in India, are organized around subcastes. For reasons not explained, the Marathi had not created such organizations. As for women, Mehta observes (lacking, unfortunately, a comparative perspective) that "a priori we should not be expecting many women at the place of service. This is so . . . because . . . the families, especially of the Gujerati and Marathi are settled in the city and therefore there is no need for these women to stay at the place of service and, secondly, Hindu women generally would not be allowed to leave their own households . . . (pp. 116–117)." Only Christian women are "free" from such familial constraints. This is partly explained by the higher percentage of Christian women living in nuclear rather than extended families (73 percent compared to 55 percent for Gujeratis and 35 percent for Marathis). Christians differ also in that Christian women are typically "ayahs" caring for children, the ill, or their mistresses, while Gujerati and Marathi women "usually perform the task of daily cleaning the various items of the household." Very few women are hired for the relatively high paying job of cook. Cooks are largely Christian males, Gujerati are usually butlers or chore boys, while Marathi are predominantly the latter. Male workers' ages differ significantly from female in that the modal age for males is under 20, while women are more normally distributed.

Another complicating factor is the servant preference not to work for wealthier members of their own caste. In terms of literacy, the male Christian and Gujerati servants are about the same (70 percent), while the Marathis are only 48 percent literate. Among the women, Christians are far more literate (27 percent) than the Gujeratis (13 percent) and Marathis (8 percent). In India in 1951 only 30 percent of males and 9 percent of females were literate (p. 235). A related fact was the high rate of unemployment among the educated in India. What is still not self-evident is why employers would prefer literate servants given the usual assumption that they would be less servile. Evidently this is not a problem in India.

Historically, Mehta feels that an important difference between European domestic service and Indian is that the latter evolved directly from slavery (which was abolished by the British in 1841) while Europe's nineteenth century servants were many generations beyond serfdom. Like the British, however, Indian servants enjoyed little protection or control by labor or welfare laws.

## ENGLAND AND FRANCE

Domestic service, as a percentage of the labor force, peaked at 15.8 percent in 1891 in England and Wales and at 14.6 percent in 1866 in France (McBride, 1976, pp. 35–36). The number of households with servants is more difficult to determine, but McBride estimates that "between 1830 and 1885, approximately 15 percent of all French households employed one or more servants (p. 34)." The author's analysis of a one percent sample of the census enumerators' household schedules for London and of published tables for England and Wales indicates that 11 percent of all households in England and Wales in 1851 had one or more domestic servants compared with 29 percent of London's households. With respect to France, McBride noted that: "The Parisian segment of the servant class continued to grow after the overall (national) decline of servants was established so that after 1880 there was an ever higher concentration of servants in the capital city (p. 34)." London's servant population peaked in 1851, as can be seen in Table 10, falling gradually there-

*Table 10.* Servant Populations of London and Paris as a Percent of Servants in the Entire Country, 1846–1921.

| Year | London | Paris |
|---|---|---|
| 1846 | — | 7.5 |
| 1851 | 21.5 | — |
| 1861 | 20.2 | 12.4 |
| 1871 | 18.9 | — |
| 1872 | — | 11.8 |
| 1881 | 17.6 | — |
| 1891 | 16.5 | 20.1 |
| 1901 | — | 21.7 |
| 1911 | 16.3 | 20.9 |
| 1921 | 14.8 | 24.3 |

*Source:* McBride, 1976, p. 36.

after, while the proportion of Parisian servants increased well into the twentieth century.

In both countries, servants were predominantly migrants, with the French being more rural and a rising percentage of English servants urban born. Servants had higher mobility rates in terms of both level and distance than workers in industrial occupations. However, England and France differed significantly in many other respects.

1. The French population growth rate was lower than the English and its immigrant stream was not augmented in the nineteenth century by a rural dependency such as Ireland. English employers enjoyed a buyers' market to a far greater extent than did the French.

2. The political and economic power of Paris was far greater early in the nineteenth century than was that of London, in spite of its being half London's size in 1810 (Sheppard, 1971, p. xviii). Eighteen fifty was the peak of England's reaction against the growing power of London. In 1801, it was eleven times the size of Britain's next largest city, Liverpool, and had 10 percent of the nation's population. (In this respect, London was like Lima vis-à-vis Peru and many other "primate" Third World capitals today.) By 1871, however, there were 16 "provincial" towns in Great Britain with populations over 100,000. However, London was still six times as large as Liverpool in 1871, which remained the second largest city. Moreover, its population had risen from 10 percent of England and Wales in 1801 to 14 percent by 1870. "London, formerly the hub of the nation's attention and the nation's industry, had now (1871) became almost isolated in the still preponderantly agricultural south (Sheppard, 1971, p. xviii)." Sheppard goes on to note that it was not until 1870 that "(t)he power of London as the seat of government was increasing once again (p. xix)."

In addition to national resentment against London's power, there was a great concern that the type of revolutionary uprisings occurring in the great cities of the continent would be repeated in London. Sheppard speculates that "paradoxically it was her enormous size as much as anything else which precluded the emergence of such a [revolutionary] force. Politically, London never overawed the rest of the nation during the nineteenth century and the accession of the middle classes to power and the rise of working class consciousness and organization were [therefore] achieved without violence on the continental scale." (p. xix)

The counter-revolutionary character of London and its high concentration of servants are not unrelated phenomena. England's major "modern" industrial development occurred in Northern towns, leaving London increasingly a trade and service center much like Third World capital cities (Chaplin, 1968b, p. 555). Thus a larger proportion of its workers was employed in occupations highly resistent to collective political action.

3. Law and actual government policy also differed sharply between England and France. Thanks to the highly organized local police forces, French social historians have much richer sources of data on the nineteenth century working class than is available in England. In France both the Church, in a more protective fashion, and the State in a repressive manner, exerted direct control over servants. In both countries, private employment agencies proliferated. But the Parisian police were obliged to control them as early as 1820, while English reform efforts in this area were still nascent at the end of the century (McBride, 1976, p. 77). The chief governmental institution affecting servants in England was the poor law and workhouses for paupers. The French government was equally interested "in the placement of domestic servants as part of the solution to the problem of poverty (p. 77)." In France, however, the greater cultural and physical distances servants traveled to find urban employment and the earlier decline in their numbers led to a mutual interest in a greater use of, and thus regulation of, employment agencies, while English servants coming relatively more from urban areas in greater numbers relied more on individual contacts, newspapers, and private associations for placement.

McBride also contrasts French and British servants with respect to family ties, the former remaining closer to their rural families since "small holding agriculture declined much more slowly than in England" (p. 82). Related to this difference is the fact that "the formal dowry was more important in France than in England and the delay of marriage was consequently more pronounced among the French . . . (p. 92)."

In both countries servants married later than others of similar backgrounds, with the result that they "maintained one of the smallest average family sizes of any occupational group (p. 95)." This pattern was, however, favorable to servant mobility, especially that of males. Their aspirations for lower middle class status are sufficiently well documented so that it would appear that this may be an area of difference compared to servants in India and South Africa who are of different ethnicity than their employers. Lower fertility is at best only a facilitator, not a guarantor of lower class mobility. French servants are known to have been industrious savings bank depositors (p. 97). (As is so often the case, comparable data on English domestics is much more fragmentary). At least a third of the servants in France were estimated to have suffered downward mobility as measured by prostitution, crime, alcoholism, and suicide. Neither country had any system for pensioning servants (although Germany had developed one under Bismarck). Therefore, those older servants who did not enjoy the paternalistic generosity of a grateful employer, shifted to the part-time non-resident "charing" which was to become the major form of domestic service in the twentieth century.

Recruitment into prostitution is apparently one of the "universals" in domestic service where single women lived in with their employers, although reliable data are rare. Again, French police records are unusually rich. The largest single former or current occupation of Parisian prostitutes in 1830 was domestic service (28 percent) (p. 105). More impressionistic data for London suggests the same pattern. Servants were also more likely to practice infanticide and abortion.

In both countries, as well as throughout the western world, domestic service ceased to be a dominantly live-in occupation after World War I. It declined continually in the twentieth century, except during the Great Depression. However, the shift to part-time, non-resident workers meant that the number of workers declined faster than the number of households served. Also, the declining middle class family size (which came earlier in France) meant that such families could limit their use of part-time servants to a shorter length of their family cycle, again enabling the surviving numbers of servants to have at least limited contact with a larger number of households. So the numerical gap between the experience of *being* a servant and *having* one widened at the expense of a much lower level of personal relationships. However, domestic service continued to be one of the largest single occupations for women throughout the Western world until World War II, and in some countries even later.

## CONCLUSION

This survey of diverse theoretical perspectives and available data has attempted to redress the scholarly neglect domestic service has suffered. Hopefully, it will also encourage more work on the topic.

The incidence of domestic service is a prime social indicator of the level and quality of industrialization and modernization. It measures the costs of development, and the point at which those "forced" into this employment finally enjoy more attractive alternative opportunities, more sensitively than the more readily available economic indicators.

Unlike most development indices, domestic service does not correlate positively with growth but peaks at the crucial turnaround stage when Marxian expectations of endlessly accelerating misery and growing inequality cease to be valid. It is, therefore, especially useful as a measure of mass welfare and development in those Third World countries where reliable data on the distribution of income, and on the non-market sector of the economy, are virtually non-existent.

As a declining occupation, it offers especially challenging methodological as well as theoretical opportunities for students of social change and development. As it "casualizes" (with more part-time, seasonal, and short-term incumbents), it appears to disappear faster than is the case. With decline being defined as fewer workers found in domestic service at any specific moment, with casualization they can still serve more households than ever before. Thus, the consuming public's perception of the "servant problem" is likely to be mistaken in this as well as many other respects.

Domestic service also reveals the ability of the worker's family to sustain its members, especially women and children. Nations, and ethnic groups within societies, differ greatly in the extent to which their women and children resort to, or are sent into, domestic service as an alternative to familial or state custody or state support. The composition, in contrast to the level, of domestic service employment is especially sensitive to this variable, especially in multi-ethnic societies. In Third World as well as in western labor markets, the supply and demand for domestic servants works quite imperfectly. Workers tend to withdraw from this occupation (especially the live-in situation) even before their net real income from alternative employment would be higher, given its free room and board, and employers find it increasingly difficult to calculate the real costs of servants as their duties shift by default to those personal services most resistant to mechanization or, external to the home, commercialization.

The Women's Liberation Movement, and the related concern with equal opportunity for minority groups, has brought into sharp focus a class conflict between the needs of middle class employed women, especially those with children, for substitute household services and the desire of lower-class women, especially in minority groups, to escape from domestic service, given its low income and status. "Liberation" for many of the latter women is popularly defined as a secure traditional status as the wife of a steadily employed husband. Conflicting attitudes toward whether employment is liberating thus focus on the common ground of who is to care for the children, the aged, and the infirm. The institutionalization of the latter two groups and a birth rate falling below replacement levels may be the American solution to this dilemma. Hopefully, alternatives developed by other developed nations will become more widely diffused as we enter the "post industrial" era.

## FOOTNOTES

*David Chaplin is Professor and Chairman of the Sociology Department, Western Michigan University, Kalamazoo. His interests include the sociology of development and historical sociology. He has recently edited *Peruvian Nationalism: A Corporatist Revolution* (1976). Preliminary results of his ongoing study of household and family structure in nineteenth century London have been published as a chapter in H. Y. Tien and F. D. Bean, *Comparative Family and Fertility Research*.

1. "The one servant plan adopted in the large proportion of American homes (1900) seems to impose conditions that would be entirely inadmissible in any other branch of industry, particularly in view of the fact that most employers insist on maintaining a degree of style compatible with the employment of several servants." (Willets, 1903, p. 1035.)

2. "Subjects in positions of personal dependence on the master of the household were excluded even in the most extreme of the electoral laws of the French Revolution. A number of otherwise very radical suffrage extensions drew the line at domestic servants, thus the Danish Constitution of 1879." (Bendix and Rokkan, 1962.)

# REFERENCES

Addams, Jane (1896) "A Belated Industry." *American Journal of Sociology* 1:536–550.

Anderson, C. Arnold and Bowman, Mary Jean (1953) "The Vanishing Servant and the Contemporary Status System of the American South." *American Journal of Sociology* 59:215–230.

Anderson, Michael (ed.) (1971) *Sociology of the Family*. Harmondsworth: Penguin.

Aubert, Vilhelm (1955–1956) "The Housemaid—An Occupational Role in Crisis." *Acta Sociologica* 1:149–158.

Bacci, Massimo Livi (1968) "Fertility and Nuptiality Changes in Spain from the Late 18th to the Early 20th Century." Part 1 and 2. *Population Studies* 22:83–102, 211–234.

Bendix, Reinhard (1956) *Work and Authority in Industry*. New York: Wiley.

——— and Rokkan, Stein (1962) "The Extension of National Citizenship to the Lower Classes: A Comparative Perspective." Paper presented to the Fifth World Congress of Sociology, Washington, D.C.

Boserup, Esther (1970) *Women's Role in Economic Development*. London: Allen and Unwin.

Bossard, James H. S. (1954) "Domestic Servants and Child Development." Chapter 12 in his *The Sociology of Child Development*. 2d ed. New York: Harper,

Broom, L. and Smith, J. H. (1963) "Bridging Occupations." *British Journal of Sociology* 14:321–334.

Chaplin, David (1964) "Domestic Service and the Negro." Pages 527–536 in A. B. Shostak, and W. Gomberg, *Blue Collar World*. Englewood Cliffs, N.J.: Prentice-Hall.

——— (1968a) "Labour Turnover in the Peruvian Textile Industry." *British Journal of Industrial Relations* 6:58–78.

——— (1968b) "Peruvian Social Mobility: Revolutionary and Developmental Potential." *Journal of Interamerican Studies* 10:547–570.

——— (1969) "Private Household Employment in the United States." Research Report to the Manpower Administration, U.S. Department of Labor.

Chapman, Dennis (1955) *The Home and Social Status*. London: Routledge and Kegan Paul.

Coser, Lewis (1973) "Domestic Servants: The Obsolescence of an Occupational Role." *Social Forces* 52:31–40.

Davidoff, Lenore (1974) "Mastered for Life: Servant and Wife in Victorian and Edwardian England." *Journal of Social History* 7:406–428.

Drake, Michael (1969) *Population and Society in Norway 1735–1865*. Cambridge, Eng.: Cambridge University Press.

Drake, St. Clair and Cayton, Horace R. (1962) *Black Metropolis*. 2d ed. New York: Harper and Row.

Eaton, Isabel (1899) "Report on Domestic Service" Pages 427–520 in W. E. B. DuBois, *The Philadelphia Negro*. Philadelphia: Ginn and Company.

Falcón, Lidia (1969) *Mujer y Sociedad*. Barcelona: Editorial Fontanella.

Galenson, Walter (1959) *Labor and Economic Development*. New York: Wiley.

Glass, D. V. (1966) *London Inhabitants Within the Walls, 1695*. London: London Record Society.

Goffman, Erving (1956) "The Nature of Deference and Demeanor." *American Anthropologist* 58:473–502.

——— (1959) *The Presentation of Self in Everyday Life*. Garden City, N.Y.: Doubleday Anchor.

Goldthorpe, J. E. (1975) *The Sociology of the Third World*. Cambridge, Eng.: Cambridge University Press.

Goode, William J. (1967) "The Protection of the Inept." *American Sociological Review* 32:5–18.

Haines, J. W. (1960) "Unethical Practices in Bringing Domestic Servants into U.S. Deplored." U.S. State Department *Bulletin* 43:365.

Haynes, Elizabeth Ross (1923) "Negroes in Domestic Service in the United States." *Journal of Negro History* 8:384–442.

Hecht, J. Jean (1956) *The Domestic Servant Class in Eighteenth Century England*. London: Routledge and Kegan Paul.

Hermet, Guy (1970) *Los Españoles en Francia*. Madrid: Guadiana de Publicaciones.

Keely, Charles B. (1974) "Effects of the Manpower Provisions of the U.S. Immigration Law." Paper presented at the Population Association of American, Annual Meeting, New York.

Leasure, J. William (1963) Factors Involved in the Decline of Fertility in Spain 1900–1950. *Population Studies* 14:271–284.

Levenstein, Aaron (1962) *Why People Work*. New York: Crowell-Collier Press.

Lewis, Roy and Maude, Angus (1950) *The English Middle Classes*. New York: Knopf.

Lynes, Russell (1963) "How America 'Solved' the Servant Problem." *Harper's Magazine* No. 233.

McBride, Theresa (1974) "Social Mobility for the Lower Class: Domestic Servants in France," *Journal of Social History* 8:63–78.

——— (1976) *The Domestic Revolution*. New York: Holmes and Meijer.

Mehta, Aban B. (1960) *The Domestic Servant Class*. Bombay: Popular Book Depot.

Michelotti, Kopp (1974) "Multiple Job Holding, May 1973." *Monthly Labor Review* 97:64–69.

Myers, Robert J. (1975) *Social Security*. Homewood IL: Irwin.

Nett, Emily M. (1966) "The Servant Class in a Developing Country: Ecuador." *Journal of Interamerican Studies* 8:437–452.

Noble, Jeanne L. (1967) *An Exploratory Study of Domestics' View of Their Working World*. School of Education, New York University (mimeo).

Oliver, L. (1911) *Domestic Service and Citizenship*. London.

Peru. Dirección Nacional de Estadística y Censos (1966) *Encuesta de Inmigración*. Lima: Lima Metropolitana No. 1.

Reynolds, Lloyd A. (1951) *The Structure of Labor Markets*. New York: Harper.

Salmon, Lucy M. (1897) *Domestic Service*. New York: Macmillan.

Sen, S. N. (1960) *The City of Calcutta: A Socio-Economic Survey 1954–55 to 1957–58*. Calcutta.

Sheppard, Francis (1971) *London 1808–1870: The Infernal Wen*. Berkeley: University of California Press.

Smelser, Neil J. (1959) *Social Change in the Industrial Revolution*. Chicago: University of Chicago Press.

Sofer, Cyril and Ross, Rhona (1951) "Some Characteristics of an East African European Population." *British Journal of Sociology* 2:215–227.

Spain (1966) Fundación FOESSA, *Informe Sociológico sobre la Situación Social de España*. Madrid: Editorial Euramérica.

——— (1968a) *Encuesta de Equipamiento y Nivel Cultural de la Familia*. Volume 1. Madrid: Instituto Nacional de Estadística.

——— (1968b) D.A.T.A. *Comportamiento y Actitudes de las Economías Domésticas hacia el Ahorro y el Consumo*. Madrid: Confederación Española de Cajas de Ahorros.

——— (1968c) *Informe sobre Emigración en 1966*. Madrid: Ministerio de Trabajo.

——— (1970) *Anuario Estadístico: 1969*. Madrid: Instituto Nacional de Estadística.

Stigler, George J. (1946) *Domestic Servants in the United States, 1900–1940*. Occasional Paper 24. New York: National Bureau of Economic Research.

Towner, Lawrence W. (1962) "'A Fondness of Freedom': Servant Protest in Puritan Society." *William and Mary Quarterly* 19:201–219.

United Nations (1962) *Demographic Aspects of Manpower: Sex and Age Patterns of Participation in Economic Activities*. Report 1. New York: Department of Economic and Social Affairs.

U.S. Bureau of the Census (1960) *Historical Statistics of the United States, Colonial Times to 1957*. Washington, D.C.: Government Printing Office.

——— (1972) *Occupation by Industry*. Washington, D.C.: Government Printing Office.

——— (1974) "Persons of Spanish Origin in the United States: March 1973." *Current Population Reports,* Series P-20, No. 264.

U.S. Department of Labor (1974) "Employment and Unemployment among Americans of Spanish Origin." *Monthly Labor Review*

——— Women's Bureau (1974) pp. 11–17 "Facts on Women Workers in Minority Races" (Mimeo).

Useem, Ruth Hill (1966) "The Servant Problem." Paper presented to Cross-Cultural Research Seminar, Indiana University, Bloomington.

Vazquez, Jesus Maria (1960) *El Servicio Domestico en España*. Madrid: Institute Nacional de Prevision, Ministerio de Trabajo.

Warner, Robert A. (1940) *New Haven Negroes*. New Haven: Yale University Press.

Whisson, M. G. and Weil, W. (1971) *Domestic Servants*. Johannesburg: South African Institute of Race Relations.

Willets, Gilson (1903) *Workers of the Nation*. Volume 2. New York: Crowell-Collier.

Young, Michael (1961) *The Rise of the Meritocracy*. Harmondsworth: Penguin.

# REVOLUTION AS CATACLYSM AND COUP: POLITICAL TRANSFORMATION AND ECONOMIC DEVELOPMENT IN MEXICO AND BRAZIL

Susan Eckstein and Peter Evans*

How can the consequences of revolutions be assessed? In comparing countries with contrasting revolutionary histories, it is hard to isolate the consequences due to the nature of revolutions themselves. Barrington Moore (1966), comparing revolutions in different centuries and on different continents, emphasizes the importance of preexisting agrarian structures and historical context in determining both the nature of revolutions and their consequences. We have tried to assess the effects of different types of revolutions by using a more "controlled" kind of comparison. While most comparative analyses of revolutions are, like Moore's, wide-ranging (e.g., Skocpol, 1976; Wolf, 1969; Trimberger, 1972), we have chosen to compare two countries which have much in common.

Mexico and Brazil are both late industrializers, products of Iberian

**Comparative Studies in Sociology—Vol. 1, 1978, pages 129–155**

**ISBN 0-89232-025-7**

colonialism which now occupy roughly similar positions within the world capitalist orbit. Both have undergone political transformations in the twentieth century that were officially labeled revolutions. The actual forms of the revolutions, however, could hardly have been of greater difference: Mexico's was cataclysmic; Brazil's were in the form of *coups*. Mexico's revolution was mass-fought and violent. Brazil's two "revolutions"—Getulio Vargas' seizure of power in the thirties and the military coup of 1964—were political discontinuities involving extra-legal seizures of power by new segments of the elite, but they involved negligible mass or working class support. Mexico's revolution is an approximate example of what Skocpol calls a "social revolution," that is "rapid basic transformation of socio-economic and political institutions . . . accompanied and in part effectuated through class upheavals from below." (Skocpol, 1976, p. 175). Brazil's more closely approximates what Moore (1966) and Trimberger (1972) have labeled "revolutions from above" or "elite revolutions."[1]

If social revolutions have different consequences from elite revolutions, then it should be possible to trace some of the differences between Brazil and Mexico in the early 1970s back to their contrasting political histories. Even though our two-case comparison can't provide definitive theoretical answers, it offers good possibilities for suggestive findings regarding the differential impact of contrasting types of revolutions.

The differences to be expected should not be exaggerated. Both kinds of upheaval are likely to occur as established controls break down, external pressure or foreign intrusion is intensified and as at least certain segments of the society begin to "modernize" (see Moore 1966; Trimberger, 1972; Skocpol, 1976; Wolf, 1969). Postrevolutionary regimes, whether products of elite revolutions or social revolutions, must establish control. A refurbished state apparatus, more bureaucratic in form and more thorough in its penetration of other social institutions, would be expected of both kinds of postrevolutionary society. The major differences would be in terms of the distribution of access to that apparatus. Other things being equal, the broader participation characterizing social revolutions should be reflected in a wider distribution of access to the postrevolutionary state apparatus.

Both kinds of regimes are "modernizing," intent on the expansion of economic resources. They may also favor a certain amount of redistribution, at least relative to the distribution that characterized the prerevolutionary society, but this should depend more on the type of revolution. Since elites are assured of participating in the benefits of expansion, elite revolutions will push economic expansion even if concentration of wealth and income is the consequence. The regimes created by social revolutions may try to press for wider dispersion of wealth and income even if dispersion hampers the pursuit of rapid expansion. Whether the prime aim is expansion or distribution the refurbished state apparatus is likely to be a principal instrument in the achievement of postrevolutionary economic goals.

Since intensified foreign intrusion is a common precursor of both kinds of revolution, both are likely to be nationalistic. Even the most nationalistic, however, are unlikely to be able to withdraw from the world capitalist economy without foregoing economic expansion. In the context of the world capitalist economy, economic expansion, and especially industrialization, requires the cooperation of foreign firms and governments. Some socialist revolutions may now have the alternative of reliance on the Soviet Union, but even these cannot ignore the international economy which is dominated by capitalist firms and nations. Nationalism may have to be attenuated to insure foreign cooperation. Since elite revolutions place greater emphasis on expansion, they should be more likely to restrict their nationalism in order to accommodate external allies.

All of these predictions assume that postrevolutionary developments will reflect the goals of the groups that undertake the revolution. Groups that foster revolutions may instead precipitate consequences that they neither intend nor desire. External forces or the persistent influence of traditional powerholders could prevent expansion, distribution, or both. The groups that were most central to the revolutionary struggle may find that the postrevolutionary regime serves other interests. If unintended consequences and external constraints prevail, revolutions will not produce predictably distinct consequences. Otherwise, the predicted differences between Brazil and Mexico are straightforward.

Mexico's social revolution should have produced a postrevolutionary society with wider distribution of both political access and economic rewards. It should also be characterized by a less attenuated nationalism. Both revolutions should have produced more rapid economic expansion and more powerful central governments. If there are differences in the rate of expansion and the power of the central government, Brazil should have had faster expansion and more centralization. Matching the historical reality of the cases with these simplified predictions produces some degree of correspondence, as well as some interesting contradictions and complications.

## DEVELOPMENT, DISTRIBUTION, AND DEPENDENCY

Until the 1940s there was no indication that the changes wrought by the Mexican Revolution would enhance the country's economic growth. The chaos created by the social revolution seemed completely incompatible with capital accumulation during the teens and twenties. The policies of Cárdenas in the thirties seemed to emphasize distribution at the expense of expansion, and nationalism at the expense of good relations with international capital. In retrospect, Cárdenas' actions may be seen as having laid the groundwork for the impressive capitalist expansion that followed him, but at the time the implications of the groundwork were by no means evident.

Only with the regime of Avila Camacho did the possibility of a positive relation between social revolution and subsequent economic growth begin to appear. In the forties Mexico became an example of the economic efficiency of revolutionary politics. The Gross National Product doubled between 1940 and 1950 (Banco de México as cited in Singer, 1969, p. 21). Throughout the fifties and sixties it maintained one of the highest, steadiest rates of growth in Latin America (Economic Commission for Latin America, 1973, p. 93; cited as ECLA). Industry has come to account for a large share of total output and the population has become predominantly urban. As Table 1 shows, agriculture now only contributes a small share to the nation's total product although it is one of the most productive agrarian economies in Latin America and the Third World in general (Edel, 1969, pp. 119–124; Balassa, 1971, p. 45). Observers of the changes have noted how both the destruction of the power structure created during the regime of Porfirio Diaz, especially in the rural areas, and the initiative shown by the "revolutionary" state since the Cárdenas era (1934–1940), created the bases for this development (see Vernon, 1963, pp. 80–86; Glade and Anderson, 1968, p. 99 and passim).

The structural transformation of the Brazilian economy over the past fifty years has produced results in many ways similar to those observed in Mexico. Like Mexico, Brazil can no longer be considered an agrarian

*Table 1.* Sectoral Distribution of Economically Active Population and Output in Brazil and Mexico, 1969.

(Percentages)

| | Agriculture | Industry | Services |
|---|---|---|---|
| Structure of Employed Population by Sectors: | | | |
| Brazil | 46.6 | 23.3 | 30.1 |
| Mexico | 47.2 | 23.3 | 29.5 |
| Share of Output by Sectors: | | | |
| Brazil | 19.9 | 36.3 | 43.8 |
| Mexico | 12.8 | 36.2 | 51.0 |

*Source:* ECLA, 1972, p. 55.

nation. Agriculture accounts for only a small proportion of the GNP and no longer employs the majority of the economically active population. Although its economy slumped in the early 1960s, in the late sixties and early seventies Brazil, like Mexico two decades earlier, could boast of one of the highest annual increases in GNP in the world, surpassing 10 percent per year between 1968 and 1973 (ECLA, 1975, p. 141).

The two countries have combined a generally favorable attitude toward private capitalism with an ability and willingness to use the economic leverage of the state in aggressive and entrepreneurial ways. The state in both countries directly and indirectly participates in the economy: it owns certain industries, collaborates jointly with private interests in others, and allocates funds and implements policies which are economically consequential. Cárdenas' nationalization of the foreign oil companies in 1938 was an early and dramatic example of state participation in the economy (see Tanzer, 1969, pp. 288–303), one which Brazil followed in 1951 with the creation of its own state-owned refining company, PETROBRAS (Cohn, 1968; Wirth, 1970, pp. 133–144). In both countries the state largely owns the electric power industry (Vernon, 1964; Tendler, 1968), participates in other productive industries such as steel, and is concerned with the traditional state functions of providing infrastructure and guiding the private sector. The public sector accounts for about 40 percent of the gross fixed investment in each country, a heavier state contribution than in most other Latin American countries (ECLA, 1972, p. 53).

The external as well as internal economic relations of the two countries bear certain common features. The way in which they are dependent on foreign trade and capital in some respects is similar. Moreover, the nature of their foreign dependence contrasts both with that of other Latin American countries today and with the situation in each country prior to their respective "revolution." Mexico and Brazil rank first and second in Latin America in terms of their accumulated external debt (ECLA, 1972, p. 105). Yet both countries have gradually freed themselves from the necessity of importing the manufactured goods consumed by their people. Their imports now consist mainly of raw materials, intermediate goods, and capital goods (ECLA, 1972, p. 90). Their success at import-substituting industrialization is also reflected in the composition of their foreign investments. In both countries over two-thirds of direct United States investment is in manufacturing industries and only a small fraction is in extractive industries (ECLA, 1972, p. 270). Similarly, Mexico's and Brazil's exports reflect the growing predominance of industry. While neither nation to date primarily exports manufactured products, Mexico has the highest proportion of manufactured goods among its exports of any major Latin American country (ECLA, 1972, p. 89), and the growth of exports of Brazilian manufactured products has been spectacular during the last few years, reaching over a billion dollars a year by the early seventies (ECLA, 1975, p. 138).

It seems, then, that similar economic transformations may occur in "dependent" capitalist countries which experience either cataclysms or *coups* largely because changes instituted subsequent to the upheavals are not inextricably linked to the "revolutionary" process. The changes reflect how heirs to the "revolutions" use the powers of the state. Cárdenas and Vargas alike responded to the Depression in ways that stimulated the domestic market and encouraged local industry (Reynolds, 1970, p. 167; Furtado, 1963, pp. 203–224), although in so doing Cárdenas was interested in destroying the economic and political power base of the landed oligarchy whereas Vargas operated primarily to protect the profits of planters. Above all, World War II provided a crucial stimulus for the growth of local manufacturing industries in the two countries (Baer, 1965, pp. 26–29; Vernon, 1963, pp. 230–224). In short, Mexico and Brazil have been affected by similar international economic forces and they have responded similarly.

Mexico and Brazil have both moved from being agrarian economies to being semi-industrialized economies, but there are differences in their economic growth which seem to reflect differences in their political evolution. Since World War II both countries have grown at an average rate of about 6 percent per year, but Mexico's growth has been more even. In the mid-sixties, Brazil's growth slipped to 3 percent (ECLA, 1976, p. 62) while Mexico's remained between 6 and 7 percent (ECLA, 1972, p. 213). Brazil's spectacular growth rates in the early seventies (ECLA, 1976, p. 219) were much more impressive than Mexico's during the same years (ECLA, 1976, p. 281), but overall Brazil's recent "miracle" must be seen as a return to the 6 percent growth rate. It seems not at all unreasonable to connect the greater steadiness of Mexico's growth to the greater steadiness of control by PRI (the party, or the "official" party) over Mexico's political economy.

Lack of political control in Brazil was also behind the uncontrollable inflation which struck the country in the early sixties. Food prices in Brazil rose by over 600 percent between 1961 and 1965 while in Mexico they rose by only seven percent (Ruddle and Hamour, 1971, p. 100). Without the kind of political apparatus that the PRI possessed, Brazilian regimes were unable to regulate the conflict between different social groups over who should get the benefits of growth. Inflation kept those who earned the minimum wage from ever benefiting in real terms from the industrial boom ushered in by Kubitschek's *desenvolvimentismo* (developmentalism) (see Fishlow, 1974, Table 2). Their continued demands, coupled with large government deficits incurred by attempts to keep other economic groups content, created the rampant inflation of the early sixties.

Brazil's response was to carry the elite revolution a step further. The military takeover of 1964 eventually brought the rate of inflation down below 20 percent but only at great cost to the mass of the population. Strikes were outlawed, wage increases were controlled and the real minimum wage dropped. After ten years of military rule the real minimum wage still had not regained its 1964 level (ECLA, 1976, p. 73), but the rate of inflation was on the rise again. In the mid-seventies, PRI's ability to control inflation seemed more questionable (ECLA, 1976, p. 289), but Mexico was still enjoying a lower rate of inflation than the Brazilian military could claim for Brazil. On the surface it might be expected that repressive elite revolutions such as the Brazilian one would be able to achieve control over inflation more easily than other regimes. As the case of PRI demonstrates, the political apparatus generated by a social revolution may in fact be more effective.

For both Mexico and Brazil, control over external economic affairs is even more problematic than control over internal economic conflicts. Again the political apparatus generated by Mexico's social revolution seems to do better than the regime created by Brazil's elite revolution, even though, as is to be expected, given its geographic proximity to the United States, Mexico is relatively more dependent on its northern neighbor for trade. In 1968 Mexico sent almost two-thirds of its exports to the United States and received a higher proportion of imports from the United States (63 percent) than any other Latin American country. Brazil, in contrast, traded only about a third of its exports and imports with the United States (ECLA, 1972, p. 92). Despite its apparently greater vulnerability to United States pressure, Mexico publicly assumes a more "nationalistic" stance.

Economic nationalism has its roots in the ideology of the revolution. The extreme predominance of foreigners during the Porfirian economic boom made opposition to foreign investment part of the revolutionary credo. For the emerging local capitalist class ideological predilictions were reinforced by the logic of self-interest. The government's espousal of economic nationalism has been very useful to them, as the "Mexicanization" laws illustrate. The "Mexicanization" decree of 1944, which gave the government the power to require, at its discretion, majority Mexican ownership, provided a base for preventing Mexican entrepreneurs from being squeezed out of their own economy (Glade and Anderson, 1968, pp. 89–90). The concept of "Mexicanization" was broadened in 1972 to include control over the conditions under which foreign technology could be imported. In 1973 it was extended still further: to regulate the conditions under which foreign management could enter the country and to tighten restrictions on the foreign purchase of equity in Mexican firms (*Business Latin America,* 1973, pp. 1–3). In the banking sector Mexico has placed stringent restrictions on foreign participation whereas Brazil at the end of the sixties was moving in the opposite direction (North American Congress on Latin America, 1971, p. 23; cited as NACLA).

The nationalist thrust of the "Mexicanization" laws never eliminated foreign investors. The laws have been applied flexibly and pragmatically so as to cajole international capital into cooperating with local entrepreneurs, to the extent that some international firms have come to see "Mexicanization" as "an appropriate way to guarantee a clear road for continued expansion and diversification." (*Business Latin America,* 1973, p. 155). U.S. "border industries" are exempt from ordinary export and import controls and most foreign firms, despite "Mexicanization," have managed to maintain complete control of their businesses. In Mexico as in Brazil, most American subsidiaries formed during the fifties and sixties had no local participation in their ownership (Vaupel and Curhan, 1969. p. 384).

As the recent work of Newfarmer and Mueller (1975) demonstrates most thoroughly, neither Brazil nor Mexico have escaped the predominance of foreign capital. Despite Mexico's more nationalist stance the pattern of multinational penetration in the two countries shows striking similarities. Yet, the effects of nationalism are still there. Newfarmer and Mueller found (1975, pp. 73, 126) that in 1972 most American multinationals had still not allowed significant local participation in the ownership of their subsidiaries in either Mexico or Brazil. But, the efforts of the Mexican government have resulted in a slightly larger proportion of joint ventures. Newfarmer and Mueller conclude (1975, p. 126) that "the Mexican policy of encouraging joint ventures has had some impact on ownership structure. Comparing the top forty privately owned industrial firms in Brazil and Mexico shows a clear tendency toward greater participation of local owners in Mexico. Slightly over half of Mexico's top forty have foreign owners, but in two-thirds of these cases foreigners have only partial control (*Business Latin America,* 1971, p. 167). In contrast, three fourths of the firms in Brazil are foreign-owned and none of these firms report partial local ownership (*Business Latin America,* 1971, p. 303). Mexico's "revolutionary tradition" appears to be a useful asset for Mexican capitalists interested in sharing power and profits with their vastly stronger international counterparts.

While Brazilian governments since 1930 have espoused a commitment to industrial nationalism they in practice have made almost continuous efforts to present an attractive climate to foreign investors. With the exception of the "Petroleo é Nosso" campaign during the second Vargas regime and the brief regime of Joao Goulart in the early sixties, attempts to protect the position of the national "bourgeoisie" from the inroads of international capital have been minimal. In fact, to the contrary, most of the measures adopted by Brazilian governments to stimulate industrial development have served mainly to benefit international capital (see Gordon and Gommers, 1962; Galeano, 1969; Tavares, 1972). The "revolution" of 1964 accentuated this tendency. Even though the current government talks of supporting private local enterprise (Bueno, 1974), the strength of the multinationals continues to increase (see Pignaton, 1973; Newfarmer and Mueller, 1975). The contest at the cupola of the industrial system now is between state and multinational enterprises, not local and foreign private capital (see McDonough and Aragão, 1973; Evans, 1974).

Thus, while revolution as cataclysm provides no insurance against dependence on international capital, the revolution as *coup* seems to more thoroughly consign local capitalists to a marginal position. The military have manipulated the state in a manner which strengthens their own economic and political power base more than that of domestic private capitalists. As Fernando Henrique Cardoso has pointed out, there is no longer even a pretense of a "calling to hegemony." (Cardoso, 1973, p. 199).

Underlying the apparently similar patterns of external economic dependency in the two countries are some interesting differences. The same is true when internal income distributions are examined. At first the similiaries are most striking. Mexico's "revolution from below" has not resulted in income being more equitably distributed to the poorest 80 percent of its population—particularly to the poorer half of the population—than Brazil's "elite revolutions." Rough estimates of the distribution of income in the two countries by the Economic Commission for Latin America (ECLA), as shown in Table 2 below, make it clear that the poorer half of the population in each country received almost exactly the same small share of total national income. With regard to the share of national income enjoyed by the poorer half of the population, both countries are among the most inegalitarian in Latin America.

*Table 2.* Incomes of Different Economic Groups in Relation to the National Average (about 1960).

| | Brazil | Mexico |
|---|---|---|
| National Average | 100 | 100 |
| Bottom 20 percent | 17 | 18 |
| Next 30 percent | 38 | 39 |
| 30 Percent Above the Median | 79 | 87 |
| Next 15 percent | 147 | 195 |
| Top 5 percent | 791 | 582 |

*Source:* ECLA, 1972, p. 65.

The different "revolutions" which the two countries have experienced appear to have different impacts on income distribution among the most affluent 20 percent. Around 1960 Brazil exhibited the greatest differential between the income received by the top 5 percent and the next 15 percent of the population of any of the Latin American countries surveyed by ECLA. The incomes of the top 5 percent were about five times larger than those of the next 15 percent. Moreover, since the 1964 "revolution" concentration of income within the wealthiest sector has increased even more (Fishlow, 1972).[2] On the other hand, in Mexico, the ratio of income that went to the top 5 percent and the next 15 percent of the population was only three to one, and income among the top 20 percent has become more equitably distributed over the last two decades (Navarrete, 1970, p. 37). The income distribution produced by the postrevolutionary Mexican society is redistributive relative to Brazil's, but only within the "middle class." The *petite bourgeoisie* (white collar workers, smaller businessmen and merchants etc.) along with some members of the organized working class seem to benefit from the legacy of the revolution from below. Unorganized workers and the *campesinos* (peasants) who provided the manpower for the revolution are no better off than their fellows in other Latin American countries who never fought a revolution.

Since land was a major factor inspiring Mexican *campesinos* to revolt and the Constitution includes an agrarian reform plank, one would expect the distributive impact of the Mexican revolution to be more impressive with regard to land than income. No doubt land is more evenly distributed than it was before the revolution, but relative to other Latin American countries the distribution of land in Mexico does not stand out as being egalitarian. Mexico and Brazil have roughly comparable proportions of landless laborers in the agricultural workforce (Stavenhagen, 1970, p. 244; Barraclough and Domike, 1966, p. 397). On first impression, land in Mexico appears more inequitably distributed than it is in Brazil. Table 3 indicates that the proportion of land in holdings of 1,000 hectares or more is greater in Mexico than in Brazil.

Land in Mexico is not, in fact, as inequitably distributed as it appears to be in Table 3, because a sizeable proportion of the largest holdings are *ejidos*. The creation of the *ejidos* was an innovation of the revolution. They are a reinstitution of communal landholding practices. The land in them cannot legally be sold, mortgaged, or rented by individual holders because it belongs to the community as a whole. The effects of the *ejidos* is evident when landholdings in Brazil and Mexico are compared according to forms of tenure. In Brazil squatters and renters account for about one quarter of the holdings. In Mexico these categories account for only three percent of the holdings while one quarter of the land was in *ejidos*.

Even if all the land in the *ejidos* is considered to be in small or family

*Table 3.* The Structure of Landholdings in Brazil and Mexico: by Size of Holding in Hectares.

(Percentages)

| | Under 10 | 10–100 | 100–1000 | 1000 + |
|---|---|---|---|---|
| *Mexico:* | | | | |
| Number of Holdings | 72.7 | 19.1 | 6.4 | 1.7 |
| Area | 1.2 | 5.2 | 15.3 | 78.4 |
| *Brazil:* | | | | |
| Number of Holdings | 44.8 | 44.7 | 9.4 | 0.9 |
| Area | 2.4 | 19.0 | 34.4 | 44.2 |

*Source:* Ruddle and Hamour, 1971, p. 189.

sized holdings, the distributions of holdings in Brazil and Mexico is not that different.[3] What is most interesting about the *ejidos* is the way in which they complement the private agricultural sector to facilitate capitalist expansion. The *ejidos* absorb large amounts of labor in small-scale subsistence farming. Large scale private agriculture occupies better quality land, absorbs private capital and the credit, irrigation, infrastructure, and marketing assistance that the Mexican government makes available to agrarian capitalists (Stavenhagen, 1970, pp. 249–251). Not surprisingly, most of the increases in agricultural production and incomes have been in this sector (Reynolds, 1970, p. 158; Cumberland, 1968, p. 370).

Mexico's social revolution has left behind a highly unequal distribution of land and also of agricultural incomes (see Weiskoff, 1971) but it has aided the creation of a profitable capitalist agriculture in two ways. First, the cataclysm of the revolution itself helped destroy the power of the

*Table 4.* The Structure of Landholdings in Brazil and Mexico: by Form of Tenure (1960).

(Percentages)

| | Mexico | | Brazil | |
|---|---|---|---|---|
| | Number of holdings | Area | Number of holdings | Area |
| Owner occupied | 94.5 | 57.3 | 69.7 | 84.9 |
| Rented | 2.5 | 4.4 | 17.3 | 7.2 |
| Squatter: "occupied without legal title" | 0.4 | 2.0 | 10.7 | 3.6 |
| *Ejido:* "collective ownership" | 1.4 | 26.3 | — | — |
| Other | 1.9 | 10.0 | 2.3 | 4.3 |

*Source:* Ruddle and Hamour, 1971, p. 185.

traditional "feudal" landholding class. Then, the buffer created by the *ejidos*[4] helped eliminate some of the social and political tensions created by the new profit-oriented rural elite. Brazil lacked the benefits of these revolutionary innovations and consequently has been slower to develop an efficient, profitable capitalist agriculture.

The power of the *latifundistas* (large, traditional landholders) eroded slowly in Brazil. There was never a sufficiently frightening threat of rural unrest to induce the elite to make a serious attempt at land reform. After the military came to power congress finally passed some land reform legislation, but the implementation of the legislation lagged (Feder, 1971, p. 242). The *latifundistas* utilized only small portions of their holdings and their low productivity made it very difficult for Brazil to feed its growing urban populations in the fifties and sixties. Agriculture was seen as a major bottleneck to economic growth and a major culprit for inflation. Government actions like price controls and export embargos, aimed at alleviating soaring food prices, only served to debilitate agriculture further (Adams, 1971, p. 48).

The military regime has worked hard since 1964 to promote capitalist agricultural development by transforming traditional landholders into capitalist farmers, particularly ones geared to the export market (Braga and Bernardes, 1974). The government has extended credits to large farmers (Adams, 1971, p. 50) and given large corporations substantial fiscal incentives to invest in agriculture. The regime's success at introducing capitalism to the countryside will be at the expense, however, of an agricultural population unlikely to be able to find work either in the new agriculture or industry. There is no buffer equivalent to the *ejido*. Colonization schemes in the Amazon which were originally to help absorb the "excess" population were soon given up. Dislocated peasants and sharecroppers are being deprived of even the modicum of paternalistic benefits that was their due in the traditional system (P. Singer, 1973, pp. 73–80). Differentials between rural and urban wages are increasing (Fishlow, 1974, pp. 30–31) and in 1970 most agricultural workers made less than 80 percent of the legal minimum wage.

By the mid-seventies it was clear that either a social revolution or an elite revolution could foster capitalist expansion. Mexico had been if anything more effective at capitalist expansion than the more openly procapitalist Brazilians. Mexico had also been more effective at keeping her growth rate steady and limiting inflation. In addition, the nationalism of the Mexican revolution seems to have helped domestic capital in its negotiations with the multinationals. Some distribution of benefits within the bourgeoisie (or middle class) characterizes the Mexican case, whereas the Brazilian elite revolution has produced concentration that benefits a much smaller group.

## POLITICAL TRANSFORMATION AND THE DISTRIBUTION OF POWER

The Mexican and Brazilian "revolutionaries" alike were faced with problems of establishing political order, bringing the political system under central control, developing the political resources of the state and regulating political participation when they assumed power. The Mexicans, however, have managed more effectively to resolve these issues without threatening the economic strength of domestic capitalists by ingeniously developing a structure whereby organized "popular" groups share the symbols of power and therefore responsibility for government policies but not actual power. As a consequence, in contrast to Brazil, social control in Mexico has been maintained with less frequent recourse to brute repression.

The heirs of the Mexican revolution inherited a political system in which fragmentation along regional lines was a crippling and immediate problem. The struggle against regionalism began in the 1920s when the central government coopted or destroyed local *caciques* and *caudillos* (local political bosses), many of whom had become powerful as a result of ten years of fighting. Central control over the states was formalized through the federal government's power to dismiss state governors. Over time, states received an ever diminishing share of the public revenues and became increasingly dependent on federal funding for public works, schools, and other social and economic services (González Casanova, 1970, pp. 24–30, 201). As a result, the political and economic power of the states and municipalities, relative to that of the federal government, has diminished.

The struggle for central government dominance of the polity also entailed a fight to undermine traditional military *caudillos*. Generals who opposed the government were eliminated. A system of rotation was introduced so that officers could not build up local political bases. Young officers were indoctrinated in "professionalism" and loyalty to the state. In addition, while Cárdenas made the military one of the four sectors when he reorganized the dominant national party in the 1930s, the military were forced to compete with the three other sectors for political patronage. Their relative importance was thereby diminished. They were further weakened as a political force when Cárdenas' successor, Avila Camacho, dropped the military sector from the party altogether. The government's success in subordinating the military to civilian leadership is reflected in the diminishing proportion of the federal budget allocated to the military: the proportion dropped from 53 percent in 1921 to 7 percent in 1963 (Wilkie, 1967, pp. 102–103).

Another dimension of centralization involved the subordination of the legislature and judiciary to the executive. Although the three organs of the federal government are formally separate, executive domination is sanctioned by the 1917 Constitution (in contrast to the 1857 Constitution). It has been further accentuated by government repression and subsequent removal of "opposition" parties from Congress in the early years of the new regime, current control of both houses—all Senatorial and approximately 95 percent of all Congressional seats—through the dominant political party which, as pointed out below, is closely linked to the government (González Casanova, 1970, pp. 17–18); little Congressional control over the federal budget (Wilkie, 1967, p. 17); and near-unanimous ratification in both houses of legislation backed by the executive (González Casanova, 1970, p. 201). Similarly, the Supreme Court generally follows the policy of the executive. The Court mainly modifies codified prescriptions drafted by the executive and settles disputes concerning the application of laws to specific cases. It neither initiates laws nor declares laws unconstitutional (González Casanova, 1970, p. 23; Cline, 1962, p. 147).

In addition, the formation of a government-subsidized dominant national party—known today as the Institutionalized Revolutionary Party (PRI)—helped consolidate the new regime, centralize power, and regulate conflict, but the party itself was not directly associated with the "revolution" and was not an inevitable by-product of it. Established by President Calles in 1929, it originally functioned as a loose umbrella organization under which regional politicians were unified and subordinated to the central regime, and regional agrarian confederations and radical agrarian leaders brought under central control. It initially served mainly as a vehicle for regulating conflict and competition between contending elites. It had no grassroots organization or distinct ideology (Cornelius, 1973).

When Cárdenas reorganized the Party, a mechanism was established through which the relationship between countervailing economic groups was instituted, occupational ("functional") as well as territorial groups were subordinated to the state, and economic and political power in the society was redistributed. The "revolutionary tradition" was a useful asset to Cárdenas in legitimizing the transformation, and subsequently the "revolutionary" political institution itself served as a basis of legitimizing other societal changes. Because the Revolution had been ostensibly fought by and for the *campesinos* and, to a lesser extent, the urban workers, and because Cárdenas needed the support of the military and federal and state bureaucrats to effectively usurp economic and political power from the then-dominant followers of Calles (Cornelius, 1973), the domestic agrarian landlords and foreign capitalists (especially in the struggle to nationalize oil), it made political and ideological sense to organize the party around labor, peasant, military, and "white collar" sections. In this manner, "popular" groups unleashed in the Revolution were guaranteed a place in the body politic which they previously had not enjoyed. However, since the sectors had to contest for political spoils *within* the party apparatus, these "popular" groups were kept somewhat divided among themselves, weakening their collective power.

While the Party has won all presidential and most other elections since its founding and has been instrumental in institutionalizing the Revolution, it mainly operates as a mechanism for political regulation, not "interest aggregation." It assumes little authoritative power in national decision-making, is run oligarchically, and is subordinated to the presidency (Brandenburg, 1964; Richmond, 1965). The leadership of the *campesino* sector tends to be controlled by nonpeasants, and sectoral leaders who hold patronage legislative seats do not vote as interest group blocs (see Scott, 1959, pp. 68–69, 163; González Casanova, 1970, p. 15). "Popular" groups, as a consequence, merely have been formally incorporated into the political system—that is, they have gained access to symbols of power but not to authoritative power.

Informal ties, influence, and bargaining outweigh formal group representation in the determination of decisions (see Brandenburg, 1964; Johnson, 1971). Thus, to influence the executive and gain access to patronage, leaders of "popular"-based groups must rely on personal ties with high-ranking functionaries and demonstrate loyalty to the regime. Given such pressures to cooperate with the national leadership of the "revolutionary family," the party structure serves as a useful mechanism of social control. Cooperation within the context of the party facilitates securing at least partial cooperation even from dissident leaders of "popular" groups which are not themselves formally affiliated with PRI (see Anderson and Cockcroft, 1969). While occasionally the government resorts to brutal repression, as in 1968, in the main it has managed since institutionalizing the political apparatus in the 1930s to regulate "popular" groups.

The formal exclusion of the agrarian, industrial, and commercial elite helps the regime sustain its ideological contentions that it primarily identifies with the lower and working classes. PRI includes no "employers" sector. Neither the officially-linked Federation of National Chambers of Commerce (CONCANACO) nor the National Federation of Industrial Chambers (CONCAMIN) are affiliated with the Party.

However, because the Party lacks authoritative power, the economic elites are not thereby deprived of the ability to influence government decision-making. During the 1920–1930 period northern cotton and livestock interests "dynastically" (Cline, 1962) controlled the government. Since then they increasingly have had to compete with industry and commercial capitalists for government favoritism. But because the interests of most capitalists are well represented in the informal deliberations central to decision-making, government policies generally favor capitalist groups. Their informal power as a class, to the extent that it is kept in check, occurs mainly through government controls over the somewhat competing separate chambers and divisions of chambers into which the diverse capitalists are organized.

Through the electoral process as well as through the Party political power appears to have been extended and redistributed since the revolution. Elections are regularly held and suffrage is universal. Yet because elections at times are rigged, PRI candidates are oligarchically-selected, two of the three registered opposition parties back PRI's presidential nominees, and PRI itself wields negligible political power, voting also serves as a mechanism whereby "popular" groups have gained symbolic but not real political power.

Irrespective of the Mexican government's apparent success at instituting political order and centralizing power, PRI's rule has been far from tranquil. Urban and rural guerilla movements, labor strikes, local electoral victories for the conservative National Action Party (PAN), and student-led protests suggest that the government's legitimacy is becoming more precarious despite continued official presidential and gubernatorial electoral landslides. These anti–status quo activities to date have remained isolated incidences mainly because the state thus far has successfully generated sufficient resources to coopt, repress, or allocate benefits to the "disruptive" groups. Its ability to regulate opposition is likely to deteriorate if economic conditions worsen and state resources decline.

In contrast to Mexico, Brazil has no myth of a widely shared revolutionary experience and no shared "revolutionary" values. It also has had no civil war to destroy conservative rural institutions. Getulio Vargas and his cohort confronted a traditional political system that was clearly ineffectual as early as 1930, but was not really transformed until decades later.

While faced with the same problems of establishing the predominance of the center over local and regional political machines and wresting power from conservative agrarian elite as were the heirs of the Mexican revolution, Vargas began the task with a different set of resources, went about it in a different style, and produced different and less institutionalized political results. Nonetheless, he managed to consolidate power in the federal government—creating the strongest federal government until that time in Brazil. Under his Estado Novo, Vargas established the rudiments of a modern "corporatist" political order, somewhat analagous to the one instituted in Mexico by Cárdenas.[5]

Because Vargas, unlike postrevolutionary Mexican leaders, had no distinct social base (see Fausto, 1970; Skidmore, 1967, pp. 3–29), he had to rely on adroit, highly personalistic political maneuvering to centralize power, generate political resources, and maintain political order. He began the task by replacing the regional politicians who opposed him. In addition, he instituted changes in the tax structure to transfer revenue from state to federal coffers, and a system of federal welfare legislation through which large amounts of nontax revenues, useful for patronage purposes, were placed in the hands of the federal bureaucracy. After seven years Vargas had diminished the strength of state politicians to the degree that he felt able to burn the traditional state flags in a public ceremony.

By 1937 it also was clear that Congress and the traditional politicians lacked the strength or determination to oppose him. Just as the early leaders of the "revolutionary" government in Mexico destroyed the autonomy of the legislature, Vargas closed down Congress and abolished all political parties. However, he eschewed any effort to establish his own political movement, even though he had few assets other than his image as a concerned patriarchal figure. At the end of his regime, he did create two parties—the Labor Party *(Partido Trabalhista Brasileiro, PTB)* and the Social Democratic Party *(Partido Social Democrático, PSD)*—but they could not perform comparable functions to PRI in Mexico because (1) they were the product of a leader who had clearly lost the confidence of most established elites, (2) did not include "popular" groups, (3) were competitive on the state and local level, and (4) were not closely identified ideologically with a national "revolution."

Vargas established the rudiments of a corporately-based political-economic order without the help of a political party. In 1930 he created the Ministry of Industry, Labor, and Commerce, and, under its auspices, official *sindicatos* (roughly unions or associations) for employers and employees. There could be only one official *sindicato* in each industry or profession and the various *sindicatos* were not allowed to unite among themselves to create national bargaining units. Compulsory labor courts were set up to handle cases which employers and employees, with the help of the Ministry, could not work out among themselves. Like the Mexican system, Vargas' brand of corporatism facilitated social control, particularly because it kept leadership of the labor movement inside the bounds set by the government.

However, Getulian corporatism remained weak and the coalition ultimately disintegrated in the 1950s. In contrast to Mexico where conflicts among elites were contained within the "revolutionary family" (Cornelius, 1973) in Brazil aspiring politicians increasingly competed with demagogic populists in bids for the vote of "popular" urban groups. The top-down "artificial corporatism" (Schmitter, 1971, p. 112) that Vargas had tried to impose began to change into a more autonomous variety. Leadership of the *sindicatos* became more diversified (Schmitter, 1971, p. 127). When the rapid economic growth of the fifties was replaced by stagnation in the early sixties, the demands of newly "mobilized" "popular" groups became more difficult to meet. Brazil entered into a kind of "crisis of attempted populism" (see Ianni, 1970, pp. 197–200), with rampant inflation the most obvious external symbol of the state's inability to exert control. Quadros, the candidate of the urban "middle class" gave up. Subsequently, Goulart, a stalwart of Vargas' PTB, tried to institute a syndicalist or "national labor" state (Jaguaribe, 1967–1968, p. 180–186). While Goulart cultivated the military, he appealed to, and defended enlisted men against the anti-Goulart officers. The officers reacted in 1964 by ousting the civilian president.[6]

Despite an antipathy to Vargas' populist style, in many respects the military's domestic policies are an extension of Vargas' disciplined corporatism. More than most elite revolutions, the Brazilian military's revolution was restorative (Schmitter, 1973). The military introduced no innovations in formal political structures. Instead, it weakened the role of civilian politicians, turned the legislative branch into a charade, curtailed the independence and power of the judiciary (see Steiner and Tubek, 1971), and "depopularized" elections by making elections indirect. Illiterates continue to be disenfranchised. The two new political parties created under the auspices of the military—the governing National Renewal Alliance and the "opposition" Brazilian Democratic Movement—hardly managed to promote the minimal political activity necessary to keep alive even the illusion of democracy during the late sixties and early seventies. Since the elections of 1974 the parliamentary opposition has been more active. But, if the experience of the first ten years of military rule is any indication, a new cycle of repression is the most likely ending for this resurgence of politics.

In addition, the military rulers have eliminated the popular and semicompetitive components of the system which gained force in the early 1960s, and restored syndicalism. They have instituted strict controls over urban and rural *sindicatos* through massive purges and subsequent control over leadership recruitment. They have also removed undesirable "radicals" from employers' syndicates. Pluralism, whether based on class or locality, has disappeared. The manipulation of "representative associations," together with the abolition of previously operating parties, has served to quell most overt opposition to the regime.

While, as Schmitter (1973) points out, authoritarian-corporatist regimes traditionally seek to establish a centrally manipulated alliance between more or less equal institutional hierarchies, the Brazilian military rulers have reasserted the power of the center so thoroughly and monopolized power so completely that other "corporations" at present are not used either to stabilize the regime or to legitimate it. In contrast to Mexico, the incumbent "revolutionary" leaders have created no monolithic ruling party, and existing representative associations have not been "harmonized" in the name of a single ideal under a unified command. The military represents an advance over the Estado Novo mainly in that its rule is not personalized in a single individual and that it has centralized power to a greater degree.

The 1964 coup not only extended the impulse toward centralization and syndicalism, but also toward the procapitalist stance implicit in the Getulian *sistema* (system). Although most officers come from the lower middle classes, the core group is associated with large industrial commercial and financial enterprises (Einaudi and Stepan, 1971, p. 88). According to Stepan the Brazilian military have more extensive institutionalized links to the private sector than their counterparts in other Latin American countries (Einaudi and Stepan, 1971, p. 102–107). To the extent that there was popular support for the 1964 coup, it was concentrated among domestic capitalists and middle-class groups trying to "save the free enterprise system" (see Hall, 1964). The local bourgeoisie backed the military because they knew that they could not rule on their own. They made the choice Marx attributed to the French ruling class of 1848, "exchanging the right to rule for the right to make money."

The military completed Brazil's elite revolution on the basis of the firm support of most of the domestic bourgeoisie, yet this group, as we have seen, fared less well in Brazil than it did in Mexico. Local capital finds itself, not in the free enterprise system that it apparently wanted, but squeezed between the oligopolistic power of the multinationals and the even more rapidly expanding power of the giant state-owned corporations that have been promoted by the military itself. The military has produced rapid capitalist accumulation, but not exactly the sort that its backers had in mind.

## THE FRUITS OF REVOLUTION

The results of our "controlled comparison" of elite and social revolutions can be rephrased in terms of some general propositions. The applicability of these propositions to other cases remains to be assessed, but they are still worth setting out. To begin with, elite and social revolutions were expected to share certain features which do in fact seem to characterize both Brazil and Mexico:

1. Both elite and social revolutions require a stronger and more active state apparatus. The technocratic central bureaucracy constructed by PRI may not have had quite the same monopoly on power that the Porfirian state possessed, but its penetration of other social and economic institutions was more thorough and more effective. The growth of the power of

the state apparatus in Brazil has been particularly rapid since 1964, despite the military's avowed predilections for "free enterprise."

2. Both elite and social revolutions can be used to eliminate the power of "traditional" elites, though it seems that elite revolutions may take longer to accomplish this task. In Brazil and Mexico the definition of traditional was lack of interest in capitalist development. Agrarian elites who did not place a premium on the accumulation of capital were eliminated or transformed relatively early in Mexico whereas in Brazil the development of a rural elite with a thoroughly capitalist orientation was still an issue in some regions in the mid-seventies.

3. Both social and elite revolutions can produce rapid economic expansion. This result almost follows automatically on the first two. The elimination or transformation of traditional powerholders combined with effective use of the state apparatus provides a good start toward rapid economic growth. What is surprising is not that the overall economic performance of elite and social revolutions can be similar, but that the political apparatus created by a social revolution may be more effective in solving certain problems of capitalist accumulation, such as inflation, than the more repressive machinery of an elite revolution.

Along with some expected similarities between the two countries there were some expected differences. The differences conformed to our expectations in the sense of being in the predicted directions, but their content was not quite as expected:

1. Elite revolution does in fact seem to be associated with greater concentration of income but the wider dispersion of income associated with social revolution does not extend to the mass of the population. If Mexico can be considered more egalitarian than Brazil it is only because of a broader distribution within the bourgeoisie and the more privileged segments of labor, not because there is less difference between the incomes of elite and mass.

2. Social revolution does seem to produce a more agressive kind of nationalism, but the primary evidence of greater nationalism in Mexico is the more effective effort of the state to help local capital gain entry into partnerships with the multinationals.

3. Social revolution does seem to result in the institutionalization of political access for a broader range of groups than are allowed access to the regimes created by elite revolutions. The representatives of organized labor and the various segments of the "middle class" may not have real power in Mexico, but in Brazil no group outside of the higher ranks of the military has any assured, institutionalized access.

Looking over the results, they do conform in general to our initial theorizing and they do provide an interesting starting point for the exploration of other cases. But, there is an undercurrent that was not anticipated. Throughout the comparisons between Brazil and Mexico, the social revolution keeps reappearing as an ideal vehicle for promoting capitalist development. Those who gained control of the postrevolutionary state used it to promote the accumulation of capital and used it well. Moore (1966) has called the American Civil War the "last bourgeois revolution," but the title might well be awarded to the Mexican Revolution.

Why Mexico's social revolution should have become the "last capitalist revolution" rather than becoming the "first socialist revolution" is a question that is raised but not answered by our analysis. Some simple answers are worth suggesting because they suggest avenues for broadening the scope of the comparison that we have attempted here. To begin with, Mexico's "revolutionary" political organization developed after the revolution, after the threat of mass violence and upheaval had subsided. If PRI had developed during the course of the cataclysm or before it, it would have started out with a greater dependence on mass participation. At the same time, the context of the Mexican revolution increased its dependence on the international economy. The Porfiriato left Mexico too "developed" to choose autarchy, but the revolution occurred before there was any possibility of choosing to depend on the Soviet Union or other socialist countries.

Mexico's inability to withdraw from the world capitalist economy and its lack of preexisting political organization combine to separate it from subsequent social revolutions, most of which are not just social but socialist. In Algeria, Angola, and Mozambique, political organization preceded and accompanied violent upheaval. Cuba never had the option of following Mexico because the United States expelled it from the international economy. Cambodia combines preexisting political organization with withdrawal from the international economy. Contemporary social revolutions are unlikely to duplicate Mexico's evolution, but this is not to say that they may not be characterized by equally wide divergence between the intentions of the groups that foment the revolution and the actions of those who control the postrevolutionary state. After all, if Brazil is a valid example, even elite revolutions may experience such divergence.

In Brazil as in Mexico those who provided the "popular base" for the revolution were not its prime beneficiaries. A large part of the Brazilian middle class finds itself politically powerless and with no larger share of the national income than it had before the military coup. Foreign corporations, working in collaboration with a state to which most of the domestic bourgeoisie find it difficult to gain access, and a few of the largest local capitalists, working in collaboration with the foreign corporations, are the prime beneficiaries. In reality, the Brazilian middle class had no more political organization than the Mexican peasantry. Like the leadership of

PRI, the Brazilian military found the pressures of the international economy more compelling than any internal constituency.

The fruits of revolution belong to those who gain control of the post-revolutionary state. A social revolution may work more to the interests of local capitalists and the local bourgeoisie as a whole than an elite revolution. An elite revolution may turn out to be more in the interests of external elites than of its own "popular" supporters. There is no reason to believe that contemporary elite revolutions are likely to be different from the Brazilian revolution. Nor is there any reason to believe that contemporary social revolutions can eliminate the uncertainties of postrevolutionary change simply by adopting an explicitly socialist ideology. Future studies of the consequences of social revolution in Angola, Mozambique, or Cambodia may well find that the examples of Brazil and Mexico are all too relevant.

## FOOTNOTES

*Susan Eckstein is an Associate Professor of Sociology at Boston University and was a Radcliffe Institute Fellow (1975–1977). She is the author of *The Poverty of Revolution: The States and Urban Poor in Mexico* and *The Impact of Revolution: A Comparative Analysis of Mexico and Bolivia*. Peter Evans is an Assistant Professor of Sociology at Brown University and formerly taught at the Universidade de Brasilia. He is the author of *Dependent Development: The Alliance of Multinational, State, and Local Capital in Brazil*.

The authors would like to acknowledge the assistance of a number of individuals who read and commented on earlier drafts, especially Kay Trimberger, whose initial support was crucial, and Philippe Schmitter, whose extensive comments helped correct some early errors. We would also like to acknowledge that some trends which emerged since we first drafted the paper (1973), such as inflation in Mexico, suggest certain modifications in our analysis which we have not been able to incorporate here.

1. Whether transformations like those that occurred in Brazil should be called revolutions at all is, of course, open to question. The ambiguities of terms like "elite revolutions" and "revolution from above" are evident in Moore's work. While using the term "revolution from above" to describe the transformations of Japan and Germany, he makes it clear that he sees these two countries as having modernized "without a popular revolutionary upheaval" (1966, p. 435) and as having tried to modernize without changing their social structures (1966, p. 442). Likewise, Trimberger (1972, p. 201) points out that the transformation of Turkey which she considers as an "elite revolution" is considered by others (e.g., Huntington, 1968, p. 269) a case of "effective reform." We have chosen to follow Moore and Trimberger even though we recognize the dangers of stretching the term "revolution" so far that it includes almost any transfer of power (see Brinton, 1952).

2. Fishlow (1972) estimates that in 1960 the top 3.1 percent of the income earners received 25.8 percent of total income, whereas in 1970 the share of the top 3.2 percent was 33.1 percent. In 1960 the share of the next 22 percent was 42.2 percent of total income whereas in 1970 the next 20.5 percent received 38.2 percent. This means that the ratio between the incomes in the uppermost group and incomes in the next group were about 4.3 to 1 in 1960 and 5.6 to 1 by 1970.

3. Looking at distributions for the entire countries obscures, of course, tremendous re-

gion variation. "Family-sized" farms are not uncommon in the southern states of Brazil, but in the west or northeast the distribution of land is probably much more inegalitarian than the overall figures for Mexico.

4. If *ejidal* land were alienable instead of being communally held, there is reason to believe that a repetition of the "land-grab" that followed the land reform law of 1856 with the consequences of dispossessing a large proportion of the *ejidatarios* would be the result (see Wolf, 1969, p. 12). Currently the ratio of manpower to output in Mexican agriculture as a whole is about 40 percent higher than the ratio in Brazil. Without the stable, labor-absorbing *ejidal* sector it is easy to envisage vast influxes of additional "marginals" to the urban areas accompanied by increasing misery and tension in the rural areas.

5. Schmitter (1971, p. 111) suggests that the "hallmark" of corporatism the existence of organized groups which engage in the "exchange of legal monopoly on representation and guaranteed access to decision-makers in return for compliance with certain limitations on behavior." The existence of these semiautonomous but cooperating groups enables the central political apparatus of the state to play a "moderating" role. Vargas was clearly aiming at the creation of a system structured something along these lines, although more ideologically pure corporatists like Oliveira Vianna felt that the Vargas' strategies of group formation were too exclusively "top-down" in their orientation (see Schmitter, 1971, p. 114).

6. The group of officers most central to the 1964 *coup* were known as the "Sorbonne Group" because of their close association with the *Escola Superior de Guerra* (ESG). The thinking on national security and development that was developed in the ESG was an important factor in legitimating at least in their own eyes, more active involvement in the direction of national affairs by the military (see Stepan, 1971, pp. 178–186; Schneider, 1971, pp. 244–250).

## REFERENCES

Adams, Dale (1971) "What Can Under-developed Countries Expect from Foreign Aid to Agriculture? Case Study: Brazil 1950–70." *Inter-American Economic Affairs* 25:47–64.

Alcazar, Marco (1970) *Las Agrupaciones Patronales en México*. Mexico: El Colegio de México.

Anderson, Bo and Cockcroft, James (1969) "Control and Cooptation in Mexican Politics." Pages 366–389 in Irving Horowitz, Josué de Castro, and John Gerassi (eds.), *Latin American Radicalism*. New York: Vintage Books.

Anderson, Charles (1967) *Politics and Economic Change in Latin America: The Governing of Restless Nations*. New York: Van Nostrand.

Baer, Werner (1965) *Industrialization and Economic Growth in Brazil*. Homewood, IL: Irwin.

——— (1969) *The Development of the Brazilian Steel Industry*. Nashville: Vanderbilt University Press.

Balassa, Bela (1971) "La Industrialización y el Comercio Exterior: Análisis y Proposiciones." Pages 45–81 in Miguel Wionczek et al., *Crecimiento o Desarrollo Economico?* Mexico: Secretaria de Educatión Publica.

Barraclough, Solon and Domike, Arthur (1966) "Agrarian Structure in Seven Latin American Countries." *Land Economics* Vol. 42 no. 4:391–424.

Beman, Lewis (1972) "How the Brazilians Manage Their Boom." *Fortune* Vol. 86 no. 6: December: 110–114.

Bergsman, Joel (1970) *Brazil: Industrialization and Trade Policies*. New York: Oxford University Press.

Black, Edie and Goff, Fred (1969) *The Hanna Industrial Complex.* New York: North American Congress on Latin America.

Blume, Norman (1967–1968) "Pressure Groups and Decision-Making in Brazil." *Studies in Comparative International Development* 3:205–234.

Braga, Teodomire and Bernardes, Luiz (1974) "O Capitalismo no campo." *Opinão* 69: March 4: 5.

Brandenburg, Frank (1964) *The Making of Modern Mexico.* Englewood Cliffs, NJ: Prentice-Hall.

Brinton, Crane (1952) *The Anatomy of Revolution.* Englewood Cliffs, NJ: Prentice-Hall.

Bueno, Richard (1974) "O Governo Saiu em Defesa da Indústria Nacional?" *Opinão* 80: May 20: 7.

Business Latin America (1967–1973) *Weekly Report to Managers of Latin American Operations.* New York: Business International Corporation.

Cardoso, Fernando Henrique (1972) "Dependency and Development in Latin America." *New Left Review* 74: July-August: 83–95.

——— (1973) *Politica e Desenvolvimento en Sociedades Dependentes.* Rio de Janeiro: Zahar Editores.

Cline, Howard (1962) *Mexico: Revolution to Evolution: 1940–1960.* London: Oxford University Press.

Cohn, Gabriel (1968) *Petróleo e Nacionalismo.* São Paulo: Difusão Europeia do Livro.

Cornelius, Wayne (1973) "Nation-building, Participation, and Distribution: The Politics of Sound Reform under Cárdenas," Pages 392–498 in Gabriel Almond *et al.* (eds.), *Crisis Choice, and Change: Historical Studies of Political Development.* Boston: Little, Brown.

Cumberland, Charles (1968) *Mexico: The Struggle for Modernity.* New York: Oxford University Press.

Eckstein, Harry (1965) "On the Etiology of Internal Wars." *History and Theory* 4: no. 2: 133–163.

Economic Commission for Latin America (ECLA) (1964) "Fifteen Years of Economic Policy in Brazil." *Economic Bulletin for Latin America* 9: December.

——— (1972) *Economic Survey of Latin America: 1970.* New York: United Nations.

——— (1975) *Economic Survey of Latin America: 1973.* New York: United Nations.

Economist Intelligence Unit (1969–1971) *Quarterly Economic Review: Brazil.* Second Annual Supplement. London: *The Economist.*

Edel, Mathew (1969) *Food Supply.* New York: Praeger.

Einaudi, Luigi and Stepan, Alfred III (1971) *Latin American Institutional Development: Changing Military Perspectives in Peru and Brazil.* Santa Monica: Rand.

Evans, Peter (1974) "The Military, the Multinationals, and the *Milagre:* The Political Economy of the 'Brazilian Model' of Development." *Studies in Comparative International Development* 9: no. 3: 26–45.

Faria, Vilmar (1969) "Dependência e Ideologia Empresarial." Paper presented at the Ninth Latin American Congress of Sociology, Mexico City.

Fausto, Boris (1970) *A Revolucão de 1930.* São Paulo: Editora Brasiliense.

Feder, Ernest (1971) *The Rape of the Peasantry.* Garden City, NY: Doubleday Anchor.

Fishlow, Albert (1972) "Brazilian Size Distribution of Income." *American Economic Review* 62:391–402.

——— (1974) "Algumas Reflexões sobre a Política Econômica Brazileira após 1964." *Estudos Cebrap* 7:7–65.

Flores, Edmundo (1970) *Vieja Revolución, Nuevos Problemas.* Mexico City: Editorial Joaquin Mortiz.

Frank, Andre G. (1967) *Capitalism and Underdevelopment in Latin America*. New York: Monthly Review Press.

Friedrich, Paul (1970) *Agrarian Revolt in a Mexican Village*. Englewood Cliffs, NJ: Prentice-Hall.

Furtado, Celso (1963) *The Economic Growth of Brazil*. Berkeley: University of California Press.

——— (1969) *Um Projeto para o Brasil*. Rio de Janeiro: Editora Saga.

——— (1972) *Análise do Modelo Brasileiro*. Rio de Janeiro: Civilização Brasileiro.

Galeano, Eduardo (1969) "Denationalization and Brazilian Industry." *Monthly Review* 21: December: 11–30.

Glade, William Jr. and Anderson, Charles (1968) *The Political Economy of Mexico: Two Studies*. Madison: University of Wisconsin Press.

González Casanova, Pablo (1970) *Democracy in Mexico*. New York: Oxford University Press.

Gordon, L., and Gommers, G. (1962) *United States Manufacturing Investment in Brazil*. Boston: Division of Research, Graduate School of Business Administration, Harvard University.

Hall, Clarence (1964) "The Country that Saved Itself." *Readers Digest* Vol. 85 no. 512: November: 135–158

Hansen, Roger (1971) *The Politics of Mexican Development*. Baltimore: Johns Hopkins Press.

Hanson, Simon (1967) *Five Years of the Alliance for Progress*. Washington, DC: Inter-American Affairs Press.

Huntington, Samuel (1968) *Political Order in Changing Societies*. New Haven: Yale University Press.

Ianni, Octavio (1970) *Crisis in Brazil*. New York: Columbia University Press.

International Labor Office (1971) *Yearbook of Labour Statistics*. Geneva: International Labor Office.

Jaguaribe, Helio (1967–1968) Political Strategies of National Development in Brazil. *Studies in Comparative National Development* 3:48–70.

——— (1968) *Economic and Political Development: A Theoretical Approach and a Brazilian Case Study*. Cambridge, MA.: Harvard University Press.

Johnson, Kenneth (1971) *Mexican Democracy: A Critical View*. Boston: Allyn and Bacon.

Leff, Nathaniel (1968) *Economic Policy Making and Development in Brazil 1947–1964*. New York: Wiley.

Lieuwen, Edwin (1968) *Mexican Militarism*. Albuquerque: University of New Mexico Press.

Lozoya, Jorge (1970) *El Ejercito Mexicano (1911–1965)*. Mexico City: El Colegio De México.

McDonough, Peter and Aragão, Ana Maria (1973) "Political Implications of Economic Concentration in Brazil." Paper delivered at the Ninth World Congress of the International Political Science Association, Montreal, Canada, August 19–25, 1973.

Marini, Ruy Mauro (1972) "Brazilian Subimperialism." *Monthly Review* 23: February: 14–24.

Martins, Luciano (1968) *Industrializacao, Burgesia Nacional e Desenvolvimento*. Rio de Janeiro: Editora Saga.

Moore, Barrington, Jr. (1966) *Social Origins of Dictatorship and Democracy*. Boston: Beacon Press.

Morse, Richard (1964) "Heritage of Latin America." Pages 123–177 in Louis Hartz (ed.), *The Founding of New Societies*. New York: Harcourt, Brace and World.

Moss, Robert (1972) "The Moving Frontier: A Survey of Brazil." *Economist* 224: September 2: 11–73.

Mueller, Marnie (1970) "Changing Patterns of Agricultural Output and Productivity in the Private and Land Reform Sectors in Mexico, 1940–1960." *Economic Development and Cultural Change* 18: January: 252–265.

Navarrete, Ifigenia de (1970) "La Distribución del Ingreso en México: Tendencias y Perspectivas." Pages 15–72 in David Ibarra et al. (eds.), *El Perfil de México en 1980*. Mexico City: Siglo Ventiuno.

Newfarmer, R. and Mueller, W. (1975) *Multinational Corporations in Brazil and Mexico: Structural Sources of Economic and Non-economic Power*. Report to the Subcommittee on Multinationals, Committee on Foreign Relations, U.S. Senate. Washington: Government Printing Office.

North American Congress on Latin American (NACLA) (1970) *U.S. Military and Police Operations in the Third World*. New York: NACLA.

——— (1971) *Yanqui Dollar: The Contribution of U.S. Private Investment to Underdevelopment in Latin America*. New York: NACLA.

Osorio, Sergio Reyes and Eckstein, Solomon (1971) "El Desarrollo Polarizado de la Agricultura Mexicana." Pages 21–44 in Miguel Wionczek et al. (eds.), *Crecimiento o Desarrollo Económico?* Mexico City: Secretaria de Educatión Pública.

Padgett, L. Vincent (1966) *The Mexican Political System*. Boston: Houghton Mifflin.

Pignaton, Alvaro (1973) *Capital Estrangeiro e Expansão Industrial no Brasil*. Brasilia: Universidade de Brasília.

Rabinowitz, Francine (1965) *The Political Feasibility of Metropolitan Planning: Mexico City, a Case Study*. Cambridge: Regional and Urban Planning Implementation.

Reynolds, Clark (1970) *The Mexican Economy: Twentieth Century Structure and Growth*. New Haven: Yale University Press.

Richmond, Patricia (1965) "Mexico: A Case Study of One-Party Politics." Unpublished Ph.D. Thesis. Berkeley: University of California.

Ruddle, Kenneth and Hamour, Mukhar (1971) *Statistical Abstract of Latin America*. Los Angeles: Latin American Center, University of California at Los Angeles.

Schmitter, Philippe (1971) *Interest Conflict and Political Change in Brazil*. Stanford: Stanford University Press.

——— (1972) "Paths to Political Development in Latin America." Pages 83–108 in Douglas Chalmers (ed.), *Changing Latin America: New Interpretations of Its Politics and Society*. New York: Academy of Political Science, Columbia University.

——— (1973) "The 'Portugalization' of Brazil." Pages 179–232 in Alfred Stepan III (ed.), *Authoritarian Brazil*. New Haven: Yale University Press.

Schneider, Ronald (1971) *The Brazilian Political System*. New York: Columbia University Press.

Scott, Robert (1959) *Mexican Government in Transition*. Urbana: University of Illinois Press.

Singer, Morris (1969) *Growth, Equality and the Mexican Experience*. Austin: University of Texas Press.

Singer, Paul (1972) *O 'milagre brasileiro': Causas e Consequencias." Cadernos CEBRAP* 6: São Paulo: CEBRAP.

——— (1973) "Desenvolvimento e Reparticão da Renda no Brasil." *Debate and Critica* 1: July-December: 67–94.

——— (1974) "Salarios e Inflação. *Opinião* 80: May 20: 10.

Skidmore, Thomas (1967) *Politics in Brazil, 1930–1964: An Experiment in Democracy*. New York: Oxford University Press.

Skocpol, Theda (1976) "France, Russia, China: A Structural Analysis of Social Revolutions." *Comparative Studies in Society and History* 18: no. 2: 175–210.

Stavenhagen, Rodolfo (1970) "Social Aspects of Agrarian Structure in Mexico." Pages 225–270 in Rodolfo Stavenhagen (ed.), *Agrarian Problems and Peasant Movements in Latin America*. Garden City, NY: Doubleday.
Steiner, H. J. and Tubek, D. M. (1971) "All Power to the Generals." *Foreign Affairs* 49:464–479.
Stepan, Alfred (1971) *The Military in Politics: Changing Patterns in Brazil*. Princeton, NJ: Princeton University Press.
Tannenbaum, Frank (1950) *The Struggle for Peace and Bread*. New York: Alfred Knopf.
Tanzer, Michael (1969) *The Political Economy of International Oil and the Underdeveloped Countries*. Boston: Beacon Press.
Tavares, Maria de Conceição (1972) *Da Substituicão de Importacoes ao Capitalismo Financeiro*. Rio de Janiero: Zahar Editores.
Tendler, Judith (1968) *Electric Power in Brazil: Entrepreneurship in the Public Sector*. Cambridge, MA.: Harvard University Press.
Trimberger, Ellen Kay (1972) "A Theory of Elite Revolutions." *Studies in Comparative International Development* 7: vol. 7: no. 3: 192–207.
Troncoso, Moises and Burnett, Ben (1960) *The Rise of the Latin American Labor Movement*. New Haven: College and University Press.
Ugalde, Antonio (1970) *Power and Conflict in a Mexican Community*. Albuquerque: University of New Mexico Press.
Vaupel, J., and Curhan, J. (1969) *The Making of Multinational Enterprise*. Boston: Division of Research, Graduate School of Business Administration, Harvard University.
Vernon, Raymond (1963) *The Dilemma of Mexico's Development*. Cambridge, MA: Harvard University Press.
——— (1964) *Public Policy and Private Enterprise in Mexico*. Cambridge, MA: Harvard University Press.
Vinhas de Queiroz, Mauricio (1965) "Os Grupos Multibillionarios." *Revista do Instituto das Ciencias Sociais* 2: pp. 48–77.
Wechstein, R. S. (1970) "Evaluating Land Reform." *Economic Development and Cultural Change* 18 (April): 391–409.
Weiskoff, Richard (1971) *Income Distribution and Economic Growth in Puerto Rico, Argentina, and Mexico*. New Haven: Yale University Growth Center, Center Paper No. 162.
Wilkie, James (1967) *The Mexican Revolution: Federal Expenditures and Social Change Since 1910*. Berkeley: University of California Press.
Wionczek, Miguel (1971) "La Inversión Extranjera Privada: Problemas y Perspectivas." Pages 199–234 in Miguel Wionczek *et al.*, *Crecimiento o Desarrollo Económico?* Mexico City: Secretaría de Educación Pública.
Wirth, John D. (1970) *The Politics of Brazilian Development*. Stanford: Stanford University Press.
Wolf, Eric (1969) *Peasant Wars of the Twentieth Century*. New York: Harper & Row.
Womack, John Jr. (1969) *Zapata and the Mexican Revolution*. New York: Vintage.
——— 1970 "The Spoils of the Mexican Revolution." Foreign Affairs 49: 677–687.

# THE ETHNIC SYSTEMS OF PREMODERN SPAIN

Thomas F. Glick*

---

The sociology of ethnic relations has emerged in the past forty years from analyses of a variety of modern societies, typically colonial and postcolonial, or those in which immigration of heterogeneous groups has played a major role. Since those societies studied manifest specific social, economic, and political forms deemed characteristic of modernity (e.g., capitalism, imperialism, industrialization), students of ethnic relations have been hesitant, perhaps justifiably, to claim the applicability of their conclusions to periods antedating the age of Western Imperialism. To cite one such caution, Schermerhorn (1970, p. 194) suggests that in studies of long-term adjustment between contacting groups "nationalistic" and

**Comparative Studies in Sociology—Vol. 1, 1978, pages 157–171**

**ISBN 0-89232-025-7**

"prenationalistic" societies may lack comparability because of the putatively lower level of stability in the latter. The stability in question refers specifically to the longevity of the ruling regime and the length of time deemed sufficient for the elaboration of a "mold," that is (I assume) an officially promoted or institutionalized model governing intergroup relations.

Such a judgment ignores structures or attitudes that underlie ruling institutions and which survive periods of instability. Premodern Spain (eighth through seventeenth centuries, spanning the transition from prenationalistic to nationalistic political forms) is an example of a society in which the persistence of institutional and juridical norms offers sufficient structural and attitudinal continuity to provide a viable test for assertions extrapolated from more recent situations.

The present study is a comparative analysis of ethnic relations in Islamic Spain (eighth through thirteenth centuries) and in Christian Spain at two points in time: the "feudal" period (eleventh through fifteenth centuries) and the imperial period (sixteenth and seventeenth centuries). Previous studies of intergroup relations in Spain have been marked by conceptual imprecision. Castro (1954; 1971) was the first to apply a caste analysis to the interrelations of Christians, Muslims, and Jews in Spain. His views, heavily inflected with idealistic concepts derived from German philosophers of history, were of a society wherein intergroup relations were controlled by factors wholly ideological and cultural and whose social ligaments were not visible or not significant. More recently, Gutiérrez Nieto (1973) has used the caste concept admirably to explicate cross-cutting relationships between caste and class in sixteenth-century Spain. Unlike Castro, Gutiérrez defines caste with sociological precision, but then, without denying the validity of a caste anlaysis, withdraws to an uncomfortable position of admitting only a "pseudocaste" structure for sixteenth-century Castile (1973, pp. 522, 525, 553).

Here I will argue that the dynamics of intergroup relations in medieval and early modern Spain are explicable not so much by the caste structure (which is not in question) of the groups themselves, but rather by the nature of differing and changing systems of ethnic stratification in which they were embedded. As a historian, my mode of analysis is primarily institutional. One may assert, as does Noel (1968–1969, p. 163) that ethnic stratification emerges only if the contact situation includes the interaction of ethnocentrism, competition, and differential power. However, since the latter two factors seem to be universal components of social and economic systems, it seems more productive to concentrate on the cultural factor, ethnocentrism, to examine the ways in which it became institutionalized in each of the cases studied, and, on the basis of this analysis, to offer some conclusions relevant to three specific areas of inquiry: (1) the emergence of ethnic stratification systems; (2) the typology of such systems; and (3) the interdependence of cultural and socioeconomic forces in intergroup relations.

The systems of ethnic relations discussed below fall broadly within two types, described by van den Berghe (1970) as *paternalistic* and *competitive*. Paternalistic ethnic relations are characterized by a horizontal bar between upper and lower castes, scant intercaste mobility, a legal system favoring the ethnic status quo, sharply structured ethnic roles, and accommodation by the lower castes to their inferior status. Violence erupts from the lower castes and is repressed with severity. In competitive systems, the bar between the castes tilts towards the vertical. The status gap between castes narrows, and within castes increases. Political ideologies reflect equalitarianism; ethnic roles are ill-defined; and there is aggression on both sides.

In van den Berghe's model the ideal types are associated with specific political-economic systems (slave-holding plantation societies and their successor states, respectively). My evidence, especially that describing the coexistence of both types within the same society simultaneously, does not support the economic basis of this dichotomy.[1] Rather, the two types are distinguished by institutional features regulating or limiting access to political power by subordinate groups. In the competitive systems of ethnic relations described below, all the participating groups had legal guarantees, and therefore expectations, of sharing political power. In paternalistic systems, subordinate groups were barred from access to power. Within these frameworks, economic relations and competition for resources may well determine the tonality of intergroup relations but they do not in themselves establish the basic rules of interaction.

## CASE STUDIES

### 1. *Islamic Spain*

In the medieval Islamic world, into which most of the Iberian peninsula was incorporated in the early eighth century, ethnic relations were ordered according to two different principles. The Qur'ān (Koran) envisioned a society dominated by Muslims (assumed to be Arabs), with provisions made for approved religious minorities, the *ḍhimmīs* or "protected peoples" (an overtly paternalistic image)—that is, Christians and Jews. This was an accurate representation of Arabian society in the time of Muḥammad but, as Arabs extended control over large numbers of non-Muslim, non-Arab peoples, the problem then became one of encompassing tremendous ethnic and religious diversity within the framework of the Qur'ān. Two strategies were adopted:

(1) Religious groups of high prestige, such as Zoroastrians and Buddhists, were accorded *dhimmī* status by analogy. *Dhimmīs* suffered civil and legal disabilities in comparison with Muslims, but they also enjoyed the security that inhered in formal juridical status that guaranteed them (unlike the Jewish minorities of Christian Europe) religious freedom, substantial community autonomy, and the free choice and exercise of occupation and economic activity (Goitein, 1964, pp. 64–88; 1971, pp. 288–289). By accepting this status, religious minorities were effectively removed from competition for power. The only way to achieve full integration in the society at large was to convert to Islam. Islamic society, by recognizing the autonomous status of religious minorities, sanctioned a relatively high degree of cultural enclosure among them. In Islamic Spain, both Jews and Christians acculturated to Arab norms quickly, but the pressures to do so were informal and not the result of official policies. Their status in society was not linked to their acceptance or rejection of Arabic culture. The system of "protected peoples" accords well with the paternalistic model.

(2) The situation of ethnic groups who accepted Islam is more complex since Islamic law did not spell out in any definitive way the relationship of such peoples to Arabs. Social scientists have noted (e.g., Noel, 1968–1969, p. 161, note 15) that equalitarian creeds have generally proven ineffective in preventing ethnic stratification. The Islamic experience confirms this conclusion. Although Islamic law envisioned a universal brotherhood of believers, ethnically stratified social systems evolved throughout the Islamic world. The usual method of dealing with the assimilation of ethnic minorities was to accord the neophyte the status of client, whereby new converts (often entire tribal groups) would attach themselves to an Arab tribe, adopting its lineage and social status. A tradition attributed to Muhammad asserts that "People are of three kinds: Arabs, non-Arabs, and clients" (Goldziher, 1963–1964, vol. 54, p. 33). Therefore, in both the cases of non-Muslim religious enclaves and non-Arab ethnic enclaves a principle of requisite variety governed social integration. Since the admissible level of group diversity was frozen in the image of Arabian society at the time of Muḥammad, mechanisms were developed whereby diverse groups could be accommodated to the model.

In Islamic Spain, power was contested by three ethnically-differentiated Muslim groups: a numerically small Arab ruling elite; a larger number of Berbers (indigenous peoples of northern Africa who had joined the Arabs in the invasion of Spain); and a large group of Hispano-Roman converts to Islam (*muwalladūn,* or Neo-Muslims) who became the majority around the first third of the tenth century. In addition to cultural cleavages, the groups were further differentiated ecologically and economically. The Arabs dominated the urban centers and the alluvial valleys of the Guadalquivir and Ebro rivers whose rich farmland was cultivated by Neo-Muslim or Christian tenants. The Berbers, herders and olive growers, were typically relegated to plateaux and mountain highlands (although some practiced irrigation agriculture in the Valencian region). Through the tenth century the Arab rulers of the emirate (later, caliphate) of Córdoba created a fairly stable polity by a process of balancing off ethnic interests, expressed in frequent uprisings characterized by shifting coalitions of Arab and Berber tribal alliances. These coalitions were typically symmetrical, Arab and Berber moieties pairing off in different combinations, attracting Neo-Muslim groups according to clientage relations. Toward the end of the tenth century the ethnic equilibrium upon which the stability of the Umayyad caliphate had been based was upset by the culmination of the process of conversion of the indigenous population, as well as by the massive influx of Berber tribesmen. The result was the replacement of the unified state by a constellation of smaller polities (the "Party Kingdoms"), organized roughly along ethnic lines, evidenced in the coalition, for example, of Berber-led states against the Arab kingdom of Seville. Such political relationships seem clearly competitive.

Several further observations will make clearer the functioning of ethnic relations in Islamic Spain. First, the Muslim out-groups (Berbers and Neo-Muslims) stressed in their political and social ideologies the universalist, equalitarian tenets of Islam which, in their view, the Arab elite had failed to honor. Examples of such political expressions are the Berber khārijite rebellions of the eighth and ninth centuries and the Neo-Muslim *shu'ūbiyya* movement of the eleventh, the former an equalitarian political crusade, the latter an intellectual campaign to stress the social and cultural equality of non-Arabs with Arabs.

Second, the substantial Arabization of Berbers did not lessen social distance with Arabs nor did the acculturation of Neo-Muslims lessen their feelings of inferiority with regard to the Arab elite. The fall of the caliphate was in part the political expression of the swamping of the Arabs by masses of converts, an added result of which was the coalition of competing groups into two monolithic blocs (Neo-Muslims in terms of numbers, Berbers in terms of military power). The reduction of a number of minor cleavages into one major one rendered the society even more susceptible to social conflict and political instability (see Williams, 1974, p. 59).

Third, the changing structure of the competitive subsystem had repercussions upon the paternalistic subsystem. For example, in the eleventh-century Zirid kingdom of Granada the Berber rulers made common cause with the Jewish middle class, members of which were given high state posts in preference to Arabs (known to be in league with the ruling dynasty of Seville) or to Christians (who had no economic power) (Handler, 1974, pp. 152–157).[2] When the relatively fluid situation of the first half of the eleventh century gave way, in the wake of successive Berber invasions in the latter part of that century, to a sharpening of the cleavage between Berber and other Muslims, owing to the virtual occupation of the country by the former, there ensued a general hardening of attitudes towards the groups in the paternalistic system, whose privileges were attenuated, leading most to emigrate.

It was a striking feature of the dual system of ethnic relations prior to the mid-eleventh century that social and cultural differentiation between groups embedded in different subsystems tended, initially at least, to be minimal, and that the mechanisms that led to increasing differentiation were primarily social and institutional, not economic. For centuries after the Islamic conquest indigenous peoples who converted to Islam (Neo-Muslims) and those who did not (Mozarab Christians) continued in their former ways of life, predominantly that of rural sharecroppers, and participated more or less equally in the burgeoning economies of the great urban centers of southern Spain. Likewise, since Islamic civilization (as distinct from Islamic law) was secular in nature, non-Muslims were able to acculturate to the norms of Arabic culture and participate in it in spite of their communal autonomy (Goitein, 1964, p. 125). Persecution of "protected peoples" came about only at times when the state was unable to carry out the dictates of the law, in contrast to the situation in Christian Spain where repression tended to be an instrument of state policy and whose severity was clearly correlated with economic trends (Ubieto, 1969).

In times of social disorganization in Islamic Spain *dhimmīs* were, on the whole, politically impotent; they could attain political power (as in the case of Granadan Jews) when invited by the ruling elite at whose whim they served and were dismissed, or they could revolt as a means of social protest but with no hope of gaining power. Thus, in the late eighth century many Mozarabs flocked to the banner of the Neo-Muslim Ibn Hafsun, whose Christian and Muslim followers were from the same socioeconomic class and were Romance-speaking or bilingual to the same degree. But when Ibn Hafsun converted to Christianity (the ultimate gesture of defiance) his cause was lost as most of his Neo-Muslim followers deserted him. Neo-Muslims, on the other hand, were able to engage in alliances with Berber and Arab groups to win specific gains: the Neo-Muslim Banu Qasi family ruled on the north-central frontier (the Upper March) for several generations by rallying the support of one Arab moiety against the other (Guichard, 1976, p. 275).

The *dhimmī* arrangement, therefore, involved a legal floor which provided reasonable security for group autonomy and economic activity plus a ceiling which placed definite limits on social mobility. In times of stability the guarantees were enforced without challenge; in times of stress, the discriminatory aspects of the covenant, which rendered subordinate groups politically powerless, were accentuated.

2. *Feudal Spain*

The Christian states that arose to oppose Islamic Spain (Portugal, León, Castile, Navarre, Aragón, Catalonia) generally had ethnically homogeneous Christian majorities until the end of the eleventh century when, as a result of military conquests of Islamic territory, substantial numbers of Muslims and Jews were added to the population. At this point, and for several centuries thereafter, relations with Jewish and Muslim enclaves were conducted according to a model borrowed from that of the "protected peoples" in Islam. As in Islamic Spain, religious minorities were accorded legal safeguards which promised the maintenance of a relatively high degree of enclosure, reinforced by spatial segregation in Jewish and Muslim quarters, a detailed law code which went so far as to require endogamy and religious orthodoxy within the enclaves, and a markedly antisecular ideology which served to reinforce social distance with alien religious groups. The typical Christian regal usage "*our* Jews" is an obvious symbol of the paternalistic mode.

As in the Islamic paternalistic system, there was no question of access to power, either for Jews (primarily an urban mercantile group who, as in Islamic Spain, provided certain technical and economic services for the elite without being permitted to join it) or for Muslims (a rural, sharecropping proletariat with some urban artisan elements). Nevertheless, the following distinctions should be noted: first, the adoption by the Christian elites of the paternalistic norm preceded the incorporation of large numbers of subject Jews and Muslims. Early legal arrangements for autonomous Jewish courts and uniform provisions for the autonomy of Muslim enclaves under the precepts of Islamic law stipulated in treaties of capitulation (see Burns, 1974, pp. 117–138) prove this point.

Second, the legal safeguards, while aping Islamic models, suffered erosion almost from the beginning. Guarantees of autonomy and security for these enclaves were enforced sporadically and often capriciously and in varying degrees of effectiveness. Policies differed from state to state and varied with local economic and demographic situations. In areas where Muslim enclaves were the majority; erosion of legal safeguards and assimilation of free rural cultivators to the status of feudal serfs seems to have been retarded. In all areas, pressure for conversion and assimilation continually increased and, with it, the potential for conflict. The directionality of such conflicts is significant. Muslim enclaves rose in revolt, frequently at first and decreasingly thereafter, as their numbers and power waned through repression and emigration (Burns, 1961). Pogroms against

Jews increased in frequency and intensity as their economic power grew, until finally they were expelled in 1492. The revolt and repression cycle characteristic of the Muslim enclaves fits the paternalistic model. Increasing Christian violence against Jews is indicative of a modal shift, analyzed below.

*Christian* minorities culturally differentiated from the general Christian population held an ambivalent status and were assimilated to the paternalistic model in direct relation to the degree of cultural distance. Note the three following examples: (1) in legal proceedings in Navarre, monolingual Basque speakers were allowed to plead in Basque and seem not to have suffered any social or economic disability. (2) Substantial colonies of French (and other foreign settlers generically called *francos*) in Navarre, Castile, and Aragón were settled in segregated quarters of towns, given substantial administrative and judicial autonomy, and their intermingling with natives was circumscribed. Yet their access to wealth and power (in the church hierarchy, for example) was not impeded and their acculturation (which in some instances took up to two centuries to complete) brought full assimilation. (3) The group exhibiting the highest degree of cultural differentiation, the Arabized Christians of eleventh- and twelfth-century Toledo suffered severe discrimination economically; they were barred from civil and ecclesiastical preferment (Pastor de Togneri, 1973); and they were the victims of racially-tinged bias due to their supposed admixture of infidel blood, as in the popular medieval etymology of *mozárabes* from *mixti arabes* (Colbert, 1962, pp. 20–21).

3. *Imperial Spain*

Toward the end of the medieval period Jewish-Christian relations began to move away from a paternalistic model and to approach a competitive one. The change is obvious in the anti-Jewish pogroms of 1391 (Wolff, 1971), a classic status panic in which lower-class Christians vented their resentment against the success of middle-class Jews. The shift is confirmed in the fifteenth century as substantial class differentiation within the Jewish caste was achieved, both through economic and demographic gains and through the emergence of a powerful group of converts to Christianity *(Conversos)* who maintained familial and business ties with the Jewish community.

After the expulsion of the Jews in 1492, a substantial Converso group, numbering in the hundreds of thousands, remained. Having become Christians voluntarily (although some, in secret, remained practicing Jews) this group moved into a wholly competitive situation as it sought the acceptance that canon law guaranteed them. The action of the Inquisition, ostensibly to root out remaining pockets of "Judaizers" but in actuality a campaign to break the substantial economic and political power of

Conversos (Kamen, 1965), supported by the infamous statutes of blood purity *(limpieza de sangre)* which prevented participation by those of "unclean blood" in civil, military, and ecclesiastical corporations, betrayed the elite's ambivalence toward the Conversos. In effect, this group, already highly acculturated, was obliged to join "Old Christian" society so long as it did not seek entrance into the elite. Thus the lessening of cultural distance (acculturation) did not lead to the lessening of social distance (assimilation) and the Conversos were just as much a caste in the sixteenth and seventeenth centuries as Jews had been previously. The difference was that the mode of intergroup relations had changed from paternalistic to competitive and, as a result, different mechanisms for maintaining group boundaries and social distance became salient. Gutiérrez Nieto (1973, p. 539) shows that the *limpieza* statutes were first applied by the nobility in order to break the political power of the middle class (of which the Conversos were the most dynamic sector); towards the end of the sixteenth century the same mechanism was used against Converso elements in the lower nobility. Ethnic differentiation was no longer an issue, and racialist arguments were used to justify the ostracism of a class whose main distinction was economic and intellectual success.

The encompassing of the Conversos within a competitive system of ethnic relations was not matched by the surviving Muslim enclave, called Moriscos after 1492. These Moriscos, also numbering in the hundreds of thousands, overwhelmingly rural cultivators, refused to abjure their religion or culture in the face of increasing formal pressures by the state. Forbidden to speak Arabic or to have Arabic names, to wear distinctive dress, or to engage in traditional secular customs, they were forcibly converted en masse, provoking a series of rebellions. In spite of all, their cultural boundaries remained high, and they were finally expelled to North Africa in the early seventeenth century. That some of the forced emigrants were accompanied to the points of embarkation by their Christian lords (who had ruled them as feudal serfs) is a fitting enough symbol of the persistence of paternalistic relations until the end.

The ethnic picture of Imperial Spain is completed by a small exotic group, the Gypsies, generally assimilated to the status of Moriscos whom they resembled socioeconomically and, to the extent that elements of the Morisco population were swarthy, somatically. In spite of all manner of formal pressures to assimilation and acculturation directed against them (in tone and in content modeled after anti-Morisco legislation), Gypsies nevertheless escaped both social assimilation and expulsion, doubtless because of their insignificant numbers, their highly specialized and useful economic roles (tinkering, animal-clipping, entertaining, and smuggling, which was important in view of the archaic system of internal customs barriers), their willingness to make an exaggerated display of Catholic orthodoxy, and the concomitant willingness of a bemused elite to put up with an exotic group (see Hoetink, 1971, pp. 128–129) without feeling threatened. The survival of the Gypsies clarifies certain points about the Moriscos, who were demographically threatening, who competed for food and other resources in times of scarcity, and who were unyielding in their opposition to the dominant religion.

## CONCLUSIONS

### 1. *Emergence and Stabilization of Ethnic Systems*

The question of the emergence and stabilization of systems of ethnic relations is a matter of considerable theoretical importance, since one body of theory posits that conflict over resources precedes and, to a certain extent, accounts for ethnocentric behavior, while another posits a reversed causal sequence (Levine and Campbell, 1972, pp. 214–215). In the cases of Islamic and medieval Christian Spain, norms of conduct towards religious and ethnic minorities were crystalized in the superordinate culture before specific economic arrangements were worked out. In the same way that societies have "somatic norm images" which regulate racial attitudes (Hoetink, 1971, p. 120) they may also have general norms regarding conduct toward ethnically or religiously differentiated groups well in mind before contact occurs.[3] In both Islamic and Christian Spain the only way a group in a paternalistic subsystem could shift to the competitive mode was by conversion.

The paternalistic norm of ethnic and racial relations as it developed in medieval Christian Spain was that which subsequently governed relations with newly encountered ethnic and racial groups in Africa and Spanish America.[4]

In competitive systems, however, ethnic relations are much more sensitive to power variables and initial norms can well change in response to alterations—demographic, political-military, or economic—in the ethnic balance of power.

### 2. *Adjustment and Stability*

*(a) Islamic Spain.* In the paternalistic system, stability was generally assured by making relations between superordinates and subordinates part of canon law (which in the Islamic world is not distinguished from civil law). Canonically-sanctioned norms underwrote consensus among all groups by making their observance a religious duty incumbent upon Muslims. Conflict most typically occurred when the "protected peoples" overstepped the bounds of the covenant (e.g., by dropping the pose of

religious passivity, as with the ninth-century martyrs of Córdoba, or by assuming unwonted power over Muslims, as did certain Jewish court officials), thereby abrogating the right to protection. In the competitive system, unstable equilibria were achieved through the constant testing of the relative power of each group, with consequent adjustment in cultural norms of interaction.

*(b) Feudal Spain.* Although officially the paternalistic model was adopted in full, the superordinates from the beginning were ambivalent in its execution. Privileges tended to be awarded or withdrawn in return for services rendered or anticipated. In general terms, economic dependence upon the minorities worked to preserve the positive aspect of the *dhimmī* model, while the growing nationalism and militant religiosity of Christians worked in the opposite direction. The policy of rulers varied pragmatically: where Muslim cultivators were needed to preserve the rural economy, they were encouraged to remain (Torres Fontes, 1971, p. 12); if not, they were expelled, particularly if rebellious (Burns, 1961; Ubieto, 1969, pp. 134–135). The same was true of Jews, an urban group whose success in getting the Christians to honor their statutory autonomy was a function of their economic services to the elite. Persecutions of Jews (competitive forms of aggression; status panics) and uprisings (paternalistic, "slave rebellions") by Muslims were frequent and easily correlated to periods of economic recession (Ubieto, 1969, p. 7).

*(c) Imperial Spain.* Since communal autonomy was now forbidden, stability was a function of accommodation by ethnic enclaves to ever more stringent pressures toward acculturation. The process worked differently according to the system of relations. In the competitive system (Conversos/Old Christians) the state used repression (the Inquisition) to achieve both a cultural goal (the obliteration of remaining Jewish traces among Conversos) and a socioeconomic one (the barring of Converso entrance to the elite). In the paternalistic system (Morisco/Old Christian) the typical pattern of violence from below and repression from above continued as Moriscos more and more came to approximate a plantation slave class. Yet their cultural boundaries remained high (resistance to conversion), doubtless because they were settled in compact, generally isolated, rural communities and thus were able to preserve a high degree of social cohesion, while the Conversos were fractionated socially and lived dispersed throughout urban neighborhoods. Moreover, in true paternalistic fashion Moriscos were protected by their lords from excesses of church and state, whereas Conversos had no such protectors but were in direct competition with the Old Christian elite.

*3. Ideological Ambivalence*

Schermerhorn (1970, p. 193) suggests that modal shifts in intergroup relations are more dependent on ideological shifts in the subordinate, rather than the superordinate group. On the whole, our evidence bears this out: conversion is the prime example.

Yet in Christian Spain, first in the medieval period and then more markedly in the sixteenth century, superordinate ideology played a significant role in changing ethnic relations. Even when norms of ethnic relations were fixed by custom and institutionalized in law, allowance must still be made for oscillation between ideological poles or for ambivalence. Frequently, as in Imperial Spain, superordinates were ambivalent with regard to a segregationist policy, even to the point of attempting both segregation and integration, either at the same time or in oscillating spurts. (The similarity to Russian/Jewish or American white/black relations is striking.) Moreover, the nature of the ambivalence (the mix of types) will differ depending upon the modal type of intergroup relations: if competitive, the emphasis will be on acculturation, with restrictions on the upward limit of mobility; if paternalistic, the emphasis will be on social segregation and ostracism, but with simultaneous efforts to break down cultural boundaries.

*4. Systemic Interdependence*

To what extent can the differences in the functioning of the two systems of ethnic relations here described be attributed to the general level of socioeconomic integration of the societies in question? If one considers Islamic Spain as an urban artisanal society; medieval Christian Spain (until around 1250 at least) as a static agrarian (feudal) society; and Imperial Spain as a nationalist, mercantile capitalist society, do these broad modes of socioeconomic organization affect modalities of ethnic relations? When one considers that protonationalist Castile, on the threshold of imperial expansion, adopted anti-Jewish strictures formulated by the Visigoths, an extreme example of a static agrarian society, one must doubt the influence of the socioeconomic structure on specific norms of ethnic relations. In paternalistic relations, the governing norms were susceptible to reinforcement by economic trends, but not to change. In competitive ethnic relations, however, the long-term trend in the cases discussed was for competition to move from the political-military arena increasingly into an economic context. The norms remained the same, but they were operationalized more in consonance with capitalistic values.

In summary, the way in which ethnocentrism is institutionalized by superordinates is independent of the gross economic structure, but interacts with it to determine the permissible ceilings of economic and social mobility accorded to subordinate groups.

On the basis of the above discussion, the following generalizations can be made about competitive and paternalistic systems of ethnic relations in the three cases examined:

1. Both competitive and paternalistic systems may operate in the same society simultaneously, but by involving different kinds of cleavages, e.g., competitive relations among culturally or socially differentiated members of the same religion; paternalistic relations between members of the religious majority and minorities.

2. Groups within the same society, sharing similar socioeconomic status and certain common cultural traits, may be embedded in different systems of ethnic relations, e.g.: in Islamic Spain, Neo-Muslims in a competitive, Mozarabs in a paternalistic relationship with Arabs.

3. In cases with both types of intergroup relations the out-groups in the competitive system will have an institutionalized right to a share of political power, while those in the paternalistic system will not.

4. Preexisting ethnocentrism defines the norms of relations between two or more groups coming into contact, just as contact generates further definition to ethnocentrism.

5. Conflict will result if the accommodation sought by the superordinates is not congruent with the expectations of the subordinates (Schermerhorn, 1970, p. 83); if expectations of superordinates and subordinates are congruent, a stable modus vivendi will be reached.

6. To the extent that such accommodation requires acculturation of the subordinate to the superordinate culture:
   (a) acculturation will not lead to social assimilation in a paternalistic system where subordinates are legally denied access to power.
   (b) acculturation will be a prerequisite of assimilation in competitive systems, but will not lead to reduction of social distance so long as the subordinate group is regarded as a social, economic, or political threat to superordinates.

7. A shift from paternalistic to competitive modes may result from:
   (a) adoption by the superordinates of an equalitarian ideology;
   (b) an administrative fiat designed to do away with a minority considered unassimilable (e.g., forced conversion);
   (c) adherence by the subordinate group to one or more of the superordinates' prerequisites for membership;
   (d) status differentiation within a subordinate group that has the result of bringing its upwardly mobile members into direct competition with, or superiority over, substantial members of the dominant caste.

8. A shift from paternalistic to competitive modes inevitably involves ideological ambivalence on the part of superordinates arising from:

(a) an unwillingness to validate the acculturation of a lower caste owing to resentment of socioeconomic competition (see Broom and Kitsuse, 1955);
(b) difficulty in shedding stereotypes and biases formed in the period of paternalistic relations.

## FOOTNOTES

*Thomas F. Glick is Associate Professor of History and Geography at Boston University. He has written extensively on cultural contact and diffusion in medieval Spain and has recently finished a Comparative History of Islamic and Christian Spain, 711–1250.

An earlier version of this paper was presented at a session on comparative social systems, American Sociological Association, San Francisco, August 1975. Criticism of earlier drafts by Professor Joseph Lopreato is gratefully acknowledged.

1. Van den Berghe (1970, p. 27) indicates the existence of societies where the two modal types coexist, citing the case of Jews as a competitive element in paternalistic (that is, feudal) Europe of the Middle Ages. It is more likely that medieval Jews, whether in Europe or in the Islamic world, were embedded in paternalistic systems of ethnic relations. The comparison with feudal society seems to me to be mixing units of analysis (class versus ethnic units).

2. Notice symbiotic relations between Berbers and Jews in modern Morocco, a society with the typical Islamic system of dual ethnic structures (Rosen, 1973, p. 161).

3. All the ethnic groups here considered perceived ethnic differences, at least in part, as somatic, and ethnicity was confused with race. The vast majority of the participants in interethnic struggles in premodern Spain—Muslims, Jews, and Christians alike—were all descended from Hispano-Romans. Of the major exogamous group, the Berbers, many individuals were fairhaired and blue-eyed.

4. The point is made explicitly by Rumeu de Armas (1967) who compares Christian attitudes toward medieval "infidels" (Jews and Muslims) with those later held toward African and American "Neo-Infidels"; and by Duviols (1971, pp. 176–177) who compares Spaniards' treatment of Peruvian Indians with their contemporaneous campaign against Moriscos.

## REFERENCES

Broom, L. and Kitsuse, J. I. (1955) "The Validation of Acculturation: A Condition to Ethnic Assimilation." *American Anthropologist* 57:44–48.

Burns, Robert I. (1961) "Social Riots on the Christian-Moslem Frontier (Thirteenth-Century Valencia)." *American Historical Review* 66:378–400.

——— (1974) *Islam under the Crusaders: Colonial Survival in the Thirteenth-Century Kingdom of Valencia.* Princeton: Princeton University Press.

Castro, Américo (1954) *The Structure of Spanish History.* Princeton: Princeton University Press.

——— (1971) *The Spaniards.* Berkeley: University of California Press.

Colbert, E. P. (1962) *The Martyrs of Córdoba (850–859): A Study of the Sources.* Washington, DC: The Catholic University of America Press.

Duviols, Pierre (1971) *La lutte contre les religions autochtones dans le Pérou colonial: l'Extirpation de l'idolâtrie entre 1532 et 1660*. Paris: Ophrys.

Goitein, S. D. (1964) *Jews and Arabs*. New York: Schocken.

——— (1971) *A Mediterranean Society*, Volume 2. Berkeley: University of California Press.

Goldziher, Ignace (1963–1964) "The Spanish Arabs and Islam." *Muslim World* 53:5–18, 91–100, 178–184, 281–286; 54:27–38.

Guichard, Pierre (1976) *Al-Andalus: Estructura antropológica de una sociedad islámica en occidente*. Barcelona: Barral.

Gutiérrez Nieto, José Ignacio (1973) "La estructura castizo-estamental de la sociedad casttellana del siglo XVI," *Hispania* 33:519–563.

Handler, Andrew (1974) *The Zirids of Granada*. Coral Gables: University of Florida Press.

Hoetink,H. (1971) *Caribbean Race Relations: A Study of Two Variants*. London: Oxford University Press.

Kamen, Henry (1965) *The Spanish Inquisition*. New York: New American Library.

Levine, Robert A. and Campbell, Donald T. (1972) *Ethnocentrism: Theories of Conflict, Ethnic Attitudes and Group Behavior*. New York: Wiley.

Noel, Donald L. (1968–1969) "A Theory of the Origin of Ethnic Stratification." *Social Problems* 16:157–172.

Pastor de Togneri, Reyna (1973) "Problemas de la asimilación de una minoría: los mozárabes de Toledo." Pages 197–266 in *Conflictos sociales y estanciamento económico en la España medieval*. Barcelona: Ariel.

Rosen, Lawrence (1973) "The Social and Conceptual Framework of Arab-Berber Relations in Central Morocco." Pages 155–173 in Ernest Gellner and Charles Micaud (eds.), *Arabs and Berbers*. London: Duckworth.

Rumeu de Armas, Antonio (1967) "Los problemas derivados del contacto de razas en los albores del Renacimiento." *Cuadernos de historia: Anexos de la revista Hispania* 1:61–103.

Schermerhorn, R. A. (1970) *Comparative Ethnic Relations: A Framework for Theory and Research*. New York: Random House.

Torres Fontes, Juan (1971) *Repartimiento de la huerta y el campo de Murcia en el siglo XIII*. Murcia: Academia Alfonso X el Sabio.

Ubieto, A. (1969) *Ciclos económicos en la edad media española*. Valencia: Anubar.

van den Berghe, Pierre L. (1970) "Paternalistic versus Competitive Race Relations: An Ideal-Type Approach." Pages 21–41 in *Race and Ethnicity*. New York: Basic Books.

Williams, Robin M., Jr. (1947) *The Reduction of Intergroup Tensions*. New York: Social Science Research Council.

Wolff, Philippe (1971) "The 1391 Pogrom in Spain: Social Crisis or Not?" *Past and Present* No. 50:4–18.

# VALUE PRIORITIES, LIFE SATISFACTION, AND POLITICAL DISSATISFACTION AMONG WESTERN PUBLICS

Ronald Inglehart*

## VALUES AND SATISFACTION: SOME PARADOXES

During the 1950s and early 1960s, one of the key concepts underpinning belief in the decline of ideology and sharp political conflict was the assumption that the more people have, the more satisfied they are. Rising levels of economic welfare, therefore, should lead to rising levels of public satisfaction. This assumption appeared to be based on robust common sense; everyone *knows* that when you get something, you feel better off than when you didn't have it.

Yet by the late 1960s it was apparent that something was wrong. The

**Comparative Studies in Sociology—Vol. 1, 1978, pages 173–202**

**ISBN 0-89232-025-7**

traditional principles of welfare economics didn't seem to be working; never before had Western publics had so much material welfare, as measured by all objective indicators—yet not since the 1930s had there been so much manifest discontent. These circumstances led to an increasing awareness of the need to understand and somehow measure *subjective* well-being, in addition to the usual economic indicators.

As Abrams (1973, p. 35) pointed out, "Before the mid 1960's such phrases as social indicators, social reporting, social accounts, and quality of life were almost entirely absent from the vocabulary of either social scientists or politicians." For decades, it was considered self-evident that a high rate of economic growth was the ultimate justification of a regime; accordingly, the implicit criterion for judging the contest between Western and Soviet systems had been, "Which one produces the highest rate of economic and technological growth?" A high gross national product per capita was the index of the good society, supplemented by such subsidiary indicators as the number of telephones, automobiles, and hospital beds per capita and the amount of energy consumed per capita. Today a concern with the subjective aspects of human welfare has become widespread. Research on subjective social indicators has been undertaken in at least eight Western nations and by the European Community (Bradburn, 1969; Campbell et al., 1976; Andrews and Withey, 1976; Strumpel, 1974; Allardt, 1973; Gurin et al., 1960). In 1974 the French government recognized the importance of the noneconomic side of welfare by creating a ministry responsible for the "Quality of Life."

This growing concern with nonmaterial welfare seems to reflect a changing emphasis among the criteria by which Western publics gauge their satisfaction: it seems to be a symptom of a process of value change. For the relationship between objective need-satisfaction and subjective satisfaction is conditioned by the aspiration levels and the values of the people concerned. The aspirations and values of Western peoples seem to be changing, with Materialist values giving way to post-Materialist values: there is a gradual shift from emphasis on economic and physical security above all, toward greater emphasis on the sense of belonging and esteem, and on intellectual and esthetic satisfaction. The theory underlying this hypothesis and a mass of supporting evidence have been presented in Inglehart (1977). The basic idea, in a nutshell, is that people have a variety of needs and give most attention to those they feel are in short supply. The generation born after World War II, having been raised during a period of unprecedented prosperity, tend to give relatively high priority to nonmaterial goals; their parents and grandparents, having experienced hunger and turmoil during their formative years, remain likely to emphasize economic and physical security.

This hypothesis implies that post-Materialists have only recently emerged in significant numbers. Even now they probably constitute a distinct minority of the populations of Western countries. Thus post-Materialists are likely to be somewhat at odds with the type of society in which they live. For the arrangements and institutions of industrial society are based on Materialist assumptions. On the whole, Western nations have been reasonably successful in achieving economic growth during the past couple of decades, but they have given relatively little emphasis to attaining post-Materialist goals. Consequently, despite their relatively favored objective circumstances, post-Materialists may tend to be relatively dissatisfied with their political systems; at the same time, economic gains have reached a point of diminishing returns for this group. Thus, objective need satisfaction can not be equated with subjective satisfaction in any simple fashion; instead, the two have a relationship which is loose at best, and sometimes seems counter-intuitive.

A recent study by Marsh (1975) illustrates the complexity of the interaction between external conditions, values, and subjective satisfaction. Analyzing a 1971 British survey that included my index of Materialist/post-Materialist value priorities he finds that the post-Materialists did *not* express higher levels of subjective satisfaction than did the Materialists.[1] This finding is anything but obvious for (as both Marsh and I find) the post-Materialists have substantially higher levels of income and education and more desirable jobs. Nevertheless, as Marsh demonstrates, the post-Materialists are no more satisfied with their lives as a whole, or even with the specifically economic aspects of their lives than the Materialists. At first glance, this might seem to be a telling blow to any interpretation based on the concept of need-satisfaction. For I have argued that the post-Materialists have distinctive goals because their lower-order needs have been relatively well satisfied. Doesn't it follow, therefore, that they should express relatively great satisfaction with their incomes, housing, jobs, health and so forth?

The answer is, No. The assumption that they would, rests on an understandable but crucial error: the failure to distinguish between *objective* need satisfaction and *subjective* satisfaction. As we shall see in a moment, a growing body of evidence indicates that the relationship between the two is surprisingly loose, and the tendency to equate them can be grossly misleading.

The need-satisfaction model postulates that human beings are goal-seeking organisms who pursue one goal after another in a more or less predictable order, starting with those which are most crucial to physiological survival; if a given need is satisfied, they tend to move on to pursuit of other "higher-order" needs. It may seem reasonable to assume (as Marsh does) that those who have attained satisfaction of the needs for economic and physical security would be likely to express relatively great *subjective* satisfaction with these domains. But *would* they? The need-satisfaction model states that those who have attained *objective* satisfaction of a given set of needs will, after a time, shift their priorities, giving greater attention to the pursuit of other needs—not that they would necessarily manifest relatively great *subjective* satisfaction concerning the "lower-order" domains. In the short run, one probably *would* express great satisfaction in regard to a need which has just been fulfilled: a man lost in a desert is, no doubt, delighted when he finally reaches water. But in an environment where water is, and always has been plentiful, would we expect that fact to give rise to continuous expressions of doubt? Hardly. In the long run people would take an adequate water supply for granted and ignore it—or even begin to complain about how it tastes.

In other words, we must distinguish between the short-term effects and the long-term effects of objective need satisfaction. As Maslow (1970, p. xv) put it, "What I have observed is that need gratifications lead to only temporary happiness which in turn tends to be succeeded by another and (hopefully) higher discontent." In the short run, gratification of a given need does lead to increased subjective satisfaction; in the long run, it does not. And my hypotheses about intergenerational value change are, quite explicitly, concerned with long-term effects. They imply that "post-Materialist" value priorities will be found mainly among those who have experienced economic and physical security for a "long" period of time—that is, throughout their formative years. In short, the post-Materialists are post-Materialist partly because they do *not* experience relatively great subjective satisfaction from their relatively favorable material conditions.

Why do the post-Materialists—who are better off than other groups by almost any objective criterion—fail to show higher overall satisfaction levels? This phenomenon seems to constitute part of a broader picture. For our concept of the relationship between objective conditions, value priorities, and subjective satisfaction suggests that overall satisfaction levels tend to be roughly constant not only across value types, but across *any* set of social categories having stable membership. Let us spell out the hypotheses which lead to this conclusion.

## VALUES, ASPIRATIONS, AND SATISFACTION IN RELATION TO ONE'S ENVIRONMENT

We view man as a goal-seeking organism, similar to any other animal in his pursuit of biological survival, but unique in his adaptability and in the wide range of nonphysiological goals he pursues. He can survive from the equator to the Arctic; his goals range from food and oxygen, to knowledge and beauty. Paradoxically, this immensely varied activity is regulated by a drive for inner homeostasis. Like other animals, man seeks to maintain a constant percentage of water in the body, a constant percentage of oxygen and sugar in the blood. When this inner balance is upset, he strives to either reposition himself in the environment or change the environment in ways that redress the balance.

Man's pursuit of nonmaterial goals seems to work in an analogous fashion. Subjective satisfaction or dissatisfaction help guide the conscious pursuit of man's varying needs in somewhat the same way as sensations of pleasure and pain help direct one toward physiological survival. Gratification of either material or nonmaterial needs produces a sense of subjective satisfaction, but it persists for only a limited time. Eventually, the salience of these needs declines and new sources of dissatisfaction become important. The net result is that, in the long run, one's overall sense of subjective satisfaction tends toward homeostasis.

Though everyone seeks "happiness," or a sense of "overall satisfaction," they are elusive, for satisfaction reflects a continually moving balance. Nevertheless, people are aware of being satisfied or dissatisfied at a given moment and can report these feelings. Analysis of such reports indicate that one's sense of overall satisfaction reflects a weighted average of satisfaction in all those domains that are important to the given individual. But the weights vary from individual to individual and, probably, from culture to culture. Hence, a sense of overall satisfaction does not automatically result from obtaining optimal physiological conditions. In any society, social, intellectual and esthetic needs also seem to be present. Insofar as such needs are emphasized, they can also have an important bearing on one's subjective frustration or satisfaction.

Thus, the balance between needs or aspirations, on one hand, and fulfillment on the other, is continually being upset and readjusted. An extremely high or low level of satisfaction is inherently a short-term characteristic. Satisfaction of a given need can provide intense pleasure; but in time one aspires to more, or to different things. In the long run, people adjust their nonphysiological needs or aspirations to external conditions.

Hence one is apt to find surprisingly little variation between the overall satisfaction levels of large groups in a given society. There is nothing inevitable about this phenomenon. It is simply the most probable outcome, given the assumption that one's aspirations tend to adapt to structural or long-term differences in external conditions. In any society, certain groups suffer from structural advantages or disadvantages. Provided that the differences in objective circumstances *are* stable—and that membership in the group is stable—aspiration levels have sufficient time to adjust to external conditions.

Short-term variation also occurs, of course: at any given moment, some people have recently done better than usual and some have done worse. But when we compare large groups, the effects of short-term variation are likely to cancel out. Does this mean that *all* short-term variation simply vanishes at the group level? Of course not. One can conceive of certain events that might suddenly raise or lower the satisfaction level of large groups of people. But those events that come to mind most readily—such as war or economic or political collapse—are apt to have their impact on an entire nation (or even several nations). Thus they could cause large changes in the satisfaction level of a given nation from one year to the next; or could bring about large disparities between one nation and another; but any given national cross-section might show little variation between social groups. The adjustment of one's aspirations to one's circumstances is never perfect; those with lower incomes and less education *are* less satisfied with their incomes and education than those who are objectively better off. But (as we shall see) the differences are smaller than one might expect; and, since post-Materialists tend to be relatively sensitive to the noneconomic shortcomings of advanced industrial society, this may lower their *overall* satisfaction levels to, or even below, the national mean.

We will undertake an empirical test of those ideas in the following section. Before doing so, let us summarize our argument. We hypothesize that:

1. Satisfaction tends to be generalized. People have a sense of overall satisfaction, which can be viewed as a weighted average of satisfaction with each of the various aspects of life that are important to the given individual.
2. One's satisfaction level is determined by the size of the gap between:
   a. one's perception of his or her current situation; and
   b. one's level of aspirations.
3. Aspiration levels gradually adjust to one's circumstances. People adjust them in two ways:
   a. By aspiring to more or less of the *same* things: one's aspirations rise with prosperity and gradually fall with adversity;
   b. By shifting emphasis to *different* domains: in other words, through change in one's value priorities. This type of adjustment is even more gradual than the former one. Once he or she has reached adulthood, a given individual's aspirations may be firmly linked to certain types of goals; for a society as a whole, a shift of emphasis from one domain to another may be largely a matter of intergenerational value change.

4. Thus, satisfaction levels vary a great deal from one individual to another, but this variance largely reflects the impact of recent changes. Ordinarily, there will be little variation across any social categories having stable long-term membership:
   a. Short-term effects tend to cancel out because those who have had favorable recent experiences are likely to be balanced off by those who have had unfavorable recent experiences, in any large sample.
   b. Structural differences tend to be offset by the fact that aspiration levels gradually adjust to *long-term* differences in objective circumstances.

Sex, for example, is a very stable characteristic. Consequently, aspiration levels have time to adjust to long-term differences in the objective circumstances of the sexes. One's income level, on the other hand, is only moderately stable. Any population sample is almost certain to contain people whose income level has recently improved or deteriorated, causing satisfaction with their incomes (and, to a lesser extent, with their lives as a whole) to vary accordingly. Since those who gained are simultaneously moving upward from one income category to another *and* from one satisfaction level to another, income and satisfaction will be correlated. Thus, one will find more variation in satisfaction levels according to income than according to sex: one's income category can fluctuate while one's sex ordinarily does not. In general, the more stable the characteristic, the less variation in satisfaction associated with it. Subjective satisfaction *is* affected by external conditions, hence there is considerable variation from individual to individual—but one will ordinarily observe only a modest amount of variation between groups having a stable membership. And there will be even less variation in *overall* satisfaction than in satisfaction with specific domains. Recent changes in a given domain may affect one's satisfaction with that aspect of life—but the impact is likely to be small when averaged in with all the domains that affect satisfaction with one's life as a whole.

Short-term changes can raise or lower overall satisfaction levels—but only for a limited time. Satisfaction of one set of needs eventually leads to increased emphasis on another set of needs—which in the long run may become a source of subjective discontent just as severe as that engendered by earlier, more material needs. Overall internal satisfaction necessarily remains roughly constant in the long run: if it were otherwise, enduring prosperity would cause goal-seeking activity to cease, for lack of inner motivation.

## INTER-GROUP VARIATION IN OVERALL LIFE SATISFACTION

*Does* overall subjective satisfaction tend to remain roughly constant across social groups? A set of surveys carried out in the nine European Community countries in 1973 contains a series of items designed to tap satisfaction in a variety of domains.[2] We will use them to test whether satisfaction levels tend to remain roughly constant across the categories of any relatively stable social characteristic.

The 1973 surveys inquired about each public's satisfaction in twelve different domains. Factor analysis of these results indicated that given individuals tend to show either relatively high or relatively low levels of satisfaction in *all* domains; the results are shown in Table 1.

The first factor clearly taps an overall satisfaction dimension. The highest-loading item concerns satisfaction with "your life as a whole," which shows a loading of 0.722. But all twelve of the domains have loadings of at least 0.400 on this factor. It seems that satisfaction tends to be generalized, as was suggested above. The first factor explains 32 percent of the total variance—a substantial amount, but we must allow for the fact that part of it is almost certainly due to response set. For these questions constituted a series of consecutive items in uniform format, with a fixed set of possible responses ranging from "very satisfied" to "very dissatisfied." This may be a quick and economical way to ask a battery of questions but it is also a classic situation in which response set is likely to

*Table 1.* Dimensions of Subjective Satisfaction in Nine European Countries, 1973.

(Loadings above 0.300 in conventional factor analysis).

| First Factor: Overall Satisfaction (32 percent of variance) | | Second Factor Socio-Political Satisfaction (10 percent of variance) | |
|---|---|---|---|
| Life as a whole | 0.722 | How democracy functions in (Britain) | 0.625 |
| Leisure time | 0.622 | Kind of society in which live | 0.580 |
| Personal income | 0.616 | Relations between generations | 0.393 |
| Work-at job, home, school | 0.613 | Work-at job, home school | −0.342 |
| Kind of society in which live | 0.577 | | |
| Relations with others | 0.572 | | |
| House, apartment in which live | 0.551 | | |
| Education for children | 0.538 | | |
| How democracy functions in (Britain) | 0.518 | | |
| Relations between generations | 0.486 | | |
| Social welfare benefits | 0.479 | | |
| Respect people give you | 0.406 | | |

become significant, with certain respondents giving relatively satisfied replies to item after item—replies which reflect their general mood as much as their appraisal of each specific item. There are various ways to adjust for the effects of response set. One way is to calculate each individual's mean score in response to *all* the items in the set, and then determine how far above or below this base line his response to given items falls. When we do so, we find a very interesting pattern: controlling for response set, the post-Materialists prove to be significantly *more* satisfied with their incomes and jobs than the Materialists; conversely (as we shall see in more detail below) they are significantly *less* satisfied with certain higher-order domains than the Materialists. This reversal of one of Marsh's findings reflects the fact that his post-Materialists were less satisfied with life *in general* than were his Materialists.

Regardless of whether or not we control for response set, we find positive correlations between satisfaction ratings from one domain to another. Consequently, we obtain an "Overall Satisfaction" dimension more or less similar to the one in Table 1. Separate country-by-country analyses were also performed. With minor exceptions, they show a pattern similar to that of Table 1. Satisfaction or dissatisfaction in the domains that are most important to a given individual seem to influence one's scores in other domains; the net result tends to be summed up by one's satisfaction with "your life as a whole."

On the basis of these analyses, an index of overall satisfaction was constructed.[3] Using this index as our dependent variable, we then tried to "explain" relative levels of satisfaction, using the following social background variables: age, sex, income, occupation, education, religious denomination, church attendance, political party identification, political information, labor union membership, region, size of community in which the respondent lives, and value type. We used the OSIRIS II Multiple Classification Analysis for this purpose (Sonquist, 1971). Satisfaction levels *do* vary according to these background characteristics and there are some interesting cross-national differences concerning which predictor variables do most to "explain" it. Similarly, subjective satisfaction varies a good deal from individual to individual. Our respondents' scores cover the range from 1 to 13; the former indicates that one is "very dissatisfied" with one's income, work, leisure and life as a whole; the latter score indicates that one is "very satisfied" with all four. The mean score for the nine-nation sample as a whole is 8.8 (somewhat above the neutral point, which is 7.0); and the standard deviations range from a low of 1.9 in Denmark, to a high of 2.4 in Ireland, with France, Belgium, Italy and Britain all clustered at 2.3.

Let us examine the actual distribution of overall satisfaction in nine Western countries. The most striking finding which emerges from multivariate analysis of data from each of the nine countries is the surprisingly small amount of variance which can be explained by social background characteristics. Across these nations, an average of only ten percent of the variance in satisfaction scores can be explained by the combined effects of all our social background variables. Let us emphasize that we have gone out of our way to use a dependent variable which shows relatively *strong* relationships with social background. Our index of "Overall Satisfaction" is based on one's satisfaction with the four highest-loading domains in Table 1. Two of these items ask, respectively, about satisfaction with one's income and with one's job. Income and occupation are among the predictor variables used in our model and they *do* correlate in the expected direction with satisfaction in these specific domains. This, of course, tends to inflate the amount of variance explained. When we use the best single indicator of "Overall Satisfaction"—"satisfaction with one's life as a whole"—as the dependent variable, our social background variables explain, on the average, only *six* percent of the variance. In other words, there is a tendency for satisfaction levels to remain constant—not only across value type, as Marsh found, but also across all of the *other* social characteristics used in our analyses. This pattern may seem astonishing but it is confirmed by results reported in other recent studies of subjective satisfaction and the perceived "Quality of Life" (Campbell, et al., 1976; Allardt, 1973; Andrews and Withey, 1974).

There are a variety of possible explanations for this striking lack of variance in levels of overall satisfaction according to age, sex, income, education, religion, and so forth. One explanation might be that our items simply do not do a very good job of measuring subjective satisfaction. Yet they seem straightforward enough, and most of them are based on items which have been widely used and tested. Another explanation might be that no real attitude exists to be measured here: in response to questions about which they know or care very little, people sometimes give meaningless answers, more or less at random. Such responses would tend to show null relationships with social background characteristics. But surely, people must know and care whether they are satisfied with their own incomes, leisure, work, and life in general; these are immediate concerns which involve them directly. One indication that a question seems remote or meaningless to one's respondents is an abnormally high nonresponse rate—sometimes running as high as 30 percent of a sample. But nonresponse rates here were extremely *low*—averaging less than four percent regarding one's income, leisure, and work, and less than *one* percent regarding one's life as a whole. Western publics seem to have very little difficulty in answering these questions. Still another explanation might be that we have simply failed to find the *right* predictor variables: some other aspect of one's background or environment which we have not measured might provide a much stronger explanation of one's level of satisfaction. Perhaps; one never knows until one tries. We can only say that we have combed through the variables available in the European Community surveys—using various combinations suggested by hypotheses of status inconsistency—without obtaining greatly differing results. The predictors employed here are standard, widely-used variables which have generally proven to be effective in explaining attitudes—but they explain little variance in overall satisfaction.[4]

Although our analyses show surprisingly little explained variance within given nations, nationality itself is a relatively strong predictor of satisfaction levels. When nationality is used as a predictor in multivariate analyses of the combined European samples, it "explains" far more variance than any of the variables mentioned above. Income, for example, explains about one percent of the variance in satisfaction with one's life as a whole; nationality accounts for nearly thirteen percent. Table 2 shows the mean satisfaction scores for a number of the social groups included in this analysis. Family income proves to be the second strongest predictor of satisfaction scores—which is not surprising, since satisfaction with one's income was one of the items used in constructing our index. Despite this fact, income makes a rather modest contribution to explaining levels of overall satisfaction: from those with incomes under $200 a month to those with incomes over $800 a month, satisfaction levels vary by less than half a standard deviation. Nationality is the *only* variable which shows really substantial variation, and for most variables the lack of explained variance is almost incredible: across age, sex, and value type, there is virtually no variation at all!

Our findings certainly tend to confirm the hypothesis of low inter-group variation. And, perhaps for the reasons suggested above, cross-national differences are far larger than those within any given nation. We will not attempt to demonstrate here to what extent the cross-national differences reflect linguistic or cultural factors and to what extent they reflect the impact of short-term forces on given nations (for a discussion see Inglehart, 1977, Chapter 6). In any event it seems clear that the nation is an important unit for the analysis of subjective satisfaction.

The data support the hypothesis that there is a *long-term* tendency for overall subjective satisfaction to remain roughly constant across social categories of a given society. The distribution of prosperity, prestige, and opportunities for self-expression is uneven across these categories. Yet we find remarkably little variation in overall satisfaction from one category to another, in each of nine Western nations. The phenomenon would not be obvious a priori. Everyone *knows* that women earn less money than men and suffer from a variety of forms of social discrimination; yet the overall subjective satisfaction levels of the two sexes appear to be

*Table 2.* Overall Satisfaction Scores by Social Background in Nine European Countries, 1973. (Mean Scores on Overall Satisfaction Index.)[a]

| Nationality | Score | (N) |
|---|---|---|
| Denmark | 10.4 | (1171) |
| Netherlands | 9.9 | (1388) |
| Belgium | 9.9 | (1214) |
| Luxembourg | 9.8 | (300) |
| Ireland | 9.5 | (1171) |
| Britain | 8.8 | (1904) |
| Germany | 8.2 | (1894) |
| France | 8.1 | (2122) |
| Italy | 7.1 | (1832) |

| Family Income | Score | (N) |
|---|---|---|
| Under $200/month | 8.2 | (1570) |
| $200–$399 | 8.3 | (2582) |
| $400–$599 | 8.8 | (2586) |
| $600–$799 | 9.1 | (1658) |
| Over $800/month | 9.4 | (2368) |
| Not ascertained | 9.0 | (2232) |

| Education (Age at which respondent left school) | Score | (N) |
|---|---|---|
| 15 years or younger | 8.5 | (7091) |
| 16–19 years | 9.1 | (4295) |
| 20 years or older | 9.2 | (1610) |

| Sex | Score | (N) |
|---|---|---|
| Male | 8.8 | (6294) |
| Female | 8.8 | (6699) |

| Value type | Score | (N) |
|---|---|---|
| Materialist | 8.8 | (6765) |
| Score = 1 | 8.9 | (2338) |
| Score = 2 | 9.0 | (1742) |
| Score = 3 | 8.9 | (1106) |
| Score = 4 | 8.8 | (749) |
| Post-Materialist | 8.7 | (673) |

| Age | Score | (N) |
|---|---|---|
| 15–24 | 8.8 | (1013) |
| 20–24 | 8.8 | (1394) |
| 25–34 | 8.8 | (2496) |
| 35–44 | 8.7 | (2390) |
| 45–54 | 8.8 | (2140) |
| 55–64 | 8.9 | (1759) |
| 65+ | 9.0 | (1801) |

| Occupation, Head of Family | Score | (N) |
|---|---|---|
| Non-manual | 9.1 | (4617) |
| Farm | 8.6 | (1014) |
| Manual | 8.6 | (4634) |
| Retired; housewife | 8.6 | (2731) |

| Church Attendance | Score | (N) |
|---|---|---|
| At least once/week | 9.0 | (4136) |
| At least a few times per year | 8.7 | (4406) |
| Never; no church | 8.7 | (4427) |

| Party Identification: Respondent feels closest to a party of the: | Score | (N) |
|---|---|---|
| Right | 9.1 | (3573) |
| None; Center | 8.8 | (5339) |
| Left | 8.6 | (4084) |

[a]A score of 13.0 (the maximum) indicates that the individual is "Very satisfied" with his or her income, work, leisure and life as a whole; a score of 1.0 indicates that the respondent is "Very dissatisfied" with all four; a score of 7.0 is neutral. Mean for total sample is 8.8. Figures in parentheses indicate the number of cases on which the given mean score is based.

identical. Everyone knows that in the United States, the objective conditions of blacks are worse than those of whites—yet the overall satisfaction levels of the two races do not differ greatly. The latter finding is astonishing, but it has been established in analysis of several "Quality of Life" surveys carried out in the United States (Andrews and Withey, 1976). Even more surprisingly, another study indicates that individuals with severe physical handicaps—muscular diseases, paralysis, missing limbs, or blindness—do not differ significantly from other people in their subjective satisfaction levels (Cameron, 1974). Surprising as it may seem, but in keeping with our hypotheses, overall subjective satisfaction tends to remain constant across social categories.

## SOCIOPOLITICAL SATISFACTION

Let us return to the finding that launched this exploration: the fact that post-Materialists show overall satisfaction levels no higher than those of Materialists. In a sense, the findings we have presented make this fact seem all the more bizarre. For we have found that satisfaction with income is one of the most important components of overall satisfaction; and that those with relatively high income *do* tend to be more satisfied with their lives as a whole than those with lower incomes. Yet the post-Materialists have higher incomes than other value types—and they tend to be *less* satisfied with their lives as a whole. How can this be?

Logically, the answer must be that other aspects of life are more important to the post-Materialsts; and, furthermore, they must be relatively *dissatisfied* with conditions in these other domains—sufficiently dissatisfied so as to pull down their overall satisfaction levels below the mean, despite the process of accommodation and averaging-out that we have just discussed.

Can we identify such a domain? Apparently yes. The dimensional analysis shown in Table 1 indicates that there are at least two types of satisfaction items—those loading on the first, or "Overall Satisfaction" factor, and those loading on the second. The two key items in the latter cluster concern satisfaction with "How democracy is functioning" in the respondent's country, and satisfaction with "The kind of society in which we live." Both of these items also have significant loading on the first factor (though they are lower than those for one's leisure, job and income) but they have something else in common which causes them to form a separate cluster in each of the nine nations for which we have data. This underlying theme is, of course, the fact that they both refer to societal rather than personal concerns.

This is precisely the type of domain in which we might expect the satisfaction levels of Materialists to differ from those of post-Materialists. In the first place, these items form a smaller, separate cluster from the broad "Overall Satisfaction" group. This distinctness implies that response to these two items is less likely to be averaged in with responses to the "Overall Satisfaction" group. Relatively free from the inertia of the much larger cluster, we might expect response to these items to be relatively heavily influenced by short-term forces having a differential impact on groups with different values. The content of these items enhances the likelihood of different types of response: by their very nature, post-Materialists are presumably less preoccupied with immediate personal needs and more sensitive to societal problems; and, theoretically, they evaluate societal performance by different criteria than those used by other value types. While there is no reason why we would expect the post-Materialists to be inherently and always satisfied with governmental and societal performance than other groups, we know that they constitute a minority in all Western nations. As a relatively small group that has only recently emerged in significant numbers, they live in societies that are predominately oriented toward Materialist goals: there would seem to be a fairly high probability that they would be overruled rather frequently. Finally, the political domain is, as we suggested earlier, one in which entire groups may experience sharply differentiated changes in their circumstances. Our cross-national data provide an illustration of this possibility. Those who support the parties of the Right were, in general, more satisfied with the sociopolitical domain than those who favor the Left. But in Germany—one of the few countries where the Left was in power at the time of our 1973 survey—the Social Democrats ranked higher on sociopolitical satisfaction than the Christian Democrats. It is possible, of course, that the German Social Democrats have *always* ranked relatively high on satisfaction in this domain; but it seems far more plausible to conclude that they were more satisfied because their party was in, rather than out.

These considerations lead us to hypothesize that sociopolitical satisfaction is more salient to post-Materialists than to Materialists; and that post-Materialsts tend to be relatively dissatisfied in this domain. Let us examine the former question first.

We have argued that if material needs attain long-term satisfaction, other needs become increasingly relevant to one's overall subjective satisfaction. Thus the *overall* satisfaction levels of the Materialist and post-Materialist value types are virtually indistinguishable; but the various *components* of overall satisfaction are not equally important for the two groups.

This fact becomes evident when we perform separate factor analyses of satisfaction levels for each value type. In these analyses, all of the items have rather high loadings, as was the case in Table 1: there is a pronounced tendency to generalize satisfaction across domains. Moreover, satisfaction with one's "life as a whole" emerges as the highest-loading item on the first factor among both the Materialist and post-Materialist subsamples: this factor taps overall satisfaction in both cases. But beyond this point, two distinct patterns appear. Among Materialists, satisfaction with one's job, one's leisure time, and one's income, are the three next highest-loading items—the domains most intimately linked with overall satisfaction. Among the post-Materialists, on the other hand, the second highest-loading item is "the kind of society in which we live," followed by "education for children," "leisure time," and "how democracy functions."

The differences between Materialist and post-Materialists in the absolute strength of the respective loadings is moderate: high scores in one domain seem to pull up one's scores in other domains, and vice versa. But the rank-ordering indicates that what happens in the societal and political spheres has more impact on the overall satisfaction of post-Materialists than of Materialists.

Our second hypothesis was that post-Materialists are likely to be relatively dissatisfied with their nation's society and political life. As Table 3 illustrates, there is a clear overall tendency for post-Materialist values to be linked with political dissatisfaction. In the nine European Community countries as a whole, 51 percent of the polar Materialist type are "satisfied" or "very satisfied" with the way democracy is functioning in their country; only 29 percent of the post-Materialists are satisfied.

Political dissatisfaction is not *inherent* in post-Materialist values, however. As Table 3 indicates, the strength of the relationship varies a great deal from one nation to another. In France, we find the post-Materialist type to be 47 percentage points less satisfied than the Materialist polar type—while there is scarcely any difference between these groups in Denmark (and the relationship is actually *reversed* in the latter case). There may be an overall probability that the post-Materialists will find themselves disappointed by the outputs of their political institutions. But these institutions vary from country to country; and at any given time, relatively change-oriented forces may hold office in one nation, while relatively conservative ones hold office in another. Thus, one can find intense political dissatisfaction at either the Materialist or post-Materialist end of the continuum.

Without question, the most striking illustration of this fact is provided by the Italian neo-Fascists. The supporters of this party are more heavily skewed toward the materialist extreme than any other electorate among fifty-two parties for which we have data. At the same time, they are politically the *least* satisfied of the fifty-two groups. In Denmark, the

*Table 3.* Political Satisfaction, by Value Type in Nine European Nations, 1973.
(Percent "Satisfied" or "Very satisfied" with way democracy is functioning in their country).

| | France | Belgium | Netherlands | Germany | Italy | Luxembourg | Denmark | Ireland | Britain |
|---|---|---|---|---|---|---|---|---|---|
| Materialist (0) | 63 | 77 | 62 | 44 | 30 | 74 | 45 | 61 | 49 |
| Score = 1 | 49 | 72 | 59 | 46 | 26 | 72 | 46 | 55 | 41 |
| Score = 2 | 41 | 66 | 58 | 46 | 27 | 46 | 48 | 49 | 40 |
| Score = 3 | 34 | 55 | 60 | 45 | 20 | 50 | 46 | 46 | 44 |
| Score = 4 | 29 | 53 | 54 | 43 | 12 | 26 | 40 | 43 | 30 |
| Post-Mat. (5) | 16 | 42 | 45 | 25 | 11 | 10 | 49 | 31 | 29 |

more or less Poujadist Progress Party constitutes another Materialist but relatively dissatisfied constituency.

Political dissatisfaction can be found at either end of the values continuum. Yet the global tendency is clear: dissatisfaction is most prevalent among the post-Materialists. A relatively small minority in predominately Materialist societies, they are relatively apt to perceive a disparity between their own values and the society that surrounds them.

Satisfaction with "the society in which we live" shows a pattern quite similar to that of satisfaction with "the way democracy is functioning." To facilite analysis of this domain, we constructed an index of "Sociopolitical Satisfaction" based on responses to these two items.[5] Using this as our dependent variable, we then carried out Multiple Classification Analyses similar to the one shown in Table 2, for each national sample and for the combined nine-nation European Community sample. Results from the latter analysis are shown in Table 4. Once again, nationality is our strongest predictor of satisfaction. But in other respects, the pattern is quite different from that governing "Overall Satisfaction" scores. For one thing, the overall mean score is slightly on the *negative* side: while European publics seem to be predominately satisfied with their lives as a whole (and with the material aspect in particular) there is more dissatisfaction than satisfaction with social and political life. Furthermore, there is virtually no variance in "Sociopolitical Satisfaction" according to income: in contrast with what we found in connection with "Overall Satisfaction," the higher income groups are not more satisfied than the lower income groups. The same holds true of occupation; in fact, while those with nonmanual occupations showed the highest *overall* satisfaction, they have the lowest *sociopolitical* satisfaction.

Finally, let us note a fact that helps explain the weakened or reversed relationships with income and occupation: post-Materialists are decidedly less satisfied than Materialists. The average "Sociopolitical Satisfaction" score for the Materialists is 4.0—which happens to be the neutral point between satisfaction and dissatisfaction. The intermediate value types fall toward progressively lower levels of satisfaction; while the group at the post-Materialist pole has a mean score of 3.2, which makes them less satisfied than eight of the nine nationalities—only the Italians rank lower. Our multivariate analysis indicates that value type is the second strongest predictor of "Sociopolitical Satisfaction." Only nationality explains more variance, among the predictors shown in Table 4. As was true with "Overall Satisfaction," the percentage of total variance explained in this analysis is small: merely 12 percent. As we suggested above, the process of accommodation probably tends to dampen the variation in satisfaction ratings. The relationship between values and "Sociopolitical Satisfac-

*Table 4.* Sociopolitical Satisfaction Scores by Social Background in Nine European Countries, 1973. (Mean Scores on Political Satisfaction Index: Maximum = 7.0).*

| Nationality | | |
|---|---|---|
| Belgium | 4.6 | (1253) |
| Luxembourg | 4.6 | (323) |
| Ireland | 4.3 | (1198) |
| Netherlands | 4.1 | (1423) |
| Denmark | 4.0 | (1199) |
| Germany | 4.0 | (1946) |
| Britain | 3.8 | (1931) |
| France | 3.7 | (2166) |
| Italy | 3.1 | (1903) |

| Family Income | | |
|---|---|---|
| Under $200/month | 3.9 | (1616) |
| $200–$399 | 3.8 | (2639) |
| $400–$599 | 3.9 | (2644) |
| $600–$799 | 4.0 | (1700) |
| Over $800 | 3.9 | (2414) |
| Income refused, not ascertained | 4.0 | (2329) |

| Education (Age at which respondent left school) | | |
|---|---|---|
| 15 years or younger | 3.9 | (7212) |
| 16–19 years | 4.0 | (4379) |
| 20 years or older | 3.7 | (1674) |

| Sex | | |
|---|---|---|
| Male | 3.8 | (6514) |
| Female | 4.0 | (6823) |

| Value Type | | |
|---|---|---|
| Materialist | 4.0 | (6765) |
| Score = 1 | 4.0 | (2338) |
| Score = 2 | 3.9 | (1742) |
| Score = 3 | 3.7 | (1106) |
| Score = 4 | 3.5 | (749) |
| Post-Materialist | 3.2 | (673) |

| Age | | |
|---|---|---|
| 15–24 | 3.8 | (3619) |
| 25–34 | 3.9 | (2448) |
| 35–44 | 3.9 | (2273) |
| 45–54 | 3.9 | (1913) |
| 55–64 | 3.9 | (1771) |
| 65+ | 4.1 | (1176) |

| Occupation, Head of Family | | |
|---|---|---|
| Farm | 4.2 | (1055) |
| Retired; housewife | 3.9 | (2806) |
| Manual | 3.9 | (4741) |
| Non-Manual | 3.8 | (4740) |

| Church Attendance | | |
|---|---|---|
| More than once/week | 4.0 | (685) |
| Weekly | 4.1 | (3599) |
| Several times/year | 3.9 | (4512) |
| Never; no church | 3.7 | (4546) |

| Party Identification | | |
|---|---|---|
| Respondent feels closest to a Party of the: | | |
| Right | 4.0 | (3677) |
| None; Center, Other | 3.9 | (5475) |
| Left | 3.8 | (4190) |

*A score of 7.0 on this index indicates that the individual is "Very satisfied" with "the kind of society in which we live in (Britain) today" and with "the way democracy is functioning in (Britain)." A score of 1.0 indicates that the individual is "Very dissatisfied" with both; a score of 4.0 is neutral.

tion'' is modest but significant; and though it varies a good deal from one setting to another, it does not seem to be spurious.

Post-Materialists are apparently *more sensitive* to the social and political aspects of life than Materialists; and significantly *less satisfied* with these aspects of life than other groups. Their relatively low sociopolitical satisfaction probably tends to pull down the post-Materialists' ''Overall Satisfaction.''

## VALUES AND PROTEST POTENTIAL

Post-Materialists tend to be relatively dissatisfied with their society and the political life of their nation. It remains to be demonstrated whether this goes no farther than lip service, or whether it may have behavioral consequences. Are post-Materialists prepared to act on behalf of their distinctive societal goals?

A scale developed by Marsh promises to provide a convincing test of whether the answer is yes of no. (Marsh, 1974; 1975). Designed to measure an individual's propensity to engage in unconventional political protest, the scale is based on respondent's expressions of approval and readiness to carry out a series of political protest acts ranging from petitions, to occupations of buildings and blocking traffic. Tested and applied in five Western nations, the scale has remarkably good technical characteristics and appears to measure, in a simple and meaningful way, just how far the individual is willing to go in acting on behalf of his views. The items on which Marsh's scale is based were included in a survey of a representative national sample of the American public carried out in July–September, 1974.[6] Using the Osiris III Guttman scaling program, ninety-eight percent of our respondents could be scaled, with a coefficient of reproducibility of 0.964.[7] The distribution of the American respondents on this scale is shown in Table 5.

Do the post-Materialists show a relatively high potential for unconventional political protest, as measured by the Marsh scale? If, as Marsh has argued, the post-Materialist phenomenon goes no deeper than lip service to currently fashionable ideals, we would expect the answer to be no. But if our typology reflects basic differences in societal values, the answer should be yes. For the post-Materialists are not only more dissatisfied with the society and political systems in which they live, but less constrained by concerns to maintain economic and physical security.

The relationship between values and protest potential is crucial, not only in its implications concerning the Materialist/post-Materialist concept, but in its substantive implications for society. It seems important to measure this relationship as carefully as possible.

*Table 5.* Distribution of Scores on Marsh "Protest Potential Scale": United States, 1974[a].

(Percentages).

*Highest level of protest activity Respondent is willing to take:*

| | Nothing | Petitions | Demonstrations | Boycotts | Rent strikes, wildcat strikes | Occupation of buildings, block traffic | |
|---|---|---|---|---|---|---|---|
| | 8 | 20 | 22 | 25 | 16 | 10 | 101 |
| N: | (136) | (339) | (364) | (418) | (260) | (163) | (1680) |

[a]Ninety-eight percent of our respondents could be scaled, with a coefficient of reproducibility of 0.964.

The indicator of value priorities used in our first investigation of the subject was a rather primitive one, based on responses to only four items. The 1974 survey contains a much richer array of values items than that available in any of our previous surveys. It may be possible to develop a more accurate and reliable indicator of the Materialist/post-Materialist dimension, based on this broader pool of items. Consequently, we will employ not only our original four-item index but also some broader-based (and, hopefully, more reliable) indicators.

In the 1974 survey, the following battery of items was used to tap the Materialist/post-Materialist dimension:

In politics it is not always possible to obtain everything one might wish. On this card, several different goals are listed.

If you had to choose among them, which would be your *first* choice?

Which would be your *second* choice?

Which would be your *third* choice?

The goals listed were:

A. MAINTAIN ORDER IN THE NATION

B. GIVE PEOPLE MORE SAY IN THE DECISIONS OF THE GOVERNMENT

C. FIGHT RISING PRICES

D. PROTECT FREEDOM OF SPEECH

On these cards are some goals and objectives people say our country as a whole should concentrate on. Of course, all of these are important to all of us in one way or another, but which *three* are *most* important to you personally?

And from these three goals, which one, for you, is

most important?

next most important?

third most important?

Please look at the rest of the cards and tell me which are the *three least* important?

Now which of these three is

least important?

next-to-least important?

third least important?

The goals offered in this group were:

A. MAINTAIN A HIGH RATE OF ECONOMIC GROWTH
B. MAKE SURE THAT THIS COUNTRY HAS STRONG DEFENSE FORCES
C. GIVE PEOPLE MORE SAY IN HOW THINGS ARE DECIDED AT WORK AND IN THEIR COMMUNITY
D. TRY TO MAKE OUR CITIES AND COUNTRYSIDE MORE BEAUTIFUL
E. MAINTAIN A STABLE ECONOMY
F. FIGHT AGAINST CRIME
G. MORE TOWARD A FRIENDLIER, LESS IMPERSONAL SOCIETY
H. MORE TOWARD A SOCIETY WHERE IDEAS ARE MORE IMPORTANT THAN MONEY

The question on which our original values index was based provides the first four-item series. This full battery enables us to obtain relative rankings for twelve important goals. Six of these items were intended to tap emphasis on the physiological or "Materialist" needs: "Rising prices," "Economic growth," and "Stable economy" being aimed at the sustenance needs; and "Maintain order," "Fight crime," and "Strong defense forces" being aimed at the safety needs. The remaining six items were designed to tap various post-Materialist needs. Our expectation was that emphasis on the six Materialist items would tend to go together, forming one cluster empirically, with the post-Materialist items in another distinct cluster. In order to test this expectation, we performed conventional factor analysis on the rankings of these goals.[8] The results are shown in Table 6.

*Table 6.* The Materialist/Post-Materialist Factor Among the United States Public, 1974.

(Loadings of value priorities items on unrotated first factor).

| Goal: | Loadings: (20 percent) |
|---|---|
| Ideas count | 0.560 |
| Less impersonal society | 0.528 |
| Freedom of Speech | 0.451 |
| More say in government | 0.438 |
| More say on job | 0.416 |
| More beautiful cities | 0.119 |
| Stable economy | −0.392 |
| Maintain order | −0.409 |
| Economic growth | −0.432 |
| Fight rising prices | −0.449 |
| Strong defense forces | −0.467 |
| Fight crime | −0.502 |

[a]The percentage of the total variance explained by this factor appears in parentheses.

Our expectations are borne out to a considerable extent. All six of the Materialist items cluster together, toward the negative pole. And five of the six post-Materialist items form a cluster at the opposite pole. A single item—the one concerning "more beautiful cities"—does not fit into either cluster. This is not an isolated anomaly. Analyses of similar data from nine European countries show precisely the same pattern: in every case, the six Materialist items form one cluster and five of the post-Materialist items form another cluster (Inglehart, 1977, Chapter 2). A single item—always the one concerning "more beautiful cities"—fails to fit into either cluster. This item clearly does not behave as anticipated; but response to the eleven other items lives up to expectations with remarkable consistency. Furthermore, this consistency cannot be attributed to such common sources of spurious correlation as response set: the items were asked in a forced-choice format which gives no clue to the "right" answer.

Eleven of the twelve items show the expected loadings and the expected polarity on this dimension. And all four of the items used in our earlier index fall into the appropriate clusters, as anticipated. Though we have encountered one puzzling anomaly, there seems to be little question that we are tapping the Materialist/post-Materialist dimension. By itself, this enlarged pool of items might well provide the basis for a more reliable measure of the underlying concept—but let us press on still farther in pursuit of improved measurement.

Thus far, we have dealt with items designed to tap one specific aspect of an individual's value priorities—the Materialist/post-Materialist dimension. It should be revealing to place this dimension in the context of one's *overall* value priorities. Rokeach (1973) has developed a battery of items that seems promising for this purpose. His items are intended to be exhaustive, rather than intensive. Rokeach concludes that they tap all major areas of human concern, with little duplication; and he has provided an impressive array of evidence in support of this conclusion. Accordingly, the Rokeach Terminal Values Survey was included in our 1974 questionnaire. If it does provide an exhaustive inventory of one's value priorities, some of its items should tap the Materialist/post-Materialist dimension—enabling us to integrate our work with that of Rokeach, and broadening our base of measurement still farther. The Rokeach battery is worded as follows:

> On the next page are 18 values listed in alphabetical order. Your task is to arrange them in order of their importance to *you*, as guiding principles in *your* life. Each value is printed on a gummed label which can easily be peeled off and pasted in the boxes on the left-hand side of the page.

Study the list carefully and pick out the one value which is the most important to you. Peel it off and paste it in Box 1 on the left.

Then pick out the value which is second most important to you. Peel it off and paste it in Box 2. Then do the same for each of the remaining values. The value which is least important goes in Box 18.

Work slowly and think carefully. If you change your mind, feel free to change your answers. The labels peel off easily and can be moved from place to place. The end result should truly show how you really feel.

The items are:

A COMFORTABLE LIFE (a prosperous life)
AN EXCITING LIFE (a stimulating, active life)
A SENSE OF ACCOMPLISHMENT (lasting contribution)
A WORLD AT PEACE (free of war and conflict)
A WORLD OF BEAUTY (beauty of nature and the arts)
EQUALITY (brotherhood, equal opportunity for all)
FAMILY SECURITY (taking care of loved ones)
FREEDOM (independence, free choice)
HAPPINESS (contentedness)
INNER HARMONY (freedom from inner conflict)
MATURE LOVE (sexual and spiritual intimacy)
NATIONAL SECURITY (protection from attack)
PLEASURE (an enjoyable, leisurely life)
SALVATION (saved, eternal life)
SELF-RESPECT (self-esteem)
SOCIAL RECOGNITION (respect, admiration)
TRUE FRIENDSHIP (close companionship)
WISDOM (a mature understanding of life)

Factor analysis of the twelve-item Materialist/post-Materialist battery plus the eighteen-item Rokeach battery reveals a complex and interesting structure. As we would expect, a number of dimensions are needed to capture the configuration of responses. But the Materialist/post-Materialist dimension remains clearly recognizable, and several of Rokeach's items show substantial loadings on it. Table 7 gives results from a second factor analysis, based on the eleven items showing significant loadings in Table 6, plus the related Rokeach items. In the Materialist cluster we find Rokeach's items "A Comfortable Life" and "Family Security"—two values having an obvious linkage with economic security; also linked in this cluster is an item relevant to the safety needs, "National Security." In the post-Materialist cluster we find "Equality" and "Inner Harmony," plus a pair of items relating to the intellectual and

*Table 7.* The Materialist/Post-Materialist Factor in the United States, 1974.

(Loading of eighteen items on unrotated first factor).[a]

| Goal: | Loadings: (16 percent) |
|---|---|
| Ideas count | 0.585 |
| Less impersonal society | 0.506 |
| Freedom of speech | 0.457 |
| WORLD OF BEAUTY | 0.318 |
| WISDOM | 0.317 |
| EQUALITY | 0.302 |
| More say on job | 0.300 |
| More say in government | 0.274 |
| INNER HARMONY | 0.268 |
| Maintain order | −0.280 |
| Stable economy | −0.302 |
| FAMILY SECURITY | −0.367 |
| Economic growth | −0.419 |
| Fight rising prices | −0.420 |
| NATIONAL SECURITY | −0.433 |
| Fight crime | −0.446 |
| COMFORTABLE LIFE | −0.461 |
| Strong defense forces | −0.496 |

[a]Rokeach items appear in all capitals.

esthetic needs: "Wisdom" and "A World of Beauty." Ironically enough, the item that we had designed to tap the esthetic needs failed to show the expected empirical relationships—but the item developed by Rokeach does.[9]

The percentage of the total variance explained among the enlarged pool of items is smaller than that accounted for by the factor in Table 6, but the theme these items have in common is unmistakably the Materialist/post-Materialist dimension. Conceivably, this larger item pool may provide the basis for a more accurate measurement of one's value priorities. We are ready to deal with the question: do post-Materialists show a higher level of protest potential than other value types?

The answer, clearly, is yes. If we take the original four-item index as our measure of value priorities, we find that 18 percent of the pure Materialist type show scores of five or six on the Marsh Protest Potential Scale—as compared with 42 percent of the post-Materialists; the intermediate types (those choosing one Materialist goal and one post-Materialist goal from the four-item set) fall about halfway between the two pure types. In other words, post-Materialists are more than twice as likely as Materialists to be willing to escalate protest activities beyond boycotts—to engage in rent strikes or wildcat strikes; or even go so far as to occupy buildings or obstruct traffic. The factor scores generated by the analysis in Table 7 show an even stronger relationship. When we collapse these scores into ten equal intervals along the Materialist/post-Materialist dimension, we find that only 9 percent of the most Materialist group shows a "high" level of unconventional protest potential (that is, scores of five or six on the Marsh scale). As Table 8 indicates, this percentage rises steadily as we move toward the post-Materialist pole: the respective figures are 14, 22, 20, 25, 33, 40, 61, 70, and 94 percent.

Table 9 shows the correlations between "Protest Potential" and value priorities as measured by our original four-item index; the factor scores generated by the twelve items in Table 6; and the factor scores generated by the eighteen items in Table 7. As we broaden our measurement base, we obtain progressively stronger correlations. A larger pool of relevant items apparently gives a more accurate measure of the underlying dimension than can be provided by a smaller pool.

To complete our analysis, we need to answer one more question: is the relationship between value priorities and unconventional protest potential spurious? Our theory implies that post-Materialists should be concen-

*Table 8.* Value Priorities and Protest Potential Among the United States Public, 1974.

| Value Type (collapsed factor scores from Rokeach and Inglehart items)[a]: | Score on Marsh Protest Potential Scale: Low | 2 | 3 | 4 | 5 | High | N |
|---|---|---|---|---|---|---|---|
| Materialist | 9% | 28 | 26 | 28 | 6 | 3 | ( 78) |
| Score = 2 | 9 | 27 | 27 | 24 | 11 | 3 | (231) |
| Score = 3 | 9 | 22 | 22 | 26 | 16 | 6 | (305) |
| Score = 4 | 10 | 21 | 25 | 24 | 14 | 6 | (156) |
| Score = 5 | 5 | 15 | 24 | 31 | 18 | 7 | (288) |
| Score = 6 | 6 | 15 | 19 | 27 | 22 | 11 | (176) |
| Score = 7 | 1 | 16 | 21 | 23 | 22 | 18 | (110) |
| Score = 8 | 2 | 5 | 5 | 27 | 24 | 37 | ( 62) |
| Score = 9 | 0 | 3 | 13 | 15 | 20 | 50 | ( 40) |
| Post-Materialist | 0 | 0 | 0 | 6 | 19 | 75 | ( 16) |

[a]This analysis included the eleven Materialist/post-Materialist items plus the seven Rokeach terminal values which had relatively high loadings on the dimension shown in Table 7.

*Table 9.* Relationship Between Marsh Protest Potential Scale and Three Measures of Value Priorities: United States, 1974.

(Product-moment correlations).

| | | |
|---|---|---|
| | Original 4-item values index | 0.202 |
| Factor socres, first dimension | 12 Materialist/post-materialist items | 0.280 |
| | 18 items (11 Materialist/post-materialist items plus 7 related Rokeach items) | 0.346 |

trated among the younger age cohorts, reflecting the relatively high levels of economic and physical security that were prevalent during their formative years; similarly, we would expect post-Materialists to be concentrated among the more affluent and better-educated strata of given age cohorts. The data bear out both of these expectations. But this gives rise to two possible alternative explanations of the linkage between values and protest potential: could it be that post-Materialists rank higher simply *because* they are younger? Or because they are better educated?

In order to determine whether there is a genuine linkage between value type and protest potential, we should control for age and education. In doing so we will control away some of the variance in value type that would be expected on theoretical grounds; but only by applying such controls can we ascertain whether the observed relationship between values and unconventional protest potential is spurious or genuine.

Tables 10 and 11 show the results of multiple regression analyses in which our respondents' "Protest Potential" scores are the dependent variable and age, education and value type are predictors. In Table 10 our indicator of value type is the factor scores generated by the twelve-item pool; in Table 11 we use the scores generated by the eighteen-item pool. In both cases, all three predictors show significant relationships with

*Table 10.* Value Priorities and Protest Potential, Controlling for Age and Education: United States, 1974.

(Multiple regression analysis using 12-item values index).

| Variable | Partial correlation with Marsh Protest Potential Scale: |
|---|---|
| Age | −0.322 |
| Years of education) | 0.230 |
| Value type[a] | 0.180 |
| | Multiple correlation = 0.494 |

[a]Value type is measured here by factor scores generated by our 12 Materialist/post-materialist items. The original 4-item index has a partial correlation of 0.145, when used with these same variables.

*Table 11.* Value Priorities and Protest Potential, Controlling for Age and Education: United States, 1974.

(Multiple regression analysis using 18-item values index)

| Variable | Partial correlation with Marsh Protest Potential Scale: |
|---|---|
| Age | −0.306 |
| Value type[a] | 0.236 |
| Years of education | 0.193 |
| | Multiple correlation = 0.508 |

[a]Value type is measured here by factor scores generated by our 12 Materialist/post-materialist items plus the 18 Rokeach terminal values.

unconventional "Protest Potential," after controlling for the effects of the other two variables. Our twelve-item values indicator is the weakest of the three predictors, though a substantial partial correlation persists even after we have controlled for age and education. Our eighteen-item values indicator ranks second among the three predictors—above education but below age. And the analysis using the eighteen-item indicator explains slightly more of the total variance in protest potential than the one using the twelve-item indicator. The linkage between values and unconventional protest potential does not seem to be spurious.

On the contrary, post-Materialists are more likely to support unconventional political protest activities than people with relatively materialistic value priorities—and this remains true even when we control for the fact that post-Materialists are younger and better educated than most respondents. Moreover, this relationship is surprisingly strong.

We observed a significant but modest tendency for post-Materialists to express less satisfaction with their political systems than other value types. We asked ourselves whether this merely reflected verbal support for change among a privileged group who didn't really want to alter their society in any fundamental way. The answer seems to be a clear-cut "No." For surprising as it may seem, the relationship with value type becomes much *stronger* when we move from a purely attitudinal variable (political dissatisfaction) to one based on reports of actual behavior and willingness to act (protest potential). We are *not* dealing with mere lip service; quite the contrary, it seems that the impact of one's values on one's actual behavior may be stronger than their impact on one's subjective *feelings* of dissatisfaction. Ordinarily, this would seem astounding. In the context of what we have just seen, it makes sense. For the concept of "satisfaction" seems to entail a powerful dampening effect: it connotes a comparison between reality and "reasonable" expectations. The fact that one's aspirations tend to accomodate to one's situation apparently reduces intergroup variation in political satisfaction levels almost as much as it reduces variation in overall life satisfaction. "Protest Potential," on the other hand, is less constrained by "reasonable" expectations—and the relatively slight differences in political satisfaction levels that we found between Materialist and post-Materialist give way to very sizeable differences in Protest Potential.

## CONCLUSION

Overall subjective satisfaction varies surprisingly little from one social group to another—a seemingly negative finding that actually must reflect an immense human capacity to adapt and change. High satisfaction levels, apparently, are inherently fragile. Favorable changes in external conditions may raise an individual's or a people's satisfaction level, but in the long run rising aspirations—and in the still longer run, changing values—tend to neutralize it.

While an increase in prosperity may produce a short-term sense of gratification, an individual gradually adjusts his aspiration level to converge with his external circumstances; in the long run, he will take a given level of prosperity for granted and aspire to more. Thus, structural differences in material welfare among groups with a stable membership are linked with surprisingly small differences in subjective satisfaction. Furthermore, generation units that have never been deprived of given needs tend to shift their value priorities to emphasize qualitatively different goals. For such groups, relatively high levels of material need satisfaction will not merely produce surprisingly small *gains* in subjective satisfaction—they may actually be associated with relatively *low levels* of overall satisfaction among individuals who experience frustration in the pursuit of other, more highly-valued goals.

Thus it is only an apparent paradox that post-Materialists fail to show relatively high levels of subjective satisfaction with their lives as a whole or even with the material aspects of life, than more Materialist groups. For by their very definition, these groups have distinctive value priorities. The former tends to place less emphasis on material welfare and more emphasis on qualitative aspects of society. Under the circumstances prevailing in the early 1970s, post-Materialists tended to show lower levels of "Sociopolitical Satisfaction" than Materialists. And, while in earlier periods political protest may have usually had its origins in dissatisfaction with material conditions and been based on low income groups, our 1974 data indicate that the relatively prosperous post-Materialists have a markedly greater potential for involvement in unconventional political protest activities than other value types.

## FOOTNOTES

*Ronald Inglehart is an Associate Professor in the Department of Political Science and Faculty Associate in the Institute for Social Research at the University of Michigan, Ann Arbor. He is currently taking part in an eight-nation study of expectations, levels of conceptualization, and conventional and unconventional participation in politics. His book *The Silent Revolution: Changing Values and Political Styles Among Western Publics* was published by Princeton University Press in 1977.

I am indebted to my colleagues in an ongoing cross-national study of Expectations and Political Action for helpful comments and criticism. An earlier version of this article was presented at the annual meeting of the American Political Science Assocaition, San Francisco, September 2–5, 1975.

1. Marsh's (1975) study is a critique of Inglehart (1971). In the original article and in Marsh's critique, the terms "Acquisitive" and "Post-Bourgeois" were used in place of the labels "Materialist" and "Post-Materialist" that have been substituted in subsequent publications.

2. These surveys were sponsored by the European Community Information Service and were designed by Jacques-René Rabier and the present author. For details concerning sample sizes and fieldwork, see Inglehart (1977, Chapter 2). The wording of the relevant questions was: "I would like to ask you how you regard certain aspects of your present situation. I will read out a number of aspects and for each of them I would like you to say whether you are very satisfied, fairly satisfied, not very satisfied, or not at all satisfied?" The respondent was asked about: "The house, flat or place you live; your income; your work (as a housewife, in a job, at school); education for children; your leisure (spare time); the social welfare benefits you would receive if you became ill or unable to work; in general terms, your relations with others; the kind of society in which we live in (Britain) today; relations between the generations; the way democracy is functioning in (Britain)." Respondents were then asked: "On the whole, are you very satisfied, fairly satisfied, not very satisfied, or not at all satisfied with the life you lead?" Finally, they were asked: "Do you think generally speaking, that people give you the respect which you deserve, or not?" These data are available from the ICPSR survey data archive, Ann Arbor, Michigan.

3. This index was constructed by summing the scores for the four highest-loading items on the first factor shown in Table 1; scores range from "1" ("Very dissatisfied" with all four items) to "13" ("Very satisfied" with all four items).

4. We can, of course, increase the percentage of variance explained for any of these dependent variables if we do either of two things: (1) increase the number of predictor variables—especially if we include attitudinal items; (2) increase the number of categories in the given predictor variables. For the sake of reliability, we collapsed many of the predictor variables used in these analyses, obtaining relatively few categories containing relatively many cases.

5. This index simply sums each individual's satisfaction levels for the two items, producing an index with scores ranging from "1" ("Very dissatisfied" with both) to "7" ("Very satisfied" with both).

6. Fieldwork was carried out by the fieldwork staff of the Institute for Social Research, University of Michigan. The number of respondents interviewed in the cross-sectional sample was 1721. This survey was part of a collaborative effort with Samuel H. Barnes and M. Kent Jennings. Fieldwork was supported by grants from the National Institute of Mental Health and the U.S. Army Research Institute for the Behavioral and Social Sciences. A set of independently financed but parallel surveys (not yet available for analysis) have been carried out in Great Britain by Mark Abrams and Alan Marsh; in Austria by Leopold Rosenmayr, Anselm Eder, Elfriede Schlage, and Inga Findl; in the Netherlands by Philip Stouthard, Cees de Graff and Felix Heunks; and in Germany by Klaus Allerbeck, Max Kaase, and Hans Klingemann. A report of this group's findings will appear in a volume edited by Samuel Barnes and Max Kaase, provisionally titled *Expectations and Political Action*.

7. The index items were dichotomized into "would do" versus "would not do" categories, with "might do" responses scored as positive only if the respondent *also* indicated that he approved of the action. A maximum of four errors was allowed, with a maximum of two missing data items.

8. Our use of factor analysis in this case is unconventional in one sense. Our items reflect relative rankings, not absolute scores; this is crucial to operationalizing our hypothesis but it means that the rankings are not independent. This would make factor analysis entirely

inapplicable with a small pool of items. With only two items, for example, the rank of the first item determines the rank of the second, automatically generating a −1.0 correlation between them. With three items, one would expect negative correlations of about 0.5. With a pool of four items, this effect is still important: the rank of the first item leaves only three possibilities, and random answering would generate negative correlations of about 0.3 between *all four* items—so that only two of them could load on the first factor. With a pool of eight items, the degree to which one item's rank determines that of another becomes smaller. The analysis in Table 6 is based on rankings from a group of eight items, plus another group of only four items. In this case, there is a tendency for all of the items in a given group to be negatively correlated; thus, the nonindependence of our rankings tends to spread the items over several dimensions, diminishing the amount of variance that can be explained by the first factor. As our empirical results show, this effect is dominated by a stronger tendency for Materialist items to be chosen together, on one hand; and post-Materialist items to be chosen together, on the other hand. With the still broader pool of items in Table 7 below, the problem of nonindependent items (Ipsivity) becomes more or less negligible.

9. Analysis of the responses to our own item concerning "more beautiful cities" reveals a quite unexpected tendency for this item to be linked with emphasis on "Fighting crime" among many respondents. Inclusion of the word "cities" in this context seems to evoke a concern with safety: the cities are unbeautiful because they are dangerous. Rokeach's item apparently taps esthetic concerns in a purer form.

## REFERENCES

Abrams, Mark (1973) "Subjective Social Indicators." *Social Trends* 4:35–48.

Allardt, Erik (1973) *About Dimensions of Welfare*. Helsinki: Research Group for Comparative Sociology.

Andrews, Frank and Withey, Steven (1974) "Developing Measures of Perceived Life Quality." *Social Indicators Research* 1:1–26.

——— (1976) *Social Indicators of Well-Being*. New York: Plenum.

Bradburn, Norman (1969) *The Structure of Psychological Well-Being*. Chicago: Aldine.

Cameron, Paul (1974) "Social Stereotypes: Three Faces of Happiness." *Psychology Today* 8:62–64.

Campbell, Angus et al. (1976) *The Quality of American Life*. New York: Russell Sage.

Gurin, Gerald et al. (1960) *Americans View Their Mental Health*. New York: Basic Books.

Inglehart, Ronald (1971) "The Silent Revolution in Europe: Intergenerational Change in Post-Industrial Societies." *American Political Science Review* 65:991–1017.

——— (1977) *The Silent Revolution: Changing Values and Political Styles Among Western Publics,* Princeton: Princeton University Press.

Marsh, Alan (1974) "Explorations in Unorthodox Political Behavior: A Scale to Measure 'Protest Potential'." *European Journal of Political Research* 2:107–129.

——— (1975) "The 'Silent Revolution,' Value Priorities and the Quality of Life in Britain." *American Political Science Review* 69:21–30.

Maslow, Abraham (1970) *Motivation and Personality*. 2d ed. New York: Harper and Row.

Rokeach, Milton (1973) *The Nature of Human Values*. New York: Free Press.

Sonquist, John (1971) *Multivariate Model Building: The Validation of a Research Strategy*. Ann Arbor: Institute for Social Research.

Strumpel, Burkhard (ed.) (1974) *Subjective Elements of Well-Being*. Paris: OECD.

# THE RELATIONSHIP BETWEEN OBJECTIVE AND SUBJECTIVE INDICATORS IN THE LIGHT OF A COMPARATIVE STUDY

Erik Allardt*

Social indicators aimed at assessing the state of a nation or the level of well-being in a society are by their very nature comparative. It is hard even to comprehend the meaning of social indicators unless they are made to enable comparisons. Findings from comparative studies can also be used for solving some of the methodological problems currently facing those who are engaged in the establishment of social indicators.

All through the "social indicator movement" of the last decade, the distinction between objective and subjective indicators has been a crucial one. In brief, the problem is whether one in assessing the level of well-being in a society should rely on measures of external, objective condi-

**Comparative Studies in Sociology—Vol. 1, 1978, pages 203–215**

**ISBN 0-89232-025-7**

tions or on the personal, subjective evaluations of the citizens. As regards the empirical relationships between objective and subjective social indicators, the similarities of findings obtained in different studies and different settings are striking. Very generally speaking, the relationship between objective and subjective indicators seems to be almost surprisingly weak. The aim of this paper is not to develop a theory of the relations of the objective and subjective indicators. The main task of this paper is to elaborate the thesis that objective and subjective indicators denote different things, and that they cannot be used as replacements of each other. This thesis will be supported by findings from a comparative study of the level of well-being in the Scandinavian countries although references will also be made to other comparative studies.

The Comparative Scandinavian Study, conducted by the Research Group for Comparative Sociology at the University of Helsinki, is based mainly on interview surveys in Denmark, Finland, Norway and Sweden taken in the Spring of 1972. In each country, a national probability sample of approximately 1,000 persons aged 15–64 was interviewed (Allardt, 1975a, pp. 1–2).

## THE MEANING OF OBJECTIVE AND SUBJECTIVE INDICATORS

Although it will not be possible to analyze all aspects of the meaning given to the terms "objective" and "subjective" indicators a short description of how the terms have been used here is necessary.

Social indicators are concerned with the good life and the good society and are as such clearly value-oriented. Thus, social indicators are variables aimed at describing social conditions but variables for which the extreme poles denote "good" and "bad" conditions. This immediately raises the question of where we get these values. Basically there have been two kinds of answers to this question. According to one view the values ought to be based on observations of what people through political or other structured activities actually strive for and under what conditions they suffer. This way of selecting values has been called objective because the emphasis is on overt behavior and external conditions. Another view, then, is that the values should be based on people's attitudes, feelings of satisfaction-dissatisfaction, preferences, etc. These are subjective in the sense that they are phenomena somehow "going on in people's heads," such as feelings, opinions, etc.

To select the basic value-dimensions important in a particular indicator-program and to develop and operationalize the indicators are, to be sure, two separate procedures. Nevertheless, the arguments used in deciding whether the choice of the basic value-dimensions should be objective or subjective are the same as those put forth in favor of objective or subjective indicators. The former refer to overt behavior and observable external conditions whereas the latter are measures of attitudes, preferences or verbally reported feelings of satisfaction-dissatisfaction. Later on in the paper some of the arguments for objective or subjective indicators will be briefly discussed.

It is probably worthwhile to emphasize that the distinction between objective and subjective indicators is here meant to refer to a difference in substance and not merely to differences in the mode of measurement (see Feinberg and Goodman, 1974, pp. 74–76). Assessments of the actual income reported by respondents in an interview survey are in this sense objective whereas the respondents' satisfaction with their income is a subjective measure. Needless to say the terms "objective" and "subjective" in this sense and as they are used here do not indicate anything about the reliability of the indicators.

## SOME FINDINGS FROM THE COMPARATIVE SCANDINAVIAN STUDY

The basic typology of the comparative Scandinavian study was developed in order to account for how the value-dimensions and indicators were chosen. The typology was based on the following two distinctions:

(1) *Welfare* versus *Happiness*. Welfare is based on needs: the amount of welfare is defined by the degree of need-satisfaction. Happiness, on the other hand, refers to subjective perceptions and experiences: the amount of happiness is defined by the extent to which people feel they are happy. This already implies that welfare is a more objective category than happiness. Individuals may misjudge the state of their need-satisfaction and what they need in order to live a "good life," or more appropriately, what they need in order not to live a "bad life." This is not true for happiness. The individuals themselves are the best judges of their happiness. On the operational level it means that the state of welfare is observed by observing and gauging overt behavior and actual social relationships, whereas happiness is studied by measuring attitudes and perceptions.

(2) *Level of Living* versus *Quality of Life*. The level of living concept refers to material and impersonal resources with which individuals can master and command their living conditions. More precisely, the level of living is here considered to be based on those needs for which

the level of satisfaction is defined by the material and impersonal resources individuals can command and master. This is true for income, housing, employment needs, etc., but it is not true for social needs such as needs for love and self-actualization. The satisfaction of love and self-actualization needs are not defined by the material resources an individual can command but by how he relates to other people and to society.

The implications of the two conceptual distinctions can be highlighted by the following fourfold table:

| | Welfare | Happiness |
|---|---|---|
| Level of living | 1. Needs for which satisfaction is defined by having or mastering *material or impersonal resources* | 3. *Subjective* feelings of *satisfaction-dissatisfaction* as regards the material living conditions |
| Quality of life | 2. Needs for which satisfaction is defined by *how the individual relates to other people, society, and nature* | 4. *Subjective* feelings of *satisfaction-dissatisfaction* as regards the relations to people, society, and nature |

The term "quality of life" has often been used to cover everything valued which is not part of the material level of living. The assumption here is that one can distinguish between objective and subjective "quality of life" as well as between objective and subjective levels of living.

It is to be noted that the term "happiness' here easily could be substituted by satisfaction-dissatisfaction.[1] In the following we will restrict ourselves mainly to comparisons of indicators located in cells 1 and 3 although we will deal with nothing contradictory to the findings concerning quality of life (cells 2 and 4).

In the study the objective level of living (cell 1) was measured by the following five (5) components: income, housing conditions, employment, education, and health. The subjective level of living (cell 3) or, in other words, satisfaction-dissatisfaction with material and social conditions was tapped by four (4) indicators. They were all attitudinal scales measuring perceptions of societal antagonisms, of existing social discrimination, of unjust privileges in one's own society, and subjective satisfaction with one's own income. Only the last mentioned measure, income satisfaction, corresponded clearly to one of the objective components studied.

According to the findings the relationships between the objective welfare components and the subjective satisfaction measures are very weak. Generally the national correlations are zero or close to zero. The only exception is that there is a weak positive correlation between income and income satisfaction in all the four countries (0.13 in Denmark, 0.14 in Finland, 0.17 in Norway, and 0.12 in Sweden) but even this relationship is clearly weaker than expected (Allardt, 1975b, pp. 150–153).

One possible explanation of the unexpectedly weak correlations could of course be the lack of reliability and validity of the measures used. However, there are reasonable grounds for considering the subjective measures good or at least acceptable. There are high intercorrelations of the items in each scale, and the scales are also positively intercorrelated.

A striking fact is revealed when the satisfaction measures are related to common background variables such as to social class defined by occupation, education, sex, age, etc. It appears that within each country the overall satisfaction level tends to be surprisingly constant across categories defined by social characteristics of the above kind. When multivariate analysis, e.g., by MCA-analysis, is performed separately for each of the four countries, a surprisingly small amount of variance is explained by social background factors. It is hard to avoid the conclusion that the expressions of satisfaction and dissatisfaction are only to a very small degree directly related to external social conditions.

There are, however, two factors which are correlated with satisfaction-dissatisfaction and which in the multivariate analysis appear as predictors of satisfaction. One is *political orientation:* in all four countries the level of dissatisfaction clearly increases when moving from right to left on the political spectrum. It is to be noted that "political orientation" as a variable is of a different nature than the other background variables. Political orientation is to a large extent an attitudinal variable and reflects a more or less deliberate choice whereas social class, education, age, sex, etc. reflect external circumstances under which the individual lives. These general tendencies do not disappear when an analysis based on the single items—instead of one based on summated scales—is performed. For each singular item, the political right-left dimension is more strongly correlated with satisfaction-dissatisfaction than are income and social class defined by occupational prestige. Furthermore, the correlations between political orientation and satisfaction-dissatisfaction are, as a rule, statistically significant, whereas the correlations between income or social class on the one hand and satisfaction-dissatisfaction on the other only rarely deviate from zero.

There is, however, another variable which also appears as a predictor of satisfaction-dissatisfaction. This variable is nationality. When the data from all four countries are combined into a Multiple Classification

Analysis *nationality* emerges as a fairly strong predictor of the variance in satisfaction-dissatisfaction. A glimpse at the national distributions also shows clear national variation. Dissatisfaction is highest in Finland, second highest in Sweden, followed by Norway and Denmark in that order. For the time being we will refrain from explanations but we will return especially to the difference between Denmark and Sweden.

## RESULTS FROM OTHER STUDIES

The general findings from the comparative Scandinavian study and other studies simultaneously conducted elsewhere are almost astonishingly similar. In almost all studies the general conclusion has been that there is a very low degree of correspondence between the external conditions and subjectively expressed satisfaction-dissatisfaction (e.g. Campbell, 1972, pp. 441–442; Abrams, 1972, pp. 454–455). The similarity of findings holds for many specific details. At a direction-giving conference on social indicators in 1973, it was reported that satisfaction with one's neighborhood varied only slightly with income (Duncan, 1974, p. 11).

At this point, it may be noted that satisfaction measures can of course be constructed in a number of ways. The satisfaction measures can be constructed to match and to correspond to certain external conditions as is the case when one simultaneously measures income and income satisfaction, housing and satisfaction with housing conditions, etc. The indicators can be constructed, on the other hand, as measures of more generalized feelings of satisfaction-dissatisfaction, as doubtlessly has been the case in the comparative Scandinavian study. There is no point in arguing against the possibility of arriving at higher correlations between objective and subjective indicators by making the objective conditions and their corresponding subjective measures match closer and closer. It is doubtful, however, that it would be fruitful to proceed in such a direction except for some specific purposes and in some specific studies. Theoretically the generalized attitudes of satisfaction-dissatisfaction are the important ones. The main point here is that it is definitely worthwhile to separate the objective and subjective indicators because they both empirically and conceptually represent different phenomena. To try to replace one by the other will lead to a loss of information.

In view of the fact that the comparative Scandinavian study dealt primarily with generalized satisfaction-dissatisfaction it is interesting to note the very strong resemblance between our results and those reported by Inglehart (1978) in a large-scale comparative study of nine countries. His nine-country study tapped satisfaction-dissatisfaction in a very thorough fashion by measures of both generalized and specific satisfaction-dissatisfaction. Nevertheless, the overall findings are strikingly similar in Inglehart's and our study. The resemblance starts with the general overall finding that the relationship between objective need-satisfaction and subjective satisfaction is almost astonishingly loose but the similarities of the findings can be also observed in details. Inglehart stresses how the overall satisfaction levels tend to be roughly constant not only across value types (Materialist versus post-Materialist) but also across any set of social categories having stable membership. In Inglehart's analysis, the only variable of predictive and explanatory importance was nationality.

In the Scandinavian study too, nationality proved to be a predictor of nonnegligible strength but also the political dimension right-left contributed to the explanation of the variance of satisfaction-dissatisfaction. One explanation of the importance of political orientation in the Scandinavian study, although it did not show up in Inglehart's study, is probably to be found in the political homogeneity of the Scandinavian countries versus the political heterogeneity of the nine countries studied by Inglehart. In any case, the similarity of Inglehart's and our results is reassuring, especially considering that he has been able to use very comprehensive measures of satisfaction levels.

The findings raise the question of how it can be explained that objective and subjective indicators yield such different results. To explain the situation here is not a matter of required routine, but is necessary in answering the problem posed in the beginning of the paper. If the explanations are reasonable then they give an argument for the fruitfulness of a clear separation of objective and subjective indicators and for simultaneous use of both.

## WHY OBJECTIVE AND SUBJECTIVE INDICATORS ARE ONLY WEAKLY RELATED: DENMARK AND SWEDEN AS ILLUMINATING CASES

The attempt at an explanation offered here will not be formulated in terms of general theory but rather in terms of the concrete, historical situation prevailing in Scandinavia in the light of the survey data. Nevertheless, some general conclusions may hopefully be drawn from the explanation given.

As a point of departure, it may be noted that by multivariate analysis a reasonable amount of variance of the objective components of the level of living can be explained by social background factors. This is true for all the four countries compared, and it should be added that the explanatory patterns throughout the study are very similar all over Scandinavia. Of course, the amount of variance explained varies depending on which background variables it is fruitful to put into the analysis, but it is in any case clear that several social categories are good predictors and explanatory factors of the variation in the objective level of living. This contrasts very strikingly with the already reported finding that subjective satisfaction-dissatisfaction does not clearly vary across social categories. As Inglehart (1978) states, it is the lack of variance for most variables that is almost incredible. It appears obvious that variations in subjective satisfaction do not have any direct relationship with the external conditions. Explanations of the variation have to be sought elsewhere.

An interesting pattern is revealed by the fact that it is specifically political orientation and nationality which appear as predictors. This gives a clue to noting interesting differences in the national political climates.

It was already mentioned that the overall subjective satisfaction level appeared to be highest in Denmark, next highest in Norway, followed by Sweden and Finland in that order. This result is easily misunderstood and misinterpreted if presented alone. However, the fact that Finland displays the lowest average satisfaction score and consequently the highest dissatisfaction score is not surprising. On an average, Finland shows a lower degree of value-fulfillment in the objective welfare components than the other three countries, and Finland has a history of strong class conflicts. What is surprising, however, is Sweden's comparatively low degree of subjective satisfaction and high degree of dissatisfaction. A comparison with Denmark is particularly instructive. Sweden displays, as can be expected, the highest amount of value-fulfillment in the welfare components. What is particularly important, however, is that Sweden is not only the richest among the Scandinavian countries but also the one with the lowest proportion of alienated persons. Three of the indicators of the quality of life can be assumed to have measured alienation. The three components have been labeled *Insubstitutability* (under the assumption that the less substitutable a person is in his job, in his organization, among his friends, etc., the more he is a person and less a thing easily substitutable), *Political Resources,* and *Doing* (rich leisure time activities). It now appears that Denmark has the highest frequency of alienated persons. The high degree of value-fulfillment, and accordingly the low degree of alienation among the Swedes are quite striking. Thus, on the average the Swedes clearly have more political resources, that is opportunities to influence politics and their own fate, than do the other Scandinavians.

Accordingly, Sweden and Denmark almost completely change positions when shifting from "objectively" measured alienation to "subjectively" measured dissatisfaction. Sweden is low on alienation and high on dissatisfaction whereas Denmark, on the contrary, is high on alienation and low on dissatisfaction. This indicates quite clearly that the high dissatisfaction levels in Sweden do not have their roots in alienation but on the contrary in a high degree of political consciousness. The Swedes are, so to say, socialized into the habit of expressing their political dissatisfactions openly.

In an inter-Scandinavian comparison it seems reasonable to characterize Sweden as a *politicalized* but Denmark as a *"privatized"* country. This interpretation is reinforced by some peculiarities in the response patterns among the Danes. As a rule they appear much less apt to stress traditional right-left issues and class antagonisms than other Scandinavians.

In any case, it appears safe to say that the subjective satisfaction scores clearly reflect the effects of political socialization, politicalization, and of the political culture of a society. Under such circumstances the satisfaction levels hardly indicate the state of the objective and external conditions. They are reflections of the degree of politicalization, and its obverse, "privatization."

The explanation offered relates to the specific situation in Scandinavia but its implications are general. The failure of the subjective satisfaction levels can, however, also be accounted for by more general theories. Thus, Inglehart (1978) offers an explanation in terms of a theory of the relationship between aspirations and satisfaction. Overall satisfaction is not a substance, as he says, but a moving balance. One's satisfaction level is among other things related to one's aspirations but the aspiration level gradually adjusts to the external circumstances.

In any case, it seems possible to account for the lacking correspondence between the objective circumstances and subjective satisfaction-dissatisfaction by explanations of different theoretical levels. This also implies that there would be a loss of information if one would try to replace the objective or subjective indicators with each other. The objective and subjective indicators yield different results but these differences can in addition be explained in terms of either the actual historical situation or general theories. This concludes the empirical argument: it casts severe doubts on the fruitfulness of trying to replace the objective and subjective indicators with each other.

## CONCEPTUAL DIFFERENCES BETWEEN OBJECTIVE AND SUBJECTIVE INDICATORS

Although the thesis advanced in this paper is mainly empirical and based on findings from comparative studies, it can be strengthened by some conceptual and philosophical arguments. In the beginning of the paper the distinction between welfare and happiness was introduced. These terms have been used in various ways, and one may of course question the wisdom of applying them here. The crucial problem is nevertheless the fact that in discussions of well-being it seems to be necessary to make a conceptual distinction between "objective" and "subjective" phenomena.

In analyzing ultimate political principles Barry (1965, pp.38–39) makes the basic distinction between *want-regarding* and *ideal-regarding principles*. Want-regarding principles are principles by which the wants of people are taken as the central point of departure and by which policy measures aim either at altering the overall amount of or the distribution of want-satisfaction. Ideal-regarding principles are defined simply as contradictory to want-regarding principles. The weakest form of an ideal-regarding principle is to start from the view that wants should form the basis of policy but nevertheless permit a policy maker to deviate from the ranking order of wants proposed by the subjects. The stronger forms of ideal-regarding principles appeal directly to explicit ideals.

The want-regarding principles stress subjective preferences and attitudes. It should be noted that Barry also shows that appealing to needs already implies an ideal-regarding principle. To say something is needed or to base a policy on needs always implies an end or purpose which is considered good. It is striking how in almost all discussions on construction of social indicators, in the last analysis one arrives at problems covered by Barry's distinction.

The conceptual difference between welfare and happiness is treated in numerous philosophical texts. It has been emphasized (von Wright, 1963, pp. 87–88) that welfare and happiness have very different relationships to time and causality. Happiness has a strong element of temporariness and accidentalness, whereas welfare is something more stable. Happiness can be assessed without considering its causes and consequences, whereas welfare judgments are always permeated with causal assumptions. Happiness, like satisfaction, comes and goes; it is not clearly and systematically anchored in definite external social circumstances. One can say that there exists in all analyses of well-being a necessity to account for the difference between welfare and happiness such as this difference has been outlined above.

## A PHILOSOPHICAL-IDEOLOGICAL NOTE

In an interesting critique of positivistic empirical science, Galtung (1972) has shown how the traditional view of science tends to provide social science with a straitjacket, to uphold (legitimize) vicious circles of underdevelopment instead of breaking them, and to provide for conservation in social affairs. This is done primarily in the name of the quest for invariance. According to Galtung, the requirement that the tenability of scientific propositions should be invariant of variations in time tends to lead to the legitimizing of vicious circles whereas the demand for space invariance in its turn tends to lead to an emphasis on social forms existing in dominant regions and countries. Of relevance here is Galtung's discussion of the demands for invariance of subject consciousness (the images held by the researchers) and object consciousness (independence from the consciousness of the persons studied). The quest for invariance of subject consciousness appears to be a striving for consensus. It is based on an assumption that from the unity of nature and the unity of man a unity of image should follow. If there is room for only one image, controversial results and pluralism will be avoided.

Galtung notes in passing that universalistic efforts in science seem to prevail in periods when the political world is strongly divided. This is not the place to analyze the epistemological consequences of Galtung's analysis. It is, however, clear that the assumption of a correspondence between the external circumstances and the images has certain ideological consequences.

It may of course be maintained that the question of subject consciousness is irrelevant to the discussion about objective and subjective indicators. What matters is the quest for invariance of object consciousness. In the natural sciences, propositions are invariant of the consciousness of the objects studied but translated into social reality, the idea, according to Galtung, has had rather curious consequences.

One is the idea that the essence of social reality is uncovered when the level of the consciousness of the objects is very low. This idea to a large extent has dominated especially experimental social psychology and social anthropology. Now in fact, as Galtung shows, one of the most efficient means of upsetting or breaking invariances found is to increase the consciousness of the objects. The moment there is consciousness, mechanisms of self-fulfilling and self-destructing prophecies may set in and destroy the invariances. It is worthwhile to recall the finding from the comparative Scandinavian study according to which political socialization or, in other words, differentials in political consciousness seem to contribute to an explanation of the lack of correspondence between the objective circumstances and the subjective satisfaction levels. It seems to be certain that a rise in the level of political consciousness will upset earlier patterns of satisfaction-dissatisfaction. Under such circumstances it is of course unwise even to try to evaluate the goodness and badness of objective circumstances by subjective indicators. The main intention of this philosophical-ideological note, however, is to emphasize how the approaches to the relationship between objective and subjective indicators are permeated by ideological assumptions.

## A SHORT FINAL CONCLUSION

Throughout the paper the text has contained warnings against attempts to try to replace objective and subjective indicators with each other. The discussion has been carried out both in the light of empirical results from comparative studies, and in terms of conceptual and ideological arguments.

However, the warnings should not be interpreted in a dogmatic way. First, it cannot be overemphasized that our discussion concerns only the kind of indicators which are also value-dimensions, that is, social indicators for which the extreme poles are considered good and bad. It is evident that many subjective phenomena can be used as predictors of certain occurrences objectively observable. Our thesis here is only that one cannot from subjective expressions of satisfactions and happiness draw inferences about the goodness or badness of the objective circumstances.

Secondly, anyone is of course entitled to try to improve the possibilities of predicting the outcome of objective and subjective indicators from each other. It is, however, fruitful to stress that there are important empirical and conceptual differences between the objective and subjective indicators. To try to replace one by the other might in the worst case imply an ideological stance detrimental to the development of social science. Whatever one does one should be careful not to forget or to destroy the differences and nuances inherent in the distinction between objective and subjective indicators. A simple replacement of one by the other can only lead to a considerable loss of information.

It is interesting to note that the problem of the relationship between objective and subjective social indicators has been elucidated both by findings stressing similarities between countries and by findings showing clear intercountry dissimilarities. In studies of a number of countries, satisfaction levels tend to be constant across categories defined by social characteristics. On the other hand, there are clear national differences in the satisfaction levels, thereby indicating the importance of the national mood in the formation of satisfaction and dissatisfaction in nations. Comparative studies based on the simultaneous use of both objective and subjective indicators render both substantial and methodological results which would be hard to obtain in studies of single countries.

# FOOTNOTE

*Erik Allardt is Professor of Sociology at the University of Helsinki. He is also Chairman of the Research Group for Comparative Sociology at Helsinki where he is directing a large scale study of the level of living and quality of life of the national populations of Denmark, Finland, Norway, and Sweden.

# REFERENCES

Abrams, Mark (1972) "Social Indicators and Social Equity." *New Society* 22:454–455.

Allardt, Erik (1975a) *Dimensions of Welfare in a Comparative Scandinavian Study*. Research Group for Comparative Sociology, University of Helsinki, Research Reports No. 9.

——— (1975b) *Att ha, att älska, att vara. Om välfärd i Norden* (To Have, To Love, To Be, On Welfare in the Nordic Countries). Kalmar: Argos.

Barry, Brian (1965) *Political Argument*. London: Routledge and Kegan Paul.

Campbell, Angus (1972) "Aspiration, Satisfaction, and Fulfillment." Pages 441–466 in A. Campbell and P. E. Converse (eds.), *The Human Meaning of Social Change*. New York: Russell Sage Foundation.

Duncan, Otis Dudley (1974) "Social Indicators, 1973: Report on a Conference." Pages 1–19 in Roxann A. Van Dusen (ed.), *Social Indicators, 1973: A Review Symposium*. Washington, D.C.: Social Science Research Council.

Feinberg, Stephen E. and Goodman, Leo A. (1974) "Social Indicators 1973: Statistical Considerations." Pages 63–82 in Roxann A. Van Dusen (ed.), *Social Indicators, 1973: A Review Symposium*. Washington, D.C.: Social Science Research Council.

Galtung, Johan (1972) "Enpiricism, Criticism, Constructivism. Three Approaches to Scientific Activity." Paper presented at the Seventh Scandinavian Congress of Sociology, Elsinore, (mimeo).

Inglehart, Ronald (1978) "Value Priorities, Life Satisfaction, and Political Dissatisfaction among Western Publics." Pages 173–202 in Richard F. Tomasson (ed.), *Comparative Studies in Sociology*, Vol. 1. Greenwich, CT:JAI Press.

von Wright, Georg Henrik (1963) *The Varieties of Goodness*. London: Routledge and Kegan Paul.

# GOVERNMENT PENSIONS FOR THE AGED IN 19 INDUSTRIALIZED COUNTRIES: DEMONSTRATION OF A METHOD FOR CROSS-NATIONAL EVALUATION

Lincoln H. Day*

I have three purposes in writing this paper: First, I hope to persuade the reader that the data available for making cross-national comparisons offer greater latitude for analysis than may be realized, and can be used more effectively than they usually are. Second, I wish to present an example of a procedure for making systematic cross-national comparisons on the basis of disparate materials. And third, in presenting this example, I hope to cast some useful light on a topic of practical interest to both social researchers and government policy makers.

**Comparative Studies in Sociology—Vol. 1, 1978, pages 217–233**

**ISBN 0-89232-025-7**

# PENSION SCHEMES AS INDICATORS OF "LIFE CHANCES"

The structure of any comparison among peoples or programs is, of course, a product of both the available data and the purposes for which the comparison is undertaken. The data available for the present comparison of pension schemes, though predictably subject to certain limitations, nonetheless extend over a fairly broad spectrum of attributes. But the particular attributes selected, and the weights assigned them, reflect, in the present instance, the fact that this comparison is one of several undertaken for the purpose of developing a set of social indicators suited to use in determining the possible relation of "life chances" (in the Weberian sense) to fertility levels among populations exercising substantial control over both fertility and mortality.[1]

This use of statutory pension schemes as an indicator of "life chances" is predicated on the assumption that industrialization (and all the countries in the study are industrialized) involves an increase in economic interdependence within populations, and that this necessitates a resort to collective means merely to forestall declines in human well-being, let alone to secure improvement.

But, of course, not all such collective means are statutory, private pension plans being a notable example. Is the existence of these nonstatutory plans—and the fact that it is virtually impossible to obtain data on their characteristics and the extent of their coverage sufficient to permit international comparisons—likely to bias conclusions about the "life chances" of the aged that are based on an analysis confined to statutory schemes? Probably not very much, if at all. A study of such schemes in eight countries (Australia, Canada, West Germany, Netherlands, Sweden, Switzerland, the United Kingdom, and the United States) found that, while there was considerable variation in the relative importance of nonstatutory schemes, and a substantial negative correlation (approximately −0.75) between the respective proportions of national income spent on statutory and nonstatutory programs, expenditure on the nonstatutory programs in no case exceeded either 2 percent of national income or 35 percent of the expenditure on statutory programs (cited in Aaron, 1967, pp. 14–15, footnote 3). That there has been a marked increase in both coverage and benefits associated with statutory schemes in the years since that study was made suggests that, if anything, the relative importance of the nonstatutory is even less today than it was then.

## METHODOLOGY

In terms of their methodologies, the cross-national comparisons of pension schemes made elsewhere can be categorized into three types: (a) those that describe the various individual provisions without endeavoring to evaluate them (e.g., U.S. Department of Health, Education, and Welfare, *Social Security Programs . . .;* Cohen, 1960); (b) those that attempt an evaluation, but essentially only in terms of the numerical attributes of the plans (e.g., Aaron, 1967; Hohm, 1975); and (c) those that, while recognizing the desirability of evaluation in terms of both numerical and nonnumerical attributes, despair of attempting it in any detail on the basis of the highly disparate materials that pertain to these schemes—settling, instead, for an essentially impressionistic assessment, e.g., the particularly sophisticated example of Kaim-Caudle (1973).

While much of value can be gleaned from studies concerned only with numerical attributes, or those whose results can be summarized in such general fashion as "higher" vs. "lower," "better" vs. "worse," or "superior" vs. "inferior," the construction of a social indicator suited to my broader research needs relating to fertility requires both greater comprehensiveness and an attempt at greater precision. Because of its bearing on the organization of the present comparison of pension schemes, a word is in order concerning this fertility inquiry.

In contrast with the usual fertility study, this one focuses not on the attributes of individuals, but on the larger social setting within which decisions about childbearing perforce take place. And in further contrast with common procedure, it does so at a level of generality not so high as to verge on meaninglessness (as contrasted, for example, with those numerous "analyses" based on the relation between national fertility levels and per capita income). The hypothesis is that fertility in populations substantially controlling both fertility and mortality will be lowest under two polar sets of conditions: where the instrumentalities through which individuals as such (i.e., as distinct from their status as family members) can satisfy their personal needs and interests are either (a) abundant or (b) scarce. Where these instrumentalities are *abundant* it is hypothesized that fertility is low because individuals typically have ample resources for meeting their needs outside the family; because, that is, they *do not feel the need* for additional children. Where, in contrast, these instrumentalities are *scarce,* it is hypothesized that fertility is also low, but low in this instance because the low expectations for meeting individual needs lead to fear of over-extending oneself; because, that is, people *do not dare* undertake the risk of bearing and rearing additional children. Relatively higher fertility (in such populations) is seen as being supported by conditions lying between these two poles of the continuum.[2] Although research is still underway, it is possible to report that, so far, we have found no reason to reject this hypothesis.

Whatever one's theoretical orientation, a truly rigorous analysis—and at a meaningful level of generality—of a society's sociocultural conditions, particularly if it is intended for use in cross-national comparisons, necessitates the development of summary indicators that can be manipulated statistically. Only in this way will it be possible to work simultaneously with more than one set of indicators. Particularly when working with disparate sorts of materials, this involves development of a "grade" or "score" on a scale from 1 to n for each country on each attribute—with the score at one extreme representing the condition hypothesized as being the least, and that at the other extreme as being the most, conducive to or depictive of whatever it is one is studying (e.g., the status of women, political equality, or, as in the present instance, individual "life chances").

Admittedly, such a method can involve considerable subjectivity. But for those who have had any experience of grading student essay examinations and term papers (or of coding open-ended survey questions), this should not be too uncongenial an exercise—especially if the justification for each grade level is appropriately specified and the grading process for any particular item is completed at one sitting for all countries under study. Moreover, there ought to be some comfort in the fact that "errors" of judgment are less likely to have deleterious consequences when the subject of "grading" is merely a country than when it is a flesh-and-blood human being.

Where it is possible to work with purely arithmetic indicators, and where the definitions are essentially the same for each country, this grading procedure is relatively simple and straightforward. Under such conditions, one can merely take a close approximation of the range of values, divide it into n equal intervals, and assign each country a grade determined by the interval within which that country's value on the item in question happens to be located. There can be some differences in grades in consequence of the selection of one point of origin rather than another, but as these differences cannot be very great, they will have little effect on the analysis. The real problem will be whether the definitions are essentially the same. If they are not, a useful way of overcoming the difficulty is to reduce the number of intervals.

Grading is a much more difficult—and less certain—undertaking where the indicators are of a nonarithmetic sort, or where there are major differences among definitions. This is probably the more usual situation in cross-national comparisons; it is certainly the case with government-sponsored old age pension systems, the summary grade for which in the present analysis is a composite of grades on eight aspects, only three of which (items 2, 3, and 5, below) are arithmetic:

1. Whether or not there is a cost-of-living adjustment.
2. How the maximum pension available to the *highest paid worker* (plus dependent spouse) compares with the average male wage in nonagriculture.
3. How the maximum pension available to the *lowest paid worker* (plus dependent spouse) compares with the average male wage in nonagriculture.
4. Whether or not there is a means test.
5. How the pension available to the *worker (plus dependent spouse) with a wage equal to the average male wage in nonagriculture* compares with that worker's wage.
6. The degree of flexibility in age at which one qualifies for a pension (i.e., whether one has a choice of retiring earlier at, say, an actuarially reduced pension).
7. The degree of universality in coverage of the population (i.e., whether any group of workers is left uncovered).
8. The degree of retirement required to qualify for a pension.

All of these attributes—and the relative weights assigned them in developing the single figure depicting each country's position—were selected in terms of the extent to which, corresponding to the requirements of the broader fertility inquiry, they appeared indicative of the degree to which aged persons could: (a) participate in the society and (b) avoid sudden or marked losses in status. Other possibilities offered themselves, but these seemed the ones appropriate to the purpose.

## THE DATA

Most of the information for the construction of these grades comes from a publication of the United States Government (U.S. Department of Health, Education, and Welfare, *Social Security Programs . . .*); the remainder, consisting of information on wages, from the *Yearbook of Labor Statistics* (International Labor Office). The sorts of information provided in the U.S. source may be illustrated by the following examples taken verbatim from the 1975 edition:

*Australia:*

1) Dates of basic laws:

First laws: 1908 (old-age and invalidity pensions)

Current law: 1947.

2) Coverage:
   Residents of limited means or over age 75.
3) Source of funds:
   *Insured person:* None
   *Employer:* None
   *Government:* Entire cost from general revenue.
4) Qualifying conditions:
   *Old-age pension:* Age 65 (men) or 60 (women); 10 years of continuous residence; and up to age 75 limited means (pension reduced by half if means exceed $20 a week, plus $14.50 for wife, and $6 for each child). Payable abroad under certain conditions.
5) Cash benefits for insured workers (except permanent disability):
   *Old-age pension* (after means test up to age 75): Up to $31 a week; couple $25.75 a week each.
   Wife's supplement: Up to $25.75 a week.
   Child's supplement: Up to $5.50 a week for each child under age 16 or dependent student.
   Single pensioner with children (guardian's allowance): Up to $6 a week if one or more children under age 6 or invalid; $4 a week in other cases.
   Rent supplement: Up to $5 a week if paying rent and substantially dependent on pension.

*Netherlands:*

1) Dates of basic laws:
   First law: 1913
   Current laws: 1956 (old age pensions)
2) Coverage:
   All residents (old-age and survivor pensions).
   Special system for public employees.
3) Source of funds:
   *Insured person:* 10.4% and 1.5% of income for old-age and survivor pensions, respectively (low-income persons exempted).
   *Government:* Contributions for exempted low-income persons, and any deficit.
   Maximum earnings for contribution purposes: 2,646 guilders a month.
4) Qualifying conditions:
   *Old-age pension:* Age 65. Contributions paid each year from age 15 through 64, for full pension; otherwise reduced pension (no decrements for pre-1957 period if resident citizen with 6 years of residence after age 59).
   Retirement unnecessary. Payable abroad.
5) Cash benefits for insured workers (except permanent disability):
   *Old-age pension:* Full pension, 642 guilders a month (666 as of April 1, 1975).
   Supplement for wife of any age: 268 guilders a month (278 as of April 1, 1975).
   Pension reduced by 2% for each unexcused year of non-contribution.
   Automatic adjustment of all pensions twice a year for changes in wage index.

*United States:*

1) Dates of basic laws:

First and current law: 1935 (last amended in 1973).

2) Coverage:

Gainfully occupied persons, including self-employed persons.

Exclusions: Casual agricultural and domestic employment; and limited self-employment (when annual net income below $4000).

Voluntary coverage for employees of voluntary institutions, most State and local governments, and some clergymen.

Applies in U.S., Puerto Rico, Virgin Islands, Guam, and Samoa, and to citizens employed abroad by U.S. employers.

Special systems for railroad employees, Federal employees, and many employees of State and local governments.

3) Source of funds:

*Insured person:* 4.95% of earnings. Self-employed. 7%.

*Employer:* 4.95% of payroll.

*Government:* Cost of special monthly old-age benefit for persons age 72 before 1968, whole cost of means-tested allowance.

Maximum earnings for contribution and benefit purposes: $14,100 a year. Automatic increase adjusted to wage levels.

4) Qualifying conditions:

*Old-age pension:* Age 65 (62–65 with reduction).

Insured: At least 1 quarter of coverage (QC) for each calendar year since 1950 to age 62; maximum, 40 QC. Pension reduced $1 for each $2 of earnings above $2,520 a year until age 72. Payment to aliens abroad if reciprocity exists.

5) Cash benefits for insured workers (except permanent disability):

*Old-age pension:* Minimum, $93.80 a month. Maximum, $316.30. Based on covered earnings after 1950 up to retirement age or death (excluding 5 lowest years).

Increment of 1% for each year worker delays retirement between age 65–72.

Automatic cost-of-living adjustment.

Special minimum benefit for service in excess of 10 years.

*Dependent's allowance:* 50% of worker's pensions paid to wife or dependent husband age 65 (reduced for 62–65) or to wife at any age caring for child under age 18 or invalid; to each child (or dependent grandchild) under age 18 (22 if student, no age limit if invalid before age 22).

Maximum family pension: Based on worker's basic pension; minimum, $140.80 a month. Maximum, $573.90.

*Special monthly benefit:* To persons age 72 not receiving pension from any other public source. Means-tested allowance: Payable to needy aged.

### *Weighting*

As these eight components are hardly of equal importance, I assigned each a weight from 1 to 4, as follows:

Whether there is a cost of living adjustment was assigned the maximum weight of 4 because of the obvious importance of this adjustment to the maintenance of one's level of living, social standing, and overall sense of worth and dignity.

For much the same reason, a weight of 4 was also assigned the level of the maximum pension available to the highest paid worker.

The slightly lower weight of 3 was assigned the level of the maximum pension available to the *lowest* paid worker; a lower weight because, while this pension level would be a determinant of all noted above as being affected by the pension level available to the *highest* paid worker, there would not be with the *lowest* paid worker the same *relative* degree of loss entailed, either in income itself or in social standing.

A weight of 3 was also assigned the extent to which there is a means test. The existence of a means test removes the pension from the status of a deferred wage and puts it into the category of charity—with all the attendant connotations—instead. However, the charitable connotations would presumably lessen as the cutoff point was raised to enable a larger proportion of all workers to qualify.

A weight of 2 was assigned the level of the pension for which the worker with an average wage would qualify. It was felt that, however personally significant to the individual recipient, as an indicator of the character of old-age pension systems this measure was of less importance than the maximum and minimum pensions available; for it is these latter that set the limits and thereby, presumably, determine the maximum extent of the retired workers' loss in status and style of life, so far as these are determined by one's income.

A weight of 2 was also assigned the degree of flexibility available in the age at which one can commence receiving the pension. This ordinarily involves a period ranging over only about five years; but at an advanced age, five years can make a big difference, as to both income and one's sense of personal worth and dignity—particularly if it enables an individual who becomes unemployed to avail himself of his pension rights instead of having to go on the dole or apply for support (usually at a lower level than that afforded by a pension) from some other source.

Finally, weights of 1, each, were assigned to universality of coverage and the degree of retirement required to qualify. Each is important, but there was relatively little difference among the countries as to universality, while the degree of retirement necessary is, to some extent, a duplication of the means test aspect.

*Grading*

The individual country grades for each of these components were assigned on a scale of 1 to 10, with 10 representing the condition presumed to be most depictive of individual "life chances." These grades, and the criteria for their determination were as follows:

1. *Cost of living adjustment*

| *grade* | *criterion* |
|---|---|
| 10 | Automatic, frequent adjustment for changes in wages or prices |
| 9 | Same, except that adjustment is either semiautomatic or not made until prices or wages increase at least a very small amount (1–2%) |
| 8 | Automatic, frequent adjustment for changes in wages or prices—but only after increases of more than a very small amount (i.e., of at least 2.5%) |
| 7 | Adjustment—but infrequent, or not automatic—for changes in wages or prices |
| 1 | No provision for such adjustment |

2. *Maximum pension available to the highest paid worker (and dependent spouse), as a percentage of the average male wage in nonagriculture*

| *grade* | *criterion* | *grade* | *criterion* |
|---|---|---|---|
| 10 | 117+ | 5 | 52–64 |
| 9 | 104–116 | 4 | 39–51 |
| 8 | 91–103 | 3 | 26–38 |
| 7 | 78–90 | 2 | 13–25 |
| 6 | 65–77 | 1 | 0–12 |

3. *Maximum pension available to the lowest paid workers (and dependent spouse), as a percentage of the average male wage in nonagriculture* (grade raised 1 point in countries in which this percentage is at or above the midpoint of the interval and a means-tested supplement to the regular pension is available)

| *grade* | *criterion* | *grade* | *criterion* |
|---|---|---|---|
| 10 | 72+ | 5 | 32–39 |
| 9 | 64–71 | 4 | 24–31 |
| 8 | 56–63 | 3 | 16–23 |
| 7 | 48–55 | 2 | 8–15 |
| 6 | 40–47 | 1 | 0–7 |

4. *Means test*

| *grade* | *criterion* |
|---|---|
| 10 | No means test, and pensions are paid all residents (or at least all resident nationals) |
| 8 | No means test for the gainfully employed; means test for everyone else |
| 7 | No means test for the gainfully employed, except for some of the "better off" among them; means test for everyone else |

4. *Means test (continued)*

| *grade* | *criterion* |
|---|---|
| 6 | No means test for the gainfully employed, except for certain classes among them (not necessarily those who are "better off"); means test for everyone else |
| 5 | a) No means test: all gainfully employed covered, but there is no provision for anyone else; or<br>b) A means test exists, but the minimum is fairly high and coverage extends to everyone |
| 4 | a) No means test: most—but not all—gainfully employed covered; no provision for anyone else; or<br>b) A means test exists, but not only is the minimum fairly low, but several categories of the gainfully employed are not covered; no provision for anyone else |

5. *Maximum pension available to the worker (and dependent spouse) whose average wage has been equal to the average male wage in nonagriculture, as a percentage of the average male wage in nonagriculture*

| *grade* | *criterion* | *grade* | *criterion* |
|---|---|---|---|
| 10 | 96+ | 5 | 56–63 |
| 9 | 88–95 | 4 | 48–55 |
| 8 | 80–87 | 3 | 40–47 |
| 7 | 72–79 | 2 | 32–39 |
| 6 | 64–71 | 1 | 24–31 |

6. *Degree of flexibility in age at which one qualifies for pension*

| *grade* | *criterion* |
|---|---|
| 10 | Age 65 for men, 60 for women—or after 35 years' contribution (= retirement age as early as 50) |
| 9 | Age 60 for men, 55 for women—or earlier if in unhealthy or onerous work, or (for women) if raised several children |
| 8 | Age 60 for both sexes |
| 7 | Age 65, and up to 5 years earlier, if so choose |
| 6 | Age 65, and up to 5 years earlier, if unemployed for one year |
| 5 | Age 60–63 at reduced amount, or for ill health, unhealthy occupation, etc. |
| 4 | Age 65 for men, 60 for women |
| 3 | Age 65 for both sexes |
| 2 | Age 68 for both sexes, declining to age 65 in 1970 |
| 1 | Age 70 for both sexes |

7. *Universality of coverage*

| *grade* | *criterion* |
|---|---|
| 10 | All residents |

7. *Universality of coverage (continued)*

| *grade* | *criterion* |
|---|---|
| 9 | All residents, exclusive of those better off financially (full effect of this taken into account in determining grade on means test aspect) |
| 7 | Gainfully occupied |
| 5 | Gainfully occupied, exclusive of those better off financially |
| 4 | Gainfully occupied, exclusive of a small number |
| 2 | Gainfully occupied, exclusive of certain poorer and disadvantaged sectors |

8. *Degree of retirement required to qualify*

| *grade* | *criterion* |
|---|---|
| 10 | Retirement not necessary |
| 5 | Retirement not necessary, but pension reduced by amounts earned in excess of approximately 50 percent of the average male wage in nonagriculture |
| 3 | Retirement not necessary, but pension reduced by amounts earned in excess of about 25 percent of the average male wage in nonagriculture |
| 2 | Substantial retirement necessary |
| 1 | Means test so low as to limit pension to persons with very modest incomes (whether or not derived from earnings) relative to the average male wage in nonagriculture |

In using the average male wage in nonagriculture as the standard it was necessary to make certain assumptions, as follows:

a) Where information was available only for male and female wages combined, male wages were assumed to exceed the male-female total by 10 percent.
b) Where no information was available specifically for nonagriculture, use was made of wages in manufacturing, instead.
c) Annual wages were assumed equal to 50 weekly wages; monthly wages to 4.33 weekly wages; weekly wages to 40 hourly wages.
d) In New Zealand, average male wages in nonagriculture in 1967 were assumed to be 50 percent higher than the legal minimum (this latter being the only information given). For the same reason, the same assumption was made with reference to Australian wages in 1975.

It was also necessary to make certain assumptions in calculating the numerators of these measures based on average male wages in nonagriculture, as follows:

a) The pensioner had worked continuously since the age of 20.
b) The pensioner had worked continuously at either the maximum wage for the calculation of benefit (in the case of the highest paid

worker), or the minimum wage for qualification (in the case of the lowest paid worker), or the equivalent of the average male wage in nonagriculture (in the case of the worker assumed to be at that wage for benefit purposes).

c) Where no maximum was specified for the calculation of an earnings-related pension, a maximum equal to twice the average male wage in nonagriculture (revalued, where applicable, for changes in wage or price levels) was assumed to obtain.

d) A pensioner's only source of income was his pension.

e) In the case of Denmark, it was assumed that pensioners had availed themselves of the opportunity provided by the Index-Related Insurance and Savings for Old Age Act, 1956, which enables persons 18–57 years of age to make "index contracts" with banks and insurance companies for annuities from age 67, the premiums of which, limited to 2,000 kroner per year, are deductible from one's tax and insured by the government. In addition, as with the better developed pension systems, there is provision for cost-of-living adjustments in both the premiums paid and the benefits received (Kaim-Caudle, 1973, pp. 149–151). As the maximum premium allowed under this act was, in 1967, equal to one paid for a regular pension on an income 2.18 times as high as the average male wage in nonagriculture, it would seem, from a practical standpoint, that the Danish government's old age pension scheme permits payment of a pension (to a worker at or above the average male wage in nonagriculture) at least equal to 100 percent of the average male wage in nonagriculture.

f) Finally, for New Zealand in 1975, it was assumed that the maximum payment from the newly-established supplementary earnings-related pension was equal to that from the universal old-age pension.

## RESULTS

The results of my labors for the years 1967 and 1975 appear, respectively, in Tables 1 and 2. Although six countries experienced a decline, the greatest decline (Belgium's) was only 13 percent. In contrast, substantial increases occurred in New Zealand, the United States, and Switzerland (61, 51, and 49 percent, respectively), and lesser—though notable—increases in West Germany, France, and Finland (21, 17, and 16 percent, respectively). In general, the losses were occasioned by failure to adjust benefits to a degree sufficient to compensate for increases in wage rates; the gains, by institution of cost-of-living adjustments where formerly

*Table 1.* Weighted Grades on Different Aspects of National Old Age Pension Systems, 19 Industrialized Countries—1967.

| *Aspect* | *Weight* | Australia | Austria | Belgium | Canada | Czechoslovakia | Denmark | Finland | France | W. Germany | E. Germany | Hungary | Luxembourg | Netherlands | New Zealand | Norway | Sweden | Switzerland | United Kingdom | U.S.A. |
|---|---|---|---|---|---|---|---|---|---|---|---|---|---|---|---|---|---|---|---|---|
| Cost-of-living adjustment | 4 | 4 | 36 | 32 | 36 | 4 | 32 | 32 | 40 | 28 | 4 | 4 | 32 | 32 | 4 | 40 | 40 | 4 | 4 | 4 |
| Max. pension available to highest paid worker | 4 | 16 | 40 | 28 | 12 | 36 | 32 | 32 | 12 | 32 | 24 | 40 | 40 | 20 | 16 | 40 | 40 | 20 | 32 | 20 |
| Max. pension available to lowest paid worker | 3 | 18 | 15 | 18 | 18 | 12 | 15 | 18 | 9 | 9 | 9 | 12 | 9 | 24 | 18 | 15 | 18 | 9 | 18 | 9 |
| Means test | 3 | 12 | 18 | 24 | 30 | 24 | 30 | 30 | 24 | 21 | 24 | 18 | 15 | 30 | 30 | 30 | 30 | 30 | 30 | 18 |
| Pension available to average-pay worker | 2 | 6 | 18 | 14 | 4 | 12 | 20 | 6 | 2 | 12 | 8 | 14 | 14 | 10 | 4 | 18 | 18 | 4 | 18 | 8 |
| Flexibility in qualifying age | 2 | 8 | 20 | 14 | 4 | 18 | 10 | 6 | 16 | 12 | 10 | 18 | 14 | 6 | 6 | 2 | 10 | 8 | 8 | 10 |
| Universality of coverage | 1 | 8 | 3 | 7 | 10 | 8 | 10 | 10 | 7 | 5 | 7 | 5 | 7 | 10 | 10 | 10 | 10 | 10 | 10 | 2 |
| Degree of retirement required | 1 | 1 | 3 | 2 | 10 | 2 | 10 | 10 | 10 | 10 | 10 | 3 | 10 | 10 | 10 | 10 | 10 | 10 | 2 | 5 |
| TOTAL | | 73 | 153 | 139 | 124 | 116 | 159 | 144 | 120 | 129 | 96 | 114 | 141 | 142 | 98 | 165 | 176 | 95 | 122 | 76 |
| COMPOSITE GRADE | | 3.65 | 7.65 | 6.95 | 6.20 | 5.80 | 7.95 | 7.20 | 6.00 | 6.45 | 4.80 | 5.70 | 7.05 | 7.10 | 4.90 | 8.25 | 8.80 | 4.75 | 6.10 | 3.80 |

*Table 2.* Weighted Grades on Different Aspects of National Old Age Pension Systems, 19 Industrialized Countries—1975.

| Aspect | Weight | Australia | Austria | Belgium | Canada | Czechoslovakia | Denmark | Finland | France | W. Germany | E. Germany | Hungary | Luxembourg | Netherlands | New Zealand | Norway | Sweden | Switzerland | United Kingdom | U.S.A. |
|---|---|---|---|---|---|---|---|---|---|---|---|---|---|---|---|---|---|---|---|---|
| Cost-of-living adjustment | 4 | 4 | 40 | 32 | 36 | 4 | 32 | 40 | 40 | 40 | 4 | 4 | 32 | 40 | 40 | 40 | 40 | 28 | 40 | 40 |
| Max. pension available to highest paid worker | 4 | 16 | 40 | 20 | 16 | 28 | 40 | 40 | 24 | 36 | 16 | 40 | 40 | 20 | 28 | 40 | 40 | 28 | 16 | 20 |
| Max. pension available to lowest paid worker | 3 | 18 | 18 | 12 | 18 | 12 | 15 | 21 | 15 | 9 | 12 | 15 | 9 | 24 | 18 | 15 | 18 | 18 | 18 | 9 |
| Means test | 3 | 15 | 18 | 24 | 30 | 24 | 30 | 30 | 24 | 30 | 24 | 18 | 15 | 30 | 30 | 30 | 30 | 30 | 30 | 18 |
| Pension available to average-pay worker | 2 | 6 | 18 | 8 | 6 | 14 | 20 | 8 | 4 | 12 | 6 | 8 | 16 | 10 | 16 | 14 | 16 | 10 | 6 | 10 |
| Flexibility in qualifying age | 2 | 8 | 20 | 16 | 4 | 18 | 10 | 8 | 16 | 12 | 10 | 18 | 14 | 6 | 6 | 2 | 10 | 8 | 8 | 10 |
| Universality of coverage | 1 | 8 | 3 | 7 | 10 | 8 | 10 | 10 | 7 | 7 | 7 | 5 | 7 | 10 | 10 | 10 | 10 | 10 | 10 | 3 |
| Degree of retirement required | 1 | 2 | 3 | 2 | 10 | 2 | 10 | 10 | 10 | 10 | 10 | 3 | 10 | 10 | 10 | 8 | 10 | 10 | 2 | 5 |
| TOTAL | | 77 | 160 | 121 | 130 | 110 | 167 | 167 | 140 | 156 | 89 | 111 | 143 | 150 | 158 | 159 | 174 | 142 | 130 | 115 |
| COMPOSITE GRADE | | 3.85 | 8.00 | 6.05 | 6.50 | 5.50 | 8.35 | 8.35 | 7.00 | 7.80 | 4.45 | 5.55 | 7.15 | 7.50 | 7.90 | 7.95 | 8.70 | 7.10 | 6.50 | 5.75 |

there had been none, and by improvements in the levels of benefit. Seven countries increased the relative benefit available to the highest paid worker, and four decreased it; six countries increased that available to the lowest paid worker, while one decreased it; and eight increased that available to the worker at the average wage, while six decreased it.

Now, a modification could be introduced into this grading system, so that the grades would all be based on a scale of 10 having a range as wide as that of the 19 country grades. Were this done, the 1967 grades, for example, would range from a high of 10 for Sweden and 9 for Norway and Denmark, to a low of 1 for both the U.S.A. and Australia. But to do this would, I think, introduce an undesirable element of rank-ordering into a grading system that ought to be based, essentially, on the researcher's view of the relative significance (from the standpoint of the assumptions and hypotheses underlying his research) of each condition considered. In the present instance, it should be theoretically possible for all 19 countries either to receive first class honors or fail completely. Moreover, grades expressed in this form, rather than as rankings, are also more amenable to experimentation with different weightings, should that prove desirable in the course of the analysis.

As it happens for both 1967 and 1975, the composite grade in the present analysis is fairly strongly associated ($r \geqslant 0.6$) with only three items: (a) whether there was a cost-of-living adjustment, (b) the maximum pension payable to the highest paid worker, and (c) the pension payable to the average-pay worker. This is perhaps not too surprising with items (a) and (b). Given the weighting system used, each accounts for 20 percent of the composite grade, but item (c) accounts for only 10 percent of this grade. However, at least in 1967, item (c) is, as one might suspect, so closely associated with item (b) ($r = 0.832$) that either could be removed altogether from the analysis with little effect on the relative positions of the countries. This is not quite the case in 1975, however, although the association between (b) and (c), that year, is still fairly high ($r = 0.688$).

What is perhaps more noteworthy is the scant association among grades on the individual items. Apart from that already noted between the maximum benefit for the highest paid worker and that for the average-pay worker, fairly strong associations ($r \geqslant 0.6$) are found only between universality of coverage and (a) the presence of a means test and (b) the degree of flexibility in qualifying age. In neither year are the grades of any country on individual items invariably at only one place on the continuum. Sweden's unweighted grades on individual items range, for example, from 10 down to 5 in both years; East Germany's from 10 to 1; and Australia's from 8 to 1.While there were seven countries in 1967 with grades extending over the whole range from 10 to 1, by 1975 the number of such countries had dwindled to only three. Nevertheless, in 1967 there were only three countries, and in 1975 still only five, with a range of grades no greater than 6.

Moreover, there is among these national schemes little general agreement concerning any particular item of the eight considered. For 1967, the least variation is in the grades relating to the maximum pension available to the lowest paid worker. Yet, even here, the grades extend from 8 to 3 for a range of 5. In 1975 the least variation is in two grades: (a) maximum pension available to the lowest paid worker and (b) the existence of a means test, where they extend, respectively, from 8 to 3 and 10 to 5 for a range of 5 again.

The highest average grade, both years (8.2 in 1967; 8.4 in 1975), is that relating to the means test, which is also the attribute concerning which there is the most agreement among the different schemes: only Australia, Austria, Hungary, Luxembourg, and the United States have 1975 grades on this item lower than 8. The lowest average grade, again for both years (4.9 in 1967, 5.2 in 1975), relates to the maximum pension available to the lowest paid worker. Although there is less agreement among the different schemes on this particular attribute, there are only two countries—Finland and the Netherlands—with 1975 grades higher than 6, while there are ten with grades no higher than 5.

## CONCLUSION

In terms of maximizing "life chances," it would appear that there is room for improvement in each of these nineteen statutory pension schemes; more in some and less in others, to be sure, but some room in each. Moreover, the fact that, with each of these attributes, at least one country is at the top of the scale (the one exception being with respect to the pension available to the lowest paid worker, where the top grade is 9 rather than 10) at least suggests that it may be possible to incorporate these improvements without unduly jeopardizing any scheme's fiscal or administrative viability—at least in the short run. Impediments to such improvements in countries at the level of economic development of those in this study would appear to be more a matter of political and ethical priorities than of economics or public administration. This is, perhaps, best demonstrated by the rapidity with which extensive overhauls of pension schemes have been carried out—as depicted, for example, in the 84 and 33 percent increases, respectively, in New Zealand's and Switzerland's composite grades between only 1973 and 1975.

# FOOTNOTES

*Lincoln H. Day is Senior Fellow in Demography, Research School of Social Sciences, Institute of Advanced Studies, Australian National University, Canberra. His more recent work has been concerned with the concept of optimum population and the likely consequences of zero population growth rates. He is currently doing research on the social setting of low fertility in industrialized countries, differential fertility in Australia, and an international comparison of death from violence.

1. "Substantial control" over mortality is defined for this purpose as a male life expectancy at birth of at least 60 years over the entire period since 1950; "substantial control" over fertility, as an average annual total fertility rate not in excess of 2,800 during a nonwar period of at least 10 years' duration.

2. This study is now in its final stages. An early description of it is contained in Day and Day (1969), and a preliminary analysis of selected data for six of the countries was reported on in Day and Day (1970). A cross-national comparison of 46 populations on one item used in this study (other than the one reported on here, and involving the—methodologically less difficult—use of exclusively numerical data) is contained in Day (forthcoming)

# REFERENCES

Aaron, Henry (1967) "Social Security: International Comparisons." Pages 13–48 in Otto Eckstein (ed.), *Studies in the Economics of Income Maintenance*. Washington: Brookings Institution.

Cohen, Wilbur J. (1960) "Income Maintenance and Medical Insurance." Pages 76–105 in Ernest W. Burgess (ed.), *Aging in Western Societies*. Chicago: University of Chicago Press.

Day, Lincoln H. (forthcoming ) "Death from Violence—An International Comparison."

——— and Day, Alice Taylor (1969) "Family Size in Industrialized Countries: An Inquiry into the Social-Cultural Determinants of Levels of Childbearing," *Journal of Marriage and the Family* 31:242–251.

——— (1970) "The Social Setting of Low Natality in Industrialized Countries." Paper presented *(in absentia)* at meeting of International Sociological Association, Varna, Bulgaria.

Hohm, Charles F. (1975) "Social Security and Fertility: An International Perspective." *Demography* 12:629–644.

International Labour Office. *Yearbook of Labour Statistics*. Geneva.

*International Labour Review* (1958) "Cost of Non-Statutory Social Security Schemes." *International Labour Review* 78:388–403.

Kaim-Caudle, P. R. (1973) *Comparative Social Policy and Social Security*. London: Martin Robertson.

U.S. Department of Health, Education and Welfare, Social Security Administration, Office of Research and Statistics. *Social Security Programs throughout the World*. Washington, D.C.: Government Printing Office, 1967 and 1975 issues.

# AN INDEX OF EVALUATED EQUALITY: MEASURING CONCEPTIONS OF SOCIAL JUSTICE IN ENGLAND AND THE UNITED STATES

Wendell Bell and Robert V. Robinson*

## PURPOSE

Social stratification and inequality, of course, are subjects of major importance to sociologists. In the United States since the early studies of "Middletown," "Yankee City," and "Elmtown," we have seen numerous case studies of particular towns and cities in which the social class structure in its many aspects is comprehensively analyzed and today national surveys give us longitudinal data on socioeconomic status for the entire country. With respect to the related subject of community power, we now have reached the point of synthesis and generalization, even of studies of studies (Clark, 1973; Gilbert, 1968; Walton, 1966). Research on social mobility is not only of substantive interest, but also has become a

**Comparative Studies in Sociology—Vol. 1, 1978, pages 235–270**

**ISBN 0-89232-025-7**

source of methodological innovation (Blau and Duncan, 1967; Goodman, 1969; Klatsky and Hodge, 1971; White, 1970). Sophistication in the study of social stratification was increased with studies of status crystallization and inconsistency, beginning with Lenski's (1954) influential article. Trends in social stratification and mobility in the United States have been assessed (Duncan, 1968). Inequality of educational opportunity and its effects (J. Coleman et al., 1966; Jencks, et al., 1972; Rosenbaum, 1976) and of educational and occupational aspiration and achievement (Blau and Duncan, 1967; Duncan et al., 1968; Sewell et al., 1969, 1970, 1975, 1976) have been frequently studied and have become considerations in policy formulation.

Moreover, most—if not all—social surveys throughout the Western World include socioeconomic information as a matter of standard procedure and the objective facts of both socioeconomic inequality (Paukert, 1973; Russett, 1965) and, following the path-breaking work of Inkeles and Rossi (1956), of prestige (Hodge, et al., 1966; Treiman, 1975) have reached a new level of maturity with cross-national studies. Even in some communist countries, where official dogma in 1933 had it that there were no social classes, and since Stalin only "nonantagonistic classes, occupational distinctions" are recognized and studies of occupational prestige have been done (Yanowitch and Fisher, 1973).

Although stratification and inequality have been widely and comparatively investigated as presumed objective facts and as subjective representations of those facts, as in reputational or subjective self-placement methods of studying influence or class structures, much less empirical social inquiry has been done into the underlying evaluations of equality and inequality in the society as a whole. Thus, we know relatively little from contemporary social science research about the factors that lead some people to accept—or at least to tolerate—inequalities and that lead others to feel grievance and to struggle against them. And we know practically nothing in a comparative framework. Although they no doubt overstate the case, there is some truth in Huber and Form's (1973, p. 160) observation that "American social scientists have tended to ignore the justice of the system of rewards. We have no rationale for a fair system." Yet such rationales, as they bear on justifications of inequality or equality, are as ubiquitous as the reality of inequality itself. Although there is no society without some form of systematic inequality, there is also no society without values—sometimes competing ones—defining how much equality or inequality for whom, compared to whom, under what circumstances is just.

In this chapter we propose an empirical method for the evaluation of inequality within a society, a way to measure whether a system of inequality is just or unjust. Specifically, we have a four-fold purpose: (1) to discuss the importance of conceptions of justice as they pertain to the amount of inequality in the society, that is the importance of evaluations of equality or inequality; (2) to propose a new index to measure "evaluated equality," that is conceptions of the justice of equality or inequality; (3) to test the reliability and validity of the index by its application to comparative data for England and the United States; and (4) to comment on the differences in evaluated equality between the two countries.

## THE IMPORTANCE OF EVALUATIONS OF EQUALITY

By equality or inequality we mean the amount of "similarity or difference between two or more individuals, populations, or collectivities of people or other units with respect to some specified characteristic such as a condition, a right, a duty, or a treatment" (Bell, 1974, pp. 8–9; Oppenheim, 1968). Equality exists when the units being compared are the same; inequality exists when the units are different, larger differences indicating greater inequality.

The social significance of attitudes toward equality—and the underlying valuations on which they are based—seems so obvious in today's world that we do not want to belabor the point here. In the United States alone, adherents of the civil rights movement, Black Power advocates, activists for the feminist cause, supporters of equal educational opportunities, and enforcers of school busing, to mention just a few examples, illustrate the driving force for social change contained in egalitarian attitudes (and, we must add, opposition to each illustrates the often equally forceful resistance to change contained in inegalitarian attitudes).

Beyond our experience of the recent past, of course, is an interpretation of history: The widely held view of a democratic and egalitarian revolution that spread from eighteenth-century Western Europe and North America carrying the values of the Enlightenment (Palmer, 1959–1964). No doubt in most human societies throughout the course of human history some inequalities have existed and have been accepted as normal and often as legitimate. Yet in spite of the

> . . . great diversity of patterns, certain trends seem to emerge from a consideration of the events of the last hundred and fifty years. Everywhere there seems to have come about a steady erosion in the legitimacy accorded to social inequality. If social inequality continues to exist as a fact, it is no longer accepted by all as a part of the natural order but is challenged, or at least questioned, at every point (Béteille, 1969, p. 366).

"Everywhere" today includes the more than 80 new states that have been formed since World War II from the African, Asian, and Caribbean former colonies of European powers. Their formation constitutes the "nationalist revolution of our time" which may be to a large extent another manifestation of a more broadly based and multifaceted "egalitarian revolution" (Bell, 1967; Emerson, 1960; Fallers, 1963; Moskos, 1967). Thus, within and between countries, developed and less developed, old and new states alike, evaluations of equality or inequality have been a source of support both for an existing social order and stability, and at other times, for conflict and change. In the modern world increasingly favorable attitudes toward equality appear to be especially a source of the latter as they clash "with traditional conceptions of hierarchy" (Béteille, 1969, p. 368). A sociological assessment of evalutions of equality, then, is a step toward answering a fundamental question concerning all social organizations, institutions, and society as a whole: How much inequality is legitimate?

Quite apart from its practical significance, this question poses a theoretical challenge to sociologists as well. Given the ubiquity of social stratification, the proper study of social order and change invites the investigation of *evaluations* of equality and inequality. Such evaluations are a window to the rationales that support or reject existing inequalities. And every system of stratification "needs to be justified because valued rewards are always in short supply and many persons get few indeed" (Huber and Form, 1973, p. 1).

## MORAL PHILOSOPHY AND EMPIRICAL SOCIAL SCIENCE

John Rawls (1971, p. 3) in *A Theory of Justice* proposes that "Justice is the first virtue of social institutions, as truth is of systems of thought. A theory however elegant and economical must be rejected or revised if it is untrue; likewise laws and institutions no matter how efficient and well-arranged must be reformed or abolished if they are unjust." One can rightly agree with Rawls and conclude that justice is a measure of the legitimacy of an institution or of an entire society. Durkheim for example even went further:

> The task of the most advanced societies is, then, a work of justice. . . . Just as the ideal of lower [less developed] societies was to create or maintain as intense a common life as possible, in which the individual was absorbed, so our ideal is to make social relations always more equitable, so as to assure the free development of all our socially useful forces . . . Just as ancient peoples needed, above all, a common faith to live by, so we need justice. . . . (1933, p. 381–382).

As other writers have said (Dworkin, 1975), a fundamental right to equality lies at the heart of Rawls' theory of justice. Rawls attempts to reveal the principles underlying the "dominant moral and political ideology of our time" which he sees as a form of liberalism. But it is "a more egalitarian liberalism than dominated the eighteenth and nineteenth centuries" (Daniels, 1975, p. xiv). His principles include equal liberty, equality of opportunity, and the notion that inequality in goods other than liberty is permissible *only if such inequalities help the least advantaged.*

As is well known, Rawls' theory is based on axiological principles and an "original position" in which judgments about equality or inequality take place behind a "veil of ignorance." Rawls' somewhat conservative and risk-averting "rational choosers" have interests, but they do not know, while deciding on a "social contract," where they are—or will be—placed in the system they are evaluating. There is a vacuum of interests within which decision making about the fairness or unfairness of inequalities takes place. Thus, Rawls' principles of "justice as fairness" result from what free and rational persons would choose if they were selecting the fundamental rules of an association they were about to begin without knowing what roles they would end up having. Therefore, presumably, the choices they make would be unclouded by special interests and, as Rawls tries to show, would result, by logical deduction, in a "just society."

Although there have been many telling critiques of Rawls' theory, including some from the social sciences (Daniels, 1975; Boudon, 1976), Rawls clearly struck a nerve, as the broad acclaim and recognition that his book has received demonstrates. Somehow, he asked the right substantive question: What rationale justifies equality or various degrees of inequality in society?

There is, however, a clear need for some social science alternative to his moral philosophical answer, an alternative that nonetheless views justice as fairness and that deals with equality and inequality. Rawls himself lays the basis for an empirical evaluation of his theory of justice when he contends that any such theory must draw on what "we believe to be true about people and social systems. It is not unrelated to the facts of life" (Daniels, 1975, p. xxxi). A number of writers have raised a question about how "ideal" theory is "related to judgments about justice in the real, nonideal world" (Daniels, 1975, p. xxxiii). Why, it has been asked, should people in real societies with real interests be willing to bind themselves to choices made by people in the original position? (Nagel, 1975; Dworkin, 1975).

Thus, we think it is reasonable to suggest that in real societies, human interests must be dealt with in formulating a theory of justice. In some real sense the legitimacy that social institutions enjoy can only come from real people occupying known positions, having real interests, and more or less known costs and benefits from a system of inequality in comparison to other people. It is such people who legitimate institutions and society in general and it is they whose collective judgments of the justice of the inequalities created and perpetuated by social institutions constitute the very definition of legitimacy. For any given time and place, such collective judgments are problematic. And just what they are is an empirical question.

## SOME PRINCIPLES OF MEASURING THE JUSTICE OF EQUALITY AS FAIRNESS

From our reading of Rawls and past efforts to measure attitudes toward equity and inequality, especially from the work on equity—including experimental studies (Adams, 1963; Anderson et al., 1969; Blau, 1964; Cook, 1970, 1975; Homans, 1961; Patchen, 1961; Weick, 1966), we formulated four elementary principles for measuring the justice of equality or inequality as fairness.

The item or question should include by direct statement or by inference:

1. The specification of something that is distributed or allocated. This can be thought of as a "good"—or "negative good"—of some kind and it can refer to an existing, past, or future condition, opportunity, input, or output. For example, income, occupation, respect, and housing can be used as such goods.

2. The specification of some other variable or variables by which people or some other unit of analysis such as neighborhoods, schools, or even countries can be classified among which a good is distributed. For example, sex and race could be used. The distribution of occupation (a good) by sex (a classification) in which men and women were compared or the distribution of income (a good) by race (a classification) in which members of different races were compared satisfy the first two principles.

One exception to a multivalued classification is when comparison is based on "all human beings." That is, the specification is that all categories of people, no matter how defined, can be compared and should be equal with respect to the good being considered, as in: "All persons should have equal respect just because they are human beings."

Any given variable or social characteristic, of course, may not be solely either a good or a means of classification. It depends on the use a researcher makes of them. For example, occupation could be a classification, if one were interested in the distribution of income (a good) by occupation. This is far from academic since social class and the cluster of variables used to define it are often used as classifications and sometimes as goods.

3. The specification of the equality or inequality of the good, either directly or indirectly, as distributed among the various categories as defined by the classification. We do not mean the "degree" or "amount" of inequality, but simply that the questionnaire item should give some indication of whether the good is distributed equally or unequally among the categories being considered. We make this principle explicit because items used in the past in an effort to measure attitudes toward inequality occasionally did not specify any inequality in a clear way. For example, if a respondent agrees that "the government should reduce poverty," one still doesn't know whether the respondent is favorable to economic equality. Perhaps, he or she wants to raise everyone's income by a constant percentage that would create still greater inequality, though reducing poverty.

4. A requirement that the respondent judge the fairness or unfairness of the equality or inequality. This may be done directly by asking the respondent, "Is it fair that. . . ?"—specifying some good (principle 1) that is equally or unequally distributed (principle 3) with respect to some classification (principle 2). Or it might be implied by stating, as has been done frequently, that some group does or does not "have a right to some good" or, more simply, by using an "ought" or a "should" in a statement about the distribution of some good among differently classified people.

What results, for example, is something implicitly similar to an equity equation:

$$\frac{\text{income (a good)}}{\text{race A (a classification)}} \quad \text{compared to} \quad \frac{\text{income (a good)}}{\text{race B (a classification)}}.$$

On the face of it, this is simply a comparison of the incomes of two races and a simple mean difference tells us something about how unequal they are with respect to income. That is, if we use only principles 1, 2, and 3. But if we add a judgment about the fairness or unfairness of the inequality, then we have a statement about social justice.

Moreover, to change the simple statement of inequality between race A and B to a comparison of ratios, past research leads us to believe that the respondent's judgment depends upon an implicit or explicit substitution of some attribute characterizing the races in the denominators. This could be nearly anything in a particular case. Let us assume, for example, that members of race A have higher incomes than members of race B. Yet members of race A compared to those of race B may be thought to work harder, make a greater contribution to society, have made more sacrifices, to have greater need, to have more responsibilities, to be graced by God, to be capable of causing more trouble if denied higher incomes, etc. The evaluation of the income difference can then be based on the difference between the races on the judgmental criterion or criteria chosen. Thus, for example,

$$\frac{\text{income of race A}}{\text{contribution of race A}} \quad \text{can be compared to} \quad \frac{\text{income of race B}}{\text{contribution of race B}}.$$

If the incomes are different and the contributions are proportionately different too, then the ratios will be equal and income inequality between the races will be judged to be fair—if one accepts "differential contribution" both as objective fact and as a legitimate rationale for income inequality.[1]

Although we consciously follow the research on equity in the above formulation, we may have strayed from Rawls less than may be apparent. Rawls' theory legitimates inequality, as we said, if it redounds to the interest of the least advantaged people. It is conceivable, in the example given, that members of race B (the less advantaged) might have higher incomes than they otherwise would *if* the still higher incomes of members of race A did in fact result in members of race A working harder, making a greater contribution to society, making more sacrifices, carrying more responsibilities, or thereby causing less trouble. One can even imagine the "grace of God" functioning in this way if it was believed that the higher income of race A therefore pleased God and made Him (or Her) more beneficent to everyone. We have more trouble fitting "greater need" into the logic of Rawls' framework, because the usual examples that come to mind where need is used to justify "inequality" of income between workers, say between men and women, are based on the assumption that there are more mouths to feed, clothes to buy, etc. This actually results in more per capita equality if all the recipients of the income are taken into account and not just the worker him- or herself. Thus, it is not entirely clear in this example who the disadvantaged are nor how they are helped by "inequality." Neither equity theory nor our respondents, however, have any trouble accepting need as a basis for judging inequality to be fair or unfair.

These principles, obviously, do not substitute for the usual principles of measurement involving empirical and theoretical import. They are in addition to them.

## SOME PAST EFFORTS TO MEASURE THE JUSTICE OF EQUALITY OR INEQUALITY

It is beyond the scope of this paper to give a complete review and critique of past social scientific efforts to measure the justice of equality or inequality and related concepts. Yet we are obliged to mention a selected few as a necessary introduction to the Index of Evaluated Equality we have constructed. Although we have decided to attempt to construct a new and, we hope, better index, we build upon the past work of others.

Several social scientists, including one of the present writers, appear to have been groping toward a measurement of conceptions of the justice of equality and inequality as fairness without having Rawls as a guide. Although occasionally close, they never were right on target with all of the items in a multiple-item index, nor consistently so in their empirical focus in the case of sets of single questions.

A question from the election studies of the Survey Research Center of the University of Michigan can serve as an example. An item used in 1956 (Robinson et al., 1972, p. 547) was: "If Negroes are not getting fair treatment in jobs and housing, the government should see to it that they do."

This item is good, by our principles, in that it specifies goods (jobs and housing), a classification (Negroes with the implicit comparison being with whites), and justice as fairness (fair treatment). It is not so good, however, in that it doesn't specify that the fair treatment is a matter of equality or inequality.

Quite apart from confounding attitudes toward jobs and housing, which was rectified in subsequent wordings of the question, there is another difficulty with the question from our point of view. That is, the focus of the question is more on the means of rectifying the situation, government action, rather than on the judgment of inequality as fair or unfair. Hypothetically, a respondent could judge inequality to be unjust while opposing government action to produce equality. Furthermore, since ideologies concerning the role of government are themselves important aspects of the concept of conservatism-liberalism, the waters are muddied. Yet, because we know from past research in the United States

(Rainwater, 1974, p. 184) that ". . . respondents regard the 'government' as ultimately responsible for improvements in the realization of equalitarian ideals," it may be justifiable to include government action in an item or two. If so, however, it should appear in only a few items of a multi-item index and should not be the chief emphasis of the item.

In Turner's (1958) study of "merited prestige" in Britain, the equality or inequality of prestige (a good) is judged using a "should" question and different occupations are the classification; Rainwater (1974) used income as the good, occupational groups as the classification, and specifically stated fairness as his criterion of judgment; and in his extended interviews-in-depth with 15 men, Lane (1959) probed the meaning of equality. These results include considerable justification for the view that the respondents' own frames of reference do contain moral judgments concerning how much equality or inequality in society is just.

Runciman (1966), being familiar with Rawls' earlier work on justice as fairness, places his conception of inequality squarely in a judgmental framework. That is, grievances (negative judgments) about inequality occur when some group is relatively deprived in its members' perceptions compared to some reference group whose rewards seem relatively too great or whose "contributions" seem relatively too little. In his empirical study, however, Runciman's major concern is with measurement of relative deprivation and reference groups rather than with conceptions of the justice of inequality as fairness.

Bales and Couch (1969) construct a multi-item scale to measure equalitarianism, but at least four of the ten items fail by our criteria, and some of the others are questionable on other grounds. A respondent might disagree with the statement, "A group of equals will work a lot better than a group with a rigid hierarchy," not because he or she thinks inequality is unjust but because he or she believes, factually, that people will work better under a rigid hierarchy. To take another item as an example, agreeing or disagreeing with "In any group it is more important to keep a friendly atmosphere than to be efficient" says relatively little about the respondent's judgment concerning the justice of inequality.

Seeman and Morris constructed an 18-item "status attitude" index that is quite close—in the case of a few items identical—to the concept of the justice of equality or inequality as fairness.[2] It measured, according to Seeman (1960, p. 7) ". . . the individual's tendency to approve or disapprove of the maintenance of status differences in a broad range of situations." Low scorers were labeled "equalitarians" and high scorers "non-equalitarians." Some of the Seeman-Morris items are quite good from the point of view of our four principles. For example, the item, "Those who have a larger investment in an enterprise ought to have a greater power in determining policy.'' (Seeman, 1960, pp. 139–140)—where the response requested is a five-valued Likert type set of categories ranging from definitely or strongly agree to definitely or strongly disagree—sets up a good, ''greater power in determining policy'' and a basis of classification, ''those who have a larger investment.''

The inequality or equality implied by an ''agree'' or ''disagree'' answer appears clear. The ''ought,'' however, might be interpreted to mean an evaluative judgment regarding fairness or it might be given a utilitarian meaning, a concept of justice that Rawls goes to considerable pains to show is inferior to his own. Thus, it could mean in the latter framework that the welfare of the enterprise would be better off if it were more in the control of those people who cared more about it because of their investment in it. And one could hold to this view while still judging inequality of power to be unfair. In Rawls' terms, of course, the justice of this inequality could be a matter for empirical determination: Are the lesser investors really better or worse off by giving power to the larger investors?

Some of the other items aren't as good. For example, ''If all the money in the United States were equally distributed among all the population sooner or later it would be back in just about the same hands as it is now because of the superior ability of some individuals'' is more of a belief about how the system works than an attitude. That is, one could judge inequality in money based on ability to be unfair even though one believed that such inequality would in fact happen unless somehow prevented.

Finally, in his influential work on the nature of values, Rokeach (1973) includes the value of equality. For his purposes, his method of measurement—asking a respondent to rank 18 values (including equality) in order of importance as guiding principles in his or her life—seems appropriate. It is inadequate, however, as a measure of the justice of equality or inequality as fairness, because ''importance'' in this context does not necessarily imply ''fairness'' and because the framework does not permit an equity equation based upon the four principles we have formulated as our guidelines.[3]

## BASIC DATA

The basic data on which this exploratory study is based are interviews averaging about an hour in length with persons 18 years of age or over in England and the United States. Interviewing in both countries was done during the summer of 1975. In the United States interviews were conducted in the cities of East Haven, New Haven, West Haven, and Woodbridge, Connecticut, which were chosen to provide a sample of individuals representing a wide range of occupational, ethnic, and racial backgrounds. Using the *New Haven City Directory, 1974* as our sample frame, we selected every nth name starting with a random number from 1 to n. We fully interviewed 113 persons—or 73.4 percent of the potential respondents after persons who had changed address leaving an unoccupied dwelling unit or were too old or ill to be interviewed had been removed.

In London, using statistics for occupation and race provided by the Population Studies Office of the Greater London Council, we chose seven wards which were as comparable demographically to the four New Haven cities as we were able to get. As our Greater London sample frame we used the *Register of Electors* covering all seven wards available in each borough hall. The *Register* included all registered voters age 18 and over. The wards were Kensal Rise, Kenton, Sudbury, and Tokyngton in Brent Borough, East Barnet and Garden Suburb in Barnet Borough, and Ruskin in Southwark Borough. We interviewed a total of 101 respondents in the London area for a 73.2 percent response rate.

The samples are adequate for the purposes of preliminary testing our index and exploring causal connections within each country. For cross-country differences, of course, gross comparisons cannot be assumed to represent the results of an overall England-United States comparison between representative samples, since neither sample, especially the English one, is representative of the entire country. Nonetheless, country differences can be meaningfully made to the extent to which we have successfully matched sampling areas on key demographic variables or have introduced relevant statistical controls.

Although we pretested our items on American respondents, a British sociologist, Michael Mann, took an active part in the formulation of the items from the beginning of the project—with an eye to their appropriateness for English respondents—and he engaged in the pretest and its evaluation as well.

## AN INDEX OF EVALUATED EQUALITY

The statements we formulated that we propose for an Index of Evaluated Equality (IEE) are given in Table 1 along with the response categories and distribution of responses for England and the United States. Each of the items meets the criteria we have specified. For the first item, the good

*Table 1.* Percentage Distributions of Respondents According to Items Composing the Index of Evaluated Equality, England and the United States, 1975.

| Items Composing the Index of Evaluated Equality | England (Percent) | United States (Percent) |
|---|---|---|
| 1. "It's fair that rich people who can pay their fines can stay out of jail while poor people may have to go to jail for the same crime." (RICH-LAW) | | |
| Strongly disagree (egalitarian) | 72 | 76 |
| Somewhat disagree | 10 | 13 |
| Undecided | 8 | 1 |
| Somewhat agree | 7 | 6 |
| Strongly agree (inegalitarian) | 3 | 4 |
| Total | 100 | 100 |
| Number of cases | (98) | (113) |
| 2. "It's unfair that people in some occupations get much more respect from others than people in other occupations." (OCCUPATION-RESPECT) | | |
| Strongly agree (egalitarian) | 38 | 45 |
| Somewhat agree | 30 | 31 |
| Undecided | 2 | 3 |
| Somewhat disagree | 14 | 13 |
| Strongly disagree (inegalitarian) | 16 | 8 |
| Total | 100 | 100 |
| Number of cases | (101) | 110) |
| 3. "Now I have a statement about housing. Landlords should be allowed to turn away prospective tenants even if they do so for racial reasons." (RACE-HOUSING) | | |
| Strongly disagree (egalitarian) | 27 | 50 |
| Somewhat disagree | 15 | 10 |
| Undecided | 5 | 4 |
| Somewhat agree | 22 | 16 |
| Strongly agree (inegalitarian) | 31 | 20 |
| Total | 100 | 100 |
| Number of cases | (99) | (111) |
| 4. "It would be more fair if people in America (Britain) were paid by how much they need to live decently rather than by the jobs they do." (NEED-INCOME) | | |
| Strongly agree (egalitarian) | 16 | 14 |
| Somewhat agree | 20 | 21 |
| Undecided | 6 | 4 |
| Somewhat disagree | 18 | 26 |
| Strongly disagree (inegalitarian) | 40 | 35 |
| Total | 100 | 100 |
| Number of cases | (100) | (112) |
| 5. "It would be a good thing if Congress and the President (Parliament) decided to distribute all the money in the United States (Britain) equally among all the population." (ALL EQUAL-WEALTH) | | |
| Strongly agree (egalitarian) | 6 | 16 |
| Somewhat agree | 11 | 4 |
| Undecided | 8 | 4 |
| Somewhat disagree | 12 | 14 |
| Strongly disagree (inegalitarian) | 63 | 62 |
| Total | 100 | 100 |
| Number of cases | (101) | (112) |

being distributed is staying out of jail and the categories of the classification are rich and poor people. In the second, the good and classification are respect and occupation respectively; in the third, housing and race; in the fourth, income and need vs. jobs as alternate and competing classifications; and in the fifth, money and all people equally as human beings. In each question there is an equality or an inequality set up between alternative categories of the classification and there is a moral judgment attached to the equality or inequality, three of the questions actually using the terms "fair" or "unfair."

The equality or inequality being measured by the IEE deals with economic aspects (rich, occupation, income, and monetary wealth) predominantly, but also social (respect, housing, and need), racial (race) and legal (law) aspects. Note the short labels in parentheses after each of the items in Table 1 which we will use in our discussion of them.

Also note from Table 1 that for four out of the five items the American respondents were slightly more likely than the English respondents to be egalitarian, that is to judge equality as being fair. We shall return to the comparison between the two countries after we have evaluated the reliability, dimensionality, and validity of the index.

The IEE scores range from a possible low of 0 to a high of 20. From Table 2, note that the highest possible score was achieved in both countries and the lowest possible in the United States. The lowest score in England was two, not much different. The distribution of IEE scores is also shown in Table 2, again showing the slightly more egalitarian responses of Americans.[4]

*Table 2.* Percentage Distribution of Total Scores for the Index of Evaluated Equality, England and the United States, 1975.

| Total Scores on the Index of Evaluated Equality[a] | England (Percent) | United States (Percent) |
|---|---|---|
| 16 or more (Most Egalitarian) | 11.9 | 18.6 |
| 11–15 | 38.6 | 40.7 |
| 6–10 | 33.7 | 31.9 |
| 5 or less (Most Inegalitarian) | 15.8 | 8.8 |
| Total | 100.0 | 100.0 |
| Number of cases | (101) | (113) |
| Highest score possible | 20 | 20 |
| Highest score achieved | 20 | 20 |
| Lowest score possible | 0 | 0 |
| Lowest score achieved | 2 | 0 |

[a]Persons who did not answer all of the items composing the IEE were given total scores based on the items which they did answer.

## RELIABILITY

Since we do not have longitudinal data in which a test-retest could have been done, we cannot measure the reliability of the IEE in the sense of stability (Cronbach, 1951, p. 298). We can, however, measure reliability in the sense of internal consistency or equivalence by showing how well each of the items agrees with the others in their ordering of the respondents according to the evaluation of equality.

Two such statistics are shown in Table 3. The first is the Scale Value Difference (SVD) ratio, which is based on an item analysis. The SVD ratio "is merely the ratio of the difference between high-half and low-half item means when the split into halves is based on the total-test score, to the difference between high-half and low-half item means when the split into halves is based on the item alone" (Bardo, 1976, p. 417). Since all SVDs in both countries are significant beyond the 0.001 level, we conclude that the items tend to measure the same thing, somewhat more so in England than the United States. The highest SVD ratio in each country is for ALL EQUAL-WEALTH and the lowest for OCCUPATION-RESPECT.

Item-total score correlations, with the item being correlated each time removed from the total score, are also given in Table 3. Again, the findings support the hypothesis that the items tend to measure the same thing. With the exception of OCCUPATION-RESPECT in England and RICH-LAW in the United States, all the correlations are significant beyond the 0.001 level and these two are significant beyond 0.005. The item-total score correlations, of course, are much higher than those shown when the item being correlated is left in the total score.

*Table 3.* Scale Value Difference (SVD) Ratios and Item-Total Score Correlations[a] for the Items Composing the Index of Evaluated Equality, England and the United States, 1975.

| Items Composing the Index of Evaluated Equality | England | | United States | |
|---|---|---|---|---|
| | SVD Ratio[b] | Correlation[c] | SVD Ratio[b] | Correlation[c] |
| RICH-LAW | 0.71 | 0.31 | 0.50 | 0.16 |
| OCCUPATION-RESPECT | 0.64 | 0.27 | 0.37 | 0.31 |
| RACE-HOUSING | 0.66 | 0.37 | 0.69 | 0.34 |
| NEED-INCOME | 0.68 | 0.42 | 0.69 | 0.43 |
| ALL EQUAL-WEALTH | 0.83 | 0.38 | 0.88 | 0.44 |
| AVERAGE | 0.70 | 0.35 | 0.63 | 0.34 |

[a]To compute these correlations the particular item involved each time was *excluded* from the total score.
[b]All SVDs are significant at greater than the 0.001 level.
[c]All item-total correlations are significant at the 0.001 level, except for OCCUPATION-RESPECT in England and RICH-LAW in the United States both of which are significant at the 0.005 level.

Two other measures which pretty much tell the same story, but are summarized for the index as a whole are Cronbach's (1951) $\alpha$ and Heise and Bohrnstedt's (1970) $\Omega$. For England alpha is 0.58 and omega is 0.59 and for the United States alpha is 0.56 and omega is 0.62. As usually interpreted for a five-item scale these results are only moderately good. One might hope for between a 0.6 and 0.7 for alpha (McKennell, 1970, p. 237) and at least 0.70 for omega.[5]

## DIMENSIONALITY

*Factor analysis.*

Another way of showing the dimensionality of the items is through factor analysis. In England a principal factor solution results in one factor that explains 100 percent of the common variance of the items with an eigenvalue of 1.15 (see Table 4).[6] In the United States, however, the results are not quite as good. Although two factors are shown for the United States in Table 4, the first factor explains 82 percent of the common variance with an eigenvalue of 1.21. The second factor, with an eigenvalue of 0.27, was not worth extracting. Thus, there is really only one factor in the United States as well.

In both countries the highest item-factor correlations with the factor were for the items NEED-INCOME and ALL EQUAL-WEALTH. All other factor loadings were very encouraging, except for RICH-LAW in the United States which was somewhat low (0.17). Potential users of the index in the future are alerted to the possibility that this item might be dropped from the index *if* on repeated use with other data it continues to do poorly in the item-factor correlation. We have kept it in the IEE here, however, because it appears to work pretty well in England—it has, for

*Table 4.* Principal Factor Matrix of Items Composing the Index of Evaluated Equality, England and the United States, 1975.

| | England Factors | | United States Factors | | |
|---|---|---|---|---|---|
| Items | I | $h_i^2$ | I | II | $h_i^2$ |
| RICH-LAW | 0.33 | 0.11 | 0.17 | 0.15 | 0.05 |
| OCCUPATION-RESPECT | 0.34 | 0.12 | 0.47 | 0.42 | 0.39 |
| RACE-HOUSING | 0.48 | 0.23 | 0.46 | −0.14 | 0.23 |
| NEED-INCOME | 0.64 | 0.41 | 0.57 | −0.02 | 0.33 |
| ALL EQUAL-WEALTH | 0.53 | 0.28 | 0.65 | −0.23 | 0.48 |

example, the second highest SVD ratio there—and because it meets the theoretical criteria stated earlier. It is, of course, an extreme item with 82 percent of the English and 89 percent of the American respondents giving somewhat or strongly egalitarian responses, the largest egalitarian response of all the items in either country. This is a meaningful finding in that it supports the contention that there is—at least in modern Western societies—more concensus regarding the justice of civil and political equality than economic and social equality.

*Guttman scaling.*

Although the items were not constructed so as to be dimensional in the cumulative sense of a Guttman (1944, 1947) scale, the items in fact do form a scale with satisfactory coefficients of reproducibility, improvements over the minimum marginal reproducibility, and coefficients of scalability if we allow some agree and disagree responses to be grouped together isolating only "strongly agree" or "strongly disagree." These statistics are not fully adequate, however, if only the "undecided" response is allowed to combine with either agree or disagree responses and the "strongly agree" and "somewhat agree" are always grouped together and separately from "strongly disagree" and "somewhat disagree," a requirement that makes intuitive sense to us.

In this case, for the five items as dichotomies the coefficient of reproducibility is 0.88, minimum marginal reproducibility 0.72, and coefficient of scalability 0.55 for England. The same figures are 0.89, 0.74, and 0.56 for the United States. Thus, although we make no claims for scalability in this sense and do not use scale scores, there is some evidence that the items tend toward cumulative dimensionality. Furthermore, the items are ordered the same way in each country in terms of the percentage of egalitarian responses. In order from most to least egalitarian response they are: (1) RICH-LAW, (2) OCCUPATION-RESPECT, (3) RACE-HOUSING, (4) NEED-INCOME, (5) ALL EQUAL-WEALTH. That is, in both countries, most respondents agreed that it was not fair that rich people who can pay their fines can stay out of jail while poor people may have to go to jail for the same crime. Somewhat fewer agreed that it's unfair that people in some occupations get much more respect from others than people in other occupations. Still fewer disagreed that landlords should be allowed to turn away prospective tenants even if they do so for racial reasons. Relatively few agreed that it would be more fair if people were paid by how much they need to live decently rather than by the jobs they do. And very few respondents agreed that it would be a good thing if all the money were distributed equally among all the population (see Table 1).

## VALIDITY AND INVALIDITY

*Internal validity.*

By internal validity we mean trait validity. That is, the degree to which the overall index as constructed and the true underlying variable it is presumed to measure, in this case evaluated equality, are correlated. A "high validity coefficient does not imply that one has measured what he set out to measure. It means only that whatever the items are measuring, the composite constructed is highly correlated to it" (Heise and Bohrnstedt, 1970, p. 123). The measure suggested by Heise and Bohrnstedt is 0.77 for England and 0.79 for the United States. These are fair to middling results, certainly tolerable, though not as high as we would like.

Their $\Psi^2$, a measure of invalidity, however, is effectively zero for both countries, 0.002 in England and 0.0020 in the United States. Thus, we can conclude that there is no variation among the index items due to causes or factors other than the one underlying variable (Heise and Bohrnstedt, 1970, p. 105).

*External validity.*

By external validity we mean whether or not the index measures what it was intended to measure. We can suggest here one external criterion which appears on theoretical grounds to make a good candidate for a correlate of IEE in some basic definitional sense. Here we accept a much smaller correlation than before in support of our hypothesis, since there are so many other considerations affecting variation in the external criterion than evaluations of equality.

If IEE measures what it is supposed to measure then we would expect a correlation with political party preference, with Labour Party supporters being more favorable to equality as being fair than Conservative Party supporters in England and Democrats more so than Republicans in the United States. We expect a higher correlation in England where the "Labour Party formally rejects inegalitarian attitudes, supporting as its ideal the classless society" (Rose, 1964). Such is in fact the case, the correlations being 0.45 in England and 0.21 in the United States.[7]

Additionally, for England there is another obvious variable that we can use as an external criterion. To begin each interview session we asked respondents, "Speaking generally, what are the things about this country of which you are most proud?" A surprisingly large number of English respondents (45) mentioned the tradition, historical background, heritage, or pageantry of England and, of those, 20 respondents specifically included the Queen, the Crown, or the Royal Family. Assuming that persons who gave such responses are more favorable to the justice of hierarchy and inequality than persons who didn't mention them at all, we expect negative correlations with IEE although they may be small because some persons who didn't mention tradition or the Queen might have done so if asked outright. The results further support the validity of the index. The correlation is −0.24 with "tradition" and −0.18 with "the Queen."[8]

## COUNTRY DIFFERENCES IN EVALUATED EQUALITY

At least since Tocqueville's *Democracy in America* was published in several volumes in 1835 and 1840, it has become commonplace to characterize American society as having relatively more equality than European societies and the American people as distinctively believing in and highly valuing equality. For example, Lipset (1963, p. 517) says that more "than any other modern non-Communist industrial nation, the United States emphasizes achievement, *equalitarianism,* universalism, and specificity. . . ."; Huber and Form (1973, p. 4) say that the "dominant ideology of American stratification is based primarily on three variables: *equality,* success, and democracy"; in his comprehensive review of the literature characterizing "what is American" from early times up to 1940, L. Coleman (1941, p. 498) concludes that "belief in the *equality* of all as a fact and as a right" is among the handful of traits mentioned in all periods; and *equality of opportunity* is included by Williams (1951, p. 387) in the "nominally dominant ideals of" American society (italics added).

Compared to American society, English society is seen as being more class-bound and its people more elitist and inegalitarian in attitudes and values (Lipset, 1967). Yet, as recently as 1975, Treiman and Terrell (1975, p. 579) said that to their "knowledge no systematic evidence exists" regarding the question of whether or not "British society is more class bound than American society." Their own data, however, show that there is less intergenerational mobility in England than in the United States. Our search of the literature finds little by way of direct systematic data in a comparative framework to indicate that the English judge equality as being less fair—or inequality as being more fair—than do Americans. For example, in his well-known study, Alford (1963, p. 109) says that in Great Britain he expects there is more class consciousness but *less equalitarianism* than in the United States; he adds that this statement is suggested by "qualitative evidence."

Complicating the predominant view of American egalitarian values and

English inegalitarian values, are a number of other considerations. First, Tocqueville (1954 ed., p. 53) himself says of the United States, "I know of no country . . . where the love of money has taken stronger hold on the affections of men and *where a profounder contempt is expressed for the theory of the permanent equality of property*" (italics added). Second, because of the linked value of achievement, the value of equality in the United States is asserted to be largely equality of opportunity, including the opportunity to be unequal (Lipset, 1967, p. 369). Kristol (1968, p. 110), for example, says that "Equality of opportunity will inevitably result in inequality of condition" and that the "American creed sanctions such inequality—but only halfheartedly." Third, it has been asserted (Roshwald, 1973, p. 38) that Americans are "almost morbidly suspicious of any kind of socialism and social-welfare state" while the British Labour Party, largely reformist though it may be in comparison to continental socialist parties, has raised the level of public services and benefits far above those in the United States and has done so, at least in part, by recourse to the conception of the justice of equality. Fourth, changes have been taking place in British society and it has been moving away from elitism and toward egalitarianism. "Industrialization, urbanization, and political democratization have all spurred the growth of universalistic and achievement-oriented values" (Lipset, 1968, p. 294). And, fifth, the United States, too, may have been changing. As Lipset (1968, p. 300) says further, "the United States' self image as a radical egalitarian democracy as opposed to the reactionary, monarchical, aristocratic, and imperialist regimes of Europe has been challenged by its recent world-wide role of supporting existing regimes against communist and sometimes non-communist revolutionary movements. . . ." It is conceivable that such a change has also resulted in altering judgments about equality for at least some sections of the American population in subtle, but measurable, ways—perhaps even against what appears to be a trend toward the justice of greater equality for more people, as, for example, minority groups and women become more incorporated in educational and economic institutions.

We have already seen from the data presented above (Table 1) that Americans were slightly more favorable to the conception of the fairness of equality than the English in four of the five items and about the same as the English on the fifth, the mean total score for the IEE in England being 10.2 and in the United States 11.5 (a difference significant at the 0.025 level).

In Table 5 mean scores on the IEE are given with controls for sex, race, and occupation. Note that in every case Americans are more egalitarian

*Table 5.* Mean Scores on the Index of Evaluated Equality Controlling for Sex, Race, and Occupation, England and the United States, and Correlations of IEE Scores with Country.

| Social Background Characteristics Controlled | Mean Score on IEE England | Mean Score on IEE United States | Mean Difference | Correlation[a] |
|---|---|---|---|---|
| No Controls | | | | 0.14 |
| All respondents | 10.2 | 11.5 | +1.3 | |
| Sex | | | | 0.10 |
| Male | 9.7 | 11.1 | +1.4 | |
| Female | 10.7 | 11.8 | +1.1 | |
| Race | | | | 0.10 |
| White | 9.7 | 10.5 | +0.8 | |
| Nonwhite | 14.1 | 16.5 | +2.4 | |
| Occupation | | | | 0.09 |
| Nonmanual | 9.6 | 10.7 | +1.1 | |
| Manual | 11.3 | 11.9 | +0.6 | |
| Sex and Race | | | | 0.09 |
| Male | | | | |
| White | 9.2 | 10.2 | +1.0 | |
| Nonwhite | 13.5 | 15.7 | +2.2 | |
| Female | | | | |
| White | 10.2 | 10.8 | +0.6 | |
| Nonwhite | 14.7 | 17.0 | +2.3 | |
| Sex, Race, and Occupation[b] | | | | 0.08 |

[a]Except for the first correlation listed for "No Controls," all correlations are partial. United States = 1 and England 0 for computation of correlations.

[b]Means are not given for the three-way breakdown because the number of cases in some of the cells is too small.

than the English. The greatest difference between countries occurs in the case of nonwhites, largely blacks in the United States and New Commonwealth (Asia, Africa, and West Indies) immigrants and their descendants in England, nonwhites in the United States being considerably more favorable to the justice of equality than nonwhites in England. Within each country there are larger differences, nonwhites being markedly more egalitarian than whites. White males are the most inegalitarian and nonwhite females the most egalitarian of all the subgroups.[9]

The simple correlation between the IEE and country is 0.14 and with simultaneous controls for sex, race, and occupation it is 0.08, still showing the partial correlation, Americans to be slightly more likely than English respondents to evaluate equality as being fair and inequality as being unfair.

Thus, the many assertions concerning more favorable evaluation of egalitarianism in America than in England are weakly supported by our exploratory study. Yet, if our findings are representative at all of the total populations in these countries, we have been somewhat misled by the stereotypes. The differences in evaluated equality between countries are very small, item-by-item the responses are quite similar, and, in terms of the percentage of agree or disagree responses, the items are ordered in the same way in each country. This leads us to conclude that there may be more to explain in the relative similarity in the two countries than their differences. That is, the English are more egalitarian and the Americans less egalitarian than we have been led to believe.

Finally, we want to point out an implication of our findings for recent work on social stratification in England and the frequent assumption made by sociologists in both countries that equality is just and inequality is unjust. A number of writers have raised the question: "Why is it that, given the prevailing degree of social inequality, there is no widely supported and radical opposition to the existing socio-political order, and that at all levels of the stratification hierarchy attitudes of acceptance, if not of approval, are those most commonly found? (Goldthorpe, 1974, p. 219)." The answers given tend to be divided into the "social psychological" or the "culturalist," according to Goldthorpe (1974). The former is exemplified by Runciman (1966) who concludes that members of disadvantaged groups tend to compare themselves with other groups fairly close to them in the system of social stratification. Thus, their sense of *relative deprivation* is not great. They do not perceive great inequalities and they have relatively little sense of grievance. "In other words, the degree of *relative* deprivation—deprivation which is subjectively experienced and which may thus influence political behavior—is primarily determined *by the structure of reference groups* rather than by the structure of inequality itself as the sociologist might describe it" (Goldthorpe, 1974, p. 220).

An example of the culturalist view is the study by Almond and Verba (1965). From this perspective grievances over inequality do not lead to the desire for radical change in the system because of the nature of the political culture. From childhood onwards "the majority of citizens come to feel a sense of unfanatical, but generally unquestioning, allegiance to the established political order (Goldthorpe, 1974, p. 221)." Citizens generally trust the political elite and believe that they can "influence political decisions and outcomes—and the system itself is not therefore seen as exploitive."

No doubt, as Goldthorpe says, these explanations are not necessarily contradictory and may go some distance in answering the question posed. Yet we wonder how far the distance is. As we have seen from our data, many people in both England and the United States simply judge some kinds of socioeconomic inequality to be fair. From this point of view the question so many writers have raised may be based on a false assumption that the "prevailing degree of inequality" is in some direct way a measure of the prevailing degree of a sense of unfairness or injustice in the system of inequality. This is emphatically not the case since only *some* of the people who perceive such inequality judge it to be unfair. If they judge inequality to be fair, then we would not expect them to support a "radical opposition to the existing socio-political order."

Our results seem to be consistent with those from the probing interviews with 15 American men done by Lane (1959, pp. 47–48). He found, among other things, that his respondents believed that "equality, at least equality of income, would deprive people of the goals of life . . . would deprive men of their incentive to work, achieve, and develop their skills." Furthermore, interviewees thought it seemed desperately wrong "to suggest that men be equalized and the lower orders raised and one's own hard-earned status given to them as a right and not a reward for effort." Of course Howans (1974) makes this same point in his discussion of distribution justice and cites Aristotle who also did more than two millennia ago.

But our results run partly counter to sociological orthodoxy in Britain where workers are viewed as accepting inequality as normal but *not* as giving it moral approval (Mann, 1970, 1973).

Here are challenging questions for social scientists: Under what conditions are equalities judged to be equitable or inequitable? Under what conditions are inequalities judged to be equitable or inequitable? It can no longer be cavalierly assumed that equality is just and should be established or maintained, nor that inequality is unjust and should be eliminated.

## CONCLUSION

In this chapter we presented a new measuring instrument, the Index of Evaluated Equality, that we propose as a tool for the comparative study of conceptions of the justice of social equality or inequality as fairness. Social inequality, social scientists have demonstrated, is ubiquitous. But so, too, are evaluations of it. Such evaluations, conflicting as they sometimes are, are sources both of support for an existing social order and for attacks against it. They are important elements in assessing the legitimacy of any social institution or society as a whole, because without some general consensus on the justice of social arrangements—and the equalities and inequalities they entail—social order may not be possible.

From past work in social stratification, equity research, and Rawls' theory of justice, we formulated four principles as a basis for evaluating measurements of evaluated equality.

Briefly stated, the four principles are that the items composing the Index of Evaluated Equality should specify: (1) some "good" that is distributed or allocated; (2) some differentiating variable by which people can be classified and among which a good is distributed; (3) the equality or inequality regarding the good as distributed among the various categories of the classification; and (4) a judgment on the part of the respondent regarding the fairness or unfairness of the equality or inequality so specified.

We think that the resulting Index of Evaluated Equality is an improvement over past sociological efforts especially in its explicit focus on the concept of the justice of equality or inequality as fairness. At the same time, since it generates empirical data regarding judgments about equality or inequality of real actors in real situations with real interests, it complements Rawls' hypothetical "original position" and his "veil of ignorance."

After showing how past efforts to measure attitudes toward equality or inequality more or less fail the test of our four principles, we show how the new items we propose as an Index of Evaluated Equality do embody them. Then, with data collected from 113 persons in the Greater New Haven area of the United States and from 101 persons in some parts of Greater London, England, in the summer of 1975, we tested their reliability, dimensionality, and validity. The application of a number of standard statistical procedures leads to the general conclusion that the Index of Evaluated Equality is moderately reliable and moderately internally valid; it is definitely dimensional in the factor analytic sense, especially for England, and nearly dimensional in the Guttman sense, although not designed to be a cumulative scale; and it is quite valid in the sense of measuring what we intended to measure, at least according to the few external criteria we used.

The cliché is that England is elitist and the United States egalitarian. Yet there is very little data from social surveys that actually *compare* English and American values with respect to the justice of equality or inequality as fairness. Furthermore, there are at least some considerations that might lead one to think that Americans might favor inequality as being fair more than the English. The great stress on achievement and equality of opportunity in America inevitably results in some approval of inequality of condition; Britain has advanced further towards the welfare state than has the United States and this advancement has been justified in part by egalitarian values; British society, with democratization, industrialization, and urbanization, has been moving away from elitism and toward egalitarianism; and the United States may have become less egalitarian as it adopted a quasi-imperialistic and sometimes reactionary role in international affairs.

Our findings show a small, but consistent and genuine, difference, with Americans judging equality to be fair more often than the English.

"Why is it," many social scientists and other writers have asked, "that in the face of great inequalities disadvantaged persons don't organize into radical opposition to the existing socio-political order?" For British society, two answers have been proposed, a social-psychological one whereby people are viewed as not being relatively deprived according to their own frames of reference and a culturalist one whereby socialization into the norms and beliefs of the culture prevent political action subversive to the socio-political system itself. Although there may be some truth in each of these explanations, our results provide an answer that seems simpler. In each country there are a considerable number of respondents, including some who are disadvantaged by objective standards, who judge inequality to be fair. That is, the system of inequality is viewed by large numbers of people to be just.[10]

Finally, we assume that in some basic sense the justice of equality or inequality as fairness—and the legitimacy for social arrangements that may or may not flow from it—resides in the collective judgments of the people involved in the situation or society. Some social scientists may object to this assumption because on the surface it may appear to do away with the possibility of "false consciousness." We do not think that it does. It does contain, though, a challenge to the social scientist. If we accept Rawls' principle that inequality is justified only when it redounds to the benefit of the disadvantaged, then we should take seriously the task of showing empirically and convincingly that particular inequalities in particular social settings do or do not in fact so redound. To do so, however, requires a research design that from the start calls into question the congenial assumption made by many social scientists that equality equals equity and inequality equals inequity and permits the possibility that equality equals inequity and inequality equals equity. In the face of what appear to many of us to be obviously inequitable inequalities such a design may seem unnecessary. Yet if general conceptions of the justice of inequality reflect "false consciousness," then such a design—and the systematic and unbiased knowledge that should flow from it—may be the only way to expose it. Three Appendices to this chapter follow, beginning page 260.

*APPENDIX 1.* CORRELATION MATRIX, MEANS, AND STANDARD DEVIATIONS OF ITEMS COMPOSING THE INDEX OF EVALUATED EQUALITY AND OMITTED ITEMS FOR ENGLAND AND THE UNITED STATES.[a]

| | Items Composing IEE | | | | | Items Eliminated from IEE | | | | |
|---|---|---|---|---|---|---|---|---|---|---|
| Items | RINH-LAW | OCCUPATION-RESPECT | RACE-HOUSING | NEED-INCOME | ALL EQUAL-WEALTH | CLASS-MIX | SEX-PAY | FEW-POWER | SEX-JOB | CONTRIBUTION-INCOME |
| RICH-LAW | — | *0.19** | *0.25*** | 0.15 | *0.11* | 0.05 | −0.13 | 0.02 | 0.13 | −0.04 |
| OCCUPATION-RESPECT | *0.15* | — | *0.16* | *0.19** | *0.18** | 0.03 | −0.12 | 0.05 | 0.17 | 0.05 |
| RACE-HOUSING | *0.03* | *0.16** | — | *0.30*** | *0.21** | 0.02 | 0.05 | −0.05 | 0.01 | −0.06 |
| NEED-INCOME | *0.07* | *0.27*** | *0.26*** | — | *0.41*** | −0.17* | −0.13 | 0.13 | 0.06 | 0.18* |
| ALL EQUAL-WEALTH | *0.11* | *0.20** | *0.33*** | *0.38*** | — | −0.04 | −0.02 | 0.07 | 0.07 | −0.18* |
| CLASS-MIX | 0.10 | −0.06 | 0.34** | −0.04 | −0.08 | — | −0.14 | −0.10 | 0.04 | 0.03 |
| SEX-PAY | 0.18* | 0.06 | 0.32** | 0.07 | 0.04 | 0.26** | — | −0.08 | −0.20* | −0.08 |
| FEW-POWER | −0.07 | −0.08 | 0.05 | −0.15 | −0.15 | 0.02 | −0.06 | — | 0.07 | 0.09 |
| SEX-JOB | 0.06 | 0.08 | 0.07 | 0.16 | 0.01 | 0.13 | 0.11 | 0.09 | — | −0.04 |
| CONTRIBUTION-INCOME | 0.06 | −0.09 | 0.18* | 0.09 | 0.03 | 0.24** | 0.25** | 0.11 | 0.12 | — |
| *Means* | | | | | | | | | | |
| England | *3.45* | *2.61* | *1.87* | *1.54* | *0.84* | 2.66 | 3.09 | 2.29 | 1.72 | 2.20 |
| United States | *3.50* | *2.92* | *2.53* | *1.52* | *1.02* | 2.96 | 3.38 | 3.05 | 1.93 | 2.48 |
| *Standard Deviations* | | | | | | | | | | |
| England | *1.07* | *1.50* | *1.64* | *1.56* | *1.29* | 1.53 | 1.36 | 1.64 | 1.41 | 1.56 |
| United States | *1.06* | *1.32* | *1.67* | *1.50* | *1.52* | 1.35 | 1.12 | 1.29 | 1.45 | 1.38 |

[a]Correlations for the English sample are above the diagonal and those for the United States below. Statistics for items in the Index are italicized.
*Significant at the 0.05 level.
**Significant at the 0.01 level.

## *APPENDIX 2.* CLASSIFICATION OF POLITICAL PARTY PREFERENCE, ENGLAND (AND THE UNITED STATES).

| | |
|---|---|
| Strong Labour (Democratic) | 7 |
| Not very strong Labour (Democratic) | 6 |
| Liberal (independent) closer to Labour (Democratic) | 5 |
| Liberal (independent) not close to either major party | 4 |
| Liberal (independent) closer to Conservative (Republican) | 3 |
| Not very strong Conservative (Republican) | 2 |
| Strong Conservative (Republican) | 1 |

## *APPENDIX 3.* ITEMS ELIMINATED FROM THE INDEX OF EVALUATED EQUALITY AT THE ANALYSIS STAGE OF RESEARCH.

In the interests of reliable and complete reporting for those readers who may want to use the IEE in the future, we give the items that were removed from the IEE in the course of the analysis and our reasons for doing so. They are contained, along with the percentage distribution of responses, in Table A.3.1. In the process of elimination we tried to keep theoretical considerations foremost, but, of course, the four criteria, as they emerged, interacted with and were reciprocally influenced by our knowledge of reliability, dimensionality, and validity as we computed these statistics.

The first item in Table A.3.1, ''It's usually better if people of the same social and economic class mix only with their own kind'' (CLASS-MIX), was omitted because, upon reflection, it seemed to be more of an ''evaluative belief'' (Bem, 1970) than a judgment about the fairness of equality or inequality. Since this was one of the items that we probed, we could tell from the open-ended responses that this was in fact the meaning often given the item by the respondents. If they agreed, it was usually because ''people would feel uncomfortable'' or ''wouldn't know what to do.'' If they disagreed, it was usually because ''it would be broadening'' or ''a good experience.'' Thus, it is closer to ''Spinach tastes terrible'' than to ''People ought to like the taste of spinach.'' Although a judgment is involved, it is not necessarily a moral judgment about the *fairness* of equality or inequality.

The two items, ''Sometimes it is all right for a company to pay women less than men for doing the same job'' (SEX-PAY) and ''Sometimes, to correct for past discrimination, it's fair if a company goes out of its way to hire qualified women instead of equally qualified men'' (SEX-JOB), were in part omitted simply because they dealt with inequality of the sexes. They will be analyzed separately in forthcoming work. SEX-PAY is, otherwise, a good item according to our four principles, although the ''all

*Table A.3.1.* Percentage Distribution of Respondents According to Items Eliminated from the Index of Evaluated Equality, England and the United States, 1975.

| Items Eliminated | England (Percent) | United States (Percent) |
|---|---|---|
| "It's usually better if people of the same social and economic class mix only with their own kind." (CLASS-MIX) | | |
| Strongly disagree (egalitarian) | 45 | 52 |
| Somewhat disagree | 21 | 22 |
| Undecided | 1 | 4 |
| Somewhat agree | 20 | 15 |
| Strongly agree (inegalitarian) | 13 | 7 |
| Total | 100 | 100 |
| Number of cases | (101) | (112) |
| "Sometimes it is all right for a company to pay women less than men for doing the same job." (SEX-PAY) | | |
| Strongly disagree (egalitarian) | 59 | 68 |
| Somewhat disagree | 18 | 18 |
| Undecided | 3 | 2 |
| Somewhat agree | 12 | 7 |
| Strongly agree (inegalitarian) | 8 | 5 |
| Total | 100 | 100 |
| Number of cases | (99) | (112) |
| "Effective government requires that political power be held by only a few people." (FEW-POWER) | | |
| Strongly disagree (egalitarian) | 36 | 55 |
| Somewhat disagree | 18 | 20 |
| Undecided | 9 | 5 |
| Somewhat agree | 12 | 14 |
| Strongly agree (inegalitarian) | 25 | 6 |
| Total | 100 | 100 |
| Number of cases | (95) | (112) |
| "Sometimes, to correct for past discrimination, it's fair if a company goes out of its way to hire qualified women instead of equally qualified men." (SEX-JOB) | | |
| Strongly agree (egalitarian) | 13 | 17 |
| Somewhat agree | 24 | 28 |
| Undecided | 11 | 6 |
| Somewhat disagree | 26 | 27 |
| Strongly disagree (inegalitarian) | 26 | 22 |
| Total | 100 | 100 |
| Number of cases | (100) | (110) |
| "In general, most people in this country receive the incomes that they deserve considering the contribution they make to society." (CONTRIBUTION-INCOME) | | |
| Strongly disagree (egalitarian) | 32 | 29 |
| Somewhat disagree | 19 | 35 |
| Undecided | 5 | 6 |
| Somewhat agree | 26 | 18 |
| Strongly agree (inegalitarian) | 18 | 12 |
| Total | 100 | 100 |
| Number of cases | (98) | (110) |

right'' may not quite specify ''fairness'' enough to eliminate the possibility of a utilitarian response. SEX-JOB, to the contrary, has an ambiguity that makes its interpretation debatable in this context. Strictly speaking, one should disagree with the item to be favorable to equality, at least with respect to the immediate situation involving hiring because for a company to go out of its way to hire qualified women instead of equally qualified men would be to treat men in a different, less desirable way, than women. In Table A.3.1 the meaning attached to the responses to this item is given in the opposite way, in accordance with our original notion that agreement, meaning as it did a favorable attitude toward ''affirmative action,'' was indicative of an extreme egalitarian response. In a long-term perspective one might justify such a view: Present reverse differential treatment ''equals out'' with past differential treatment. As stated, however, ''true egalitarians'' theoretically might go either way, agreeing or disagreeing. Thus, although we find this item useful as an indicator of attitudes toward ''affirmative action'' in the case of sex, we have eliminated it from the IEE.

The item, ''Effective government requires that political power be held by only a few people.'' (FEW-POWER), is an evaluative belief and says little, if anything, about the justice of equality or inequality. That is, one could *judge* a few people holding political power to be unfair, but also to *believe* that effective government requires it.

Finally, the item, ''In general, most people in this country receive the incomes that they deserve considering the contribution they make to society.'' (CONTRIBUTION-INCOME) permits two opposite interpretations of disagreement. One could be egalitarian, ''No, lower income people deserve more.'' Another could be inegalitarian, ''No, higher income people deserve more,'' as in the case of a person who might think that doctors, considering their contributions to society, are not paid enough. Thus, this item, too, was eliminated from IEE.

We did factor analyses, Guttman scaling, reliability and validity tests on all 10 items as we did for the 5-item IEE presented in the text. The story is pretty much contained in the Scale Value Difference ratios and item-total score correlations, with the item correlated being excluded from the total score as before, shown in Table A.3.2.

For England, the items included in the final version of the Index of Evaluated Equality all have higher SVD ratios than the items excluded. Also, they all have higher item-total score correlations. In the United States, however, the superiority by these criteria of the items included in IEE is less clear. In fact, the highest SVD ratio (0.79) is for SEX-PAY. Yet in England this item has an SVD ratio of only 0.17 and is actually negatively correlated (−0.22) with the total score.[11] FEW-POWER should obviously be removed, if one were using these statistics as criteria, and

*Table A.3.2.* Scale Value Difference (SVD) Ratios and Item-Total Score Correlations for the Ten Items Originally Intended to Compose the Index of Evaluated Equality (IEE), England and the United States, 1975.

| | England | | United States | |
|---|---|---|---|---|
| Items | SVD Ratio | Correlation[a] | SVD Ratio | Correlation[a] |
| Items Included in IEE | | | | |
| RICH-LAW | 0.60 | 0.26 | 0.44 | 0.19 |
| OCCUPATION-RESPECT | 0.39 | 0.28 | 0.27 | 0.18 |
| RACE-HOUSING | 0.58 | 0.25 | 0.78 | 0.48 |
| NEED-INCOME | 0.63 | 0.35 | 0.53 | 0.31 |
| ALL EQUAL-WEALTH | 0.56 | 0.25 | 0.52 | 0.22 |
| AVERAGE | 0.55 | 0.28 | 0.51 | 0.28 |
| Items Excluded from IEE | | | | |
| CLASS-MIX | 0.10[b] | −0.07[c] | 0.42 | 0.24 |
| SEX-PAY | 0.17[b] | −0.22 | 0.79 | 0.31 |
| FEW-POWER | 0.34 | 0.05[c] | 0.03[b] | −0.05[c] |
| SEX-JOB | 0.33 | 0.09[c] | 0.36 | 0.18 |
| CONTRIBUTION-INCOME | 0.25 | 0.03[c] | 0.34 | 0.24 |
| AVERAGE | 0.24 | −0.02 | 0.39 | 0.18 |

[a]To compute these correlations the particular item involved each time was excluded from the total score.
[b]SVD ratios not significant at 0.001 level.
[c]Correlations not significant at 0.05 level.

RACE-HOUSING should be included, as was done in each case. OCCUPATION-RESPECT, however, has a lower SVD ratio than four of the items omitted and a lower item-total score correlation than three. Thus, especially in the case of the United States our decision to include or exclude items was influenced not only by the results of our data manipulations, but also by our rethinking of the theoretical considerations involved, the four principles we formulated, and the meaning of the items as interpreted by us and by our respondents.[12]

## FOOTNOTES

*Wendell Bell is Director and Robert V. Robinson a graduate student trainee of the Comparative Sociology Training Program, Yale University. In 1974 they did a restudy of attitudes of elites in the new Caribbean state of Jamaica, twelve years after political independence. Bell recently coedited *Ethnicity and Nation-Building* (Sage, 1974) and is writing a book on equality and social justice entitled *A Modern Theory of Equality*. Robinson is beginning a multicountry comparative study of social stratification.

A revised version of part of a paper read at the annual meetings of the American Sociological Association, New York, 30 August–3 September 1976. The authors gratefully acknowledge financial assistance from the National Institute of Mental Health through the

Yale Comparative Sociology Training Program (Grant No. 5-T01-MH12133) and from the Yale Concilium on International and Area Studies. Also, we thank the Shell Companies Discretionary Grant to the Department of Sociology, Yale University for supplemental financial support. Additionally, we thank our colleagues Janet Grigsby, Candace M. Kruttschnitt, H. Wesley Perkins, and Robert H. Ross for their important contributions; Michael Mann of the London School of Economics and Political Science, England for his advice in designing the study; and George W. Bohrnstedt, Scott A. Boorman, George C. Homans, Bernice A. Pescosolido, Albert J. Reiss, Jr., and Harry Laracuente, for their helpful comments on an earlier draft of this paper.

1. The equation shown in the text is convenient for getting across the simple idea involved in the comparative judgment regarding equity. A more complicated equation, however, is necessary in order to deal with negative numbers (Walster et al., 1976):

$$\frac{O_A - I_A}{(|I_A|^{k}A)} = \frac{O_B - I_B}{(|I_B|^{k}B)}$$

Where: A is person A;
B is person B;
O is outcomes either postive (rewards) or negative (costs);
I is inputs, either positive (assets) or negative (liabilities);
$k_A$ = sign ($I^A$) x sign ($O^A - I^A$);
$k_B$ = sign ($I^B$) x sign ($O^B - I^B$).

2. The Seeman-Morris index in full or in part has also been used by Seeman (1960), Bell (1964), Duke (1967), and Mau et al. (1961).

3. Other studies that are more or less relevant to the measurement of attitudes toward equality include Centers (1949), Form and Rytina (1969), Feagin (1972), Leggett (1963), McClosky (1964), Moorhouse and Chamberlain (1974), Nowak (1969), Watts and Free (1973), and Westie (1965).

4. We reduced the chance of acquiescence bias by writing the items so that the respondent had to disagree with two and to accept three in order to give an egalitarian response. Also, note that the item with the most egalitarian responses required the respondent to disagree to be classified as favoring equality and the two items with the most inegalitarian responses required the respondent to disagree to be classified as favoring inequality.

5. Personal communication from George W. Bohrnstedt.

6. See Appendix 1 for the correlation matrices on which the factor analyses are based.

7. See Appendix 2 for the classification of political party preference used in computing the correlations.

8. Since Cicourel's (1964) important critique of measurement in sociology, sociologists have become more sensitive to the problems of meaning in the interpretation of questionnaire items. The five items in the final Index of Evaluated Equality we present here are—in a very real sense—survivors of a relatively long process of formulation, reformulation, and, finally, elimination. We used the pretest in the New Haven area to probe the meaning of the items for our respondents, before our final framing of the items. Then, in the final interview schedule in which we used ten items, we still included in the case of three of them probes which were used after the respondents had given their closed-end responses. They were: "Could you tell me why you say that?" "Why do you say that?" "Could you explain your answer?" The interviewers were instructed to continue probing in order to discover the respondent's frame of reference, the meaning of the item to him or her. We have used such

information to help select the five items in the IEE and assume that validity has been improved thereby. See Appendix 3 for the items eliminated from the index and a discussion of the reasons for their elimination.

9. We will not discuss within country differences any further here because they are the subject of another paper. See Robinson and Bell (forthcoming).

10. This is not to say that there aren't correlations between objective deprivations and evaluations of equality. There are, with the underprivileged generally more likely to be egalitarian than the privileged.

11. The finding concerning SEX-PAY, of course, constitutes an interesting question of differences between England and the United States on the role of women which Janet Grigsby is now trying to answer.

12. See Appendix 1 for the intercorrelations of all 10 items. The average item-item correlation for the five items composing the IEE is 0.22 for England and 0.20 for the United States. This compares with the average correlation of items included in the IEE with items excluded from the IEE of 0.01 for England and 0.05 for the United States.

## REFERENCES


Adams, J. Stacey (1963) "Toward an Understanding of Inequity." *Journal of Abnormal Psychology* 67:422–436.

Alford, Robert R. (1963) *Party and Society: The Anglo-American Democracies.* Chicago: Rand McNally.

Almond, Gabriel A. and Verba, Sidney (1965) *The Civic Culture: Political Attitudes and Democracy in Five Nations.* Boston: Little, Brown.

Anderson, Bo, et al. (1969) "Reactions to Inequity." *Acta Sociologica* 12:1–12.

Bales, Robert F. and Couch, Arthur S. (1969) "The Value Profile: A Factor Analytic Study of Value Statements." *Sociological Inquiry* 39:3–17.

Bardo, John W. (1976) "Internal Consistency and Reliability in Likert-type Attitude Scales: Some Questions Concerning the Use of Pre-built Scales." *Sociology and Social Research* 60:403–420.

Bell, Wendell (1964) *Jamaican Leaders: Political Attitudes in a New Nation.* Berkeley and Los Angeles: University of California Press.

——— (ed.), (1967) *The Democratic Revolution in the West Indies.* Cambridge, MA: Schenkman.

——— (1974) "A Conceptual Analysis of Equality and Equity in Evolutionary Perspective." *American Behavioral Scientist* 18:8–35.

Bem, Daryl J. (1970) *Beliefs, Attitudes, and Human Affairs.* Belmont, CA: Brooks/Cole.

Béteille, André (1969) "The Decline of Social Inequality?" Pages 362–380 in André Béteille (ed.), *Social Inequality: Selected Readings.* Baltimore: Penguin.

Blau, Peter (1964) "Justice in Social Exchange." *Sociological Inquiry* 34:193–206.

——— and Duncan, Otis Dudley (1967) *American Occupational Structure.* New York: Wiley.

Boudon, Raymond (1976) "Review of John Rawls' *A Theory of Justice,*" *Contemporary Sociology* 5:102–109.

Centers, Richard (1949) *The Psychology of Social Classes: A Study of Class Consciousness.* New York: Russell and Russell.

Cicourel, Aaron V. (1964) *Method and Measurement in Sociology.* New York: Free Press.

Clark, Terry N. (1973) *Community Power and Policy Outputs: A Review of Urban Research.* Beverly Hills, CA: Sage.

Coleman, James S., et al. (1966) *Equality of Educational Opportunity*. Washington, DC: Government Printing Office.

Coleman, Lee (1941) "What is American?: A Study of Alleged American Traits." *Social Forces* 19:492–499.

Cook, Karen (1970) "An Extensive Review of the Sociological Literature on the Problem of Inequity." Stanford University, (Mimeo).

——— (1975) "Expectations, Evaluations, and Equity." *American Sociological Review* 40:372–388.

Cronbach, Lee J. (1951) "Coefficient alpha and the Internal Structure of Tests." *Psychometrika* 16:297–334.

Daniels, Norman (1975) "Introduction." Pages xi–xxxiv in Norman Daniels (ed.), *Reading Rawls: Critical Studies on Rawls'* A Theory of Justice. New York: Basic Books.

Duke, James T. (1967) "Egalitarianism and Future Leaders in Jamaica." Pages 115–139 in Wendell Bell (ed.), *The Democratic Revolution in the West Indies*. Cambridge, MA: Schenkman.

Duncan, Otis Dudley (1968) "Social Stratification and Mobility: Problems in the Measurement of Trend." Pages 675–719 in Eleanor Bernert Sheldon and Wilbert E. Moore (eds.), *Indicators of Social Change: Concepts and Measurements*. New York: Russell Sage.

——— et al. (1968) *Socioeconomic Background and Achievement*. New York and London: Seminar Press.

Durkheim, Emile (1933) *The Division of Labour in Society*. Translated by George Simpson. New York: Free Press.

Dworkin, R. (1975) "The Original Position." Pages 16–53 in Norman Daniels (ed.), *Reading Rawls: Critical Studies on Rawls'* A Theory of Justice. New York: Basic Books.

Emerson, Rupert (1960) *From Empire to Nation*. Cambridge, MA: Harvard University Press.

Fallers, Lloyd (1963) "Equality, Modernity, and Democracy in the New States." Pages 158–219 in Clifford Geertz (ed.), *Old Societies and New States*. New York: Free Press.

Feagin, Joe R. (1972) "Poverty: We Still Believe that God Helps Those who Help Themselves." *Psychology Today* 6:101–110, 129.

Form, William H. and Rytina, Joan (1961) "Ideological Beliefs on the Distribution of Power in the United States." *American Sociological Review* 34:19–31.

Gilbert, Claire W. (1968) "Community Power and Decision-Making: A Quantitative Examination of Previous Research." Pages 139–156 in Terry N. Clark (ed.), *Community Structure and Decision-Making: Comparative Analyses*. San Francisco: Chandler.

Goldthorpe, John H. (1974) "Social Inequality and Social Integration in Modern Britain." Pages 217–238 in Dorothy Wedderburn (ed.), *Poverty, Inequality, and Class Structure*. Cambridge, Eng.: Cambridge University Press.

Goodman, Leo A. (1969) "How to Ransack Social Mobility Tables and Other Kinds of Cross-Classification Tables." *American Journal of Sociology* 75:1–40.

Guttman, Louis (1944) "A Basis for Scaling Quantitative Data." *American Sociological Review* 9:139–150.

——— (1947) "The Cornell Technique for Scale and Intensity Analysis." *Educational and Psychological Measurements* 7:247–280.

Heise, David R. and Bohrnstedt, George W. (1970) "Validity, Invalidity, and Reliability." Pages 104–129 in Edgar F. Borgatta and George W. Bohrnstedt (eds.), *Sociological Methodology 1970*. San Francisco: Jossey-Bass.

Hodge, Robert W., et al. (1966) "A Comparative Study of Occupational Prestige." Pages 309–321 in Reinhard Bendix and Seymour Martin Lipset (eds.), *Class, Status, and Power*. 2d ed. New York: Free Press.

Homans, George C. (1961) *Social Behavior: Its Elementary Forms.* New York: Harcourt, Brace and World.

——— (1974) *Social Behavior: Its Elementary Forms.* 2nd Edition. New York: Harcourt, Brace and World.

Huber, Joan and Form, William H. (1973) *Income and Ideology: An Analysis of the American Political Formula.* New York: Free Press.

Inkeles, Alex and Rossi, Peter H. (1956) "National Comparisons of Occupational Prestige." *American Journal of Sociology* 61:329–339.

Jencks, Christopher, et al. (1972) *Inequality: A Reassessment of the Effect of Family and Schooling in America.* New York: Basic Books.

Klatzky, Sheila R. and Hodge, Robert W. (1971) "A Canonical Correlation Analysis of Occupational Mobility." *Journal of the American Statistical Association* 66:16–22.

Kristol, Irving (1968) "Equality as Ideal." Volume 5, pages 108–111 in *International Encyclopedia of the Social Sciences.* New York: Macmillan and Free Press.

Lane, Robert E. (1959) "The Fear of Equality." *American Political Science Review* 53:35–51.

Leggett, John C. (1963) "Uprootedness and Working-Class Consciousness." *American Journal of Sociology* 68:682–692.

Lenski, Gerhard E. (1954) "Status Crystallization: A Non-Vertical Dimension of Social Status." *American Sociological Review* 19:405–413.

Lipset, Seymour Martin (1963) "The Value Patterns of Democracy: A Case Study in Comparative Analysis." *American Sociological Review* 28:515–531.

——— (1963) *The First New Nation.* New York: Basic Books.

——— (1968) "Anglo-American Society." Volume 1, pages 289–302 in *International Encyclopedia of the Social Sciences.* New York: Macmillan and Free Press.

McClosky, Herbert (1964) "Consensus and Ideology in American Politics." *American Political Science Review* 58:361–382.

McKennell, Aubrey (1970) "Attitude Measurement: Use of Coefficient Alpha with Cluster or Factor Analysis." *Sociology* 4:227–245.

Mann, Michael (1970) "The Social Cohesion of Liberal Democracy." *American Sociological Review* 35: 423–439.

——— (1973) *Consciousness and Action in the Western Working Class.* London: Macmillan.

Mau, James A., et al. (1961) "Scale Analyses of Status Perception and Status Attitude in Jamaica and the United States." *Pacific Sociological Review* 4:33–40.

Moorhouse, H. F. and Chamberlain, C. W. (1974) "Lower-Class Attitudes to Property: Aspects of the Counter-Ideology." *Sociology* 8:387–405.

Moskos, Charles C., Jr. (1967) *The Sociology of Political Independence.* Cambridge, MA: Schenkman.

Nagel, Thomas (1975) "Rawls on Justice." Pages 1–16 in Norman Daniels (ed.), *Reading Rawls: Critical Studies on Rawls'* A Theory of Justice. New York: Basic Books.

Nowak, Stefan (1969) "Changes and Social Structure in Social Consciousness." Pages 235–247 in Celia S. Heller (ed.), *Structured Social Inequality: A Reader in Comparative Social Stratification.* New York: Collier-Macmillan.

Oppenheim, F. E. (1968) "The Concept of Equality," Volume 5, pages 102–108 in *International Encyclopedia of the Social Sciences.* New York: Macmillan and Free Press.

Palmer, R. R. (1959–1964) *The Age of the Democratic Revolution: A Political History of Europe and America, 1760–1800.* Volume 1: "The Challenge." Volume 2: "The Struggle." Princeton, NJ: Princeton University Press.

Patchen, Martin (1961) "A Conceptual Framework and Some Empirical Data Regarding Comparisons of Social Rewards." *Sociometry* 24:136–156.

Paukert, Felix (1973) "Income Distribution at Different Levels of Development." *International Labor Review* 108:97–125.

Rainwater, Lee (1974) *What Money Buys: Inequality and the Social Meaning of Income.* New York: Basic Books.

Rawls, John (1971) *A Theory of Justice.* Cambridge, MA: Belknap Press of Harvard.

Robinson, John P., et al. (1972) *Measures of Political Attitudes.* Ann Arbor, MI: Center for Political Studies, Institute for Social Research, The University of Michigan.

Robinson, Robert V. and Bell, Wendell (1978) "Equality, Success, and Social Justice in England and the United States." *American Sociological Review* 43:125–143.

Rokeach, Milton (1973) *The Nature of Human Values.* New York: Free Press.

Rose, Richard (1964) *Politics of England: An Interpretation.* Boston: Little, Brown.

Rosenbaum, James E. (1976) *Making Inequality: The Hidden Curriculum of High School Tracking.* New York: Wiley.

Roshwald, Mordecai (1973) "Order and Over-Organization in America." *British Journal of Sociology* 24:30–42.

Runciman, W. G. (1966) *Relative Deprivation and Social Justice: A Study of Attitudes to Social Inequality in Twentieth-Century England.* Berkeley and Los Angeles: University of California Press.

Russett, Bruce M. (1965) *Trends in World Politics.* New York: Macmillan.

Seeman, Melvin (1960) *Social Status and Leadership: The Case of the School Executive.* Columbus: Bureau of Educational Research and Service. Ohio State University.

——— *A Status Factor Approach to Leadership,* with the assistance of Richard T. Morris. Columbus: Personnel Research Board, Ohio State University. (Mimeo, no date).

Sewell, William H., et al. (1969) "The Educational and Early Occupational Attainment Process." *American Sociological Review* 34:82–92.

——— (1970) "The Educational and Early Occupational Status Attainment Process: Replication and Revision." *American Sociological Review* 35:1014–1027.

——— (1975) *Education, Occupation, and Earnings: Achievement in the Early Career.* New York: Academic Press.

——— (1976) *Schooling and Achievement in American Society.* New York: Academic Press.

Tocqueville, Alexis de. *Democracy in America.* Volume 1. New York: Vintage, 1954.

Treiman, Donald J. (1975) "Problems of Concept and Measurement in the Comparative Study of Occupational Mobility." *Social Science Research* 4:183–230.

——— and Terrell, Kermit (1975) "The Process of Status Attainment in the United States and Great Britain." *American Journal of Sociology* 81:563–583.

Turner, Ralph H. (1958) "Life Situation and Subculture: A Comparison of Merited Prestige Judgements by Three Occupational Classes in Britain." *British Journal of Sociology* 9:299–320.

Walster, Elaine, et al. (1976) "New Directions in Equity Research." Pages 1–42 in Leonard Berkowitz and Elaine Walster (eds.), *Equity Theory: Toward a General Theory of Social Interaction.* New York: Academic Press.

Walton, John (1966) "Discipline, Method, and Community Power: A Note on the Sociology of Knowledge." *American Sociological Review* 31:684–689.

Watts, William and Free, Lloyd A., (eds.) (1973) *State of the Nation.* New York: Universe Books. See especially pages 170–176.

Weick, Karl E. (1966) "The Concept of Equity in the Perception of Pay." *Administrative Science Quarterly* 11:414–439.

Westie, Frank (1965) "The American Dilemma: An Empirical Test." *American Sociological Review* 30:527–538.

White, Harrison (1970) *Chains of Opportunity: System Models of Mobility in Organizations.* Cambridge, MA: Harvard University Press.

Williams, Robin (1951) *American Society: A Sociological Interpretation.* New York: Knopf.

Yanowitch, Murray and Fisher, Wesley A. (eds.) (1973) *Social Stratification and Mobility in the U.S.S.R.* White Plains, NY: International Arts and Sciences Press.

# A FORMULA FOR GENOCIDE: COMPARISON OF THE TURKISH GENOCIDE (1915) AND THE GERMAN HOLOCAUST (1939–1945)

Helen Fein*

---

At the beginning, there was no word. There was no word adequate to label and mentally assimilate the murder of two of every three million European Jews in states occupied by and/or allied to Nazi Germany in World War II.

Lemkin (1944, pp. 79–95) abstracted the essence of this newly discerned class of events, coining the term "genocide" to denote an attempt to destroy a nation or an ethnic group by direct extermination and other means, including deliberately creating conditions increasing mortality and diminishing birth rates.

**Comparative Studies in Sociology—Vol. 1, 1978, pages 271–293**

**ISBN 0-89232-025-7**

What was defined as a new crime, a crime against humanity—rather than a war crime—at the International Military Tribunal at Nuremberg was the premeditated attempt to destroy a group. However, only thirty years earlier, the *New York Times* headlined the story that "Young Turks said to have declared annihilation of Armenians" (6 May 1915). Had such trials been instituted after World War I, the Western allies might have recalled the extermination of the Armenians in 1915, a genocide memorialized in the United States and Britain by denunciations, mass meetings, petitions and promises. But the Armenians had not been awarded an opportunity for public judgment, and the promises (encouraged by all allies) of an independent Armenia outside the Soviet Union were betrayed by the Peace Treaty of Lausanne in 1923.

Housepian (1966) points out that the political utility of mass murder was appreciated by Hitler. He justified the annihilation of Polish civilians in 1939 in a speech to his chief commanders before the Polish invasion by reference to his predecessors' success: "Only thus shall we gain the living space (Lebensraum) which we need. Who, after all, speaks today of the annihilation of the Armenians?" (quoted from Housepian, 1966, citing Lochner, 1942, p.2).

But the similar implications of both crimes were not generally noted. Both victims could compare their losses to earlier experiences as objects of collective violence—violence against persons as members of a religious, racial, or ethnic category. Historically, they had repeatedly been targets of collective violence for a long period, stretching in the case of European Jewry over their two millenia in diaspora and for the Armenians over the five centuries they had been subject to Ottoman domination. *Violence was legitimated* against them because *both* Jews and Armenians *had been defined outside the sanctified universe of obligation* by the dominant religion, as are pariahs in a caste order. Politically, they were usually powerless, lacking autonomy (except in intra-group relations) and sovereignty. Both diasporas often served as a "middleman minority," (Blalock, 1970, p. 84), filling distinct needs and incurring risks and opprobrium attached to such functions.

The Jews had been accused by the founders of the Christian church of the greatest crime of history, deicide, and their exile was viewed as God's punishment (Isaac, 1964; Ruether, 1974). Until emancipation, terms for their toleration were decreed by the dominant church which authorized civic discrimination, segregation, compulsory stigmata and ghettos from the twelfth to the sixteenth century of the Christian era. They were slain by roaming Crusaders accruing spiritual credits by murdering the infidel from the eleventh to thirteenth centuries, expelled from Western and Central Europe from the twelfth to the fourteenth century, intermittently lynched after accusations of spurious crimes—poisoning of wells, killing

Christian children to extract their blood, desecrating the host—up through the twentieth century, massacred by their neighbors during revolts for independence (as in the sixteenth and twentieth century Ukraine), killed in pogroms organized by the declining Czarist Empire in the nineteenth century, and in "excesses" by marauding revolutionary and counter-revolutionary armies after World War I. Although motives given for attacks on Jews changed, the definition of them as alien to the community rationalized their victimization.

The Turks, as Muslims, defined non-Muslim "People of the Book"—Christians and Jews—as *dhimmīs* or infidels who might be conditionally tolerated, protected in exchange for their accommodation to civil discrimination, ritual subordination, powerlessness, and oppression.

> [T]heir evidence is not accepted against that of a Moslem in a Kadi's court; the Moslem murderer of a *Dhimmī* does not suffer the death penalty; a *Dhimmī* man may not marry a Moslem woman, whereas a Moslem man may marry a *Dhimmī* woman. In the second place, *Dhimmīs* . . . are forbidden to ride horses or to carry arms. (Sarkissian, 1965, pp. 7–8, quoting Gibb and Bowen).

They were termed *rayah* or sheep who might be fleeced. Although all Christians and Jews were subjected to discriminatory taxes, Armenians endured extra burdens in the poll tax, military exemption tax, hospitality tax, and the *kishlak,* the duty of boarding Kurds in the winter, which frequently made the hosts prey to looting, rape and other violations by their "guests."

Was genocide simply the culmination of such traditions, which were latent despite emancipation and secularization? Can it be understood in terms of its function by assuming that extermination serves the same functions as did earlier discontinuous campaigns of collective violence? Although collective violence against oppressed classes and "middleman-minorities" serves to enhance the social control of the dominant group, redistribute property and opportunities, and deflect expression of class conflict among different classes within the dominant group, elimination of the victim deprives the dominant group of a target for future abuse. What ends, then, can genocide serve?

To understand genocide, it must be first appreciated as rational, premeditated action by its perpetrators, before one relates its causes and preconditions theoretically or empirically to collective violence generally. This means firstly we must concentrate on the problem confronting its architects to understand their ends. I will attempt to show that genocide is a rational function of the myth chosen by a ruling elite which serves as a *"political formula"* (Mosca, 1939, pp. 70–72) *to legitimate the existence of the state as the vehicle for the destiny of the dominant group, a circle based on underlying likeness (mechanical solidarity) from which the victim is excluded by definition.* Such a formula assumes (or creates) a myth exalting the unique origins of the dominant group and reifying the idea of the people so that the "real" nature of the group cannot be judged by the performance of its members. Arendt (1966, pp. 226–227) called this phenomenon "tribalism," Sugar and Lederer (1969, p. 11) referred to it as "messianism," and others simply call it fascism (overlooking the varieties of fascisms). This kind of myth, I suspect, is most apt to be chosen by leaders of states in which there is low underlying solidarity between major groups, a lack of correspondence between borders of the state and regions of settlement of the dominant nationality, and in which the state has suffered recent defeat or decline in territorial claims. The state's *raison d'être* as a competitive enterprise is in doubt. Since the old political formula which arose in the nineteenth century instigated the creation of new states, stirring people then to deny legitimacy to foreign authorities, a new political formula which rationalized the domination of the state by decreeing the creation of a mass-master race was plausible.[1]

While the liberal ideal of nineteenth century nationalism justified removing authorities which were deemed illegitimate because they did not represent the people, the new formula justified eradicating peoples to assure the legitimation of the state's authority. One way to excise elements that did not fit into this new nation was to assimilate them, another was to eliminate them by expulsion or annihilation. To be sure, choosing the latter path does not imply that the selected strategies—expulsion or annihilation—are discrete or unilateral choices: they may be complementary or evolve as costs and opportunities change. While expulsion and annihilation are open choices from the perspective of the ruling elite, flight is the only rational choice of the victims if they lack the defense capacity to fight in order to avoid extinction. The threat of annihilation, then, mobilizes people to flee, serving to expel them, while the lack of outlets stimulates the will and ability of leaders to exterminate victims. The strategy chosen must take into account the opportunities, costs, and sanctions attached to each policy. The visibility of violence may instigate external sanctions, increasing costs. War diminishes visibility and obligations within the international system, thus facilitating extermination. But leaders could not have chosen the elimination of the victims had not the group been previously defined as outside the universe of obligation. This was the necessary precondition making extermination a conceivable option: since there was no obligation to protect the class of victims, there was no deterrent once it became practically possible.

Not only were the victims defined as alien, they were both members of international or multi-national collectivities. Both Armenians and Jews could be readily labeled enemies as they had observable bonds to other

Christians and Jews. Massacres of Armenians and pogroms against Jews had evoked protests throughout the Western world in the nineteenth century, leading to diplomatic interventions on their behalf. Hostility could freely be projected upon the victims once they were labeled enemies. Thus, both groups could be readily accused of disloyalty if the particularism—*volkish* or Turkish—of the dominant collectivity became the norm. The will to exterminate them becomes predictable once the political formula adopted altered the basis of allegiance to the state. But the need for a new formula was instigated by the state's own prior failure.

The need for a new order was apparent to German and Turkish contenders for power in the turbulent years after the victory of the Young Turks in 1908 and in the post-World War I, post-depression Weimar Republic. Both the Ottoman Empire and Germany had suffered military defeats within their generation and lost territories. Any elite seeking to capture the state needed a political formula to justify its rule which addressed the critical question of the nation's existence; the right of a master-race or unique people to dominate others was such a formula. War was used in both cases (an opportunity anticipated and planned for by Germany but simply seized by Turkey after World War I began) to transform the nation to correspond to the ruling elite's formula by eliminating groups they defined as alien.

War enabled both states to murder with impunity; it obscured the visibility of their action and insured freedom from sanctions. Common accounting processes may be noted. To invent post facto justifications of the program, leaders of both states accused the victim of aiding the enemy, betraying them, or causing the war. Such accusations aided the perpetrators to rationalize their acts by the prevalent paradigm justifying collective violence; it was a just punishment (or reprisal) for a crime committed by the victim (Fein, 1977). But the perpetrators knew already they did not have to fear sanctions, only censure, for they had already tested the ground by oppression and calculated violence against the victims for eight years in the case of Germany and forty years in the case of Turkey. I will attempt to briefly compare the development of both cases, and later explore the German extension of genocide to the Gypsies, restricting discussion of the Holocaust to German Jews and Gypsies, relating their murder to the selective extermination of the "unfit" in Germany in 1939.

## EXTERMINATION OF THE ARMENIANS

The majority of Armenians in 1914 inhabited western Asia, divided between Persia and the Russian and Ottoman Empires. Although figures on ethnicity and religion of the population in the six *vilayets* (provinces) in which Armenians were concentrated vary, Armenians constituted a minority there—from 27 to 39 percent—because of the Ottoman rulers' policy of resettling the Kurds in Armenian regions to serve as governing agents (Bryce, 1916; Boyajian, 1972).

Armenians (as were Greek Christians and Jews) were organized as a community in a separate *millet* headed by their Patriarch. The system enabled each group to govern its religious and social life as a corporate endogamous body subordinated with the Empire to the oppressive rule of the dominant Ottoman tribe. Legally barred from bearing arms (until 1911), and subjected to periodic violence and exploitation by their Kurdish chieftains, the Armenians had been known as the *sadik millet* or faithful community (Sarkissian, 1965, p. 11).

The Ottoman Empire, which extended in mid-seventeenth century from Persia to Hungary, began losing ground two centuries before Nicholas I of Russia labeled it (1853) the "sick man" of Europe. The Sultan and the Ottoman governing class of the nineteenth century could not conceive of any transformation of the Empire that would accommodate the aspirations of its many nationalities so as to counter the credo of national liberation filtering through Europe. There was no way to legitimate Ottoman domination for there was no basis of solidarity among its subjects—no notion of a common nationality, no religious bond, and no representative mechanisms. By 1908, the Ottomans had withdrawn from all of Europe except Salonica and Albania, accepting Greek emancipation and the independence of Bulgaria, Rumania, Albania, and Serbia in the nineteenth century. The British had helped them to check the process, fearing Russian penetration of the Straits. Britain viewed with alarm the Czar's expansion into Asia, and his declarations of concern for the Christian subjects of the Turk; thus it rushed to defend Turkey in the Crimean War. But the Turks' oppression of their Christian subjects, which manifestly instigated Russian intervention, obliged its allies to press the Sultan to institute reform. Responding to such pressures, a series of Sultan's edicts, most to implement peace treaties, were issued in 1839, 1856, and 1878 granting all subjects equal rights, opportunities, and justice under the law. None were enforced.

The nationalist awakening throughout Europe and expansion of foreign Christian missions within the Ottoman Empire attracted the Armenians and led to a new collective self-consciousness among them during the nineteenth century. Louise Nalbandian's (1967) *The Armenian Revolutionary Movement* describes how such a movement evolved. Fraternal organizations and secret societies sprung up among Armenians and began collecting and distributing arms so that peasants could defend themselves when attacked. Revolutionary parties were formed, first among Armenian students studying abroad in Switzerland, France, and Russia: foremost among these were the Hunchaks and Dashnaks, the latter a federation of Armenian revolutionaries in Russia. Their goals and program were heavily influenced by the ideology of the Marxists and the Russian *narodniki* (populists). The revolutionaries stressed socialism and equal civil and political rights, the Dashnaks being willing to remain within the Ottoman Empire if it guaranteed communal autonomy. To gain supporters among other groups, they addressed propaganda to the Kurds and other minorities in their own languages and established ties to Balkan dissidents and the Young Turks. Their program contrasted with that of the first national Armenakan Party, which sought only liberation of the Armenians and rejected alliances with non-Armenians. Within the Ottoman Empire, the revolutionaries attracted followers principally among the educated classes, although there was much opposition to them among wealthy and influential Armenians.

During the last decade of the century, the physical security of the Armenians became more precarious. Terror by the Kurds against Armenians was organized by the government, as the British Consul Clifford Lloyd observed in 1890, acknowledging the responsibility of Great Britain, whose tolerance of the Porte's refusal to enforce its treaty obligations encouraged the government to retaliate against the Armenians. He also observed that the government's allegations of wide-spread Armenian preparation for rebellion were not substantiated—Armenian peasants were usually defenseless (Boyajian, 1972, pp. 36–38).

Nevertheless, such terror did not dampen the revolutionaries' confidence in their strategy of collective self-assertion and defense, which might invite foreign intervention on their behalf if it did not elicit direct concessions. The Hunchaks organized public demonstrations in Constantinople in 1890 and 1895 to present their petitions to the Sultan but were blocked by troops and many demonstrators were slain in the ensuing disorders. Rebellions which led to severe repression were organized among Armenians at Sassun, Zeitun, and Van between 1894 and 1896. The revolt at Sassun was also an uprising by Armenians against Kurds; the former refused to pay the conventional tribute to the latter.

The Sultan, Abdul Hamid, responded to signs that the "faithful community" was no longer submissive by organizing the Hamidye, special regiments of Kurdish tribesmen modeled after the Russian Cossaks who committed massacres against the Armenians resembling the pogroms the Black Hundreds in Russia committed against Jews during the same period. Can one doubt he expected this would dampen the revolutionaries' hopes for Kurdish-Armenian cooperation? But although there were reprisals and occasional acts of terror committed against the Kurds by Armenian revolutionaries, their ideology was not directed against the minorities nor against the Turks—indeed the Dashnaks supported the Young Turks—but against the government. The revolutionaries' willingness to disarm, and trust the Young Turks in 1908 may be accounted for by their addiction to ideological principles which were not changed by evidence of how deadly Muslim collective behavior could be when agitated by pan-Islamic rallying cries.

In a daring bid to invite foreign intervention to obtain the autonomy of the Armenian *vilayet,* twenty-six young revolutionaries (Dashnaks) occupied the partly foreign-owned Imperial Ottoman Bank in Constantinople on August 24, 1896, threatening to blow it up if their demands were not met. A third of them were blasted by the bombs they hurled to repel invaders, but the others—still alive and well—were led out within a day by a Russian emissary who caused them to believe their demands would be acted upon. They sailed from Constantinople, but other Armenians were not so fortunate. The government responded immediately by organizing random massacres of Armenians and other Christians in Constantinople: more than 6,000 are estimated to have been slain.

These activities, and allegations that the Armenian revolutionaries conspired with Russia (which were incorrect but credible: they conspired in Russia, a state whose own internal policies then encouraged discrimination against Armenians) caused the Sultan to incite more massacres in which the educated, the class from which revolutionaries were likely to arise, were special targets, regardless of whether they were revolutionary sympathizers or not. Between 1895 and 1908 (when the Sultan's despotism ended), 100,000 to 300,000 Armenians were estimated to have been killed (Hartunian, 1968; Boyajian, 1972).

The decline of the Empire provoked Turkish officers to challenge the government. The party of the "Young Turks," the *Itahad* (Committee of Union and Progress), was headed by a central committee, the *Jemiyet,* which following two years of army mutinies, demanded and secured in 1908 the Sultan's restoration of the 1876 Constitution. The party's slogan was "Freedom, Justice, Equality, Fraternity." Its victory was welcomed by Muslims, Christians, and Jews. *Itahad* attracted the cooperation of Armenian revolutionary committees in exile who expected Armenians to obtain full civil and political rights.

The Young Turks who made the revolution "did not want only to save the state in its existing form . . . . [but] wanted to revive it and make it a going concern in the modern world" (Ahmad, 1969, p. 156). But the route of the Turks accelerated in North Africa and the Balkans, attacked by Italy invading Tripoli in 1911 and a coalition of Bulgaria, Serbia, and Greece in Macedonia during the First Balkan War of 1912. (However, Turkey regained some territory from a divided coalition in the Second Balkan War of 1913). Against this background, Djemal Pasha, *Itahad*-appointed Governor of Constantinople in 1913, explained that there seemed to be no way that the new men of power could simultaneously retain the Empire and accept the demands of minorities which included the emerging pan-Arab movement, Maronite Christians, Greek Christians, Macedonians, Albanians, and Armenians (Djemal, n.d., pp. 249–252). To justify their domination, the ruling elite adopted a credo based on Pan-Turanianism, which alleged a prehistoric mythic unity among Turanian peoples based on racial origin, to be implemented by "Turkification," instituting the Turkish language throughout, demanding Mohammedan (Zaravend says "read Turkish") supremacy and centralization of rule from Constantinople (Zaravend, 1971, pp. 37–38).

Djemal Pasha (n.d.) tells us that all the minorities refused to accept *Itahad's* bid to disband and join the Committee, declining to be assimilated, to cease to exist for themselves. Although opposition within *Itahad* was suppressed, *Itahad* was unable to prevent the formation of a new Liberal Party, and overcame its liberal Turkish opposition by a coup in January 1913, instituting a dictatorship.

In 1913, Russia, responding to Armenian petitions, again proposed reforms to guarantee the Armenian rights by instituting mixed police, judiciary, and local control over officials to be supervised by foreign inspectors. After some modifications were made by Germany and Britain, the Ottoman Empire signed an agreement with Russia on February 8, 1914. Djemal Pasha states that the *Itahad* viewed this as the first step toward a Russian protectorate, and realized that the World War was an opportunity to liberate itself from such obligations.

> [I]t was our one hope to free ourselves through the World War from all conventions, which meant so many attacks on our independence. . . . This is not to say, however, that we had not the earnest intention of introducing reform in our country. On the contrary, we had determined on radical reform, as we were inspired by the conviction that otherwise we could not continue to exist (Djemal Pasha, n.d., p. 272).

The Turks opportune entry in World War I on the side of the Central Powers, created the opportunity for such "radical reform," diminishing their opponents' influence and oversight. Lord Bryce, honorary author of the definitive British report on the genocide (prepared by Arnold Toynbee) concluded that: "It is evident that the war was merely an opportunity and not a cause—in fact, that the deportation scheme, and all that it involved, flowed inevitably from the general policy of the Young Turkish Government (Bryce, 1916, p. 633)."

The Turks' initial thrust in the winter of 1915 against Russia was unsuccessful; they were pushed back by a Russian Army which included units of Russian Armenians. But the English set back in early spring of 1915 at

Gallipoli withdrew the threat of an invasion, increasing the self-confidence of the Turkish leaders (Moorehead, 1956, p. 98); it insured their inviolability and turned off the spotlight the allies had earlier focused on the Armenians.

The first notification of the plan began with an accusation blaming the victim. The *Jemiyet* telegraphed governors of the Armenian *vilayets* on February 28, 1915 that:

> Periodic news arriving from Cairo recently indicates that Dashnagtzoutium (the Armenian Revolutionary Federation) is preparing a decisive attack upon the *Jemiyet*. . . .
>
> *Jemiyet* has decided to free the fatherland from the covetousness of this accursed race and to bear upon their shoulder the stigma that might malign the Ottoman history.
>
> Unable to forget the disgrace and bitterness of the past, filled with vengeful episodes, *Jemiyet,* hopeful about its future, has decided to exterminate all Armenians living in Turkey, without allowing a single one to remain alive and to this regard has given the Government extensive authority (Boyajian, 1972, pp. 315–316).

There was never any doubt as to who the victims were, as Jews were required to register in Germany in 1935. They were known to tax collectors, public officials, and neighbors. The campaign began with measures that stripped the victims of the means and social organization to resist. Armenians were ordered to hand in their weapons, and they usually hastened to find some weapons (even if they had to buy them) for fear charges of noncooperation would be used as evidence of disloyalty and then employed to provoke violence against them. Armenian men in the Army were segregated into special units ("labor battalions"), disarmed, and later slain. On the night of April 24, 1915, some 1000 prominent Armenians were arrested in the capital and secretly murdered, leaving the others numbed by terror (Sarkissian, 1965, p. 29). The few remaining males in each village were summoned by the town crier to report immediately, were led out of town and slain. Women and children and a few infirm males previously exempted were then bidden by the crier to prepare themselves for deportation. They were driven into the desert by soldiers, staggering along until they dropped from drought, starvation, epidemics, the lash, or their festering wounds. The military was aided by surrounding Kurdish and Circassian tribesmen who looted and raped the women, kidnapping a favorite, or murdering another used vessel of their desire. For months, packs of bedraggled survivors wound through the deserts of western Asia until they dropped or were slain. Toynbee, assessing all the evidence, estimated that two-thirds of the 1.8 million Armenians in the Ottoman Empire in 1914 were annihilated or deported to the desert (Bryce, 1916, pp. 649–650).

The Turkish Minister of the Interior Talaat Bey—"whose correspondence authorizing the annihilation was discovered after the war—never did deny his government's responsibility . . ." (Morganthau's recounting his experience as American Ambassador, 1918, pp. 336–339). But the ruling junta attempted to deter foreign protests by lowering the visibility of the "deportations;" thus, they did not deport the Armenians in Constantinople and Smyrna, cities with many foreign residents.

German Ambassadors first denied and then tried to overlook the policy of their ally but finally protested (Trumpener, 1968, pp. 204–208). German Ambassador Count Wolf-Metternich arrived in Constantinople in December 1915, seeking a statement which would disassociate Germany from Turkish crimes in order to repudiate allegations abroad that Germany had instigated them. But the Count soon began to understand that protest was useless unless there was force behind it. He explained to the Reich Chancellor in June 1916 that winning the war was not the Turks' first objective:

> I have discussed with Talaat Bey and Halil Bey the deportation of the Armenian workers from the Amanus [railroad] stretch, which deportation hampers the conduct of the war. These measures, I told the ministers, among other things, gave the impression as if the Turkish government were itself bent on losing the war. . . . But no one any longer has the power to control the many-headed hydra of the Committee, to control the chauvinism and the fanaticism . . . there is not much to gain any longer from the Armenians. The mob is therefore preparing for the moment when Greece, forced by the Entente, must turn against Turkey and her allies. Massacres of far greater scope will occur then. The victims are more numerous and the booty more enticing. Greekdom constitutes the cultural element of Turkey and it will be destroyed like the Armenian segment if outside influence will not put a stop to it. "Turkification" means to expel or kill everything non-Turkish . . . (quoted in Boyajian, 1972, pp. 116–117).

To repel petitions, the Turkish government magnified its accusation that it had been attacked by its victims. The victims' guilt was demonstrated by the few cases in which Armenians, having heard of the deportations of neighboring villages, defended themselves against the Turkish militia. The beleaguered defenders scarcely ever saved themselves except in instances of intervention by allied forces or rescue by ships, such as that of the Russian Army at Van and the French Navy at Musa Dagh. The government repeated the stab-in-the-back legend that Turks had been betrayed by Armenians conspiring with Russia, later even extrapolating evidence of Armenian reprisals in 1918 to account for the Turkish annihilation of Armenians in 1915.

Djemal Pasha's account (n.d., pp. 279–298) justifying the genocide and that of Talaat Bey, (who authorized it) reveal their definition of Armenians as the enemy simply because they were Armenians. Talaat Bey said in an interview in 1916 with the *Berliner Tageblatt:* "We have been reproached for making no distinction between the innocent Armenians and the guilty; but that was utterly impossible, in view of the fact that *those who were innocent today might be guilty tomorrow.*" (italics in the original; quoted in Bryce, 1916, p. 633).

Talaat Bey was assassinated in Germany in 1921 by an Armenian who acted on behalf of the Armenian revolutionary federation. Dr. Johannes Lepsius, testifying for the assassin's defense, asserted that the Armenians had been defined as the prime enemy because of the allies' rhetoric on their behalf and their simultaneous refusal to protect them during the previous century. This had simply incited the Turks against the Armenians further, while proving to them the powerlessness of the Armenians.

> In the game of chess between London and Petersburg the Armenian was the pawn, sometimes pushed forward, sometimes sacrificed. The humanitarian causes, "protection of Christians," were pretexts. When in 1895 Abdul Hamid was forced to sign the plan of reforms presented by England, Russia and France, he had already set in motion a number of Armenian massacres. Lord Salisbury announced that as far as England was concerned, the Armenian question had ceased to exist. Prince Lobanov indicated to the Sultan that he had nothing to worry about because Russia pays no attention to the execution of reforms. The Sultan drew his own conclusions (Boyajian, 1972, p. 287).

When the Young Turks attempted to establish their power with a new formula, annihilating the Armenians completely became a rational means to fulfill their ideal. This superficially seemed to be an extension of the policy of Abdul Hamid who had attempted to fortify Islamic unity and cement loyalties to the state by instigating massacres of Armenians, often using the services of and providing booty for non-Turkish Muslims. However, Islamic traditionalism assumed the continuous existence of the "People of the Book" while Pan-Turanianism did not. Their annihilation was also a way of proving Turkish independence by eliminating a body perceived as foreign which did not incur the costs that an attack on Greek Christians would have provoked. The calculation of the Young Turks was proved correct and the Armenian reliance on petitions to the allies was proved to be based on false trust; the Young Turks reestablished their domination after World War I and the allies abandoned promises of an autonomous Armenia or Armenian protectorate under an American mandate.

## THE EXTERMINATION OF THE JEWS

Germany, defeated by the allies in World War I, renewed political existence as a republic after aborted revolutions and right-wing coups. Adolf Hitler, sentenced to three years imprisonment in 1923 for his role in the unsuccessful *putsch* in Munich, was only one of many agitators demanding militant national action to redress German grievances and failure. But the failure was never acknowledged as defeat in his oratory, or his testament *Mein Kampf* (1924) which was written in prison; instead it was attributed to internal enemies, especially the Jews, who had stabbed Germany in the back. Hitler was appointed Chancellor in January 1933 and later named President after Hindenburg's death in 1934, fusing both offices and transforming the former parliamentary bureaucracy into a totalitarian state with legal sanction from the *Reichstag*. Parties and persons not swayed by his charisma were repressed by the brown-shirted Nazi paramilitary (SA) in the streets and in concentration camps. But the populist violence of the SA was soon replaced by that of the SS, which Taylor (1946, pp. 215–216) stresses, constituted a political stratum: "Hitler discovered a 'Hitler class,' his unshakeable resource in extremity . . . the S.S.—the middle class of education but no property."

What did Hitler promise the German people and what did he expect of them? The ends which Hitler promised to achieve and the themes of his speeches which triggered most audience approval were not novel, as Dawidowicz (1975) shows in *The War Against the Jews,* but resonated with German ideologies and popular notions fully developed fifty years before the beginning of World War II, and which have been traced by Mosse (1964) in *The Crisis of German Ideology* and Massing (1967) in *Rehearsal for Destruction.* The German nationalist ideologies united romantic nationalism with anti-Semitism and modern racism. They assumed an underlying mythical identity, or essential likeness among the German people *(Volk)* based on "blood." The Jews were not *Volk* but aliens to whom the Germans should owe no obligation as put forth in the Nazi party program of 1920. While the Germans belonged to the Aryan race, whose supremacy to the Slav and to nonwhite races they unhesitatingly asserted, the Jews, according to the Nazis, did not belong to any human race but were nonhuman; bloodsuckers, lice, parasites, fleas, bacilli. The hidden agenda seems an obvious implication from the definition of the problem itself; these are organisms to be squashed or exterminated by chemical means. The mythical Jew was alternately subhuman and superhuman. These ideologues were obsessed with envy of the Jews, their cohesion and alleged claim to chosenness—a vulgar misinterpretation of the covenant bond, which implies special obligations but not special origins (Silver, 1974, pp. 29, 42). The explanatory power of anti-

Semitism was expanded by the diffusion of the fraudulent *Protocols of the Elders of Zion* published by the Czar's secret police and spread by anti-Bolshevik emigrés to reactionary circles in Germany after World War I. The *Protocols* depicted a Jewish world-wide conspiracy, making Jews responsible for the victory of Bolshevism which was, Cohn (1969) shows in his study of their use, a *Warrant For Genocide*.

The metahistory of the *Volk* differed from the actual history of the Germans, for whose misfortunes actual Germans were not responsible. They had been destroyed, stabbed in the back, by the enemy within—the Jew. The *Volk* had a messianic mission and right to exist over others. They demanded not only equality with other nations—freedom from Versailles Treaty restrictions—but additional room to expand, *Lebensraum*. Other nationals of German blood *(Volksdeutsche)* who could be reclaimed resided from the Rhine to the Vistula. The nations which they inhabitated would become incorporated into the Reich in the next decade or colonized by it. Natives of colonized nations belonging to the inferior Slavic race would be stripped of rights, reduced to subliteracy, exploited ruthlessly, and frequently subjected to collective violence.

During the first five years of the Nazi regime, Germany prepared itself for European domination before intervening openly in 1938 in Czechoslovakia. It repudiated war reparations but attempted to show pacific intentions by signing a treaty respecting the Polish frontiers and issuing diplomatic assurances to Western nations. The program to isolate the Jews by successively processing them in a functional sequence—first in order to expel them, later to annihilate them—was not rationalized until 1938 when it was tested out by Eichmann in Vienna (Schleunes, 1970). In Germany itself, the regime wavered before initiating new steps, reacting to the consequences of earlier steps upon the primary goal of that period, rearmament and economic autarchy. Jews were stripped of offices in the government and schools by local administrative actions initally in 1933, and an anti-Jewish boycott was instigated against marked Jewish enterprises. But only in 1935 were Jews (as differentiated from non-Aryans) defined. They were classified by lineage, corresponding to the Nazi belief that Jews were a race rather than a religious community, and new intermarriages and cohabitation were prohibited to prevent Jews from evading their fate by assimilation and to protect Aryans from being polluted by them. Identification mechanism were only perfected in 1938 with marked identification cards and passports preventing free movement within Germany and easy exodus.

Allegedly responding to the assassination of a German diplomatic official in Paris by a Jewish boy whose parents had been brutally dumped over the Polish border, the Nazi Party instigated its own pogrom to punish the Jews on November 10, 1938, burning nearly 300 synagogues, shattering windows of Jews' shops, interning 20,000 male Jews in concentration camps. The night of the broken glass, *Kristallnacht,* was to be, as Hitler vowed, the SA's "final fling (Schleunes, 1970, p. 24, citing Kochan)." Thereafter, anti-Jewish policies were planned and coordinated by the SS. No concentration was instituted in Germany since the few remaining Jews had been completely segregated and isolated within the German sea before being compelled to wear the yellow star in September 1941, expediting the policeman's future tasks. At least two of every three Jews in Germany in 1933 had left Germany before Jews began receiving notices of deportation (meaning extermination) in October 1941.

The processing of Jews throughout Europe in German-occupied states toward their own destruction, from definition through expropriation to concentration and annihilation, was first (1961) analyzed organizationally by Hilberg in *The Destruction of European Jewry* (1967). Although Germany sought to lessen observability or perception of extermination in the old Reich, the organization of genocide, Hilberg points out, involved all agencies of the state: "The machinery of destruction, then, was structurally no different from organized German society as a whole: the difference was only one of function. The machinery of destruction *was* the organized community in one of its special roles" (p. 640). Although there is no evidence that bureaucracy is in itself a cause of the choice of destructive ends, bureaucratization facilitates their accomplishment by routinizing the obedience of many agents, each trained to perform their role without questioning the ends of action. Max Weber (1930, p. 181) foresaw society becoming an "iron cage" in his classic analysis of modernity. But he did not anticipate that the cage could become an elevator, descending mechanically to crush the members excluded from the universe of obligation. The passengers within shrank from observing the walls around them, denying or repressing their vision of former members being systematically extruded to the pit below, accustomed as they were to assigning direction to the Führer—the only operator.

When did the Final Solution begin? The answer depends on which phase of the plan, from conception to execution, we focus upon. Its execution depended on success of the plan of conquest first.

It was established at Nuremberg that the order to devise implementation of an annihilation plan was transmitted orally from Hitler to Göring in the spring of 1941 and from Göring to Reinhard Heydrich, Chief of the Reich Security Main Office (RHSA) on July 31, 1941, instructing him to make "all necessary preparations . . . for bringing about a complete solution to the Jewish problem"—code words as usual—and these plans were communicated to all bureaucracies at the RHSA conference at Wannsee (near Berlin) on January 20, 1942. Orders to massacre Jews during invasion of the territory formerly occupied by the Soviet Union were given by

Hitler to the Army High Command and the RHSA chief during the spring of 1941 (Hilberg, 1967, pp. 177–187, 261–266; International Military Tribunal, 1946, p. 297).

German Foreign Office and RHSA correspondence had led some scholars (Yahil, 1974) to believe that the aim of Hitler in 1940 was to expel the Jews from Europe and resettle them in a penal colony in Madagascar, a French possession. Others (Reitlinger, 1968, pp. 80–82) believe this was an alternative tactic to their extermination. Discussion of the Madagascar plan may have served not only as a smokescreen but as a mechanism to allow the bureaucracy to adjust by stages to the Final Solution by showing that the resettlement of Jews in Madagascar—first proposed by Poland in 1936—was impracticable. To insiders, it was surely "a sick joke," as Dawidowicz (1975, pp. 118–119) puts it, "that Philip Bouhler, the head of Hitler's chancellery, was slated to become governor of the Madagascar reservation. Bouhler headed the so-called 'Euthanasia Program,' the first mass murder by gassing, experience that doubless qualified him to run a reservation for Jews that would become truly their final destination." Moreover, the pretrial interrogation of Adolf Eichmann (repudiated during the trial) in Jerusalem lends credence to the interpretation that RHSA chief Heydrich and Eichmann were fully aware that the ultimate goal was the annihilation of the Jews when Heydrich in September 1939 instructed the chiefs of his Security Police as to the strategy of entrapment of Polish Jews.[2]

Schleunes (1970) sees the Final Solution as evolving from the failure of earlier programs, the enlargement of the number of Jews in the domain occupied by the Reich and finally, the domination, only achieved in 1938, of the SS over all aspects of Jewish policy. But Hitler had to resolve the problem not simply to fulfill his convictions but because:

> It was the Jew who helped hold Hitler's system together—on the practical as well as the ideological level. . . . The continued search for a solution of the Jewish problem allowed Hitler to maintain ideological contact with elements of his movement for whom National Socialism had done very little." (p. 261).

How then, one may ask, could one rid Germany of the Jews if they were the cement making the blocks of National Socialism cohere? One may infer that only when Germans were mobilized behind an external enemy could they live without their internal enemy. Therefore, it was both a functional and tactical move to proceed against the Jews only after the Germans were immersed in war. Hilberg, and many others, see Hitler's speech of January 30, 1939 to the *Reichstag* as warning of his intentions, masked by his projection of his own intent onto the Jews in paranoid style:

> And one thing I wish to say on this day which perhaps is memorable not only for us Germans: In my life I have often been a prophet, and most of the time I have been laughed at. . . . Today I want to be a prophet once more: If international-finance Jewry inside and outside of Europe should succeed once more in plunging nations into another world war, the consequence will not be the Bolshevization of the earth and thereby the victory of Jewry, but the annihilation [*Vernichtung*] of the Jewish race in Europe (quoted in Hilberg, 1967, p. 267).

Only nine days earlier, he had told the Czechoslovakian Foreign Minister "We are going to destroy the Jews (Dawidowicz, 1975, p. 106)." Certain associates knew this earlier. A British Consul who had gone to Germany to rescue a friend from Dachau concentration camp while on leave in November 1938, had talked with a senior member of Hitler's Chancellery who told him "that Germany intended to get rid of her Jews, either by emigration or if necessary by starving or killing them, since she would not risk having such a hostile minority in the country in the event of war." The official added that Germany "intended to expel or kill off the Jews in Poland, Hungary, and the Ukraine when she took control of those countries (Sherman, 1973, p. 183)." The invasion of Poland in 1939 swelled the Jewish population under Nazi rule to 2,657,000, making it clear that emigration was only a talking point.

The war was a necessary condition to justify and cover mobilization for extermination, but not itself a cause. Needs stemming from the war effort were often put second to the imperatives of "The War Against the Jews." Hilberg (1967, pp. 644–646) has noted that the elimination of Jewish labor and diversion of equipment was counterproductive to military mobilization. Ridding Europe of the Jews was an absolute end to Hitler, the only one he attempted which was virtually fulfilled. Felix Kersten, Himmler's masseur, states that had Germany won, the Jews of North and South America were next on Hitler's list for gassing (1947, p. 174).

## EXTERMINATION OF THE GYPSIES

The Jews were not the only group in Germany stigmatized as alien, but the only stigmatized group of political significance whose elimination had been publicly promised by Hitler twenty years before it began. The Gypsies were also designated for destruction, although scarcely any publicity was devoted to the "Gypsy problem." We are indebted (except where otherwise stated) to Kenrick and Puxon (1972) authors of *The Destiny of Europe's Gypsies* for this documentation. Gypsies had also been defined outside the universe of obligation sanctified by the Christian churches. They have been accused of crime and corruption since their entry into Europe, charged with assistance at the crucifixion, unnatural copulation, cannibalism, necrophiliac activity, and spreading filth and disease. The first response of European states from the fifteenth to the eighteenth century was to expel them; 148 such laws were passed by German states alone between 1416 and 1774. Violence was commonly employed for enforcement and deterrence. As late as the nineteenth century, Gypsy hunts (like fox hunts) occurred in Denmark. Only after drives for expulsion and extermination had failed did states attempt to assimilate them, by denying the right of Gypsies to live together, by encouraging settlement and criminalizing the nomads' life. By 1933, police in France, Baden, and Prussia already had files with finger-printed identification of Gypsies there.

Gypsies were officially defined as non-Aryan by the same Nuremberg laws of 1935 which first defined Jews; both groups were forbidden to marry Germans. Gypsies were later labeled as asocials by the 1937 Laws Against Crime, regardless of whether or not they had been charged with any unlawful acts. By May 1938 SS Reichsführer Himmler established the Central Office for Fighting the Gypsy Menace which defined the question as "a matter of race," discriminating pure Gypsies from part-Gypsies as Jews were discriminated, and ordered their registration. In 1939 resettlement of Gypsies was put under Eichmann's jurisdiction along with that of the Jews. Gypsies were forbidden to move freely and in 1939 were concentrated in encampments within Germany. These were later transformed into fenced ghettoes (1941), from which Gypsies would be seized for transport by the criminal police (aided by dogs) and dispatched to Auschwitz in February 1943. The common fate of Gypsies and Jews was signified by the agreement between German Justice Minister Thierack and SS Reichsführer Himmler on September 18, 1942. Thierack wrote, "I envisage transferring all criminal proceedings concerning (these people) to Himmler. I do this because I realize that the courts can only feebly contribute to the extermination of these people. . . (Kenrick and Puxon, 1972, p. 87)."

Although Himmler did not authorize the extermination of the German Gypsies until 1944—apparently pausing while he considered sparing certain tribes, the "so-called pure Gypsies," as Martin Bormann put it—three-fourths of them are estimated to have been killed through starvation, disease, and abuse as live experimental subjects as well as by direct gassing.

## CREATING A RACE "OF PURE BLOOD"

The plan to transform the German people into a race of pure blood, first intent on selective population increase by encouraging eugenic breeding, was radically expanded at the start of World War II. On September 1,

1939, Hitler allowed Dr. Karl Brandt and Philip Bouhler, his Chancellery Chief, to authorize "certain physicians" to grant "incurable" persons a "mercy death." These were considered in Nazi ideology to be people unfit to breed and those who consumed food uselessly. German victims included the mentally ill, deformed or retarded children, tuberculars, and arteriosclerotic adults; other victims were foreign workers who became ill or disabled and concentration camp prisoners, including Jews (U.S. Military Tribunal, 1949, pp. 795–896). Wertham declares (1966, pp. 156–158) that this program, which led to the death of an estimated 270,000 Germans among the institutionalized mental patients alone, has been falsely labeled "euthanasia" when it was simple murder.

It served as a pilot program as well. The same staff had developed the gas chambers for the special killing centers within Germany developed the massive installations at Auschwitz. The gassing of German children transported by the busload to such centers was halted by Hitler's edict in response to German protests and widely expressed revulsion and fears; however, their individual murder was continued by less visible means, such as the injection of poisons. The gassing of German Jews was never stopped; Germans felt no need to observe or protest their absence.

The fantasy of a pure race also inspired the *"Lebensbörn"* ("well of life") program, first established by Heinrich Himmler within the SS in 1935 to enlarge and purify the Aryan race by selective mating from existing stock. During the war, maternity homes and clinics were established throughout Europe for the birth of the progeny of SS men and women of diverse nationality whom the officers had impregnated, thus fulfilling their duty (dictated by Himmler) as SS officers (Thompson, 1971, p. 69). Pregnant mothers had to pass racial screening tests (as did their fathers to become SS officers) for admission. The children of unmarried parents became the legal wards of Himmler and could not be claimed by their parents. Robert Kempner, Chief US prosecutor at Nuremburg (1946–1949) estimates that 50,000 to 100,000 children were born under *Lebensbörn* auspices (Henry and Hillel, n.d., p. 20). *Lebensbörn* obtained homes in Germany, Austria, Czechoslovakia, the Netherlands, and Poland by taking over Jewish property and hospitals. Secondly, children of suitable racial characteristics (screened in orphanages, schools, and special centers) in the Protectorate, Poland, and the occupied eastern territories were openly kidnapped, institutionalized and later (if they passed all racial tests) adopted by German parents. Those not selected died in concentration camps. It is estimated that 200,000 children were snatched from Poland alone.[3] The plan for the suppression of the Polish nation—Poles might remain alive but not as Poles—was supplemented by selective extermination of especially vulnerable groups: Polish workers in Germany who became incapacitated for some reason and those in mental institutions in Poland. An attempt (not successful due to German opposition) was also made to exterminate tubercular Poles in institutions (Bucheim, 1968, pp. 377–378). The Germans attempted to extinguish Poland as a nation by destruction of the intelligentsia, reducing the masses to subliteracy, kidnapping Polish children, lowering the population growth (raising the minimum marriage age, depressing the standard of living, penalizing out-of-wedlock births), physical resettlement, and racially stratifying the population to induce or coerce Poles classified (often arbitrarily) as of German blood to become "re-Germanized (International Military Tribunal, 1946, pp. 1023–1038; U.S. Military Tribunal, 1948, pp. 45–102)."

The kingdom of death established throughout Europe between 1941 and 1945 was devised for the dominion of an ideal race, not yet existent. Just as Hitler ordered the annihilation of Germans that were less than perfect in 1939, when the Germans proved unwilling to make sacrifices he demanded in 1945, Hitler ordered the destruction of basic resources that would have radically diminished survival and reconstruction-potential of the German people because he believed they no longer deserved to live (Speer, 1972, pp. 475, 520, 523). It was never the real people but the ideal *volk* which dictated his programs.

## CONCLUSION

The extermination of the Jews, the Gypsies, and Armenians was instigated by ideological imperatives stemming from the "political formulas" adopted by the ruling elites of Germany and the Ottoman Empire to legitimate their domination.

The annihilation of the Jews and Gypsies was made possible by the German conception of them as alien, non-*Volk,* and their idealization of the *Volk* as an imminent, pure, and transcendant race. Hitler's drive to transform Germans into such a pure race, justifying their domination over other races, dictated the categorical annihilation of such aliens and selective murders of Germans who did not contribute towards the goal. The Turks' annihilation of the Armenians was dictated by the ruling elite's concept of an underlying Turkish identity which alone could justify the continued existence of the Ottoman Empire. When the Young Turks attempted to establish their power with a new formula, annihilating the Armenians became a rational means to fulfill their ideal.

In both cases, world wars diminished the visibility of extermination and provided immunity from sanctions by the western allies and Russia, enemies of the Ottomans in World War I and of Germany in World War II. Although Germany apparently desired to halt the extermination of the

Armenians, she was generally unwilling to impose any sanctions and did not exert any counterforce to check her Turkish ally.

Extermination of the victims was a prime end-in-itself. Military needs were subordinated by the Turks in order to exterminate the Armenians, as they were by the Germans who neglected their own needs for labor and transport while exterminating the Jews.

The victims were marked as potential targets for centuries earlier. While the political formulas justifying the extinction of the groups selected were the tools of new leadership, the victims had earlier been decreed outside the universe of obligation by Koranic injunctions and by Christian theodicy. However, churches holding out the possibility of conversion to all must assume a common humanity and therefore may not sanction unlimited violence. But a doctrine which assumes people do not belong to a common species imposes no limits inhibiting the magnitude of permissible crime.

The functional value of propaganda against the victims differed for these regimes as did the degree of premeditation of the genocides. The Nazi (NSDAP) campaign against the Jews in Germany was almost twenty years old by 1939 and Jew-hatred had clearly been instrumental in terms of attracting followers: solving the "Jewish problem" was a commitment of Hitler from the beginning. However, the Young Turks proclaimed a liberal national credo in 1908. Turkish chauvinism and Pan-Turkism were used by the triumvirate usurping power in 1913 to justify domination, rather than as a tool of mass mobilization. The efficiency of the German genocide can be accounted for by the length of its premeditation, the generally higher level of technical innovation and social organization in Germany in 1939 compared with Turkey of 1915 and the German leaders' fear of popular violence within the Reich. They feared the consequences of liberating repressed violence directly, as during the *Kristallnacht* pogrom. Then, the Nazis acted out sentiments most often expressed rhetorically against Jews. The Turks, however, exploited a tradition of popular collective physical violence against infidels.

Finally, the actual political role of the victims in both states differed, although all were powerless once stripped of rights. In their statelessness no European nation-state was obligated to protect them. The Armenians were organized as a collectivity, and had demonstrated their capacity for guerrilla warfare as well as public demonstration under the Sultan's despotism ending in 1908. Although Armenian leaders demonstrated their loyalty to the new regime publicly, the military capacity shown by the Russian Armenians reinforced their type-casting as potential enemies. They were a substantively numerous, cohesive and a significantly located minority inhabiting the land bridge overlapping Persia and the

Russian and Ottoman Empires, whom the dominant Turks would have had to recognize and bargain with to coexist within a democratic state.

By contrast, German Jews were apt to be assimilated within German society, integrated within German political parties (excepting the anti-Semitic parties) and only organized in self-defense associations to protest collective slanders by apolitical means. German Gypsies were neither integrated nor organized to participate politically. Neither Jews nor Gypsies made demands for special representation. Although there has been controversy over the wisdom of past political strategies among Armenians and Jews, there is no evidence to suggest that the strategies chosen by either group influenced the Turkish and German leaders' choice of exclusive political formulas leading toward their extermination.

At the beginning of the crime was an ideal. But the ideal could only be realized by an organized movement which was not checked. War between nations and internal war now (as then) diminishes the possibility of observing and checking genocide. To observe it, we will have to look with fresh eyes, for it will appear again masked by new ideologies which justify it among nations to whom racism is a stigma. Only by focusing on the identity of the victim and the perpetrator can we strip the mask of ideology and accounting mechanisms used by perpetrators to disguise their responsibility.

## FOOTNOTES

*Helen Fein is a political sociologist concerned with collective violence and genocide. She is the author of *Imperial Crime and Punishment: The Massacre at Jallianwala Bagh and British Judgement 1919–1920* (University Press of Hawaii, 1977) and has recently completed *Accounting for Genocide: National Responses and Jewish Victimization During the Holocaust,* to be published by The Free Press, New York, in 1978. She is currently at Queens College, New York.

1. The concept of a master race has emerged both among pan-movements appealing to people without a nation-state and nation-states with weak solidarity. See Arendt (1966, pp. 235, 412) on the varying implications of this.

2. Eichmann concurred with the implication of Heydrich's memorandum before his trial apparently without realizing that it also implicated him because of his presence at the conference referred to in the memorandum. See Hauser (1966, pp. 55–56).

3. The kidnapping of Polish children was documented by a Polish state investigation commission, as reported by Henry and Hillel (n.d.) in "Of Pure Blood." For Himmler's authorization of screening Polish schoolchildren in the German-occupied area of Poland, see International Military Tribunal (1946, p. 640). Arendt (1966, p. 342) reviews other documents showing that "in June, 1944, the Ninth Army actually kidnapped 40,000 to 50,000 [Polish] children and subsequently transported them to Germany."

# REFERENCES


Ahmad, Feroz (1969) *The Young Turks: The Committee of Union and Progress in Turkish Politics 1908–1914*. Oxford: Clarendon Press.

Arendt, Hannah (1966) *The Origins of Totalitarianism*. New York: Harcourt, Brace and World.

Blalock, H. M., Jr. (1970) *Towards A Theory of Minority-Group Relations*. New York: Capricorn Books.

Boyajian, H. (1972) *Armenia: The Case for a Forgotten Genocide*. Westwood, NJ: Educational Book Crafters.

Bryce, Viscount (1916) *The Treatment of Armenians in the Ottoman Empire 1915–1916*. Prepared by Arnold Toynbee. London: H.M.S.O.

Bucheim, Hans (1968) "Command and Compliance." Pages 305–396 in H. Krausnick et al. (eds.), *Anatomy of the S.S. State*. Translated by Richard Barry et al., New York: Walker.

Cohn, Norman (1969) *Warrant for Genocide: The Myth of the Jewish World-Conspiracy and the Protocols of the Elders of Zion*. New York: Harper Torchbook.

Dawidowicz, Lucy S. (1975) *The War Against the Jews 1933–1945*. New York: Holt, Rinehart and Winston.

Djemal Pasha (n.d.) *Memories of a Turkish Statesman, 1913–1919*. London: Hutchinson, [ca. 1922].

Fein, Helen (1977) *Imperial Crime and Punishment: The Jallianwala Bagh Massacre and British Judgement 1919–1920*. Honolulu: The University Press of Hawaii.

Gibb, H. A. R. and Bowen, Harold (1962) *Islamic Society and the West*. Volume 1. London: Oxford University Press.

Hartunian, Abraham (1968) *Neither to Laugh Nor to Weep*. Boston: Beacon Press.

Hausner, Gideon (1966) *Justice in Jerusalem*. New York: Harper & Row.

Henry, Clarissa and Hillel, Marc (n.d.) "Of Pure Blood." Filmscript of documentary by Agence Française. Translated by the B.B.C.

Hilberg, Raul (1967) *The Destruction of the European Jews*. Chicago: Quadrangle Books.

Housepian, Marjorie (1966) "The Unremembered Genocide." *Commentary*. Volume 37, September: 55–61.

International Military Tribunal (1946) *Nazi Conspiracy and Aggression*. Volumes 2, 3. Washington, DC: Government Printing Office.

Isaac, Jules (1964) *The Teaching of Contempt: Christian Roots of Anti-Semitism*. Translated by H. Weaver. New York: Holt, Rinehart and Winston.

Kenrick, Donald and Puxon, Grattan (1972) *The Destiny of Europe's Gypsies*. New York: Basic Books.

Kersten, Felix (1947) *The Memoirs of Dr. Felix Kersten*. Translated by E. Morwitz. New York: Doubleday.

Kochan, Lionel (1957) *Pogrom: 10 November 1938*. London: André Deutsch.

Lemkin, Raphael (1944) *Axis Rule in Occupied Europe*. Washington, DC: Carnegie Endowment for International Peace.

Lochner, Louis (1942) *What About Germany?* New York: Dodd, Mead.

Massing, Paul W. (1967) *Rehearsal for Destruction: A Study of Political Anti-Semitism in Imperial Germany*. New York: Fertig.

Moorehead, Alan (1956) *Gallipoli*. New York: Harper.

Morgenthau, Henry, Sr. (1918) *Ambassador Morgenthau's Story*. Garden City, NY: Doubleday, Page.

Mosca, Gaetano (1939) *The Ruling Class*. Translated by H. Kahan and revised by Arthur Livingston. New York: McGraw-Hill.

Mosse, George L. (1964) *The Crisis of German Ideology: Intellectual Origins of the Third Reich*. New York: Grosset and Dunlap.

Naim Bey (1964) *The Memoirs of Naim Bey: Turkish Official Documents Relating to the Deportation and Massacres of Armenians*. Compiled by Aram Andonian. Newton Square, PA: Armenian Historical Research Association.

Nalbandian, Louise (1967) *The Armenian Revolutionary Movement: The Development of Armenian Political Parties Through the Nineteenth Century*. Berkeley: University of California Press.

Reitlinger, Gerald (1968) *The Final Solution: The Attempt to Exterminate the Jews of Europe 1939–1945*. 2d ed. Cranbury, NJ: Thomas Yoseloff.

Reuther, Rosemary (1974) *Faith and Fratricide*. New York: Seabury Press.

Sarkissian, A. O. (1965) *Martyrdom and Rebirth*. Published by the Armenian Church of America. New York: Lydian Press.

Schleunes, Karl A. (1970) *The Twisted Road to Auschwitz*. Urbana, IL: University of Illinois Press.

Sherman, A. J. (1973) *Island Refuge: Britain and Refugees from the Third Reich, 1933–1939*. London: Paul Elck.

Silver, Daniel Jeremy (1974) *A History of Judaism*. Volume 1: *From Abraham to Maimonides*. New York: Basic Books.

Speer, Albert (1972) *Inside the Third Reich*. Translated by Richard and Clara Winston. New York: Macmillan.

Sugar, Peter F. and Lederer, Ivo J. (eds.) (1969) *Nationalism in Eastern Europe*. Seattle: University of Washington Press.

Taylor, A. J. P. (1946) *The Course of German History: A Survey of the Development of Germany since 1815*. New York: Coward-McCann.

Thompson, Larry (1971) "*Lebensborn* and the Eugenics Policy of the *Reichsfuhrer-SS*." *Central European History* 4:54–77.

Trumpener, Ulrich (1968) *Germany and the Ottoman Empire 1914–1918*. Princeton, NJ: Princeton University Press.

United States Military Tribunal (1949) *Trial of War Criminals Before the Nuremberg Military Tribunals Under Control Council Law No. 10*. Case VIII, Volume 1. Washington, DC: Government Printing Office.

Weber, Max (1930) *The Protestant Ethic and the Spirit of Capitalism*. Trans. by Talcott Parsons. New York: Scribners.

Wertham, Frederic (1966) *A Sign for Cain*. New York: Macmillan.

Yahil, L. (1974) "Madagascar—Phantom of a Solution for the Jewish Question." Pages 315–334 in Bela Vago and George L. Mosse (eds.), *Jews and Non-Jews in Eastern Europe 1918–1945*. New York: Wiley.

Zaravend (pseud.) (1971) *United and Independent Turania: Aims and Designs of the Turks*. Translated by V. N. Dadrian. Leiden: E. J. Brill.

# IMPERFECTLY UNIFIED ELITES: THE CASES OF ITALY AND FRANCE

G. Lowell Field and John Higley*

Patterns of elite unity and disunity, and the consequences which these have for the stability of political institutions as well as for the values of liberty, equality, and democracy, are a major focus of comparative political sociology (Aron, 1950; Putnam, 1976, pp. 107–132). With respect to unified elites, two types are commonly recognized. The first, represented by Russian and East European elites, displays a marked ideological consensus. The second, typified by Western liberal elites, like the American, British, Dutch, and Swedish, lacks any overt ideological consensus, but its members seem to share a commitment to defend and to abide by existing institutions and rules of political contest. According to a theory

**Comparative Studies in Sociology—Vol. 1, 1978, pages 295–317**

**ISBN 0-89232-025-7**

we have advanced (Field, 1967; Higley, Field and Grøholt, 1976), the unity of these two elite types is the last best explanation for the stability of political institutions characteristic of the societies in which they are found.

But a third type of elite also obviously exists. This is the disunified elite, among whose members there is neither ideological consensus nor an underlying commitment to existing institutions and rules of political contest. Where an elite is disunified, political institutions are more or less constantly threatened with violent overthrow, and such overthrows occur frequently enough to make the pursuit of democracy, and with it a liberal and fair society, largely pointless (Field and Higley, 1973, pp. 19–20). Disunified elites are by far the most common type of elite now and in history. Indeed, so many cases of elite disunity may be observed in Europe, Latin America, the Middle East, and Asia that there is little agreement about the subtypes most significant for a general theory of elites.

The theory we have advanced distinguishes two subtypes of disunified elites. The first is the pure type containing several distinct and highly antagonistic factions. Where adventitious subcultural and regional groupings are not present, these are usually seen as comprising a right, a left, and sometimes a center. This pure type of disunified elite occurs in societies at lower levels of socioeconomic development, as the latter concept is measured by work force differentiation. The consequence of this disunity is a succession of irregular seizures of power by force, or the widespread expectation that such seizures will occur. The earlier political histories of most European societies, the entire political histories of nearly all Latin American societies, and the recent political histories of nearly all Third World societies clearly display this type of disunified elite with its consequent political instability.

The other type of disunified elite is what we call the imperfectly unified elite. It occurs only in societies which have attained a relatively high level of socioeconomic development at which it is sometimes possible to mobilize stable conservative voting coalitions that last for long periods of time. This has the effect of depriving right-wingers of any incentive to upset constitutional arrangements. At the same time it makes it imprudent for left-wingers to contemplate political measures other than the mere solicitation of voting support. In essentials, an imperfectly unified elite represents a distinct attenuation of the sharp antagonism and the political warfare characteristic of elite disunity in its pure form. Although it still contains left, right, and center factions, all direct their efforts to electoral politics and suspend any serious consideration of insurrectional attempts. Most elite persons express a willingness to abide by electoral and other institutional outcomes without, however, fully trusting that their opponents will do the same. In other words, the mutual trust and shared commitment of the elite that is fully unified around the desirability of existing institutions and political rules is hardly present in an imperfectly unified elite. Important cleavages still exist. Typically, the largest portion of the elite, the right and center factions, is more or less fully allegiant to existing institutions and rules, while a smaller portion, the left faction, is regarded as only tentatively allegiant to these at best, and as deceptive in its profession of this allegiance at worst.

These distinctions between an imperfectly unified elite, a fully unified one, and a fully disunified one are important, even if they are too seldom made in the sociology of elites. Commonly, sociologists blur the distinctions, putting the imperfectly unified elite into either the fully unified or fully disunified categories. Thus the Italian and French elites, we shall argue, have been imperfectly unified for a number of years, after having been disunified for many decades. Yet it is a commonplace in political sociology to treat these elites as interchangeable with the fully unified Anglo-American and Scandinavian elites. This is a mistake, for what one can predict about the likely behavior of one kind of elite does not readily hold for the other.

In our view, the central question about imperfectly unified elites is whether they can achieve full unification. The evidence on this question is, as yet, quite equivocal. On the one hand, several elites that were imperfectly unified have indeed become fully unified. We refer to the Norwegian and Danish elites around the time of the Second World War, and to the Austrian elite sometime after postwar military occupation ended. Yet none of these cases represents a straightforward unification of an imperfectly unified elite independent of exogenous forces. In the Norwegian and Danish cases the German occupation, and local resistance to it, probably strongly facilitated elite unification. Similarly, the influence of occupation forces in Austria immediately after the war in selecting a new political leadership had much to do with the eventual formation of a unified elite in that country. None of these three elites contained strong Communist or Fascist factions at the time of their unification. On the other hand, two elites that until recently had been imperfectly unified for long periods, the Uruguayan and Chilean elites, have in this decade broken apart into obvious disunity.

Given this equivocal evidence, whether imperfectly unified elites can "of their own accord," so to speak, achieve full unification remains unproven. This is why we view recent and current processes among French and Italian elites with the greatest theoretical interest. During the past 15 years, the elite antagonisms that accounted historically for five irregular changes of regime in France since 1789, and for highly turbulent politics before the Fascist take-over in Italy, seem to have attenuated steadily. At present many observers believe that these two elites are poised to allow their large Communist factions a major, possibly a decisive, role in government for the first time in any Western democracy (except for the geographically idiosyncratic Finland and Iceland). However, these observers are also quite disagreed about what consequences for liberal democratic politics this change may have. In this article we examine the attenuation of elite disunity in France and Italy, and we assess the likelihood of its continuation until full elite unity is achieved.

## IMPERFECTLY UNIFIED ELITES[1]

Unified elites of the sort that involve ideological consensus are created in two ways. In the generic Russian Communist, Italian Fascist, and German Nazi cases they arose out of the victory of radical forces in revolutionary circumstances (Hagopian, 1975, pp. 341–365) and the subsequent imposition by those forces of a single ideology on all persons who aspired to elite and subelite positions. In all other cases this kind of elite unity has been imposed by conquering foreign military forces (as in Austria just before World War II and in Eastern Europe and North Korea after it) or has resulted from victory in organized civil warfare (as in Yugoslavia, Albania, China, North and South Vietnam, Cuba, Cambodia, and Laos). In other words, the creation of an ideologically unified elite without protracted warfare is a rare occurrence. All the evidence suggests, however, that such an elite, once established is reliably self-perpetuating until the regime it operates is defeated in warfare or the military forces which imposed it are no longer available to shore it up.

Unified elites of the sort that involve a shared commitment to existing institutions and political rules are created in two ways, and there is the possibility of a third (which is the one this article investigates). The first way is through a deliberate and sudden reorganization of a previously disunified elite so that most influential persons are assured that under the reorganization they need not constantly fight each other to retain their elite status. We can find only three instances of this kind of elite reorganization by the elite itself, however: England in 1689, Sweden in 1809, and Mexico in 1933. In all three instances the elites concerned were small numerically and they were effectively isolated from popular pressures in the mainly agrarian societies over which they presided.

The second and most frequent way in which unified elites of this kind have been created has been through successful struggles for independence after the elite in question had already gained substantial experience in representative or "democratic" politics. The generic case was the American elite in the late eighteenth century, presumably preceded by the

Dutch elite in the late sixteenth century and followed by the Swiss, Canadian, New Zealand, and Australian elites in the nineteenth century, and the South African and Irish elites in the first part of the twentieth century. Whether any elites in the developing societies that gained independence after World War II (e.g. India, Kenya, Tanzania, Tunisia, the Philippines) have achieved this kind of unity is open to question in view of their more limited experience, while still in colonial status, with representative politics, not to mention the serious subcultural and regional divisions which beset their societies today. But because colonialism is now a dead letter, this most frequent way in which unified elites of this type were created is currently unavailable. Unless there is a third route to elite unity, then, our theory contends that, except as the outcomes of wars may permit, the political future of nearly all developing societies can only be one of uninterrupted elite disunity and political instability.

But possibly there is a third way in which this kind of unified elite can be formed. This would be the transformation of disunified elites into imperfectly unified ones, and then their further transformation into fully unified ones. We have already said that this seems to have been what happened in the Norwegian and Danish cases, although the circumstances of World War II had a muddying effect so far as a clear demonstration of the process is concerned. We have also said that at least two imperfectly unified elites, in Uruguay and Chile, have clearly failed to unify fully and have instead broken apart. Thus there seems to be nothing inexorable about the process, an observation which can be supported by a more detailed examination of what is involved.

Imperfect elite unity is created after the discovery by a portion of the elite stratum that it commands a relatively conservative electoral majority on which it can rely for support in any election, referendum, or similar peaceful registration of mass sentiment. The discovery that it commands such a majority enables this body of elite persons gradually to give representative institutions and the rules by which they operate greater allegiance. Instead of constantly preparing to counter the actions of their opponents with whatever means necessary, it becomes possible for these elites to relax their guard, to proclaim themselves "democrats," and to engage confidently in competitive electoral politics. Consequently, expectations that veto groups such as the police and military are likely to intervene and impose forcible solutions on elite struggles diminish over time.

It should be obvious, however, that relatively conservative electoral majorities of the sort to which we refer are not available to elites in most societies. They come into existence only when a society attains a level of socioeconomic development sufficient to vest a majority of voters with an interest in maintaining roughly the existing unequal distribution of goods and privileges. In societies at lower levels of development, in which populations constitute a largely undifferentiated and alienated mass, such majorities simply do not exist. If they are allowed to vote at all when the elite is not fully unified and if they are not swayed by adventitious appeals to their cultural conservatism, or nationalism, such populations vote in antisystem directions. But at high levels of development this is not the case. Indeed, it has never happened that a majority of voters in an industrialized society has voted to level seriously that society's extended hierarchies of wealth, power, and privilege. Because the creation of imperfect elite unity depends on elites realizing the essentially conservative nature of majority sentiment in such developed societies, it follows that imperfectly unified elites only occur in substantially developed societies.

Less abstractly, an imperfectly unified elite consists of an elite stratum that is divided into two parts, each of which is substantially alienated from the other. On the one hand, there is a large body of elite persons, located in the center and right-of-center of the political spectrum, who are unified around the desirability of existing institutions and rules of political contest. They profit from the political reality of a voter majority opposed to any sharp alterations in the status order. The reliability of this majority is manifested through successive elections, the outcomes of which always provide enough support to enable these elite persons to form government coalitions that effectively exclude the other major group in an imperfectly unified elite. This other group consists of elite persons who head up parties, organizations, and mass followings opposed to the existing status order and who are on record as intending to alter it dramatically if and when they obtain power. In actual cases these are ordinarily persons leading Communist and/or Socialist movements. They comprise an out group not merely because of their distinctive ideology and antisystem stance, but also because they are able to mobilize only a minority of voters. These voters tend in varying degrees to be hostile toward center and right-of-center forces and supporters. From time to time they engage in violent mass protests and disorders directed against constituted authority. Although leftist elite persons may not actually organize these riots, disruptions, and political strikes, they cannot afford to oppose them publicly. Consequently, where there is an imperfectly unified elite political stability is always seen to be precarious, especially by those who have not noticed the reliability of the conservative electoral majority.

The dynamic component of an imperfectly unified elite is this leftist body of elite persons. This is because the repeated demonstration of majority support for the unified portion of the elite creates a genuine dilemma for the leftist faction which it must seek to resolve sooner or later. Insofar as they can be separated, the horns of this dilemma are intellectual and practical. Intellectually, the leftist elite faction is forced to consider that its continued adherence to egalitarian goals means an indefinite, probably permanent, exclusion from power. One alternative would be to attempt to seize power by force, but this is ordinarily not a practical possibility in view of the political base of the regime. The other alternative is gradually to disavow enough of those tenets of its egalitarian ideology as are least appealing to potential supporters in order to attract additional support.

But it is at this point that the leftist elite faction faces the practical horn of its dilemma. For to disavow ideological tenets is a tricky process that risks alienating hard core supporters. It is in this respect that the difference between the situation of an imperfectly unified elite and that of disunified ones like the English, Swedish, and Mexican at the time of their unifications is most clearly seen. The factions which comprise an imperfectly unified elite are not isolated from mass pressures to anything like the degree that the three elites just mentioned were. Even if they privately have no serious commitments to the ideologies with which they have long appealed for mass support, the factions which make up the left in an imperfectly unified elite can only with great danger to their political survival discard these ideologies in order to gain more support. They risk being replaced by more fervid leaders whose only contribution would be to exacerbate already serious elite divisions. The importance of this mass constraint on elite maneuverability is that in an imperfectly unified elite leaders of other factions recognize this pressure on leftist leaders to redeem long-standing ideological promises. Because of this recognition, few elite opponents of the left will usually be prepared to find out what might happen by allowing the left to govern in its own right.

We trace here the vicious circle in which an imperfectly unified elite is ensnared. Conceivably, external pressure can break this circle and open the way to full unification. This may have been the significance, for example, of the German occupation of Norway and Denmark. Just as conceivably, however, portions of an imperfectly unified elite will try to break the circle precipitously only to push the situation into full disunity. This may have been the significance of allowing Allende to govern alone even though his forces had captured less than two-fifths of the popular vote in the 1970 election. But it is also conceivable that an imperfectly united elite would have enough political good sense not to take great risks while still encouraging further attenuation of its divisions where and when circumstances permit. As we said, there seems to be little that is inexorable about this process. Rather, like all deliberate political change, it depends on large amounts of political acumen and accidental good fortune. We now inquire whether political acumen and good fortune seem to be present in sufficient quantity in France and Italy at present to make a full unification of their elites likely.

## THE FORMATION OF IMPERFECTLY UNIFIED ELITES IN FRANCE AND ITALY

Throughout their histories as nation states prior to World War II, except for the period of the Fascist dictatorship in Italy, and for some years after the war, French and Italian elites were disunified. Deep hostilities between left and right elite factions in France, fueled by bitter memories of the Revolution, created highly unstable political institutions throughout much of the nineteenth century. Only a very precarious stability was attained under the Third Republic after 1870. The same kind of hostility brought Italy to the brink of civil war in the early 1920s and was followed by a fascist repression of the left under Mussolini.

At the end of World War II, left-wing forces in both countries were strong and inclined toward revolutionary action. But the American and British forces that had defeated and expelled the previously dominant German forces were essentially in control, as conquerors in Italy, and as somewhat reluctant supporters of a provisional regime under General de Gaulle in France. Because they prudently considered that these "liberating" forces would support right-of-center elite factions in a confrontation, leftist leaders abstained from overt revolutionary measures. Partly because their association with the hated Germans had discredited them, and partly because they too felt sure that the liberators would side with them in a confrontation, those inclined to strict conservatism in both countries also refrained from fully reopening the political struggles of the prewar years. These circumstances made possible a liberal democratic constitution in each case, and, initially, governments representing all factions (including the Communists) that had not been thoroughly discredited during the war.

With the onset of the Cold War in 1947, however, the Communists were excluded from ministerial office. Both governments thus came to be made up of more or less extended coalitions of the noncommunist parties. In Italy the Christian Democrats, closely associated with the Catholic Church and with the help of small parties, were strong enough to retain control until the present time. They always had until 1976 the option of making a majority in alliance with the right. During most of the 1960s they chose, however, to ally formally with the Socialists. Because the other option remained available, Socialist influence on governmental policy remained weak. The Socialists lost support through such participation and eventually withdrew. Sometimes the Christian Democrats have been in office alone although a minority. This was possible because the right would refrain from voting against them if they did not adopt leftist measures and the strictly leftist vote had always (up to 1976) fallen short of a majority.

Thus in Italy in election after election in the fifties and sixties an anti-Communist majority repeatedly demonstrated its existence. Probably this was facilitated by the distinctly communal and highly organized nature of Italian society in which many persons saw the Catholic Church as a useful stabilizing force (Lange, 1975). In any event, the repeated demonstration after 1945 that right-of-center forces (principally the Christian Democrats and the Liberals), assisted by various splinter groups, could count on control of parliament has two theoretical implications. First, it accords with our conceptualization of the line-up of forces which underlie the formation of imperfectly unified elites. Second, it meant that sooner or later the radical left would have to face up to the dilemma which such an elite arrangement poses for it.

The Italian Communists adjusted to this situation as best they could (Tarrow, 1974). During the early postwar years the probability that the Anglo-American occupying forces might intervene on the side of their opponents in the event of revolutionary action forced them to concentrate instead on parliamentary politics. Since they refrained from terrorist or similar actions that would have threatened other politicians individually, over a decade they became accepted in parliamentary circles as entitled to at least minor consideration even by Christian Democratic deputies. During the first postwar decade, moreover, the principal Socialist faction was in a position of subordination to the Communists. This means that the Communists did not have to act on their revolutionary program in order to keep pride of place on the left. It is sometimes argued that from its origins Italian communism was more democratic than other national communisms. We need not decide this question since actual events can be explained adequately merely by noting that during the 1950s a large Communist parliamentary contingent adhered to liberal democratic procedures of necessity because no other course of action was reasonably open to it.

In France, however, such relatively clear-cut elite and electoral alignments did not emerge so readily. Possibly because French society is not seriously communal, and because French upper strata were accustomed to seeing their political convictions as highly individualistic matters, no right-of-center vehicle similar to the Christian Democrats could be fashioned. Consequently, the prewar system of *tendances,* as distinct from fully organized national parties, revived as the means by which French conservatives labeled themselves electorally. At the same time, larger conservative movements—Gaullist and Poujadist—formed and re-formed without establishing themselves as permanent parties. While on the whole some amalgam of right-of-center *tendances,* temporary movements, and moderate centrists comprised a parliamentary majority, the residues of France's unique historical divisions prevented this majority from appearing as a single right-of-center force. Thus until 1958 there was no clear demonstration of a reliable, relatively conservative electoral majority in France.

The crisis of 1958, which arose out of the double rebellion in Algeria, must be seen as a turning point for French elite alignments. The outcome of the crisis was to allow de Gaulle to return to political life under circumstances that brought about the consolidation and demonstration of what had previously been the *de facto* conservative majority. Faced in Algeria with an ongoing native rebellion and with a second rebellion by Europeans and military commanders against government policies, the 1958 government of the Fourth Republic saw its authority rapidly disappearing. A military seizure of Paris, which would have precipitated civil war, was in fact being planned. At the time, de Gaulle remained in retirement, having only recently repudiated the last organized movement that had centered around his name. Evidently, the political leaders of the Fourth Republic recalled that de Gaulle had never ruled in strict defiance of electoral sentiment. He had resigned as head of the provisional government in 1946 in the face of political difficulties. While he had probably expected to be recalled as an indispensable man, it remains true that he did not attempt to rule on the sole basis of military power. In any event, on June 1, 1958, de Gaulle was invested as prime minister, and the threat of military revolt subsided.

General de Gaulle promptly set about transforming the French political system into an ambiguously "presidential" one that in due course gave him, as president, a central position in the new Fifth Republic. At the same time, his friends and associates rapidly organized a wide-ranging political movement for his support, the U.N.R. For at least the first 3 years, until the Algerian war was finally settled, the single clear issue facing French voters was de Gaulle or civil war. In a reversal of national political habits, many voters supported him in successive elections and referenda solely on pragmatic grounds. Victories in these gave de Gaulle authority to act in ways appropriate to the changing situation. In a process of highly ambiguous politics he eventually liberated most of the French colonial empire, in addition to Algeria, and he also crushed a subsequent military revolt.

During these tense years, conservative electoral majorities came more and more to be taken for granted. The Communists had little choice but to conform to the sitaution as de Gaulle defined it. Presumably, they were as reluctant as most other factions to engage in the sanguinary and doubtful civil war, which would almost certainly follow any upset of the Gaullist regime until the colonial issue was eliminated. This Communist acquiescence in the established system was demonstrated conclusively in the events following the 1968 student uprising when the Communists used their strong influence in the trade unions to curtail labor support for the uprising. It appears as if they then allowed de Gaulle to win one last parliamentary election by allowing him to blame them falsely for the student disruptions.

To summarize, although Italy and France both avoided illegal seizures of power by force during the thirty years which followed World War II, both elites were clearly more disunified than unified, especially during the earlier part of the period. For elite persons in both countries the possibility of such a seizure was never far from consideration. In other words, few Italian or French leaders trusted that their opponents' commitments to existing institutions and rules of political contest were sufficiently deep to make such seizures more or less unthinkable. Moreover, throughout most of the period from 40 to 50 percent of the voters in both countries supported parties that were at least formally committed to a doctrinally defined socialism or communism. At least formally, these persons could not approve of, or even condone, existing socioeconomic arrangements. While no portion of this bloc was part of the parliamentary majority in France after 1958, in Italy one or both of the two socialist parties were in governing coalition with the Christian Democrats during much of the 1960s. The major Italian socialist faction was strongly torn between its desire to keep the democratic government going and its affinity in doctrine, belief, and symbolism to the opposition Communists. Thus neither national elite was marked by an underlying agreement on essentials. Rather, both showed a continuing division between a dominant center and right-of-center group and an antagonistic left-of-center one. But in both countries the trend of greatest significance over the period was the repeated demonstration of the right-of-center group's electoral supremacy.

## THE CURRENT STATE OF COMMUNIST ELITES IN FRANCE AND ITALY

For a number of years the Communist parties in both countries have gradually been modifying their doctrines. Since the overthrow of Allende in Chile, the Italian Communist Party has sought a governing coalition that would include even the Christian Democrats. By the 1976 national elections, the Italian party had repudiated much of its traditional doctrine and practice. Moving less rapidly, the French Communists waited until the winter of 1975–1976 to repudiate, clearly and convincingly its aspiration to exercise a "dictatorship of the proletariat." However, because their past behavior led to less widespread contacts in French governing circles than the Italian Communists enjoyed, this repudiation still lacks some of the Italians' credibility. In addition, the French Communists as yet aspire only to govern in a narrow coalition, with the Socialists as their main ally.

As a consequence of these doctrinal modifications, the broader elites in both countries are now seriously contemplating the prospect of Communist participation in cabinets in the near future. This prospect has created an air of crisis. For it is evident that large numbers of non-Communist leaders remain unsatisfied that the Communists can be trusted. In the terms of our theory, the attenuation of division among the elites may not have gone far enough to make a regression to greater disunity under a partly Communist coalition government unlikely.

What stands in the way of complete unification of the two elites? Mainly, it is the historical character of the official world Communist movement from 1919 to the present, or at least what remains of this heritage in each country—rather more in France than in Italy. Full unification requires that all or most of the elite structure of the present Communist parties be absorbed into the wider political elite on a basis of trust and acceptance. Yet, this has never happened before in any country.

In previous cases where imperfectly unified elites became fully unified, it was Socialist, not Communist, parties that dominated the estranged left elite faction. In Austria, Denmark, and Norway it was Socialist party and union leaders that were absorbed into the broader political elite in order to create full unity. While it is true that socialist movements may range from doctrinal facsimilies of communism to a mere sentimental egalitarianism, the important difference is that socialist movements have no strong international organization. Therefore, they can be judged by their current, local behavior. Generally, this behavior has changed in the direction of accepting the political norms of nonsocialist elite factions during the postwar period in Europe and elsewhere. Consequently, socialist parties today are accepted for what they say they stand for.

But it seems to have been precisely this possibility that the structure and practice of Leninist communism, especially its long organization as an international movement, was designed to prevent. As Kriegel (1966) has pointed out, in the specifics of its historic structure, communism is primarily a device for protecting its working class following from cultural *embourgeoisement*. It is unnecessary to review here the ideological and factual considerations that long made it impossible to accept communist parties as mere partners in liberal democratic states. But these must at least be summarized because they are essential to understanding the current problem in Italy and France.

The Communists professed a strong and unyielding doctrine of class struggle. They insisted that the proletariat's triumph over other classes was the only solution to the world's problems. Communist organizations existed precisely to provide the necessary leadership for the proletariat, both before and after it achieved power. Communists claimed to know what needed to be done at all stages of the revolutionary process and even in its aftermath. Consequently, although they were inclined toward a crude and simplistic democracy, practical aspects of democracy, such as free debate, were of little or no value to them. Moreover, they were militant, secretive, and unscrupulous in fighting other forces, except when expediency dictated otherwise, because they regarded other political groups not merely as mistaken but as agents of the class enemy. These considerations made it reasonable to believe that communists wanted to seize power for themselves after which they would not allow opposition forces to try to unseat them. Except for the postwar behavior of the Italian and French Communist parties, most evidence from before the war and from after it in other countries tended to confirm the stereotype that only a fool would trust communists unless he were one himself.

France and Italy belong to that group of countries in which advanced industrialization means that political power can be exercised only by persons located in strategic positions in a variety of highly bureaucratic organizations. This is because only persons so situated have direct, regular access to the communication channels through which attitudes are formed and actions are taken. Broadly, such strategically located persons comprise the political elite in these societies. Although anomic protests and uprisings in very rare situations of extreme stress may impede or even break down these channels, such disruptions can only be temporary. The general dependence on bureaucratic organizations for most essential services assures their rapid restoration. This was demonstrated very clearly in France in May and June of 1968. Without a severe, drastic, and prolonged dismembering of bureaucracy, advanced industrial societies cannot resort to simpler forms of production and policing because most people in them no longer know how to operate in simpler contexts. The implication of this is that Communist leaders in Italy and France by now frequently engage in typical bureaucratic tasks. In this fundamental respect, they have become similar in attitudes, habits, daily problems, and expectations to all other elite persons in those countries.

Yet our designation of Italian and French elites as disunified until a few years ago, and as imperfectly unified since then, points to a continuing division of these elites into two parts which are alienated from each other. On the one hand, there is the now unified body of center and right-of-center elite persons who respect Western traditions of liberal democracy. As well, these persons adhere to the residues of capitalist doctrine as regards the provision of "rational" incentives in the economic sphere. While these economies, particularly that of Italy, involve considerable government ownership, departures from entrepreneural methods of operation are not conspicuous. These unified elite groups hold the key posts in cabinets, the higher civil service, business companies and associations, and in a variety of public bodies such as most of the parties, the churches, media organizations, and perhaps some of the trade unions.

Functioning as a "counterelite," on the other hand, are officials of the Communist parties themselves, trade union leaders, and some Communists and Socialists who have entered the school and university systems, the media, the civil service, and other organizations over which the unified portion of the elite presides. These persons comprise a "counterelite" not so much because of clear differences between their attitudes on current issues and those of the unified elite. They comprise a counterelite primarily because they respect quite different political and economic traditions. Generally, they do not view previous Western political and economic development in a favorable light. They have different explanations for this development, and they oppose its continuation. But in the main, and for many years now, these persons have avoided serious revolutionary gestures. While they do not closely associate with the main body of unified elite persons, they nevertheless speak for interests, negotiate these, and administer them just as the unified portion of the elite does.

When we discussed the formation of imperfectly unified elites in these countries, we indicated how this ambiguous division came about in the early postwar period. But we need to emphasize again that because they found possibilities for revolutionary action blocked by the war's outcome, Communists and those Socialists who most resembled them, particularly in Italy, were forced into what they must have thought was temporary and purely defensive political action. They adopted what might be called a "tribunician" strategy (Lavan, 1969) which involved defending the plebian strata least able to defend their own interests in the way in which ancient Roman tribunes were specifically empowered to intervene on behalf of the lower class, the plebs. On this basis, Communists established themselves in parliament and in trade union bureaucracies. Because of the deep alienation of most working class circles in the two countries, the Italian and French Communists thus established a strong and stable mass following of workers who regarded them as their spokesmen.

In fact, support from this stratum of the working class, which was often more stable than the enrolled party membership, dates back to the late 1920s in France and to the anti-Fascist resistance in Italy. Immediately after World War II it made possible the election of large contingents of Communist deputies in both countries. This and even higher levels of support were maintained in subsequent elections. Considerable bodies of French and Italian workers thus rewarded Communist interventions on their behalf even if the workers themselves probably held few illusions about the ease with which the economic system could be changed. For them it was enough that Communist leaders displayed their clear allegiance to the working class. To always speak for the working man, to live without ostentation, to make occasional demands on behalf of working people (when expedient), and to provide counsel, celebration, and some services for the working class was essentially what the immediate prewar and postwar generations of French and Italian workers demanded of their Communist leaders.

This kind of working class support hardly created a need to change Communist ideology. Because it was stable, and because the workers' expectations were on the whole limited, there was no necessity to tinker with a satisfactory set of ideological symbols. This was especially true in France where Communist party functionaries, themselves recruited from the working class, made very few alterations in the party's image between its initial bolshevisation in the middle 1920s and the 1970s. The French party performed its "tribunician" function for a relatively undemanding rank-and-file with an ideology which defined the working class narrowly while at the same time proclaiming these workers' ultimate triumph.

The circumstances of Italian Communist leaders were somewhat different, however. Not only was Italy as a whole less industrialized, but the society was more closely knit than French society has been at least since the widespread withdrawal by French workers of their allegiance to the Church in the nineteenth century (Lange, 1975). Moreover, leading Italian Communists seem to have come from more educated backgrounds than their French colleagues. As a consequence of the long Fascist dictatorship, when Communists could act only from exile or underground, the "tribunician" strategy had not been as firmly implanted. Unlike the French, Italian Communists could not expect to increase their mass following step by step merely as industrialization created more workers. They could not be sure that unorganized voters whom they failed to reach would not be mobilized by some other group.

The strong position of the Catholic Church alone made this last assumption dangerous for the Italian Communists. Generally, Italian workers, and especially those among them who were recent recruits to the urban working class, had ramifying family and village connections. Either they were Catholics or they were so tied to Catholics in one way or another that they could not easily exclude all the rest of society from their concerns in order to focus solely on a Communist organization which simply made demands on behalf of the working class. In other words, issues of freedom, of representation, of morality were inevitably present among all Italian strata, including even the relatively stabilized portions of the working class. If Communists did not face these issues, then someone else—very likely the Catholic clergy—would. Thus the Italian Communists could not, unlike the French, establish a stable and exclusive relation with a politically and socially isolated portion of the working class. Instead, they were forced to plunge into the society, to associate closely with Communist and Catholic believers and nonbelievers, and to establish a presence wherever they could (Tarrow, 1974). They had to meet an active and a questioning public on its own ground. In the process, their distinctive Communist characteristics and doctrines suffered considerable erosion.

In the years after World War II, therefore, there was a conspicuous evolution in Italian Communism. Seriously involved in the electoral and representational processes of a liberal democratic state, they could not waste time in communications with Moscow over every issue that arose. Barred for the time being from social revolutionary activity, they began to operate more and more as their competition did in the democratic representational process. A Communist deputy in parliament could not just ignore his non-Communist constituents. He had to be helpful to them as well as to his ideological brethren. Given the weakness of Italy's centralized bureaucracy, a Communist mayor was far too powerful to be able to ignore local business interests. He had to make frequent decisions which, if mistaken, could easily paralyze the local economy and eventually incur national intervention. For these efforts the Italian Communists acquired power, prestige, and recognition.

To survive in these politics of multiple interests and constant claims from all quarters, Italian Communist politicians had to calculate forces and make numerous concessions to political expediency. By the middle 1950s they had already learned much more than they could possibly have transmitted to Moscow for approval. At the same time, they were more and more successful politically. They had at that time no wish to dissociate themselves from the worldwide Communist movement, but they saw themselves as contributing substantially to that movement. In short, their deference to Russian leadership was limited and declining.

Thus it was not surprising that the Khrushchev revelations of 1956 were promptly met by Italian disavowal. Togliatti, the Italian Communist leader, declared that the conduct of the Russian party was obviously not a compulsory model for other Communist parties to follow. He spoke of "polycentrism" and urged individual national Communist parties to think for themselves. This was the first instance since the consolidation of the world Communist movement in the middle 1920s of an open dissent from Moscow that was not followed by expulsion of the offending persons or of the whole party. For the Russians to say that a large and influential party was no longer genuinely "Communist" when they obviously had no chance of setting up a serious rival in the country concerned was futile. Sensibly, the Russians refrained from doing so.

Thereafter, a steady differentiation of the Italian Communists from the model and standards of the international movement occurred. The party allowed its membership to grow to the point where it could no longer seriously claim to be an organization of professional revolutionaries. Its cell structure apparently deteriorated. Increasingly, local party life took place in large "sections" not unlike those of the social democratic parties. As yet, however, this looser structure has not resulted in organized, public intraparty struggles for control. Seemingly, something like the "democratic centralism" of the standard Communist party still prevails. But in the party press and at party congresses a wide range of elite and intellectual positions is tolerated. Probably this organizational and relative ideological cohesion is sustainable only so long as the party is confined to representative and defensive gestures on behalf of its mass following. Until now the more divisive situations of revolutionary action or majority control of the existing government have been out of the question. In any event, it is clear that party members are by now unaccustomed to severe internal party supervision or control. If and when divisive issues arise it is unlikely that their discussion can be seriously curtailed or controlled by methods other than those routinely available to the leaders of any democratic party.

As its internal structure probably now requires, the Italian Communist party stresses more and more, in a variety of statements and actions, its commitment to the democratic process and its lack of any interest in imposing a "dictatorship of the proletariat." It condemned the Russian intervention in Czechoslovakia in 1968. Since the overthrow of the minority Allende government in Chile, it has repeatedly stated its desire to govern not merely with the support of like-minded socialist parties. Rather, it looks to a grand coalition of all "anti-Fascist" parties, which in Italy would include almost all factions. In February 1976 Berlinguer, the party leader, made clear that the party was in no sense demanding the socialization of all means of production. Rather, he foresaw a continuing role for private enterprise. Moreover, he said the party did not want Italy to withdraw from NATO. The dissolution of this and other defensive alliances could only come about gradually through the process of detente. In a later interview he admitted that Italy's NATO membership was essential to his own liberty and to that of his party.

Meanwhile, differentiation of the French Communist party from the international movement and the Leninist model has been much slower and less convincing to outsiders. The limited political role of the French Communists has not forced an evolution in their doctrines and practice. In parliament the party's role has continued to be strictly oppositional. Because the strong and prestigious French national bureaucracy holds municipalities on a tight rein, the party has enjoyed little scope for political leadership in the numerous municipalities that have elected Communist mayors and councillors. Even to retain municipal elective office in France, it is necessary to defer in important matters almost wholly to the national government. Thus the adjustments which French Communists have made toward liberal democratic principles are not seen to arise out of the necessities of everyday political experience. Like the party's eventual differentiation from the Moscow line and model, they are seen as expedient and belated concessions.

When Togliatti was first speaking of "polycentrism" in the 1950s, the French party was among his severest critics. French Communists were still saying that a conflict of interest with the Russians was unthinkable and that the Red Army would be welcome if it invaded France. However, by 1963 the party withdrew its unconditional support of the Soviet party, at the same time assuring French voters that it did not support the mistaken Stalinist idea that only one party should be permitted under socialism. In actuality, there is a good deal of evidence which indicates that the French party has supported the French political system ever since the Popular Front venture in 1936. Lavan (1969) contends that it accepted all the norms of a democratic system after 1936, but that it refused to admit publicly that these norms were followed in other Western countries and that they were not respected in Russia or the East European states.

But the continuing tribunician function of the French Communist party makes it difficult to evaluate such contentions. In its organization and membership, the French party is still a highly limited party of cells. And although French intellectuals are frequently attracted to communism, the party in no sense seems to welcome them or to give them any authority. Unlike the Italian party, the concerns of intellectuals have little serious effect in French party discussions.

Nevertheless, the party's reaction to the "days of May" in 1968 seemed to confirm that it was no longer seriously revolutionary. Moreover, in strictly technical terms, the French party has moved nearly as far from the Soviet line as has the Italian party. Thus French Communists found it impossible not to join in condemning Russian intervention in Czechoslovakia. Gradually during the 1960s French Communist theoreticians, under the hostile critique of Soviet publicists, elaborated rather obscure Marxian doctrines to contend that under "advanced democracy" the attainment of socialism is merely a gradual process of adjusting economic matters (Davidshofer, 1976). This destroys the Marxian concept of "revolution" as a sudden and final change in the dominant class. In 1972 the party negotiated a "Common Program" with the French Socialists. In this they agreed to abide by electoral outcomes even if these should require going back into opposition. In November 1975 French and Italian Communist leaders joined in a statement which stressed their acceptance of a multi-party system and their intention to achieve power through parliamentary means. From time to time, the French Communists have joined the Italians in denouncing instances of Soviet brutality and repression. Finally, in February 1976 the French party congress voted to drop from its statutes all references to the "dictatorship of the proletariat."

At present, the French Communist party seeks an electoral and parliamentary majority for the "left" and for the "Common Program" at the next general election. However, it continues to conceive of the "left" rather narrowly as embracing essentially only the Communists and the Socialists. Similarly, it conceives of the Common Program as a rather narrow, tightly negotiated platform binding these two parties.

## CONCLUSIONS

The unifications of elites can only rarely be pinpointed as occurring at some specific point in time. In mainly agrarian societies where elites are small and isolated from mass pressures this is perhaps less the case. In England in 1689, in Sweden in 1809, and in Mexico in 1933 it is possible to identify specific sequences of events from which a self-perpetuating unified elite emanated. But in societies that are at all seriously industrialized there are too many elite actors who are too subject to complex and contradictory mass and elite pressures to permit sharp, clear elite reorganizations which can then be dated precisely. Thus the full unification of Danish and Norwegian elites seems to have occurred over the fifteen years, 1930 to 1945. Similarly, the unification of Austrian elites probably began while the country was under military occupation from 1945 to 1955, and it probably was not completed until the first really competitive national election in 1966.

This process has been even more complex in France and Italy because in these countries elites have moved toward two analytically distinct stages of unification in a relatively short 30 years. First was the imperfect unification which began with the postwar period. During the 1950s the repeated electoral dominance of the Christian Democrats in Italy seems to have created this imperfect unity. At least from 1961, the year of the Christian Democrats' "opening to the left," right and center factions were sure of their ultimate ability to control the government on the basis of electoral support. In addition, the possibility of an irregular seizure of power by leftist and rightist factions has diminished, initially because the presence of Allied forces deterred the left from revolutionary action, and later because the right was satisfied that the Christian Democrats and their allies had the situation under reliable control.

The real threat of a *coup d'etat* by the French military in 1958 was prima facie evidence that until that year French elites remained disunified. Thus it was not until sometime in the 1960s that imperfect elite unity was achieved. What was required was the demonstration of a repeated Gaullist majority and the training which the Gaullist regime gave mainly centrist and right-wing voters to vote pragmatically for specific referenda positions and to accept large and loose parliamentary factions. The unprecedentedly large Gaullist electoral victory in June 1968, immediately after the "days of May," probably drove home once and for all the lesson that a clear, moderately conservative majority existed and that all other factions would have to come to terms with that political fact. Thus it is plausible to say that, from at least 1968, French elites have been imperfectly unified.

In the years since 1961 in Italy and 1968 in France, the Communist counterelite in both countries has more and more abandoned the formal doctrinal commitments that seemed to bar it from unrestricted acceptance in the countries' governing processes. By 1976, however, this process of ideological moderation may well have undermined the essential presumption that makes an imperfectly unified elite viable: the assurance that majorities will reliably support moderately conservative governments. In other words, it is now very much an open question whether a majority of voters will any longer prevent the left, and most especially the Communists, from coming to power.

There are both long- and short-term reasons for this current electoral uncertainty. Among the former is the fact that the working class for which the Communists always spoke, especially in France, is now much less clearly defined than ever before. During the 1920s and the 1930s, and possibly during even the 1950s and 1960s, it was a fair assumption that Communists in power would initially favor the manual proletariat. As a corollary, it was assumed, not unfairly, that they had so little sympathy for the other, more or less "bourgeois" parts of the population, that both the old and new middle classes would suffer seriously as a consequence of the drastic policy changes which a Communist government would bring. But such assumptions are not nearly so plausible today. This is because manual workers, along with many technicians and lesser white-collar personnel have some property, some money, and some expectations of future holiday and retirement benefits accruing to them from combinations of pension funds and private savings. Many of these people are Communists. By the same token, many Italian and French working class families now contain members of what would earlier have been thought of as a higher social class. To confuse matters still further, many of those who are today most egalitarian (and usually anti-Communist) in France and Italy are persons who come from distinctly privileged backgrounds and who continue to possess substantial funds, status, and perquisites even while pursuing radical goals. In these several respects, *embourgeoisement* has gone very far.

Thus there is no way in which anyone, Communist or otherwise, could easily draw sharp class distinctions within the bulk of today's Italian and French populations. The evolution of social status and the institutionalization of collective bargaining, social security, and many other benefits has removed the plausibility of the idea for many moderately well-off persons that they personally would be discriminated against if social radicals came to power. Moreover, the short-term factors of the 1973–1976 economic recession and the CIA, airplane and other purchasing scandals which American investigators have opened up in Italy and other capitalist countries add to the temptation to try new leadership. It is therefore entirely possible, but by no means a foregone conclusion, that in the French election of 1978 the Communists and Socialists will win a majority and will attempt to govern. Similarly, although the 1976 Italian election did not quite provide such a majority, the same thing can eventually happen there.

Would the coming to power of the Communists in Italy and France force a final unification of these elites? In our theoretical perspective the answer is that the exact way in which the Communists eventually achieve a governing role is all-important. A simple leftist electoral victory could not be expected to complete the unification of these elites as such victories evidently did earlier in Norway and Austria. For one thing, the Norwegian and Austrian cases involved Socialists, not Communists. For another, they occurred in periods of economic growth, before the recent discovery of serious ecological limits to growth and before the recent attempts of Third World countries to capture a greater share of world production. In the late 1970s or early 1980s, therefore, a left precariously in power in France or Italy might well find itself in an economic situation where keeping its own supporters satisfied would leave no room for serious protection of established middle-class interests. We agree with what is evidently the view of the Italian Communists, derived from their observation of Chile, that such a situation would be exceedingly dangerous both to the left-wing coalition in power and to the continuation of democratic processes. After all, a long tradition of democratic government in Chile was destroyed in a similar situation.

Earlier we cited evidence that, once in power, the Italian and French Communists would be inclined to respect democratic norms. But whatever may be the strength of this evidence, it seems clear that the whole Italian and French populations are in no sense reconciled to being governed by them. Certainly the large segments of these populations which are in one sense or another "middle class" are not prepared to make serious sacrifices at the demand of movements which they are accustomed to seeing as hostile to themselves. Thus instead of leading to a full unification of the elite, a leftist electoral victory followed by a narrow left-wing governing coalition, would, under the restrictive economic conditions that are foreseeable, be more likely to restore full elite disunity. In all probability that would soon lead to a highly reactionary military dictatorship.

What we are saying is that neither in France nor in Italy have the Communists gone far enough in differentiating themselves from their former identifications so that their accession to power, alone or with an ideologically compatible partner, would be fully accepted by the rest of the elite. Under such accession, defections of other elite persons from support of existing institutions and from obedience to established rules of contest would occur. Thereafter either the left or the right would soon be in the position of ruling undemocratically or losing power to the other side. The Communists' own commitment to present themselves in a democratic and tolerant light would probably operate against them in such a situation. Right-wing forces would almost certainly be able to use weapons ruthlessly enough to bring the situation under their control.

On the other hand, a broad alliance in which the Communists were included along with such strictly non-Marxist forces as the Italian Christian Democrats or the French Gaullists (or large secessions from such parties) presents a different prospect. Something like the German Grand Coalition of 1966 to 1969 might be needed. In such a broad coalition it would be difficult for proletarian followers to pressure Communist leaders for dramatic concessions to their interests. Such a governing coalition, committed to some degree of reform and to practical management of the economy, would be unlikely to encounter serious challenges to its authority from either the left or the right. Moreover, their membership in such a coalition would further distance the Communists from their past commitments. Possibly it would divide them organizationally in ways that would further efface those commitments. Under such circumstances, it is quite possible that in a relatively short time the full unification of the French and Italian elites would be accomplished.

## FOOTNOTES

*G. Lowell Field and John Higley are on the faculties of the University of Connecticut, Storrs and the Australian National University, Canberra, respectively. They have recently been collaborating in the development and application of a theory specifying the elite and mass elements determinative of major variations in political systems. With Knut Grøholt they collaborated on the recent Columbia University Press book: *Elite Structure and Ideology, a Theory with Applications to Norway.*

1. In order to elaborate the concept of imperfectly unified elites, this section merely touches on some of the contentions of the general theory (Field, 1967; Higley, Field and Grøholt, 1976). Similarly, we here only allude to the important ways in which under the theory nonelite circumstances affect elite behavior.

# REFERENCES

Aron, Raymond (1950) "Social Structure and Ruling Class." *British Journal of Sociology* 1:1–16,126–143.

Davidshofer, William J. (1976) "Advanced Democracy: The French Communist Challenge to the Soviet Theory of People's Democracy." Paper presented to the New England Slavic Association, University of Connecticut, Storrs.

Field, G. Lowell (1967) *Comparative Political Development: The Precedent of the West*. Ithaca, NY: Cornell University Press.

——— and Higley, John (1973) *Elites and Nonelites: The Possibilities and Their Side Effects*. New York: MSS Modular Publications.

Hagopian, Mark (1975) *The Phenomenon of Revolution*. New York: Dodd,Mead.

Higley, John, Field, G. Lowell, and Grøholt, Knut (1976) *Elite Structure and Ideology*. New York: Columbia University Press.

Kriegel, Annie (1966) "Les communistes français et le pouvior." Pages 93–221 in Michelle Perrot, (ed.), *Le socialisme français et le pouvior*. Paris: Centre d'études socialistes.

Lange, Peter (1975) "La politica delle alleanze del PCI e del PCF." *Il Mulino* no. 240:499–527.

Lavan, Georges (1969) "Le parti communiste dans le système politique français." Pages 7–81 in Fondation Nationale des Sciences Politiques, *Le communisme en France et en Italie*. Volume 1: Le communisme en France. *Cahiers*, No. 175. Paris: Armand Colin.

Putnam, Robert (1976) *The Comparative Study of Political Elites*. Englewood Cliffs, NJ: Prentice-Hall.

Tarrow, Sidney (1974) "Le parti communiste et la société italienne." Pages 1–53 in Fondation Nationale des Sciences Politique, *Sociologie du communisme en Italie*. *Cahiers*, No. 194. Paris: Armand Colin.

# IMPERIAL DEVELOPMENT: THE CASES OF AMERICAN PUERTO RICO AND SOVIET GEORGIA

Barry B. Levine and Ralph S. Clem*

Many of the important political, economic, and social trends of this century have been associated with two processes: 1) the disintegration of the vast European colonial empires, and 2) the rise to superpower status of the United States and the Union of Soviet Socialist Republics. These two processes are related, for both the United States and the Soviet Union are imperial powers in their own right. The relationships they have with their dependencies are imperialistic in nature despite their characterizations of them as "a brotherhood of peoples," "a dynamic federalism," "the proletarian solution of the nationality problem," "the best form of mutual assistance," "the highest form of cooperation between peoples," "the

Comparative Studies in Sociology—Vol. 1, 1978, pages 319–336

ISBN 0-89232-025-7

most hopeful example in the Americas of how to develop an underdeveloped community in the clean atmosphere of freedom,'' and so on.

Although the perpetuation of the American and Soviet empires has obvious benefits for the colonial powers, such as strategic military or favorable economic purposes, the justification for the retention of the territories is generally given as something resembling an advanced case of ''white man's burden'': to develop the dependencies, a prolonged association between colonial power and colony must be maintained. To the extent that any choice has been granted to the colonies regarding continued association with the dominant powers, the alternative to dependency has been the bleakest sort of an ''all or nothing'' arrangement. Gordon Lewis (1963, p. 21) has characterized the situation with respect to Puerto Rico, for example, as one in which ''. . . America throughout has confronted the island population with a Hobson's choice between a political status that gives them food with shame or one that offers them poverty with dignity.'' The non-Russian nationalities of the U.S.S.R. were warned by Stalin that secession would endanger the consolidation of power by the working class, a situation which would be tantamount to threatening social and economic development.

Against the background of the dissolution of the European empires, the prolongation of the Soviet and American colonial dependencies seems at first glance an anachronism and an international political liability. In fact, however, both the United States and the U.S.S.R. have utilized, or at least attempted to utilize, their colonies as ''showcases'' in the worldwide development competition. The contemporary dichotomy of ''developed'' and ''developing'' countries has resulted in a rivalry between socialist and capitalist development models, in which the United States and the Soviet Union point to their colonies as examples of what can be accomplished under their respective economic and ideological systems. Thus, the United States government is willing to tolerate the periodic raising of the ''Puerto Rican question'' in the United Nations under the hope that delegations of Latin Americans, Africans, and Asians can be impressed by ''Operation Bootstrap.'' The Soviet Union similarly hopes that their development efforts in the non-Russian republics will be noticed by Tanzania, India, and other African and Asian areas in need of a development model to emulate.

Given the importance of the development process in political, economic, and social terms, there is good reason to analyze and assess the performance of the United States and Soviet governments in effecting modernization in their dependencies. Many social scientists have called for ''comparative studies of socialist and nonsocialist cases of national development'' (Berger, 1974, p. 102). Yet, except for so-called convergence theories, studies that propose the possibility of social and cultural comparisons between socialist and capitalist countries are rare. One reason for this is ideology; scholars are reluctant to suggest that there might be some similarity between negatively-viewed processes in one's adversary's society and those in one's own.

A second reason is philosophical or methodological, and derives from the Marxist evolutionary tenet that each historical stage in the dialectic progression is characterized by specific economic and social relationships. This kind of evolutionary theory leads to conceptualization of the various periods as mutually exclusive, thereby ruling out comparative studies that cross historical boundaries. Contributing further to the methodological separation of socialist from capitalist social science is the attitude of many Western scholars that the totalitarian nature of the Soviet Union in some way invalidates otherwise accurate cross-cultural statements. Finally, comparative studies in the social sciences which examine socioeconomic features of capitalist and socialist countries are inhibited by the practical difficulties which stand in the way of any comparative study: a large volume of information to be digested and synthesized, language differences, data comparability, and similar problems.

This paper represents initial efforts at a comparative study of the development processes of dependencies of the United States and of the U.S.S.R. At the outset, the assumption was that we were talking about Russian imperialism versus American imperialism, socialist development versus capitalist development—processes apparently worlds apart. To examine these imperial relationships we focus on the Soviet colonial relationship in the Georgian Soviet Socialist Republic (Georgia—one of the fifteen constituent republics of the U.S.S.R.) and the American colonial relationship in Puerto Rico (a "freely associated state" of the United States).

Our intention had been to study the differences in the American and Soviet imperial relationships. Yet, when we began a comparison of the two circumstances, we were forced to recognize that there are more similarities than normally realized. We characterize the similarities in these relationships as *imperial development*. While we underscore those similarities that we call imperial development, we want to emphasize that many important and obvious differences in the Puerto Rican and Georgian cases do exist; clearly there are differences in political styles, tolerance of dissent, economic systems, rate of development, and even of social psychology. These differences notwithstanding, we maintain that there are important benefits to be gained by viewing the American and Soviet cases as instances of a broader, multi-faceted process, imperial development.

Imperial development is a specific concept applicable only to certain specified cases. By *imperial development* we mean a political relationship in which a dominant, ethnically distinct power controls the ultimate prerogatives of sovereignty, generally through some federal political mechanism, and is obliged to promote economic and social development in the dependent territory as a condition of this arrangement. Instances of imperial development, one might note, are examples that contradict so-called dependency theory where dependency is thought to preclude development.

Imperial development differs from classical imperialism insofar as economic and social change are an integral part of the former and not of the latter. In classical imperialism, to the extent that there was any social and economic development at all, it was generally peripheral to the ideological justification of the relationship. More importantly, imperial development differs from other avenues of development (such as satellization, brokered development, or self-development) in that the political relationship between the dominant power and the colony formalizes dependence and preempts sovereignty. Clearly not all development is imperial nor all imperialism development.

This paper leaves many questions unanswered. For example, is the concept of imperial development applicable only to the superpowers? Can the concept be applied to such cases as the Yugoslav relationship in Macedonia, Chinese hegemony in Sinkiang, the Canadian one with regard to Quebec, the Spanish situation in Catalonia? Would the concept be viable should Third World countries take on imperial ventures? In an imperial development context, what happens when there is a failure at development, i.e., the French experience in Africa? Or a failure to develop, i.e., the Portuguese experience in Angola and Mozambique?

To help explain what we mean by imperial development, we have elaborated eleven theses which, together with examples from the Puerto Rican and Georgian cases, should explicate the dimensions of the phenomenon.

## THESIS ONE: Imperialism today necessarily means imperial development

We live in a world in which the *goal* of development is largely beyond question in all except some circles of the developed countries. This reality invariably causes critical sectors of the underdeveloped nations to search for its local implementation. The circumstances of imperialism produce the logical possibility that the source of development might derive from the imperial relationship. The underdeveloped colony demands from the imperium the necessary support to allow and foster development in return for the continuation, however tentative, of the imperial relationship. It is, therefore, today no longer practical for imperial powers to practice benign neglect, at least not overtly.

In addition to guaranteeing to the dominant power the benefits of classical imperialism (for instance, a captive or mercantilist market and military-strategic advantages), imperial development also provides a more active economic relationship usually enhanced by no-tariff trade arrangements and a more lucrative market for the goods produced in the developed country.

Beyond these obvious tangible benefits, modernization by imperial development has a showcase or propaganda value for the imperial power to offset any politically embarrassing aspects of the arrangement. Thus, the imperium demonstrates the worth of imperial development first to the locals and then to their neighbors.

In the early 1940s the Puerto Rican government attempted to promote development in the island with the formation of the Puerto Rican Development Company *(Fomento). Fomento's* initial activities included the establishment and running of several industries. These industries "created 2,000 jobs, but 200,000 were needed. Its investment was generating perhaps $4 million a year of new income when something like another billion dollars of income were needed" (Wells, 1969, p. 149). The Puerto Rican government changed strategy—it looked to the United States for the source of its development. The plan for this "industrialization by invitation" (Best, 1970, p. 6) was called "Operation Bootstrap," a plan to take advantage of American capital to create jobs for Puerto Ricans. "Operation Bootstrap" was introduced with the hope that the debate over the status of Puerto Rico could be suspended while the economy was being improved.

Tax exemptions, aid in plant construction, inexpensive labor, inclusion with the American tariff walls—these and other advantages have lured massive amounts of capital investment by American corporations to the island. The result has been that Puerto Rico has developed both her productive capacity and degree of consumption to levels higher than those of any other country in the Caribbean or Latin America. When one questions the fact that Puerto Rico is an American colony one is usually apprised of those areas of political autonomy that Puerto Rico has in fact eked out. But more importantly, one is shown the economic progress that the island has gained and these gains are considered by proponents of continued association with the United States to be worth any loss in political sovereignty. Puerto Rico has become "the showcase of America in the Caribbean;" it is a showcase of development American style. Rather than suspending the debate on the status of Puerto Rico, "Operation Bootstrap" has been incorporated into it.

Similarly, the Soviet government has long recognized, at least in theory and rhetoric, the necessity of promoting the social and economic development of previously backward, non-Russian nationality homelands (such as Georgia). The development of non-Russian lands within the U.S.S.R. has been a tenet of Soviet policy at least since the X Party Congress in 1921. The XV Party Congress, charged with initiating the first Five-Year Plan in the late 1920s, stated that attention would be paid to the development of all nationality regions, thereby ". . . liquidating their economic and cultural backwardness" (Clem, 1975, Chapter 2). Lenin, among others, made it plain that a requirement for the establishment of a viable multinational federation was the elimination of social, political, and economic inequalities among the various ethnic groups; the economic development of non-Russian areas can be considered as a response by the Soviet government to the perceived dangers inherent in underdevelopment. By promoting the economic growth of regions inhabited by non-Russians, it was assumed that eventually the indigenous population would be drawn into the development process. The centrally-directed socialist economy was the key to this policy, inasmuch as control over investment, technology, and manpower would enable the government to plan and implement the modernization directives. Clearly, Georgia and other non-Russian areas of the Soviet Union have served as showcases for the Soviet development model in Asia, Africa, and Latin America, with frequent comparisons being made between the U.S.S.R. and various countries of the world in terms of economic growth and social change.

## THESIS TWO: Imperial development takes place under special political status relationships designed to distract attention from the nature of the arrangement

Development today facilitates imperialism. Imperial development is based on a dependent political status which evolves as the development proceeds. These evolving political relationships distract attention from the imperial nature of the association.

These status arrangements between the dominant power and the colony include the formal recognition of the ethnic group's claim to privilege in their homeland, and at the same time subordinate that privilege to the new status. These new political structures typically are in theory of a federal nature, since blatant colonial relationships are now considered to be politically inexpedient: it would clearly be impolitic to establish a "crown colony" today. Moreover, as the Puerto Rican and Georgian examples illustrate, these political arrangements are progressively "sweetened," ostensibly to promote developmental possibilities.

By the end of the nineteenth century, the United States expressed a desire to "acquire" Puerto Rico. The Spanish-American War in 1898 concluded with Spain ceding Puerto Rico to the United States. One of the invading American generals, James Wilson, proclaimed shortly after the war that:

> Puerto Rico will at first be governed by a military regime, then it will be declared an American territory, and later it will achieve the category of sovereign state within the Union. The duration of these periods will depend more or less upon the merits of the country (quoted in Wagenheim, 1970, p. 67).

The Foraker Act (1900) ended military rule and declared Puerto Ricans to be "citizens of Porto Rico"—neither Americans nor citizens of a self-governing nation. The Act established mechanisms of governance, subject to American manipulation and veto. The Jones Act (1917) further incorporated Puerto Ricans into American life; it awarded them American citizenship (without asking if they wanted it) and made them subject to being drafted into the American Army. In 1948, Puerto Rico gained its first elected governor. In 1950, Congress passed Public Law 600 which allowed Puerto Ricans to draft their own constitution establishing the commonwealth relationship. Puerto Rico became a "freely associated state" of the United States in 1952. Then-governor Luis Muñoz Marin declared that the "last juridical vestiges of colonialism have been abolished" (Wagenheim, 1970, p. 79). Regardless of what autonomy the Commonwealth gained, "paramount power" still resided in the U.S. Congress.

Georgia, on the other hand, was at the beginning of the nineteenth century an independent country caught between two expanding imperial powers, the Tsarist Russian Empire to the north and the Ottoman Empire to the south. In 1801, choosing what must have appeared to them as the lesser of these two evils, the Georgians chose incorporation into the Tsarist state. With the fall of the Russian Empire and the subsequent seizure of power by the Bolsheviks in 1917, the Georgians took advantage of the political and military dislocations of the postrevolutionary period to declare their independence, and established a republic in May, 1918. Despite having signed a formal treaty of mutual recognition and noninterference with the fledgling Soviet government in 1920, Georgia was invaded by troops of the Red Army in 1921 and was reincorporated into the Russian-dominated multinational state. Granted varying degrees of regional autonomy in the early years of Soviet power, manifested in the U.S.S.R. by the ranking of an ethnic area in a hierarchy of unit-type, the Georgians were accorded Union Republic status in 1936, making the

Georgian Soviet Socialist Republic one of the fifteen most important and in theory most autonomous units in the Soviet Union. The creation of the U.S.S.R. has been characterized as a shrewd political response to the exigencies of the troubled postrevolutionary period, during which the major non-Russian nationalities had opted for self-determination. By granting these groups political recognition as nominally self-governing republics within the Soviet federation, while in practice limiting their prerogatives, this arrangement gives the appearance of autonomy and at the same time allows for the imposition of central authority.

## THESIS THREE: Imperial development brings to the fore questions concerning ethnicity and its relation to nationhood

In the contemporary world, the legitimate expression of ethnicity is believed to be nationalism, ultimately culminating in nationhood and political independence. Where the colonial power is ethnically distinct from the subordinate colony, imperial development is thought (by the dominant power) to counter such an attitude. Yet, imperial development brings to the fore questions concerning ethnicity and its relation to nationhood.

Once the political arrangement between the dominant power and the subordinate group is formalized, the fortunes of the ethnic group become intertwined with the future of that relationship. Curiously, the new relationship *forces* the articulation of ethnic identity, while at the same time modulating its maturation. The greater the threat of ethnic nationalism, the greater the need for development. Yet, apparently contradictory, the greater the imperial development the greater the focus on the ethnic nationality of the subordinate power.

Puerto Ricans are extremely self-conscious people. Their political status encourages this self-examination. Each time a Puerto Rican fills out an application asking for his nationality an identity crisis ensues: "Is he an American or a Puerto Rican?" Any modification in the political status of the island is always considered in terms of its effects on ethnic identity. *Independentistas* rail against statehood as the elimination of the Puerto Rican identity. Assimilationists argue that the political integration of the island would not mean the loss of *puertorriquenidad*. Consider the curious argument of ex-governor Luis Ferre: "'Nation' is a concept of political, social, and human identification. 'Homeland' is the hearts' affection for the place of birth. Our nation, the United States. Our homeland, Puerto Rico" (quoted in Wagenheim, 1973, p. 288).

One hears Ferre talking of Puerto Rico as if it were the land from which he had emigrated. He argues that the loss of nation status will have no effect on the meaning of Puerto Rican nationality. And yet it is the exercise of nationhood that will determine the content of that Puerto Rican nationality.

The Georgian ethnic identity, tracing its direct origins back to the sixth century B.C., is one of the oldest in the Soviet Union and perhaps in the world. The formalization of the political relationship between Georgia and the Soviet Union by the creation of the Georgian S.S.R. has resulted in a strengthening of Georgian identity, while at the same time Georgia's membership in a multinational state dominated by Russians has the effect of submerging the identity within the broader Soviet context. This is summed up in the well-known Stalinist slogan "national in form, socialist in content." Thus, because the federal political relationship between Georgia and the Soviet Union is ethnically-based, the Georgians receive in return for their continued participation in this arrangement the overt recognition of their homeland as an area in which they have some prerogatives. On the other hand, Soviet theorists on ethnicity, who are generally proassimilationist, argue that the ethnically-defined units may have outlived their usefulness, and that their demise would encourage the abandonment of the parochial ethnicity and the adoption of a supranational identity usually referred to as the "new Soviet man." Any such suggestion by the Soviet government that implies changes which might reduce the importance of the ethnic-territorial structure traditionally meets with strong protests by the Georgians. Clearly, both nationalists and assimilationists recognize the pivotal role that the Georgian Republic plays as a focus of ethnic identity.

## THESIS FOUR: In imperial development, the ideology of progress is now complemented by the economic capacity to carry it off

If development is one key to maintenance of an imperial relationship today, then the imperial powers must have the economic capacity to carry it off. Given this capacity, the greater the political integration the greater the need to perform economically, since otherwise the status arrangement itself would be called into question.

Whatever one's feelings about the political status of Puerto Rico, one must admit that tremendous economic growth has occurred on the island. Between 1940 and 1970, the GNP went from 287 million to 4.6 billion dollars. During the same time the number of automobiles rose 20 times, the number of telephones, 17 times. *Per capita* income rose from $118 to $1,425, average family income from $611 to $6,132. Similar indications of spectacular growth can be found in many other indices. The first American civilian governor of the island claimed in 1901 that:

> The introduction of fresh blood is needed and when the American capitalist realizes . . . that property is as well protected here as in the United States, that his own forms of court procedure prevail here as at home, that there is a surplus of labor accustomed to the tropics and adapted to the kind of work likely to be undertaken here, that the return to capital is exceedingly profitable, it is my feeling that he will come here not only with his capital, but with the push and energy which always accompany his undertakings, and, with the cooperation of the native, will proceed to make at least five spears of grass grow where one has grown before, to the immense and permanent prosperity of the island. (Allen, 1971, pp. 8–11)

The capitalist came, the Puerto Rican cooperated, and the growth is obvious. But this growth has created new expectations. It is significant that separatist activity has increased these last couple of years as the economy has taken a downturn much as it was significant that nationalist activity was at its height in the 1930s, a time of grave economic problems.

The success of the Soviet government in fostering economic growth in formerly backward areas of the U.S.S.R. is generally universally conceded. Economic growth in the Georgian Republic has been impressive in both the industrial and agricultural sectors. Most significant have been the rapid expansion of manufacturing and extractive industries, which were virtually nonexistent under the Tsarist regime: according to Soviet sources, growth in the industrial sector increased by a factor of 62 between 1913 and 1966, while agricultural production increased by about six times during this period. In Georgia, such increases in economic production are now taken for granted.

## THESIS FIVE: Resistance to imperial development where development is promoted is more frequently resistance to the dominant power. Resistance to classical imperialism where development was accidental is more frequently resistance to change

In classical imperialism, the problem for the local population was the destruction of traditionally held norms. Imperial development, in contrast, convinces most members of even the subjugated ethnic group that new norms have some value, at least in economic terms. Consequently, the problem for the local population is the choice and implementation of a set of new norms free from external restraints.

There is little resistance to modernization *per se* in Puerto Rico. Except for an insubstantial group of Catholic *independentistas* wishing a return to past days of glory under Spain, there is little political expression against modernization and "progress." Indeed, each of the three political parties is in favor of modernization. One group asserts that it has brought the progress, another that it will be the future source of progress, and another that progress can only come through socialism. Indeed, federal agencies often attempt to restrain certain local practices that are adopted in the name of progress. When resistance is expressed, it is not antimodern but anti-American. On the political level there are clear protests that Puerto Ricans and the Puerto Rican government rather than the Americans and the American government should control the modernization of the island. Beneath the overt political level there is a broader resentment against the American presence.

One of the highest priorities of the Soviet government with regard to modernization has been the formation of skilled cadres of indigenous nationalities which would provide personnel for integration into the advanced sectors of society and the economy. Clearly, major gains have been made in this field, and in Georgia, as in other republics of the U.S.S.R., there is a substantial new elite which has a stake in the furtherance of development. Indeed, the major complaint of the young, educated Georgians seems to be that they are not afforded enough opportunity for advancement in the modernized sectors. Thus, the importance or value of modernization is generally not questioned, but the fact that development is directed by the Russians has led to dissent. Georgia presents somewhat of a unique situation in the Soviet Union in that Georgians have developed to a very sophisticated degree a "shadow" economy existing on the legal margin or even beyond the law. By perfecting a black market and by bending the rules of the legal economy, Georgians have been able to adapt to the rigidly controlled system imposed upon them from Moscow. Recent attempts by authorities to crack down on the Georgians were met by bombings and arson, the message here being that progress Soviet style is fine only within certain limits.

## THESIS SIX: In imperial development, the local political machinery is limited to strictly local matters and becomes bound up with external political realities

By the very nature of the relationship, the dominant power assumes the responsibility of control over such concerns as foreign policy, the judicial system, and the regulatory bureaucracy. Consequently, local government is relegated to minor issues, such as local policing and utilities. However, the existence of a local government provides a focal point to pressure for greater local autonomy. A delicate balance is achieved between the local government acting for the imperium and the local government squeezing benefits from the dominating power.

Local government in Puerto Rico in many ways resembles state governments in the United States. The ultimate determination of the law and its major bureaucratic execution is a federal prerogative, as is foreign policy. Once these questions are defined, the local government insures that they are carried out. Yet, these ultimate prerogatives are beyond their decision. As a consequence, the political parties all have stances as to how they relate to the "paramount powers." To the extent that they do not advocate rejection of the imperial relationship they then have the option of advocating one method or another of how to take advantage of it; Puerto Rican politicians often try to take credit for getting this or that federal program for the island. They demonstrate their effectiveness as politicians insofar as they can claim good contacts with the federal government. The ability to get the United States food stamp program to apply to Puerto Rico is such an example. The island government is presently trying to convince Congress that greater autonomy is needed in the areas of minimum wages, environmental controls, tariff, and immigration regulation. The party in power claims that should the Congress grant them this autonomy they will be more able to promote development and thus combat pressures from the separatists. The *independentistas,* of course, see such "grants" of autonomy as attempts to perfume the basic colonial relationship.

The prerogatives of the various republics of the U.S.S.R. and those reserved for the central government were originally delimited by the Soviet constitution of 1924 and later modified by the second Soviet constitution of 1936. Basically, all governmental functions other than social security and education are controlled directly by the central government or are subject to some type of consultation-veto procedure. Despite the fact that the state apparatus of the U.S.S.R. is, as a federation, theoretically decentralized, the Party exerts *de facto* control through a rigid, highly centralized system of parallel authority. In Georgia, this has meant in practice that although Georgians may be represented in the republic government, Russians occupy key posts and dominate the Party bureaucracy where the real political power is vested. Furthermore, the highly disciplined Party machinery attempts to prevent split loyalties where local officials might put local interests before national ones. This should not, however, be taken to mean that there is no element of local self-interest in Georgian government. Indeed, substantial evidence exists which suggests that whenever the opportunity presents itself, such as in the location of the Rustavi iron and steel plant, local government attempts to further its own development, even at the expense of the national economy. Thus, during the economic decentralization of the Khrushchev period, there was widespread criticism of republic governments for excessive "localism" in planning and allocating production.

## THESIS SEVEN: In imperial development, the structure of the local economy (both the agricultural and industrial sectors) is reorganized to the style of the dominant power and is designed to complement the dominant power's economy

Given the political realities facing the colonies, the way to gain optimum economic advantage is to orient themselves to the new structure of opportunities, and conform more or less to the system and style of the imperial power. Whether or not choice between systems actually exists, there is latitude for manipulating the system for maximum economic benefit.

When the Americans took over Puerto Rico they changed its agriculture from family farming to large plantation agriculture. Moreover, the agriculture was diverted from production of food crops for internal consumption to production of the "after-dinner" crops (coffee, sugar, tobacco) for external export. Similarly, manufacturing became Americanized with the success of the *Fomento* program in the 1950s and the influx of American manufacturing capital to the island. The industry is primarily for export and Puerto Rico has been put in the peculiar position of producing what it does not need and needing what it does not produce. Since the *Fomento* program sought to seduce the American capitalist, the "socialist experiment" of the 1940s where the government owned several factories had to cease. By 1950 it was all "capitalist."

The implementation of the Soviet-planned economy, with all responsibility and control reserved for the central government, obviously dramatically changed the economic system which existed in Georgia before 1917. Before the advent of Soviet power in Georgia, agriculture was basically feudal in nature, and the limited manufacturing and trading sectors were in the hands of a small commercial bourgeoisie. After the late 1920s, agriculture in Georgia was collectivized, and the private sector in industry and commerce was eliminated. Thus, within a relatively short period, the economy of Georgia was transformed to comply with the total Soviet economy. Interestingly, just as was the case with Puerto Rico, Georgian agriculture is concentrated mainly in specialty crops such as tea, citrus, and wine, and not in staple crops for self-sufficiency.

## THESIS EIGHT: In imperial development, education becomes an ideological tool as well as a training ground for the newly required skills and roles

The educational system becomes reorganized along the lines of the dominant power, both in structure and content. Heavy emphasis is put on learning the skills and roles required in the new bureaucracy and economy, especially the language of the dominant power. The educational system either purposefully or inadvertently expresses the ideology of the dominant power.

Literacy in Puerto Rico went from less than 70 percent in 1940 to near 90 percent in 1970. In 1950, about 60 percent of the school age population, grades 1–12, were in school; in 1970, the figure was 88 percent. Puerto Rico today has more college students in proportion to its population than any other country except the United States. Schooling has become very important in Puerto Rico. Education is conceived of to be the proper mechanism of social mobility. It is in school where one learns the roles, techniques, and skills needed in the new industry. If one cannot take advantage of education itself, then one hopes that one's children will so avail themselves. The American reverence for education has been successfully transplanted to Puerto Rican soil. Almost as soon as the Americans landed they began to change the educational system to the American style. They immediately demanded that the language of instruction be English rather than Spanish. By 1948, when it was finally realized that this policy was counterproductive, the language of instruction was changed back to Spanish, but English was a required second language and has become recognized as the language of economic success.

After the Soviet regime had consolidated its authority in Georgia, educational reforms were implemented which altered in radical fashion the existing local or Tsarist school systems. Historically, education in Georgia was controlled by the clergy and was limited to a very small segment of society: Tsarist rule in this region did not effect any significant changes in the educational system. The Soviet government eventually expanded both the number of schools and the number of students, instituting mandatory education for boys, and, importantly, for girls as well. Illustrative of the extent of the Soviet reforms is the fact that the number of students in Georgia increased from 157,000 in 1914 to 928,000 in 1966.

In addition to the expansion of the educational system under the Soviets, there were dramatic changes as well in the curriculum and, obviously, in the function of schools in Georgia. Typically, the Soviet educational system is heavily vocational, with the emphasis being on the attainment of skills required by the modern society. One of these skills is the knowledge of the Russian language, so much so that Russian is a required subject. Ideology, as is well known, is overtly expressed in Soviet schools through courses of study, through ideologically determined interpretation of certain subjects, and through extracurricular activities. With regard to the structure, function, and content of schools in Georgia, there is a high degree of conformity to the Soviet model.

## THESIS NINE: In imperial development, there is an inevitable cultural hegemony of the dominated culture. Most of the local culture that continues to emerge is in reaction to or in favor of the dominant power

The overbearing presence of the dominant power sooner or later places its stamp on both traditional and new cultural forms. In the first case, old styles are penetrated, and in the second new styles are often in response, pro or con, to the influence of the dominant culture.

The American presence in Puerto Rico is not only massive but also all-pervasive. The mass media—television, radio, movies, newspapers—brings a barrage of information to the islander about a desired American way of life. Against this barrage there is little that one can do except complain: that taste in music should be more traditional, that dress no longer conforms to old codes, that fast foods are not Puerto Rican, or that "Spanglish" is replacing Spanish. New art and culture, when not openly emulative of exogenous styles, take the form of statements criticizing the penetration by the alien culture.

The penetration of Russian or Soviet culture in Georgia has been pervasive in both form and content. Traditional forms of nationality culture have in many instances been supplanted by new forms such as television and movies. Further, the content of existing cultural forms has in most instances been made to conform to ideologically sound themes; thus, the traditional Georgian theater may present works extolling the virtues of industry or the Red Army. This is not to say that the traditional forms have been entirely adapted to the new Soviet norms; indeed, at least in some instances, traditional forms are encouraged as a means of strengthening nationality identity among Georgians. Yet, there is little evidence of an indigenous cultural expression utilizing a new form not conforming in content to the official view.

## THESIS TEN: Imperial development becomes the mechanism for introducing those demographic and socioeconomic changes normally associated with modernization. Though these changes are general processes, credit or discredit is assigned to the dominant power

Historically, a number of demographic and other socioeconomic changes occur with modernization, apparently without regard for the political or economic system or the cultural background. For example, development, whether imperial or otherwise, entails such profound trends as a decline in mortality and fertility, migration, urbanization, secularization, and a change in the status of women. Given the pervasive nature of the imperial relationship, and the fact that ideology becomes so important, change, whether viewed positively or negatively, is often attributed to the status arrangement.

Development in Puerto Rico has had dramatic demographic and socioeconomic implications. The decrease in mortality levels after World War II occurred at a rate unprecedented in human history, with life expectancy at birth rising from 46 years in 1940 to almost 70 years by 1960. Birth rates in Puerto Rico, another key demographic variable affected by modernization, fell from 41 per thousand in 1930 to 25 in 1969. Urbanization has proceeded at a rapid rate: rising from 15 percent in 1900 to about 58 percent by 1970, with the most significant gains taking place since the war. Exposure to American influence has broken the Catholic dominance of religious life on the island and in general religion has undergone a process of secularization. Similarly, modernized life styles have given new roles to women. If these processes are appreciated the American influence is thanked, if they are not so appreciated the American influence is damned. Nor do Americans fail to take credit for the modernization whenever they are given a chance.

Under the Soviet regime in Georgia, there have been a wide range of important demographic and socioeconomic changes resulting from modernization. The government has implemented public health and other measures which sharply reduced mortality levels, and modernization has resulted in substantial fertility declines. Urbanization has increased significantly in Georgia since the Revolution; in 1926, less than 20 percent of the population of Georgia lived in cities, whereas that figure now stands at over 50 percent. Clearly, one of the most important changes in Georgia has involved secularization; the Soviet government early on took steps to reduce the influence of the Orthodox Church in education and society in general. Credit for these trends is actively taken by the Soviet government, while those desiring a more traditional Georgian identity deplore such changes.

## THESIS ELEVEN: In cases of imperial development, the dominant power has a clear military advantage over the subjugated group

The military as a local political institution is by-passed, reducing the possibility of overt resistance to the central authority. The role of the military in society and politics is absorbed by the dominant group's military. For example, the possibility of the *coup d'etat* as a means of effecting change on the local level is eliminated.

When a Puerto Rican wants to join the army he joins the American Army; there is no such thing as the Puerto Rican Armed Forces. The armed forces are those of the United States, commanded mostly by Americans, even on local bases. The American Army operates as a school of American skills and as a teacher of the English language. Likewise, under the Soviet system, control over the armed forces is a clearly-defined constitutional prerogative of the central authority. There are no territorial or ethnic units in the Soviet Armed Forces, and those military units stationed within Georgia are almost always commanded by Russians or by members of other nonindigenous groups. As was the case above, the Soviet armed forces serve to train and educate non-Russians in skills and in the Russian language.

## CONCLUSION

In summary, the foregoing examples largely support our theses proposed as representative of a phenomenon which we have termed imperial development. Gross indications are that even given different economic and ideological systems, the impact of development under an imperial relationship upon society, culture, and the economy of the dependencies in these two cases, normally considered to be widely divergent, has in fact been essentially the same. We conclude that the critical variable in such arrangements is the nature of the political association between the dominant power and the colony, a status which in the cases of Puerto Rico and Georgia has placed upon the respective imperial powers the burden of facilitating development. Further study is warranted for inasmuch as imperialism and emerging nationhood are of such importance, the articulation and assessment of imperial development should provide valuable insights into the nature of international political, economic, and social change, insights which will challenge ideological claims of diversity.

## FOOTNOTE

*Barry B. Levine chairs the Department of Sociology and Anthropology at Florida International University, Miami. He was cofounder and coeditor of *Caribbean Review*. He coedited *Problemas de Desigualdad Social en Puerto Rico*. Ralph S. Clem teaches in the Department of International Relations at Florida International University. He coauthored *Population Change and Nationality in Russia and the U.S.S.R.* and edited both *The Soviet West* and *The City 2000 A.D.*

Paper presented to the 71st annual meeting of The American Sociological Association, New York, August 1976

## REFERENCES

Allen, Charles H. (1971) "First Annual Report of Charles H. Allen, Governor of Puerto Rico." Excerpted and reprinted as "Let Us Construct A Water Closet." *Caribbean Review* 3:8–11.

Berger, Peter L. (1974) *Pyramids of Sacrifice*. New York: Basic Books.

Best, Lloyd (1970) "Black Power and Doctor Politics." *Caribbean Review* 2:6.

Clem, Ralph S. (1975) "The Changing Geography of Soviet Nationalities." Unpublished Ph.D. Dissertation, Columbia University.

Lewis, Gordon K. (1963) *Puerto Rico: Freedom and Power in the Caribbean*. New York: Harper and Row.

Wagenheim, Kal (1970) *Puerto Rico: A Profile*. New York: Praeger.

——— (ed.) (1973) *The Puerto Ricans*. New York: Praeger.

Wells, Henry (1969) *The Modernization of Puerto Rico*. Cambridge, MA: Harvard University Press.

**RESEARCH IN LAW AND SOCIOLOGY**
**An Annual Compilation of Research**

**Guest Editor: Steven Spitzer, Department of Sociology, University of Northern Iowa, Cedar Falls**

Volume 2 May 1979 Cloth Approx. 365 pages
ISBN NUMBER: 0-89232-111-3

**TENTATIVE CONTENTS:**



Published 1978

# RESEARCH IN POLITICAL ECONOMY

## An Annual Compilation of Research

**Series Editor: Paul Zarembka, Department of Economics, State University of New York, Buffalo.**

This series of annual volumes develops an approach to understanding society that completely breaks with any approach via separate social science disciplines. The approach here, consistent with classical Marxism, treats society as an integrated whole, the separate parts of which make little sense when studied in isolation. The essential tool is class struggle within a mode of production and the relation between modes of production. With emphasis on the capitalist mode of production, some attention is also given to pre-capitalist modes, as well as to socialism as a structural break from the capitalist mode. Both theoretical abstraction and case studies are and will be included.

Volume 1. Published 1978 Cloth 350 pages Institutions: $25.00
ISBN NUMBER 0-89232-020-6 Individuals: $12.50

**CONTENTS: The Capitalist Mode of Production,** Paul Zarembka, State University of New York, Buffalo. **There is Nothing Simple about a Commodity,** Jesse C. Schwartz, San Diego State University. **The Political Economy of U.S. Steel Prices in the Post-War Period,** Edward Greer, Roosevelt University. **Unproductive Labor and the Rate of Surplus Value in the United States, 1947–1967,** Edward N. Wolff, New York University. **Monopoly Accumulation, Hegemonic Crisis and Francoist Dictatorship,** Juan-Pablo Perez Sainz, Institute of Social Studies. **The Changing Class Structure of South Africa: The African Petit-Bourgeoisie,** Harold Wolpe, University of Sussex. **Transnationals and Cheap Labor in the Periphery,** Raul Trajtenberg, Latin American Institute of Transnational Studies, Mexico City. **Proletariat Dictatorship and the Development of Productive Forces in China,** Gek-Boo Ng.

A 10 percent discount will be granted on all institutional standing orders placed directly with the publisher. Standing orders will be filled automatically upon publication and will continue until cancelled. Please indicate which volume Standing Order is to begin with.

**JAI PRESS INC.**
P.O. Box 1285
321 Greenwich Avenue
Greenwich, Connecticut 06830

(203) 661-7602 Cable Address: JAIPUBL.

# OTHER SERIES OF INTEREST FROM JAI PRESS INC.

*Consulting Editor for Sociology:* Rita J. Simon, Director, Program in Law and Society, University of Illinois

**COMPARATIVE STUDIES IN SOCIOLOGY**
Series Editor: Richard F. Tomasson, University of New Mexico

**POLITICAL POWER AND SOCIAL THEORY**
Series Editor: Maurice Zeitlin, University of California—Los Angeles

**RESEARCH IN COMMUNITY AND MENTAL HEALTH**
Series Editor: Roberta G. Simmons, University of Minnesota

**RESEARCH IN LAW AND SOCIOLOGY**
Series Editor: Rita J. Simon, Director, Program in Law and Society, University of Illinois

**RESEARCH IN RACE AND ETHNIC RELATIONS**
Series Editor: Cora B. Marrett, University of Wisconsin, and Cheryl Leggon, University of Illinois, Chicago Circle

**RESEARCH IN SOCIAL MOVEMENTS, CONFLICTS AND CHANGE**
Series Editor: Louis Kriesberg, Syracuse University

**RESEARCH IN SOCIAL PROBLEMS AND PUBLIC POLICY**
Series Editor: Michael Lewis, University of Massachusetts

**RESEARCH IN SOCIAL STRATIFICATION AND MOBILITY**
Series Editor: Donald J. Treiman, University of California—Los Angeles

**RESEARCH IN SOCIOLOGY OF EDUCATION AND SOCIALIZATION**
Series Editor: Alan C. Kerckhoff, Duke University

**RESEARCH IN SOCIOLOGY OF KNOWLEDGE, SCIENCES AND ART**
Series Editor: Robert Alun Jones, University of Illinois

**RESEARCH IN THE INTERWEAVE OF SOCIAL ROLES: Women and Men**
Series Editor: Helena Z. Lopata, Center for the Comparative Study of Social Roles, Loyola University of Chicago

**RESEARCH IN THE SOCIOLOGY OF HEALTH CARE**
Series Editor: Julius A. Roth, University of California—Davis

**RESEARCH IN THE SOCIOLOGY OF WORK**
Series Editor: Ida Harper Simpson, Duke University, and Richard Lee Simpson, University of North Carolina, Chapel Hill

## OTHER SERIES OF INTEREST FROM JAI PRESS INC.

*Consulting Editor for Sociology:* Rita J. Simon, Director, Program in Law and Society, University of Illinois

**STUDIES IN SYMBOLIC INTERACTION**
Series Editor: Norman K. Denzin, University of Illinois

*ALL VOLUMES IN THESE ANNUAL SERIES ARE AVAILABLE AT INSTITUTIONAL AND INDIVIDUAL SUBSCRIPTION RATES.*

*PLEASE WRITE FOR DETAILED BROCHURES ON EACH SERIES*

A 10 percent discount will be granted on all institutional standing orders placed directly with the publisher. Standing orders will be filled automatically upon publication and will continue until cancelled. Please indicate which volume Standing Order is to begin with.

**JAI PRESS INC.**
P.O. Box 1285
321 Greenwich Avenue
Greenwich, Connecticut 06830

(203) 661-7602 Cable Address: JAIPUBL.